Beyond Forty Acres and a Mule

UNIVERSITY PRESS OF FLORIDA

Florida A&M University, Tallahassee
Florida Atlantic University, Boca Raton
Florida Gulf Coast University, Ft. Myers
Florida International University, Miami
Florida State University, Tallahassee
New College of Florida, Sarasota
University of Central Florida, Orlando
University of Florida, Gainesville
University of North Florida, Jacksonville
University of South Florida, Tampa
University of West Florida, Pensacola

Beyond Forty Acres and a Mule

African American Landowning Families since Reconstruction

Edited by Debra A. Reid and Evan P. Bennett

Foreword by Loren Schweninger

University Press of Florida
Gainesville · Tallahassee · Tampa · Boca Raton
Pensacola · Orlando · Miami · Jacksonville · Ft. Myers · Sarasota

Copyright 2012 by Debra A. Reid and Evan P. Bennett
All rights reserved
Printed in the United States of America on acid-free paper

First cloth printing, 2012
First paperback printing, 2014

Library of Congress Cataloging-in-Publication Data
Beyond forty acres and a mule : African American landowning families since Reconstruction / edited by Debra A. Reid and Evan P. Bennett ; foreword by Loren Schweninger.
p. cm.
Includes bibliographical references and index.
ISBN 978-0-8130-3986-2 (cloth: acid-free paper)
ISBN 978-0-8130-6036-1 (pbk.)

1. African American farmers—United States—History. 2. African Americans—Land tenure—United States—History. 3. African American farmers—United States—Economic conditions. 4. African American farmers—United States—Political conditions. 5. Freedmen—United States—Economic conditions. 6. African American farmers—Southern States—History. 7. African Americans—Land tenure—Southern—History. 8. African American farmers—Southern States—Economic conditions. 9. United States—Race relations. 10. Southern States—Race relations. I. Reid, Debra Ann, 1960– II. Bennett, Evan P.
E185.6.B49 2012
305.5'6308996073075—dc23   2012001107

The University Press of Florida is the scholarly publishing agency for the State University System of Florida, comprising Florida A&M University, Florida Atlantic University, Florida Gulf Coast University, Florida International University, Florida State University, New College of Florida, University of Central Florida, University of Florida, University of North Florida, University of South Florida, and University of West Florida.

University Press of Florida
15 Northwest 15th Street
Gainesville, FL 32611-2079
http://www.upf.com

Contents

List of Maps / vii
List of Figures / ix
List of Tables / xi
Foreword / xiii
List of Abbreviations / xv

Introduction / 1
Debra A. Reid

Part I. Historiography and Philosophy

1. The Jim Crow Section of Agricultural History / 21
Adrienne Petty

Part II. Farm Acquisition and Retention

2. Out of Mount Vernon's Shadow: Black Landowners in George Washington's Neighborhood, 1870–1930 / 39
Scott E. Casper

3. James E. Youngblood: Race, Family, and Farm Ownership in Jim Crow Texas / 63
Keith J. Volanto

4. Benjamin Hubert and the Association for the Advancement of Negro Country Life / 83
Mark Schultz

Part III. Agrarianism and Black Politics

5. Black Populism: Agrarian Politics from the Colored Alliance to the People's Party / 109
Omar H. Ali

6. "The Lazarus of American Farmers": The Politics of Black Agrarianism in the Jim Crow South, 1921–1938 / 132
Jarod Roll

Part IV. Farm Families at Work

7. Land Ownership and the Color Line: African American Farmers in the Heartland, 1870s–1920s / 155
   Debra A. Reid

8. Of the Quest of the Golden Leaf: Black Farmers and Bright Tobacco in the Piedmont South / 179
   Evan P. Bennett

9. "Justifiable Pride": Negotiation and Collaboration in Florida African American Extension / 205
   Kelly A. Minor

Part V. Legal Activism and Civil Rights Expansion

10. Black Power in the Alabama Black Belt to the 1970s / 231
    Veronica L. Womack

11. "You're just like mules, you don't know your own strength": Rural South Carolina Blacks and the Emergence of the Civil Rights Struggle / 254
    Carmen V. Harris

12. Between Forty Acres and a Class Action Lawsuit: Black Farmers, Civil Rights, and Protest against the U.S. Department of Agriculture, 1997–2010 / 271
    Valerie Grim

Researching African American Land and Farm Owners: A Bibliographic Essay / 297
Debra A. Reid

List of Contributors / 317
Index / 321

Maps

2.1. Mount Vernon District No. 3 / 41

2.2. Detail, Mount Vernon District No. 3, showing Gum Springs and property owned by Susan Quander and Sandy Alexander / 46

6.1. County distribution of Universal Negro Improvement Association divisions in the rural South, 1920–35 / 135

Figures

I.1. J. R. Dean, landowner living with a hotel keeper in Ashville, Alabama, 1915 / 8

I.2. L. C. Carter, a farmer near Butler Springs, Alabama, c. 1918 / 13

2.1. Marriage license, 1908 / 49

3.1. James Thomas Youngblood (1833–1891) / 65

3.2. Eliza Youngblood (1842–1924) / 67

3.3. James E. "Squire" Youngblood (1869–1946) / 70

3.4. "Squire" Youngblood's farmhouse, between 1901 and 1915 / 72

4.1. Portrait of Benjamin F. Hubert / 89

4.2. Camilla-Zach Log Cabin Center, 1932 / 97

5.1. Walter A. Pattillo / 117

5.2. Picking cotton in Mississippi, 1890s / 122

6.1. Promotional broadside, National Federation of Colored Farmers, 1933 / 144

7.1. Thomas Green, landowner in Pleasant Ridge, Wisconsin, c. 1936 / 157

7.2. John Summer and family, Kansas, 1880 to 1885 / 165

7.3. Blacks and whites performing similar labor, but white oversight prevailed, c. 1899 / 170

7.4. Laborers harvesting wheat on the W. P. Ridley farm near Columbia, Tennessee, June 14, 1921 / 172

8.1. Farm owned by Wes Cris[p], 1939 / 181

8.2. Farmer talking with warehouse man, 1939 / 192

8.3. Farmer buying patent medicine outside tobacco warehouse, 1939 / 192

8.4. Stock barn on the B. C. Corbett farm, 1939 / 194

9.1. Canning demonstration, Washington County, Florida, 1919 / 208

9.2. Newspaper clipping of Mrs. Ethel Anderson, 1946 / 210

9.3. Okra patch at home garden of Rosa Walker, Rock Hill Community, 1952 / 212

9.4. Mrs. Smith and a friend installing foundation shrubbery, 1952 / 213

9.5. The Stewart family of Micanopy and their guests, 1951 / 216

9.6. Mrs. Rosa Walker bakes in her kitchen, Leon County, Florida, 1952 / 217

9.7. Estelle Jenkins improved her home, 1956 / 219

Tables

3.1. Property of James E. Youngblood, 1893–1910 / 71

7.1. African American Farms, North-Central States, with Comparative Data, 1900 / 160

8.1. Rates of Black Ownership, Virginia–North Carolina Piedmont, 1900–1950 / 186

8.2. Plantation Counties in the Virginia–North Carolina Piedmont, 1860–1920 / 201

8.3. Peripheral Counties in the Virginia–North Carolina Piedmont, 1860–1920 / 202

10.1. Farmers in Selected Alabama Black Belt Counties, 1930 / 236

10.2. Black Owners, Tenants, and Sharecroppers in the Alabama Black Belt, 1930 / 237

10.3. Black Agricultural Workers in the Alabama Black Belt, 1930 / 241

Foreword

Considering the proliferation of scholarship on various aspects of the African American experience after slavery, it is surprising that comparatively little attention has been devoted to black farmers. Following Emancipation, as former slaves sought to adjust to their new life in freedom, the great majority of freedmen and freedwomen began their new lives with virtually nothing. In the decades that followed, in the southern states, where 90 percent of the black population lived, the number and percentage of African Americans who acquired their own farms rose steadily for more than a half century—from about 17,783 or 2.2 percent of farm families in 1870, to 208,647, or 23 percent in 1920—before beginning a slow decline until 1950 and then plummeting during the next thirty years to only 27,000 farm families. In 2007, according to U.S. Department of Agriculture census data, that number has remained unchanged.

The articles in this anthology deal with some of the most perplexing issues facing black farmers in the South. Building on the work of Steven Hahn's *A Nation under Our Feet: Black Political Struggles in the Rural South from Slavery to the Great Migration* (2003), the authors discuss the importance of kinship and family connections among blacks in acquiring farm land and other property, the difficulties blacks faced obtaining credit and purchasing land, and the class tensions between black farm owners and black tenant farmers and sharecroppers. They discuss rural cooperatives as well as individuals and groups who attempted to bridge the racial divide. They examine the dual nature of American capitalism and black separatism.

The authors make their most important contribution when they address the seemingly contradictory philosophies that emerged as African Americans acquired and protected their real property. Many farmers advocated and practiced separatism, creating all-black farming communities and all-black organizations to support land acquisition, self-governance, and cultural autonomy. Such attitudes undermined opportunities for political alliances, both during the Populist era of the 1890s and in the Great Depression. The authors write about the back-to-the-country movement during the early twentieth century in Georgia, combining the self-help philosophy of Booker T. Washington with the separation of the races. During the 1920s, following the decline of Marcus Garvey's movement, the National Federation of Colored Farmers took up many of his radical ideas, especially the separation of blacks and whites, arguing that self-reliance and autonomy through land ownership would "save the race." As several of the articles indicate, despite the fact that in most rural areas members of both races raised the same crops, slaughtered the same livestock, and shared access to and frustrations with markets, there were few efforts to come together in a common cause.

The anthology ends with an article on the successful multi-year struggle of black farmers against the U.S. Department of Agriculture, an agency they called the "Last Plantation." After winning a $1.25 billion award, about $18,000 per individual among the 70,000 or so affected, President Obama said, "My hope is that the farmers and their families who were denied access to USDA loans and programs will be made whole and will have the chance to rebuild their lives and their businesses." Congress, however, did not authorize the release of funds. In short, this anthology takes us on a journey from the beginning of freedom to the present day, offering new insights into the social, cultural, and political attitudes of black farmers as well as their struggles to overcome the racism that looms so large in our nation's history.

Loren Schweninger

Abbreviations

AAA—Agricultural Adjustment Act

AANCL—Association for the Advancement of Negro Country Life

ACP—Agricultural Conservation Program

AHC—Austin History Center (Texas)

AME—African Methodist Episcopal Church

ANSR—Annual Narrative and Statistical Reports of State Offices and County Agents

ASCS—Agricultural Stabilization and Conservation Service

BFAA—Black Farmers and Agriculturalists Association

BFH—Benjamin Franklin Hubert

BFH Papers—Benjamin Franklin Hubert papers, Hargrett Rare Book and Manuscript Library, University of Georgia, Athens

Brewington—*Cecil Brewington et al. v. Dan Glickman, Secretary, U.S. Department of Agriculture*, Civil Action No. 98–1693 (PLF) (D.D.C. April 14, 1999); consolidated with *Pigford*

Briggs—*Harry Briggs, Jr., et al. v. The Board of Trustees for School District Number 22, Clarendon County, South Carolina, R. W. Elliott, Chairman, et al.*, 1950 Case No.: 2505; and *Harry Briggs, Jr., et al. v. R. W. Elliott, et al.*, 1950 Case No. 2657. These cases originated in the U.S. District Court for the Eastern District of South Carolina. The decision in *Briggs v. Elliott* (1950 Case No. 2657) was appealed to the U.S. Supreme Court as *Harry Briggs et al. v. Elliott et al.*, 342 U.S. 350 (SCOTUS, 1952); consolidated with *Brown v. Board of Education*

Brown I—*Oliver Brown et al. v. Board of Education of Topeka et al.*, 347 U.S. 483 (SCOTUS, 1954)

Brown II—*Oliver Brown et al. v. Board of Education of Topeka et al.*, judgment on relief, 349 U.S. 294 (SCOTUS, 1955)

CCIA—Clarendon County Improvement Association

Census—U.S. Federal Census

Cobell—*Elouise Cobell et al. v. Bruce Babbitt, Secretary, Department of the Interior* (D.D.C., filed June 10, 1996), subsequently *Cobell v. Norton*; *Cobell v. Kempthorne*, 569 F. Supp.2d 223, 226 (D.D.C. 2008); *Cobell v. Salazar* (*Cobell XXII*), 573 F.3d 808 (D.C. Cir. 2009)

Colored Alliance—Colored Farmers National Alliance and Co-Operative Union, a.k.a. Colored Farmers Alliance

CRAT—Civil Rights Action Team, U.S. Department of Agriculture

CRAT Report—*Civil Rights at the U.S. Department of Agriculture* (Washington, D.C.: Government Printing Office, 1997)

CUL—Clemson University Libraries, Clemson University, Clemson, South Carolina

D.C. Cir.—U.S. Court of Appeals for the District of Columbia Circuit

DDC—U.S. District Court for the District of Columbia

ELF—Emergency Land Fund

EWG—Environmental Working Group

FAMU—Florida Agricultural and Mechanical University

FCA—Farm Credit Administration

FCHR—Fairfax County Circuit Court Historical Records (Virginia)

FES—Federal Extension Service

FLAG—Farmers' Legal Action Group

FmHA—Farmers Home Administration (1946)

FSA—Farm Security Administration (1935)

FSA—Farm Service Agency (1994)

FSC—Federation of Southern Cooperatives

FSCW—Florida State College for Women, Tallahassee

FSL—Florida State Library, Gainesville

Land Tax Books—Fairfax County Land Tax Books—South, 1911: Colored/Mount Vernon District (Virginia)

LCCMHR—Lowndes County Christian Movement for Human Rights

LCFO—Lowndes County Freedom Organization

LDS—Church of Jesus Christ of Latter-Day Saints

LFU—Louisiana Farmers' Union

Love—*Rosemary Love et al. v. Dan Glickman, U.S. Secretary of Agriculture*, No. 00-2502 (D.D.C., filed October 19, 2000); consolidated with *Garcia*; subsequently *Love v. Veneman, Love v. Johanns, Love v. Schafer, Love v. Vilsack*

NAACP—National Association for the Advancement of Colored People

NAD—National Appeals Division

NARA—National Archives and Records Administration

NBFA—National Black Farmers Association

NFCF—National Federation of Colored Farmers

NNHW—National Negro Health Week

NOI—Nation of Islam

OEO—Office of Economic Opportunity

PLF—Paul L. Friedman, Judge, U.S. District Court for the District of Columbia, acronym affixed to case numbers designating his decisions

Pearson—James Pearson, an infant, by Levi Pearson, his next friend and *Levi Pearson v. County Board of Education for Clarendon County, et. al.*, 1948 Case No. 1909, U. S. District Court for the Eastern District of South Carolina, Charleston Division (1948)

Pigford (Pigford I)—*Timothy C. Pigford et al. v. Dan Glickman, Secretary, U.S. Department of Agriculture*, Civil Action No. 97-1978 (PLF) (D.D.C., April 14, 1999), consolidated with *Brewington*; consent decree approved, 185 F.R.D. 82 (D.D.C. 1999); consent decree affirmed, 206 F.3d 1212 (D.C. Cir. 2000); subsequently *Pigford v. Veneman, Pigford v. Johanns, Pigford v. Schafer, Pigford v. Vilsack*

Pigford II—Term used to distinguish claimants admitted into the *Pigford* class in 2000 from those who met the original *Pigford* filing deadline of October 12, 1999 (*Pigford I*); the 2008 farm bill (P.L. 110-246) included provision for funding these late claims, but appropriations lag behind

Plessy v. Ferguson—*Homer A. Plessy v. J.H. Ferguson*, 163 U.S. 537 (SCOTUS, 1896)

RA—Resettlement Administration

RG 33, NARA—Records of the Extension Service, 1888–1991, Record Group 33, National Archives and Records Administration, College Park, Maryland

RG 33.6, NARA—Annual Narrative and Statistical Reports, 1908–66, 3,590 lin. ft. and 7,167 rolls of microfilm, Records of the Extension Service, Record Group 33.6, National Archives and Records Administration, College Park, Maryland

SCOTUS—Supreme Court of the United States

SCU—Share Croppers' Union of Alabama

SHLRC—Sam Houston Regional Library and Research Center, Liberty, Texas

SNCC—Student Nonviolent Coordinating Committee

STFU—Southern Tenant Farmers' Union

Tri-State—Tri-State Tobacco Growers' Cooperative

UF—University of Florida, Gainesville

UFSC—University of Florida Special Collections, Gainesville

UNIA—Universal Negro Improvement Association

USDA—U.S. Department of Agriculture

WHS—Wisconsin Historical Society, Madison

WPA—Works Progress Administration

Introduction

DEBRA A. REID

John W. Boyd Jr., who founded the National Black Farmers Association (NBFA) in 1995, described himself as a "fourth-generation black farmer" with roots in tobacco country. When not engrossed in his numerous duties as a nonprofit director and advocate for black farmers, he farms in Bakersville, Virginia. Boyd grew up in urban New Jersey, not on the family farm, but he spent a lot of time there helping his grandparents before he eventually committed himself to farming and activism. Gary R. Grant, president of the Black Farmers and Agriculturalists Association (BFAA), founded in 1997, grew up in Tillery, North Carolina, a community that the Farm Security Administration created to resettle selected black farm families. Both the NBFA and the BFAA emerged as other organizations such as the Federation of Southern Cooperatives (FSC), founded in 1967, and the Farmers' Legal Action Group (FLAG), founded in 1986, became even more vigilant advocates for black farmers.[1]

Farmer organizations and collective action increased public awareness of African American landowning farm families, but few scholars have committed to the painstaking research necessary to document their existence and explicate their pasts. Studies of the Colored Farmers Alliance, which appealed to tens of thousands of politically conscious farmers during the late 1880s and early 1890s, tend to focus on the leaders. Paltry evidence makes it difficult to document the rank and file or arrive at conclusions about farmers who joined the movement. Yet, knowing more about the farming communities that sustained political organizations generally could increase understanding of the activism that farmers engaged in historically, and could provide needed context for the activism that occurred during the nadir of black farming later during the twentieth century.

W.E.B. Du Bois studied black landowning farmers operating at the turn of the twentieth century and indicated the status that landowners held and the respect they commanded. Such influence had apparently all but disappeared by 1967 when the Federation of Southern Cooperatives called attention, in the post–Civil Rights Act context, to another inalienable right under assault, the right to own land. The Black Economic Research Center's director, Robert Browne, published *Only Six Million Acres* in 1973, which documented African American land acquisition and loss over one hundred years, and Browne founded the Emergency Land Fund (ELF) the same year to provide financial support to reverse the trend. The ELF, under Browne's direction and with USDA funding, researched the causes of black land loss and completed "The Impact of Heir Property on Black Rural Land Tenure in the Southeastern Region of the United States" in 1980. By 1990 such activism culminated in the first lawsuit on behalf of black farmers against the national government. When little came of that effort, the FSC organized the first "Caravan to Washington" in 1992 to generate attention, and in 1997, FLAG with the FSC filed a lawsuit that became *Pigford v. Glickman*, the largest class action lawsuit in U.S. history, citing racial discrimination as the class grievance.[2]

The settlement of the consent decree in *Pigford* remains a work in progress, but it generated fresh interest in a forgotten class—black landowners. Associated Press reporters serialized the drama of black landownership in three installments in late 2001. Other newspaper coverage of black farm ownership caused Evan Bennett to reflect on African Americans' embrace of their rural and farm heritage as an act of empowerment. He cited as evidence the *New York Times* story "Black Landowners Fight to Reclaim Georgia Home," which explained how the U.S. government's seizure of land by eminent domain during World War II to build an airfield destroyed a community and how former members tried to return to it seventy years later. Stories such as this, according to Bennett, imply that "African Americans are [discovering] some lost rural tradition, [when] it has been there all along!"[3]

Documentary film, exhibits, and accompanying publications had helped inform even broader audiences. Evocative historic and contemporary photographs combined with personal narratives of African American farmers at work, at community gatherings, and in conversations with family about farm management make clear the love-hate relationships that develop as farm families struggle to retain their land. Filmmaker Charlene Gilbert put the experiences of her landowning farm family in Montezuma, Georgia, into context in the 1998 documentary film *Homecoming*. She approached the film "as a historical investigation" and captured well the conundrum of "the importance of the land to those who continue to work it and in working it honor those who spilled their blood to escape it." Photographer John Francis Ficara documented sixty farm-owning families across six southern states from the Carolinas to Louisiana, and one northern state, Michigan, starting in 1999. The stories they shared conveyed the common struggle to keep "their fields sufficiently productive to provide enough income to hold onto the land that has been in their families for generations.... They sweat and pray for what most of us take for granted—a reasonable income and independence." Traveling exhibits, First Lady Michelle Obama's good-food advocacy, and seed catalogues advertising African American heritage vegetables sustain interest in African Americans and agriculture in 2010.[4]

Black farm families would virtually disappear from both the contemporary and the historic farming landscape without sustained efforts to keep them visible. Contributors to this collection have taken the time to document black land and farm owners and their families, many of whom left little more than a ripple of historic evidence. The contributors did so to correct some narratives that oversimplify African American roles in American history. First, African Americans were not the only farmers constrained by cotton monoculture; nor were they the only farmers debilitated by crop liens. Second, city life did not define African American experiences as much as the concentration on urban history and black culture studies implies. Third, the historiographic emphases on urban experiences contrasted with rural impoverishment have cast the Great Migration as little more than an escape from the rural South. This interpretation implies that nothing of value occurred in the rural South after the talented youth left for different opportunities in cities, and it implies that change happened only because of northern urban influences. Charlene Gilbert conveys this oft repeated assumption when she describes the land that her family farmed as "the same land that held up the world for the young 'smart Negro' children of the [1950s] and [1960s] who dreamed of lives off the farm, who dreamed of labor free of sweat, and who dreamed of giving their sons and daughters a world of choices beyond forty acres and a mule." Essays in this volume challenge assumptions that the smartest or more militant rural youth left the South and only the subservient stayed behind. Contributors provide ample evidence that those who remained on the farms and in their rural communities did not submit to the status quo. Instead, they managed their businesses (their farms) in which they had much invested, participated in their communities, reacted to changing local, state, national, and international conditions, and risked all to secure their rights.[5]

Urban bias has most obfuscated rural contributions to the civil rights movement, particularly farm family activism. Dr. Hasan Kwame Jeffries, native of Brooklyn, New York, and graduate of southern urban universities, told delegates to the 2010 Agricultural History Society conference that rural areas have been ignored by scholars of the Black Power movement. His research helped him realize that evidence must document the movement over the *longue durée* and must integrate rural and farm perspectives. Greta de Jong, a New Zealander and student of Nan Woodruff, approached her history of rural Louisianans' involvement with the Congress of Racial Equality knowing that "black activism in the rural South before the arrival of civil rights workers has largely gone unnoticed." Both make it clear that rural people can no longer be ignored as a force for change, or worse, vilified as the antithesis of change, in the context of African American experiences, and that black land and farm owners need to be added to the list of activists who, de Jong claims, "provided the backbone of the . . . freedom movement."[6]

Essays in this collection concentrate on black landowning farm families who exercised their civil rights from the end of the Civil War to the present. They operated farms, helped create communities, and developed social, economic, and political infrastructure, but they remained nearly invisible in the historical record nonetheless. Sociologist Arthur Raper claimed, in 1936, that the black farm owner "provides leadership and much of the support for the local institutions of his race. With an abiding interest in the land he cultivates, in the stock he raises, in the trees he plants, and in the community where he lives, the Negro owner, like the white owner, stands in sharp contrast with the landless farmer who moves every two or three years from one barren farm cabin to another." J. William Harris concluded, based on Raper's comment, that "black landowning families were a small minority, but important in the African American community out of proportion to their numbers."[7]

Scholars have been slow to analyze black landowning farm families, in general. They have not addressed the factors that gave black landowners a status comparable to their white peers and that made them distinctive from their landless white and black peers. Few social scientists documented black land ownership during the forty years in which rural blacks accumulated their land holdings, a period stretching between the end of Reconstruction and the end of World War I. W.E.B. Du Bois devoted the most scholarly attention to the phenomenon during the late nineteenth and early twentieth century. Luther Porter Jackson and others studied property accumulation among free African Americans prior to the Civil War, but paid less attention to property accumulated by freedpeople after the war. Economic historians Robert Higgs and Robert Margo quantified property accumulation among rural blacks, but the most comprehensive treatment remains Loren Schweninger's *Black Property Owners in the South, 1790–1915*. Schweninger explained the correlation that African Americans made between the right they had to own property and their status as American citizens: Did African Americans "equate ownership with power, prestige, and status," as did other Americans? Did property ownership provide the means by which people of African descent became American? He focused his inquiry on the region of the United States where 90 percent of all African Americans lived until the late 1910s, specifically in fifteen southern states and the District of Columbia. He concluded that blacks "clung to the values and attitudes . . . that acquiring land and property [c]ould somehow free them . . . [but] it never would."[8]

Black property owners, in fact, personified the "ambiguous tension between race consciousness and the strong impulse of so many blacks to 'integrate' themselves into American civilization."[9] Many white southerners went to any length to prevent integration, but one of the most innocuous measures entailed an ideological construct that linked landownership with the white race and landlessness with the black race. Many white southerners knew that the distinction was inaccurate. Lily Hardy Hammond, a social reformer and advocate for interracial cooperation who lived in Augusta, Georgia, argued that middle-class blacks and whites had much in common. "Our problem is not racial, but human and economic. The coincidence to so great extent in the South of the property line and the color line has confused our thoughts. We hold the Negro racially responsible for conditions common to all races on his economic plane."[10] Hammond's comment confirmed the social constructions that conferred a lower economic status on black farmers than their white peers—but also challenged the construct as misguided. Racism obfuscated the factors that trapped whites as well as blacks in a lower economic status but also blinded people to the strategies shared by farmers who accumulated property.

Historians have slowly moved beyond the stereotypes. J. William Harris, who compared three southern regions in *Deep Souths*, observed that "many . . . generalizations about black farmers apply equally well to whites. The status and incomes of African Americans was determined, as it had been for generations, partly by race, [but] partly by other factors." Few have attempted to put aside race and address those other factors, but Neil Canaday's study of property accumulation in a South Carolina cotton county and Neil Canaday and Charles Reback's study of literacy and real estate purchases stand as notable exceptions that take into account factors in addition to race.[11]

Members of both races subscribed to agrarian rhetoric that had helped define the nation, but race consciousness caused their convictions to diverge. Thomas Jefferson popularized agrarianism during the 1780s as a foundation for national policy. Agrarianism elevated farmers as the chosen citizens of the nation, morally upright and beyond corruption due to their status as independent landowners. Jefferson believed that government policy should ensure distribution of public lands in the interest of creating a nation of landowning farmers. After 1865, white southerners remained committed to Jeffersonian agrarianism but southern Democrats modified their agrarianism on notions of black inferiority. Freedpeople, on the other hand, built their agrarianism on the foundation that they had used to end slavery and oppose white supremacy. Steven Hahn has identified the "disruptive and communal behaviors" that slaves and free blacks used to make the Civil War into a war to end slavery. Freedpeople who sought land used the same strategies to realize their goals; they practiced individual choice in acquiring land, and they used it to develop communities. They mobilized their resources, formed organizations, and identified spokespersons to convey their agenda. Thinking about black agrarianism in this context, as fundamentally defiant, can recast rural landowner enclaves as something other than accommodations to second-class citizenship, and something other than economic opportunism. Some communities of landowning families developed because of biracial cooperation, but most became bastions of racial separatism, tangible evidence of accomplishments, and symbols of black empowerment when little else conveyed that lesson.[12]

White southerners did their best to deemphasize the potential offered by landownership. In 1889 historian Philip A. Bruce linked real property acquisition to full citizenship: "Not until the negro becomes a property owner, not until he has an interest in the soil, do the whites expect to see him as an estimable citizen." Yet Bruce denigrated the goal by criticizing landowning black families as marginalized and impoverished, elderly and addled, preferring to exercise their liberty rather than enjoy the comforts that the plantation masters stood willing to provide.[13]

Regardless of how white southerners such as Bruce misrepresented them, black farmers who owned land held a different status than the majority of residents in many rural communities. Their elevation as business owners instead of laborers pleased social scientists who interpreted this as evidence of economic growth. W.E.B. Du Bois commented on class divisions becoming more evident among residents in Farmville, Virginia, in 1898 and between landowners and other rural residents in Georgia in 1901. The class division that Du Bois identified did not go unnoticed, but as Hammond intimated, the division manifested the tension that existed between race consciousness, on one hand, and integration into the American capitalist system, on the other. Evidence abounded that some blacks had secured the American agrarian dream of landownership, but fear of retribution prompted some to conceal their accomplishments from those whites intent on maintaining economic as well as social inequality. Owners could assume economic, social, and civil leadership positions within segregated rural enclaves but outside of those they adopted non-controversial self-help rhetoric.[14]

Evan Bennett urges us to lift the veil, as it were, and see black landowners for who they were and what they represented. As is, black landowners seems "analogous to free blacks in the antebellum period. . . . [free blacks existed] but antebellum slave owners' logic (to be black was to be a slave) clouds our vision." Not until Melvin Ely's *Israel on the Appomattox* appeared did historians "consider free blacks as something other than anomalies whose presence did not alter the story." The same applies for black landowners. Relatively few black farmers became landowners, but if scholars assume that all black farmers were sharecroppers, then they accept "the basic logic/assumption of the postbellum white power structure"—that all blacks had been slaves; that all blacks were laborers—and scholars will continue to "see the landowners as anomalies."[15]

Black landowning farm families can become part of the mainstream, and no longer anomalous, if research incorporates factors in addition to race. For example, studies could compare farm ownership and literacy rates, could map the relationship of property tax payments and farm-to-market road proximity, and could determine the correlation between diversity in

Figure I.1. J. R. Dean owned a two-hundred-acre farm but was too old to work. Instead he lived with a hotel keeper in Ashville, Alabama, February 1915. Source: McCormick-International Harvester Collection, WHi-9464, Wisconsin Historical Society.

production and propensity for farm ownership. More needs to be done to determine the ways that agricultural policy, including but not limited to the relief, recovery, and reform agenda of the New Deal, affected farmers, white as well as black. This requires scholars to move beyond race as a factor that limited rural prosperity.

Those who assume that blacks generally operated as unfree landless laborers may also assume that all landowners were rich and all tenants and sharecroppers poor. Certainly a correlation existed between the value of farmland and the status of the owner, but land ownership did not necessarily translate into a higher standard of living for black farmers. Du Bois indicted that materially, landowners' property visibly conveyed their class superiority. The landowners improved their homes modestly, and slowly, adding a porch to a former slave cabin, putting in glass windows, and adding sheds. They did this as they restored their soil and invested in other permanent improvements. Many did not invest in their own creature comforts. Former slave J. R. Dean borrowed four hundred dollars to purchase two hundred acres after the Civil War and still owned the farm in

1915, but he was too old to work and lived with a hotel keeper in Ashville, Alabama. His living arrangements implied poverty, but his landholdings documented an alternative reality (figure I.1). Another former slave from Missouri, Thomas Green, bought land for $1.50 an acre in Pleasant Ridge, Wisconsin, after 1863. He lived into his mid-nineties on his farm in comfort but not pretension.[16]

Farm owners' political ideology warrants further study. Many assume that black farmers shared political goals because they were black. Political scientist Adolph Reed confirmed that "black Americans' racial status always at least partly shaped the character of their political involvement [but] the goals of those involvements were by no means always exclusively, or even primarily, racial. . . . Black farmers organized and acted as black farmers . . . even as they linked those activities to the larger goal of improving the race's condition."[17] In fact, black farmers organized and acted as *farmers*, and then further refined their political identity because farm owners had different agendas than tenants or sharecroppers. Did African Americans forge political alliances across class divisions during the Jim Crow era, or did disfranchisement help elevate the owners because their property gave them the resources they needed to pursue other forms of political speech than the vote? Owners paid property taxes, which gave them some influence in local decisions, if not in state and national debates. Hahn's comprehensive treatment of rural political struggles in the former Confederacy goes a long way toward explaining rural influence. As he argues, gains made by "freedom's first generation" to maintain attachments "to people, to place, and more generally to the land . . . created dense webs of black community life, . . . [gave] tangible meaning to the notion of uplift through social separation, and [testified] to the value of their many and varied mobilizations."[18] Black landowning families warrant additional dedicated study to understand the significance of these mobilizations within and beyond the community.

The essays in *Beyond Forty Acres and a Mule* take a sober look at black landowning families generally and at farm owners specifically. Essays identify the opportunities they created for themselves, the divisions that united and separated them from other rural residents, and the ways they managed their farms, their livelihoods. It took the near extinction of black farmers by the end of the twentieth century to galvanize public support for them. These essays collectively try to recapture the complexity of rural life to explain why so few remained so committed to a way of life, a business, a reform agenda, a social outlet, and a community identity that allowed them to exert influence out of proportion to their number.

* * *

Authors conceptualize black farmers in relation to personal, regional, and national issues. Adrienne Petty, in her essay, "The Jim Crow Section of Agricultural History," challenges readers to reconsider the prevailing method of analysis for studying agriculture in the American South. She argues that black farmers were distinct but not separate from their white peers. Therefore, scholars should not set them apart for study and analysis as though they existed in a separate society. Scholars must recognize the ways that racism affected the prospects of black farmers, but race-specific approach obscures the fact that the exploitation of both white and black farmers was of a piece, and that they farmed the same crops on adjacent land and depended on the same markets. To understand any nuances in this general exploitation that may be a consequence of racism demands a common approach to studying farmers as a single class.

Three case studies focus on farm acquisition and retention as practiced in three regions of the South, Virginia, Georgia, and Texas, between the end of the Civil War and the start of World War II. Scott E. Casper uses court records and kinship networks to trace the process by which African Americans in Mount Vernon's shadow acquired farmland and other real and personal property over the years. "Out of Mount Vernon's Shadow: Black Landowners in George Washington's Neighborhood, 1870–1930" explores the connections that landowning families created to help protect their investments, and Casper indicates how internal tension and external pressures made it difficult for the poor and undercapitalized black families to retain their possessions. He identifies the class tensions that created distance between farm owners, operators, and agricultural laborers, and the ways that personal conflicts undermined African American solidarity. In addition, this case study of people who self-identified as "farmers" indicates the variety of meanings that rural and urban blacks associated with the term "farming." Some owned acreage adequate to dedicate their lives to production agriculture, but most worked in a variety of agricultural occupations including market gardening. Such pursuits could sustain black farm families but did not always translate into recognition of accomplishments by their contemporaries or subsequent researchers.

Keith J. Volanto, in "James E. Youngblood: Race, Family, and Farm Ownership in Jim Crow Texas," traces the history of one biracial man from his progenitors' trek to Texas through his acquisition and management of sizeable land holdings. Volanto delves into the complicated relationships that caused light-skinned James E. Youngblood to secure land through association with his extended white family more than his freedmen relatives. Racial ambiguity (association with whites as a bound laborer and social distance from his black family) allowed Youngblood to emerge in post-Reconstruction Texas as one of the leading property holders in the county. He secured such wealth through domination of his own large hardworking family and through connections with markets. These gave him economic security but not full citizenship rights. Youngblood gained his property holdings and his family gained its status not because of deep connections within African American communities but almost despite these associations. Instead, connections to extended white kin allowed Youngblood to become the "Squire of Limestone County."

Mark Schultz delves into the life of Benjamin F. Hubert, a rural reformer in Georgia who participated in the back-to-the-country movement during the early twentieth century, in his essay "Benjamin Hubert and the Association for the Advancement of Negro Country Life." Georgia, in 1900, had the lowest proportion of black landowners in the southern states. Hubert tried to stem the flood away from farming by establishing a viable independent black town, the Log Cabin Community. Hubert allied with other African American agrarian reformers who believed that property, well managed, could help rural blacks secure an independent life separate from whites and buffered against white supremacy and unequal citizenship.

Two essays address farmers in politics and political divisions among farmers. Omar H. Ali, in "Black Populism: Agrarian Politics from the Colored Alliance to the People's Party," explains the ways agricultural interests helped define rural third-party politics during the 1880s and 1890s. Black farm owners sought economic stability, rights protection, and political influence. They constructed a viable strategy based in moral reform, community uplift, and political activism to realize these goals. Racism marginalized black farmers from full participation in white populist organizations, so Black Populism emerged as a distinctive movement with its own organizations, leaders, and tactics. Yet, dissention arose over class interests when farm owners became uneasy with the radical activism that farm laborers pursued, particularly when cotton picker strikes threatened farm owners' property.

Jarod Roll, in "'The Lazarus of American Farmers': The Politics of Black Agrarianism in the Jim Crow South, 1921–1938," explores the evolution of black agrarianism between the Great Migration and the Great Depression. He does so by analyzing the membership of the Universal Negro Improvement Association (UNIA) and the National Federation of Colored Farmers (NFCF). He connects the two organizations, showing that members of the UNIA, predominantly landowners, shifted allegiance to the NFCF when the UNIA dissolved during the 1920s. He indicates that both organizations gained membership because of their race-conscious goals, but UNIA members, predominantly farm owners, believed that self-reliance and autonomy through landownership could save the race. The NFCF celebrated similar goals until economic conditions worsened. By the early 1930s NFCF leaders articulated a new agrarian protest rhetoric that emphasized labor as patriotic and worthy of national government protection. The NFCF did not prosper, however, but the ultimate failure of the UNIA and the NFCF should not be considered proof of their irrelevance. Instead, studying the demise of one and the rise and eventual decline of another agrarian organization can help explain the contested nature of farmer politics during an era of farm consolidation and changing agricultural practices.

Crop cultures dictated work routines that created common experiences for black and white farm families. Yet shared work routines and shared catastrophes did not obliterate the racism that limited opportunities available to African American farm families. Crop cultures reified various divisions of labor so that sex, class, age, and skill, in addition to race, must be addressed as we consider the meanings of the rituals and rhythms of the seasons.

Cotton grew in importance as a cash crop and came to dominate southern agriculture over the same time period that the number of black farmers who owned their land increased. Black owners grew the crop, but their legal relationship to the crop differed from that of landless cash renters or sharecroppers who grew it. In fact, farm owners told stories about their ability to make cotton pay because they had the freedom to devote labor to crops and stock in addition to cotton. During the mid-1910s L. C. Carter, a farmer near Butler Springs, Alabama, explained to a reporter from *Harvester World* magazine that he could profit from his nine-bale cotton crop because he had planted a garden to help feed his family and forage crops to feed his livestock (figure I.2). Thus he could hold his cotton "till he [could] get a fair price for it; otherwise he would have to sacrifice it . . . to get enough money to buy groceries to live on."[19]

But what of the situation in states where cotton was not king and where relatively few black farm families lived but where their ownership rates

Figure I.2. L. C. Carter, a farmer near Butler Springs, Alabama, next to the shed where he stored his nine bales of cotton. Originally published in *Harvester World* magazine (June 1918), 2. Source: McCormick-International Harvester Collection, WHi-44199, Wisconsin Historical Society.

exceeded 50 percent of the total black farmer population? Debra A. Reid's essay addresses the tensions that emerged in a border area where North met South, rural met urban, and ethnic met American. She considers the ways that urban markets and ethnic diversity created different dynamics that African Americans negotiated to try to cross the color line that kept them landless in the post-Reconstruction Midwest. Farmers near the city raised wheat, cut cordwood, and raised hogs, as did many of their neighbors. Such economic diversity kept the families busy and mobile across race boundaries. They interacted at market, worried about crop and stock prices, and helped one another as need arose. Yet black landowning farmers and their white peers remained ideologically separate, and this undermined the potential that a biracial class alliance might have offered prior to the Great Depression.

Other crop cultures offered different opportunities. No region better illustrates the relationship between crop culture and farm-family potential than the bright tobacco area that straddled the Virginia and North Carolina border. Evan P. Bennett's essay "Of the Quest of the Golden Leaf: Black

Farmers and Bright Tobacco in the Piedmont South" focuses on the precarious position of landowning farmers, the role of tobacco agriculture in their lives, and the agrarian vision that resulted and rang as true during the 1930s as when voiced by the National Black Farmers Association in 2010.

Kelly A. Minor's essay "'Justifiable Pride': Negotiation and Collaboration in Florida African American Extension" explores the relationships between agents of the Negro Division of the Florida Agricultural Extension Service and African American farm families in a state with a nearly 50 percent land ownership rate among black farmers. Minor argues that the farm families influenced the programs delivered by home demonstration agents over the entire history of the Negro Division's existence. She explains the institutional structure of the division as well as the chain of command within the division and between the division and the white service. Such a structure implies that forces of reform flowed directly out and into communities and farm homes. Yet black farm families, communities, governing bodies, and funding sources all influenced the work that agents delivered. Black women had to balance lack of resources and lack of support with practical steps that could improve rural standards of living. The history shows frustration as well as failure as gender bias, racism, sexism, and poverty compromised reform. Ultimately, the informal education that black home demonstration agents provided helped farm families, because even though farmers selectively adopted the advice, the services gave families support that they otherwise lacked.[20]

Black reform agendas such as those promoted by the African American agents employed in agricultural extension services across the South helped black farm-owning families remain viable even as government policy conspired against landless farmers and agricultural laborers. Competing political organizations likewise fueled political activism, legal activism, and civil rights expansion. Three essays address factors that drew black farmers into grassroots politics and made them both advocates for and critics of government involvement in twentieth-century rural reform.

Veronica L. Womack in "Black Power in the Alabama Black Belt to the 1970s" argues that white land control, an impoverished working class, and violent race relations resulted in a distinctive form of Black Power. African Americans purchased land despite this, but Alabama still had the second lowest rate of black land ownership among black farmers in the South in 1900. Most black farmers in the state operated farms on the cash-rent system. Others operated on the shares, and they, along with agricultural laborers, suffered at the hands of merciless landlords. Sharecroppers and laborers briefly allied with the Communist Party during the 1930s and challenged the capitalist system that entrapped them in exploitive monoculture. White supremacists responded with violence. These competing agendas between black landowners, cash- and share-rent tenants, and laborers created fertile ground for the emergence of militant Black Power and overtly separatist goals pursued by Black Muslims through the Nation of Islam in the aftermath of the signing of the Civil Rights Act of 1964.

Rural African Americans may be perceived as being economically conservative and averse to risking their investments by challenging the racial status quo. Yet African American agricultural extension service employees helped develop a community spirit that came to fruition in the *Briggs v. Elliott* case, one of the five cases consolidated into the *Brown v. Board of Education of Topeka, Kansas* ruling of the Supreme Court of the United States in 1954. South Carolinians Harry Sr. and Eliza Briggs, Levi Pearson, and the Reverend Joseph Delaine tried to destroy segregation and ensure equal educational opportunities for their children. The rural dimension of *Briggs v. Elliott* and its reverberations in Clarendon County, South Carolina, however, have largely been overlooked. Carmen V. Harris addresses this oversight in "'You're just like mules, you don't know your own strength': Rural South Carolina Blacks and the Emergence of the Civil Rights Struggle."

Many of the plaintiffs in the *Briggs* case were farmers, most of them independent landowners. They remained steadfast in pursuing equal opportunity even as whites who dominated the predominantly black county disrupted and, in some cases, destroyed the black farm families' agricultural livelihoods. In the aftermath of the *Brown v. Board of Education* ruling, African American farmers in the Elloree community in Orangeburg County began to pursue equal opportunities that the Supreme Court's rulings in *Brown I* and *Brown II* affirmed. In this second rural community, African American farmers again faced white economic reprisal but remained resolute. A decade later Afro-South Carolinian farmers in other counties confronted the inequalities of integration in the extension service and asserted their right to determine agricultural progress in their own communities.

Valerie Grim indicates that black farmers have still not won the long struggle for equal rights. In 1999, for the first time in American history, black farmers brought a successful class action law suit against the U.S. Department of Agriculture, the institution they called the "Last Plantation." For years black farmers claimed discrimination in federally funded agricultural programs. They alleged that their civil rights were violated and that the USDA did nothing to prevent local and state agricultural agencies charged with implementation of its federal farm programs from establishing oppressive and racist operational practices and procedures. In "Between Forty Acres and a Class Action Lawsuit: Black Farmers, Civil Rights, and Protest against the U.S. Department of Agriculture, 1997–2010" Grim claims that black farmers placed their land loss and other related agricultural and farming struggles right in the middle of the continuous civil rights struggle in America.

The contributors to this collection increase understanding of the ways that black landowning farm families responded to adversity historically and pursued equity, justice, and human and civil rights. Ultimately these essays inform us of the variety of personal agendas, grassroots politics, educational initiatives, and economic strategies that helped African American landowning farm families challenge white agrarianism and white supremacy even as they pursued their own American democratic ideals.

Notes

Evan P. Bennett's comments improved this introduction. I thank him for his clarity in editing and for his solid grounding in agricultural history. He and I hatched the idea for this collection at the 2006 American Historical Association meeting, and it could not have come to fruition without his support. I thank Shawn Hale for suggestions that improved this work, Sumner Hunnewell for indexing, and Jacqueline Wehrle for proofreading.

1. "Biography," Dr. John W. Boyd Jr., at http://www.johnboydjr.com/bio.html; National Black Farmers Association Web site, http://www.blackfarmers.org/ (accessed August 13, 2010); Gary Grant, homepage of the Black Farmers and Agriculturalists Association, http://www.bfaa-us.org/index.html (accessed August 13, 2010).

2. The Federation of Southern Cooperatives maintains a timeline at http://www.federationsoutherncoop.com/landloss.htm (accessed February 21, 2011). Robert S. Browne, *Only Six Million Acres: The Decline of Black Owned Land in the Rural South* (New York: Black Economic Research Center, June 1973; repr., March 1975). Emergency Land Fund, "The Impact of Heir Property on Black Rural Land Tenure in the Southeastern Region of the United States" (1980), released to the USDA/Farmers Home Administration (1984). For decisions, court orders, arbiter and mediator statements for *Pigford v. Glickman* (and its permutations), see the Office of the Monitor, http://www.pigfordmonitor.org/ (accessed June 2, 2010). The Environmental Working Group and the NBFA investigated USDA compliance with the consent decree and subsequent court orders. The report and tables based on 2004 data appear at http://www.ewg.org/reports/blackfarmers (accessed June 2, 2010).

3. E-mail, Evan P. Bennett to Debra A. Reid, August 12, 2010. The series consisted of Todd Lewan and Dolores Barclay, "Torn from the Land, Part I: Black Americans' Farmland Taken through Cheating, Intimidation, Even Murder" (December 2, 2001); Todd Lewan, Dolores Barclay, and Allen G. Breed, "Torn from the Land, Part II: Landownership

Made Blacks Targets of Violence and Murder, an AP Investigation Shows" (December 3, 2001); Dolores Barclay, "Torn from the Land, Part II: A Man Is Jailed for Defending His Land" (December 3, 2001); Todd Lewan, "Torn from the Land, Part II: Taking Away the Vote—and a Black Man's Land" (December 3, 2001); Todd Lewan and Dolores Barclay, "Torn from the Land, Part III: Today, Developers and Lawyers Use a Legal Maneuver to Strip Black Families of Land" (December 9, 2001); and Todd Lewan, "Torn from the Land, Part III: With Help from Their White Lawyer, A Black Mississippi Family Loses a Farm" (December 9, 2001), all available through *The Authentic Voice*, http://www.theauthenticvoice.org/Torn_From_The_Land_Intro.html (accessed August 9, 2010). "Black Landowners Fight to Reclaim Georgia Home," *New York Times* (June 30, 2010), at http://www.nytimes.com/2010/07/01/us/01harris.html (accessed August 13, 2010); printed in *New York Times*, New York edition (July 1, 2010), A16.

    4. Charlene Gilbert, producer and director, *Homecoming* (Independent Television Service, 1998). Charlene Gilbert and Quinn Eli, *Homecoming: The Story of African-American Farmers* (Boston: Beacon Press, 2000), 3. John Francis Ficara, photographer, Juan Williams, essay, *Black Farmers in America* (Lexington: University Press of Kentucky, 2006), xvii. Margaret A. Hutto and Nona R. Martin, curators, "Distant Echoes: Black Farmers in America," Reginald F. Lewis Museum of Maryland African-American History and Culture, a traveling exhibit based on sixty of Ficara's images, opened on February 3, 2006. "The African American Heritage Collection," *Landreth 2009–2011 Catalog* (New Freedom, Penn.: D. Landreth Seed Company, [2009]), 3–4, electronic version at http://www.landrethseeds.com/catalog/african_american.php (accessed August 13, 2010).

    5. Gilbert, *Homecoming*, 3–4.

    6. Hasan Jeffries, *Bloody Lowndes: Civil Rights and Black Power in Alabama's Black Belt* (New York University Press, 2009). Jeffries presented as part of the panel "Recent Books in Rural African-American History," Agricultural History Society, June 10, 2010, notes in author's possession. Greta de Jong, *A Different Day: African American Struggles for Justice in Rural Louisiana, 1900–1970* (Chapel Hill: University of North Carolina Press, 2002), quotes at 2, 9.

    7. Arthur Raper, *Preface to Peasantry: A Take of Two Black Belt Counties* (Chapel Hill: University of North Carolina, 1936), 22, quoted in J. William Harris, *Deep Souths: Delta, Piedmont and Sea Island Society in the Age of Segregation* (Baltimore: Johns Hopkins University Press, 2001), 259–60.

    8. Loren Schweninger, *Black Property Owners in the South, 1790–1915* (Urbana: University of Illinois Press, 1990), 2–3, 236–37. W. E. Burghardt Du Bois, *The Negroes of Farmville, Virginia: A Social Study*, U.S. Department of Labor, Bulletin 3, no. 14 (Washington, D.C.: Government Printing Office, January 1898), 1–38, and his *The Negro Landowner in Georgia*, U.S. Department of Labor, Bulletin 6, no. 25 (Washington, D.C.: Government Printing Office, July 1901), 647–777, both reprinted in Herbert Aptheker, compiler and editor, *Contributions by W.E.B. Du Bois in Government Publications and Proceedings* (Millwood, N.Y.: Kraus-Thomson, 1980), 7–44 and 97–228, respectively. Luther P. Jackson, *Free Negro Labor and Property Holding in Virginia, 1830–1860* (New York: D. Appleton Company, 1942). Robert Higgs, "Accumulation of Property by Southern Blacks before World War I," *American Economic Review* 72, no. 4 (September 1982): 725–37; Robert A. Margo, "Accumulation of Property by Southern Blacks before World War I: Comment and Further

Evidence," *American Economic Review* 74, no. 4 (September 1984), 768–76; Robert Higgs, "Accumulation of Property by Southern Blacks before World War I: Reply," *American Economic Review* 74, no. 4 (September 1984), 777–81.

9. Schweninger, *Black Property Owners in the South*, 5.

10. Harris, "Essay on Sources," in *Deep Souths*, 431, mentions Lily Hardy Hammond as an example of a southern reformer conscious of class issues, citing her *In Black and White* (1914; repr., New York, 1972). For Hammond's quote see Lily Hardy Hammond, *In Black and White: An Interpretation of Southern Life*, edited by Elna C. Green (Athens: University of Georgia Press, 2008), xxix–xxx, n.104.

11. Harris, *Deep Souths,* 260. Neil Canaday, "The Accumulation of Property by Southern Blacks and Whites: Individual-Level Evidence from a South Carolina Cotton County," *Explorations in Economic History* 45, no. 1 (2008): 51–75; Neil Canaday and Charles Reback, "Race, Literacy, and Real Estate Transactions in the Postbellum South," *Journal of Economic History* 70, no. 2 (June 2010): 428–45.

12. Barbara J. Fields, "Ideology and Race in American History," in *Region, Race, and Reconstruction: Essays in Honor of C. Vann Woodward*, edited by J. Morgan Kousser and James M. McPherson (New York: Oxford University Press, 1982): 143–77. Steven Hahn, *A Nation under Our Feet: Black Political Struggles in the Rural South from Slavery to the Great Migration* (Cambridge, Mass.: Belknap Press of Harvard University Press, 2003), 15.

13. Philip A. Bruce, "Renters and Land-Owners," in *The Plantation Negro as a Freeman: Observations on his Character, Condition, and Prospects in Virginia* (New York: G. P. Putnam's Sons, 1889), 211–27, quote on 219.

14. Du Bois, *The Negroes of Farmville, Virginia*; Du Bois, *The Negro Landowner in Georgia*.

15. E-mail from Evan P. Bennett to Debra A. Reid, August 12, 2010. Melvin Patrick Ely, *Israel on the Appomattox: A Southern Experiment in Black Freedom from the 1790s through the Civil War* (New York: Knopf, 2004). See the bibliographic essay of this volume for suggested readings, underutilized resources, and potential research topics.

16. Du Bois, "The Negro Farmer," in Aptheker, *Contributions by W. E. B. Du Bois*, 238–39, 243, 273–74. J. R. Dean photograph caption, McCormick-International Harvester Collection, Wisconsin Historical Society, Madison. Dave Stevens, "Only One Survivor of Negro Colony," *Telegraph-Herald* (Dubuque, Iowa), June 1, 1958, clipping in Charles Shepard Papers, 1850–1958, Wisconsin Historical Society, Madison.

17. Adolph Reed Jr., *Stirrings in the Jug: Black Politics in the Post-Segregation Era* (Minneapolis: University of Minnesota Press, 1999), 28.

18. Hahn, *A Nation under Our Feet*, 457.

19. The article about L. C. Carter appeared in *Harvester World* magazine, June 1918, 2; L. C. Carter photograph and caption, McCormick-International Harvester Collection, Wisconsin Historical Society, Madison.

20. In 1900, 48.4 percent of black farmers in Florida owned land. Du Bois, "The Negro Farmer," 259.

I
Historiography and Philosophy

1

The Jim Crow Section of Agricultural History

ADRIENNE PETTY

When news of Shirley Sherrod's forced resignation broke, I was writing this essay, which relates to the underlying point of the speech that propelled her into the national spotlight. Sherrod was an anonymous political appointee, the U.S. Department of Agriculture's director for rural development in Georgia, when she addressed a local chapter of the National Association for the Advancement of Colored People in March 2010. Her speech concerned an experience almost a quarter century ago, long before she worked for the federal government, which amounted to an awakening. But the anecdote that animated her talk pointed to a different way of understanding the problem of the nation's small farmers, the subject of this essay.[1]

In her address Sherrod recounted her work with a white farmer, Roger Spooner, when she was a case worker with the Federation of Southern Cooperatives Land Assistance Fund, which helped black farm owners organize cooperatives and hold onto their land. She remembered thinking that she could not justify helping Spooner when "so many black people have lost their farmland." When she had first decided to stay in the South after the murder of her father by a white neighbor, she explained, "I was making that commitment to black people only." But Sherrod had an epiphany after witnessing Spooner's unfair treatment at the hands of a white lawyer. "Working with him made me see that it's really about those who have versus those who don't, you know. And they could be black; they could be white; they could be Hispanic. And it made me realize then that I needed to work to help poor people—those who don't have access the way others have," she said.[2]

The episode involving Shirley Sherrod comes in the midst of growing attention to black farm owners. The news media are closely following the story of black farmers who are still awaiting $1 billion from the settlement of the 1999 *Pigford v. Glickman* case, which established that the United States Department of Agriculture discriminated against black farmers. In addition, rising numbers of historians are studying black farm owners.[3] One indication of the increasing saliency of this historical group is the inclusion of an "African American Landowners" entry in *The New Encyclopedia of Southern Culture*, a departure from the classic 1989 edition.[4] A focus on land ownership has exposed intriguing new stories of African Americans who prospered, including those who were landlords over large plantations.[5] Although the majority of black farmers have lived in the South, historians also are beginning to investigate black farm owners in other parts of the country.[6] As the work in this volume shows, the study of black farmers is poised to continue growing.

Sherrod's speech to the NAACP holds advice that historians would do well to consider in examining black farm owners of the past. Just as Sherrod realized that she could not tackle the problems facing poor farmers if she only tackled them when they affected black people, would a less segregated approach to the study of black farm owners enhance historians' understanding of southern agriculture and American society as a whole? This essay applies the important insights of Sherrod's speech and historian Michael Rudolph West's essential book *The Education of Booker T. Washington: American Democracy and the Idea of Race Relations* to the realm of agricultural history.[7] In particular, it interrogates some of the existing literature on black farm owners and explores what new understanding of the Jim Crow South and American agriculture at large might emerge if historians rethink the enduring idea and conceptual approach that West labors to clear away: race relations.

West establishes that Booker T. Washington created the idea of race relations. He invented it as a way to settle the contradiction of disfranchisement and segregation in a purportedly democratic society during the Jim Crow era. Democratic politicians, reacting to the agrarian protests and Populist agitation of the late nineteenth century, found African Americans a convenient target to remove from the body politic. Rather than attacking the denial of citizenship to the vast majority of black Americans, Washington focused on encouraging harmonious interactions between black and white Americans as a way to measure the progress of society.[8]

The Shirley Sherrod episode reveals how journalists, pundits, and politicians keep Washington's idea alive. After Spooner, his wife Eloise, and a look at her whole speech vindicated Sherrod, many commentators celebrated Sherrod's success in saving the Spooners' farm as an instance of good race relations. The *New York Times* quoted Jesse Jackson as saying, "In the end, it's such a redemptive storybook ending. I wish that Shirley Sherrod and the Spooner family could be invited to the White House and give them the credit they're due, because it is a great American story. A rural white family in Georgia and a black woman, overcoming years of segregation."[9]

Whether they use the term *race relations* or not, many historians who study black farm owners also employ this approach, either analyzing African Americans' successful attainment of land primarily in racial terms or interpreting their motivations and attitudes toward land ownership as totally distinct from those of similarly situated farmers of other backgrounds. They also assume that only black farm owners faced barriers to accumulating wealth. In this rendering, black farm owners stand out as a singular historical group facing problems completely different than other farm owners rather than as one part of a national—indeed, global—contingent of farmers facing common problems and the aggravating factor of racism. As West argues, "ritualizing race and casting every situation in terms of race ... obscures a wider reality by isolating and coloring the experience of African Americans."[10]

What do historians miss when they set the experience of black property holders apart from the larger whole? One clue comes from the ongoing debate over why black people's capacity to build wealth through the accumulation of land and other property varied across the South. Loren Schweninger, who has produced the most influential book to date on black property holders in the South, argues that black people's ownership of farms was not evenly distributed across the South. While half of all black farmers in the upper South states of Virginia, Delaware, Maryland, West Virginia, and North Carolina achieved ownership of at least modest property by 1910, only 19 percent did so in the deep South states of Louisiana, Mississippi, Alabama, and Georgia.[11]

What accounts for this glaring disparity? Schweninger argues that African Americans in the upper South obtained land more readily than those in the deep South because "in the Upper-South, whites gradually became less resistant to the idea of selling land to Negroes."[12] In other words, "race relations" were better in the upper South than in the lower South, so black farmers fared better in obtaining land there. Many scholars have echoed this interpretation, and, of course, there is evidence to support the idea that white landowners refused to sell land to black people or sold them only marginal or undeveloped land.[13]

Yet other historians deny that black people were less likely to gain land in parts of the South characterized by large cotton plantations. Robert Higgs, an economic historian, concludes, "The Georgia blacks who succeeded best in accumulating wealth before 1910 tended, *ceteris paribus,* to inhabit counties with extensive plantation agriculture and cotton cultivation, relatively high population densities, relatively low levels of black tenancy and illiteracy, and relatively cheap agricultural land."[14] However, Higgs and Margo concluded this without applying their detailed econometric analysis to the experiences of white farm owners of limited means.[15]

Would reconsidering the question of the upper South–deep South differential beyond the framework of race relations produce a different, perhaps fuller, explanation? Evidence that white landowners snubbed prospective black buyers because of racism can be a starting point for further analysis, but other explanations emerge if we resist the urge to see race relations as the final answer. A racist belief in the inferiority of African Americans may very well have served as the ideological rationale for refusing to sell land to black people in the deep South or for a form of rural redlining that confined African Americans to the rockiest land. However, the reason behind the refusal was not the ancestry of the land-hungry person of African descent. It might be useful to evaluate the social, economic, and political imperatives underlying the unabashed racism apparent on the surface.

Two studies of Georgia offer strong evidence that prerogatives of power and wealth, not race relations, could partly explain differences of land ownership rates between regions, within states, and even within one county. In *The Rural Face of White Supremacy: Beyond Jim Crow,* which focuses on Hancock County in central Georgia, Mark Schultz found that landowners who controlled prime land sought to keep this valued resource in their control. If their sole purpose had been keeping the land in lily-white hands, perhaps more white small farmers would have had premium land. Instead, small white farmers lived predominantly in the northern, upland section of the county, where, not coincidentally, black farmers also had "the greatest success" in buying land. "A few large planters lived in this area, but mostly the planters had settled on the richer, less rocky soil that spread through the center of the county. . . . Side by side these black and white middling farmers derived a decent living from land that the big planters had passed by."[16]

However, we should not be lulled into framing this as evidence of good race relations. The fact that black and white smallholders shared a section of Hancock County stemmed from their social, political, and economic standing with respect to larger farmers, not their ability to live harmoniously. This example also suggests that racism against small black farm owners did not benefit small white farm owners.

On the other hand, a study of neighboring and more fertile Taliaferro County revealed that African Americans were able to acquire 5 percent of farm acreage by 1910. The author used this "relatively high level of black ownership" on prime land in the deep South to argue against the accepted wisdom that black farm owners were confined to marginal land.[17] Seeking to debunk the tautological argument that black farmers lost their land because they were marginal farmers on marginal land, Peggy Hargis insightfully concludes that "viewing variations in African American landholding as simply a reflection of racial inequality or as differences in human capital masks the degree to which local factors affected ownership."[18]

What I have found in my own research suggests that migration and changes in land use also played a role in creating new opportunities for landownership. In parts of the lower Cape Fear region of North Carolina, ownership of land increased among farmers who held farms of sixty acres or fewer in a very specific swath of the county that was further from the coast than the traditional plantation belt. The land became available for smaller farmers to purchase not out of any feeling of goodwill on the part of owners but because of the decline in turpentine production after the Civil War. During the antebellum period, the piney woods of the region had supported the state's burgeoning turpentine industry. Having exhausted the pines by the 1880s, many of the large landowners involved in turpentine production migrated to Georgia and Florida. Both black and white farmers carved new small farms out of the piney woods.[19] It is possible that we would arrive at a fuller and more nuanced understanding of the differences between the upper South and deep South if we paid attention to the degree to which white farmers were able to gain land for the first time in each subregion. Taking Hargis's analysis one step further, a promising project would be to trace the degree to which white farmers who had not previously owned land were able to buy land in the plantation district of Taliaferro County. How large were their farms? When were they able to purchase them? How successful were they in keeping them? We also must take into account antebellum and postbellum differences between regions within the South: between old cotton or rice areas and new ones, between capital-intensive sugar production and labor-intensive cotton and tobacco production, between the enormous concentration of land ownership in the Mississippi Delta and the more widespread ownership of land among smallholders, black and white, in Southside Virginia and the North Carolina piedmont.

A 2010 study of land ownership in Tennessee offers a refreshing approach to the question of whether African Americans' ability to buy land varied across time and space. Using a sample of rural and urban real estate transactions from 1880, Neil Canaday and Charles Reback examined land purchase dates, the amount paid per acre, and rates of literacy for both black and white people in plantation and nonplantation areas. In addition, they considered the number of acres purchased, which allowed them to distinguish between disadvantages the black purchasers faced because of racism and disadvantages they faced because they were buying small properties (which, admittedly, could have been a consequence of racism). They found that black people paid a mean price per acre of $24.13, compared with the $16.54 that mulattoes paid and the $15.28 that white people paid. "When only properties of ten acres and larger are considered," Canaday and Reback argue, "the racial gap narrows considerably, as mean prices per acre were $11.68 for blacks, $11.27 for whites, and $9.23 for mulattoes."[20]

A related issue in the study of black farm owners has to do with the role of white people who granted land to black people or ran interference for them in their quest to buy land from others. In Hancock County, Schultz finds that "African Americans needed white assistance to navigate a system that was intentionally studded with legal and illegal barriers to black landownership." In some cases, he argues, "interracial kinship ties smoothed an African American family's path to landownership" by enabling black people to acquire land through inheritance, gifts, or different types of assistance from white relatives.[21] Some historians recognize this as a form of noblesse oblige, a vestige of paternalism. To varying degrees, all of these studies rest their interpretations on the idea of race relations rather than analyzing the fundamentally unequal circumstances that placed an elite group in a position to assist or block at their own whim the aspirations of their social inferiors. More studies that analyze small farmers, black and white, as a single group would likely reveal that small white farmers had similar class-based relations. Evan P. Bennett, one of the editors of this volume, mentioned that his grandfather, a white farmer in Poinsett County, Arkansas, applied to purchase a tract of land that the Farm Security Administration (FSA) sold around 1937. A prominent planter who knew the aspiring landowner vouched for his reputation as a hardworking cotton farmer. The FSA selected him rather than numerous other applicants as a result.[22]

The role of white elites in easing or obstructing the path to ownership calls into question another aspect of the approach to studying black farm owners that historians need to rethink: land ownership as an example of black people's success. This approach casts black people's ownership of land almost exclusively as an achievement in spite of racism. Thad Sitton and James H. Conrad's *Freedom Colonies: Independent Black Texans in the Time of Jim Crow* exemplifies scholarship that delves into land ownership to highlight the resourcefulness and initiative of African Americans. Although they concede that the "main story" of African Americans in the Jim Crow countryside "is that of discrimination, disadvantage, and economic exploitation, maintained by an ever-present threat of violence," they argue that "this focus on black Southerners as victims . . . must not blind us to their achievements against long odds" in establishing independent rural enclaves that they called "freedom colonies."[23] They tell the story of people who formed all-black communities in the backwoods of eastern and southern Texas, giving primacy to people's determined actions rather than how others acted upon them. The goal of these farmers was to isolate themselves from the racist exclusion and violence that characterized life in Texas during the Jim Crow era. But Sitton and Conrad's work, offered as a critique of scholarship that emphasizes the crushing power of Jim Crow, unintentionally but perhaps necessarily underscores the fact that the experience of African American farm owners was "that of discrimination, disadvantage, and economic exploitation, maintained by an ever-present threat of violence." Although they emphasize the triumph that land ownership represented, their own evidence shows how contingent black farm owners' triumph was upon factors beyond their control. Many black farmers relied upon the assistance of better-placed white people to set up their farms in the first place, a large indication of the acute disadvantage under which they were forced to operate—a disadvantage that was not confined to black people, as the story of Bennett's grandfather reveals. In the same vein, black landowners kept their homes unpainted for fear of retaliation from white people who resented their property holdings. Keeping their ownership off the public record out of fear of reprisals, many of the landowning patriarchs of the freedom colonies neglected to leave wills. Because many died intestate, their lands were often subdivided for multiple heirs into properties so small that making a living from the land ceased to be viable.[24]

Focusing on a more prosperous group of landowners, another study by Robert C. Kenzer aimed to disabuse us of the tendency to think of the post–Civil War prospects for African Americans in "monolithic terms."[25] Kenzer's book *Enterprising Southerners* reveals that a small but connected group of black North Carolinians achieved a modicum of economic independence as farmers, doctors, and business owners. Paying particular attention to how social and political factors contributed to economic opportunity, the author argues that being "mulatto," being a free person of color during the antebellum period, having a non-agricultural occupation, and living in an urban locale made it easier for North Carolinians of African descent to gain land.[26]

Yet these very factors call into question the framework of race relations for understanding landownership, an aspiration that was dependent upon too many factors beyond the farmers' control. It is a well-meaning but misguided attempt to assign a level of autonomy to people that they simply did not have. What would happen if we were to explore these "enterprising southerners" in order to understand the overall structure of society during the Jim Crow era rather than as an exception to it? When we interpret land ownership and other measures of success as manifestations of success in overcoming bad race relations, we close off other questions and produce ugly contradictions. If better race relations produced land ownership, why did some landowners need assistance? Perhaps land ownership is better understood as success in the context of racism rather than as success in spite of racism.

It cannot be denied that attention to black farm owners' achievements have contributed to new ways of understanding freedpeople in the postbellum era. Sharon Ann Holt's *Making Freedom Pay: North Carolina Freedpeople Working for Themselves, 1865–1900*, for example, shows in breathtaking detail how crucial household production and dual tenure were to helping freedpeople achieve land ownership. Having women, men, and children engaged in all manner of tasks—hunting, gardening, berry picking, sewing, basket weaving—enabled freedpeople to squirrel away enough cash to buy land eventually. She shows that many worked others' land as well as their own—what she calls dual tenure—as a way to stay afloat. At the same time, however, Holt is careful to balance her emphasis on freedpeople's work on their own behalf with equal attention to the circumstances that constrained them and other farmers, especially the growth of farm tenancy, the role of debt, and agricultural depression.[27]

Schultz's focus on black landowners moves toward another promising way of understanding land ownership. His interest in this group seems to derive from the counterpoint they present to the classic narrative of the rural South. He writes, "Independent black farmers have become largely invisible when we imagine the landscape of the American South. If we think of rural African Americans, we usually think only of sharecroppers and wage laborers. If we think of the black middle class, our minds typically turn automatically to the urban centers. To the extent that we indulge these stereotypes, however, our imaginations are overruling our statistics."[28] He uses the story of black farm owners to dispel the myth of "a 'Solid South' period of black docility and white solidarity in the first decades of the twentieth century."[29]

More than any of the studies to date, Schultz's book tells us something new about the South during the Jim Crow era by unearthing a culture of personalism and violence. In this rural county, black and white people worked, ate, worshipped, celebrated, and lived together. The ties that bound them to one another were social, economic, and even familial. Schultz argues persuasively that land ownership among African Americans represents another crack in our conception of the Solid South. Schultz found that by 1910, the high water mark of landownership for African Americans throughout the South, 9 percent of Hancock County's landowners were black, while overall, black people made up 70 percent of the county's population. Although their numbers were low, Schultz argued that land ownership gave African Americans more control over their time, their labor and that of their children, their money, and their lives. In memorable words, Roy Roberts, one of the two hundred men and women Schultz interviewed, put it this way: "'Most black people hired themselves out to whites,' remembered Roberts. 'If they said, 'Get up at six o' clock and go to work,' they had to get up. If they said, 'Fifty cents a day,' that's all they got. But we didn't have to get up for nobody, because we were home. We had our own land—our own everything—and it made a difference. It made a difference.'"[30]

But were black farm owners as independent as Roberts remembered? Although it does much to enhance our understanding of life during this era, Schultz's book and other studies run the risk of ascribing too much independence to black farm owners. Two studies on postbellum Maryland and the South Carolina and Georgia upland and sea islands argue that independence proved elusive. "Farming their own land may have enhanced black people's sense of freedom, independence, and accomplishment," Barbara J. Fields argues in *Slavery and Freedom on the Middle Ground*. "It may also—though this is much more dubious—have added to their standing in the eyes of the community at large. But it certainly did not suffice to place even the tiny minority concerned upon the high road to economic security."[31] J. William Harris argues that farm owners were only partly able to maintain a self-sufficient lifestyle, but that land ownership gave them "a crucial margin of independence."[32] Working within the framework of agency heightens the risk of historians taking independence for granted without analyzing the substance of farm owners' experience. One promising avenue for exploration, however, is to delve more deeply into the specific meaning that black farm owners attached to their land and status, as Debra Reid convincingly discusses.[33] As the literature on black farm owners increases, scholars will offer fresh interpretations of the degree to which it afforded them independence.

I am not suggesting that historians never stop to consider how black farm owners fit into the broader context of southern agriculture or that they never compare white and black farmers. They frequently do so. For instance, scholars acknowledge that black farmers faced hardships common to all farmers across space and time.[34] In addition, they concede that black farmers have had to contend with challenges besetting all farmers during the years since the Civil War, including increasing reliance on one-crop commercial agricultural production. But after granting that there were common hardships, they invariably proceed to offer in-depth analysis only of those hardships that they assume were peculiar to black farm owners, and they tend to settle upon racism as the main explanation rather than as the ideological formulation that requires picking apart and explaining. There is no denying the importance of studying the impact of racism or analyzing ways that African Americans circumvented barriers that the perpetrators of racism placed in their way. This line of inquiry has led to innumerable insights about the rural South, including Pete Daniel's recent discussion of the racism prevalent in local committees that administered federal agricultural programs.[35] I am only suggesting that we probe the social, economic, and political conditions upon which racism rests. For example, one scholar seems to take much for granted in arguing that "long-term discrimination against African American farmers has made it difficult for them to acquire significant landholdings and to expand their operations." But were all white farmers large landowners and were they all more insulated from the politics that swirled around water rights and irrigation, the topic of the study, than were black farm owners?[36]

Even though historians and other scholars largely interpret black farm owners as encountering a different set of challenges than everyone else, they do not hesitate to compare the numbers, percentages, farm value, and acreage of black farm owners and white farm owners. The problem is that black southerners tended to own smaller farms, and that white owners of the largest farms significantly skew the average. Anyone who has worked with the Census of Agriculture knows that it is not an ideal source for determining the number of farm owners in the first place. One problem is that the census counted all farms as separate units, whether they were operated by owners, tenants, or sharecroppers. This meant that the owner of a 480-acre farm who rented out his land to eight different tenant farmers would not appear in the census as a farm owner, and his land would appear as eight separate tenant-operated farms. But even though the largest farms do not always show up in the census figures, we are, in effect, setting the smallest farmers side by side with the largest, most prosperous farmers, even though their access to power, privilege, opportunity, credit, land, and labor were vastly unequal.[37]

As historians continue to write black farm owners into American agricultural history, it helps to bear in mind why many historians of the post-Reconstruction South have not studied black farm owners in much depth. For them, taking note of black farm owners is like finding a flock of healthy brown pelicans in the Gulf of Mexico's oil-contaminated waters despite the rig explosion: a glimmer of hope in a sea of distress and devastation. Most historians seem to have accepted the sober assessment C. Vann Woodward made nearly sixty years ago, and justifiably so: "The lives of the overwhelming majority of Negroes were still circumscribed by the farm and plantation. The same was true of the white people, but the Negroes, with few exceptions, were farmers without land." The existence of black landowners simply did not seem to rate sustained attention given the overwhelming economic, political, and social inequality that marked life in the South. Similarly, Harold Woodman noted, "Although some black agricultural workers succeeded in their pursuit of acquiring land, almost all African Americans, nevertheless, remained landless and owned little other property, a fact that clearly differentiated the white and black experience."[38]

Woodward and Woodman are right, in an important sense. Even at the height of black land ownership in 1910, the vast majority of black farmers in the South remained landless. When considered as one and the same with small white farm owners, however, their story could acquire larger significance for understanding the Jim Crow South. Whether they were former slaves or embattled white yeoman farmers, all small farm owners likely sought not to fall under the dependency and close supervision that was entrapping so many at the dawn of the Jim Crow era. Above all, they sought a democratic commerce. Whether they were landed descendants of former slaves or inheritors of their family's small farms, all small farm owners likely sought protection of their interests under New Deal agricultural programs. Whether they are Roger Spooner or Timothy Pigford, the lead plaintiff in the black farmers' class action suit, small farm owners today seek strategies for competing with larger, better-capitalized farmers in the United States and in other countries. Racism surely aggravated the circumstances of black farm owners. Did racism ultimately place the entire class of small farm owners at a disadvantage as well? When the USDA denied loans to black farm owners for all those years, it is doubtful that the funds were instead made available to white farmers of the same class, by and large. Rather, the loans likely benefited large farm owners. As Sherrod testified, "God helped me to see that it's not just about black people—it's about poor people."[39]

Notes

1. This chapter is an expanded version of a paper I presented at Region, Class and Culture: New Perspectives on the American South, a conference in honor of Pete Daniel, June 13, 2009, at Rhodes College. Special thanks to Pete Daniel and Nan Woodruff for their helpful comments. Jonathan Weisman, "Worker Fired in Video Flap Gets White House 'Sorry,'" *Wall Street Journal*, July 22, 2010, A3.

2. Greg Bluestein, "Father's Death Turning Point for Fired Agriculture Official," *Washington Post*, July 22, 2010, http://www.washingtonpost.com/wpdyn/content/article/2010/07/22/AR2010072205405.html (accessed July 25, 2010); video of Shirley Sherrod, http://www.naacp.org/news/entry/video_sherrod/ (accessed July 25, 2010).

3. Economic historians have undertaken the most recent work on African American property owners. See Neil Canaday, "The Accumulation of Property by Southern Blacks and Whites: Individual-Level Evidence from a South Carolina Cotton County, 1910–1919," *Explorations in Economic History* 45 (2008): 51–75; Neil Canaday and Charles Reback, "Race, Literacy, and Real Estate Transactions in the Postbellum South," *Journal of Economic History* 70, no. 2 (June 2010): 428–45. Other recent works include Spencer D. Wood and Jess Gilbert, "Returning African American Farmers to the Land: Recent Trends and a Policy Rationale," *Review of Black Political Economy* 24, no. 4 (Spring 2000): 43–64; Jess Gilbert, Spencer D. Wood, and Gwen Sharp, "Who Owns the Land? Agricultural Land Ownership by Race/Ethnicity," *Rural Conditions and Trends* 17, no. 4 (Winter 2002):

55–62; John Francis Ficara and Juan Williams, *Black Farmers in America* (Lexington: University Press of Kentucky, 2006); and Charlene Gilbert and Quinn Eli, *Homecoming: The Story of African American Farmers* (Boston: Beacon Press, 2002), a companion book to the 1998 PBS documentary *Homecoming: Sometimes I Am Haunted by Memories of Red Dirt and Clay*.

4. Mark Schultz, "African American Landowners," in Melissa Walker and James C. Cobb, eds., *The New Encyclopedia of Southern Culture*, vol. 11: *Agriculture and Industry* (Chapel Hill: University of North Carolina Press, 2008), 31–32. The original edition does not include such an entry. Charles Reagan Wilson and William R. Ferris, eds., *Encyclopedia of Southern Culture* (Chapel Hill: University of North Carolina Press, 1989).

5. Valerie Grim, "African American Landlords in the Rural South, 1870–1950: A Profile," *Agricultural History* 72, no. 2 (Spring 1998): 399–416.

6. For a new study of contests over land between Native Americans, white Americans and African Americans in Oklahoma, see David A. Chang, *The Color of the Land: Race, Nation, and the Politics of Landownership in Oklahoma, 1832–1929* (Chapel Hill: University of North Carolina Press, 2010); for an article that discusses landownership among black people in the Midwest, see Debra A. Reid, "'The Whitest of Occupations'? African Americans in the Rural Midwest, 1940–2010," in J. L. Anderson, ed., *The Rural Midwest since World War II* (DeKalb: Northern Illinois University Press, forthcoming).

7. Michael Rudolph West, *The Education of Booker T. Washington: American Democracy and the Idea of Race Relations* (New York: Columbia University Press, 2006).

8. West, *Education of Booker T. Washington*, 15–16.

9. Sheryl Gay Stolberg, Shaila Dewan, and Brian Stelter, "With Apology, Fired Official Is Offered a New Job," *New York Times*, July 21, 2010, http://www.nytimes.com/2010/07/22/us/politics/22sherrod.html (accessed July 25, 2010).

10. West, *Education of Booker T. Washington*, 15–16.

11. Loren Schweninger, "A Vanishing Breed: Black Farm Owners in the South, 1651–1982," *Agricultural History* 63 (Summer 1989): 41–60. Schweninger's *Black Property Owners in the South, 1790–1915* (Urbana: University of Illinois Press, 1990) was the first book-length treatment that focused on black property ownership throughout the South. He and other contemporary scholars have built on the pioneering work of William Edward Burghardt Du Bois: "The Negro in the Cotton Belt: Some Social Sketches," *Department of Labor Bulletin*, no. 22 (May 1899): 401–17; "The Negro Landholder of Georgia," *Department of Labor Bulletin*, no. 35 (July 1901): 647–777; and "The Negro Farmer" in *Negroes in the United States*, Bureau of the Census, Bulletin 8 (1904). With the exception of Schweninger and a few other social historians, the economic historians, sociologists and economists have been far more prolific in analyzing black farm owners. See Edward H. Bonekemper III, "Negro Ownership of Real Property in Hampton and Elizabeth City County, Virginia, 1860–1870," *Journal of Negro History* 55, no. 3 (1970): 165–81; Charles F. Oubre, *Forty Acres and a Mule: The Freedmen's Bureau and Black Landownership* (Baton Rouge: Louisiana State University Press, 1978); Robert S. Browne, *Only Six Million Acres: The Decline of Black-Owned Land in the Rural South* (New York: Black Economic Research Center, 1973); Robert Higgs, *Competition and Coercion: Blacks in the American Economy, 1865–1914* (Chicago: University of Chicago Press, 1977); Robert Higgs, "Accumulation of Property by Southern Blacks before World War I," *American Economic Review* 72

(September 1982): 725–37; Robert Higgs, "Accumulation of Property by Southern Blacks before World War I: Reply," *American Economic Review* 74, no. 4 (1984); 777–81; Robert A. Margo, "Accumulation of Property by Southern Blacks before World War I: Comment and Further Evidence," *American Economic Review* 74, no. 4 (1984): 768–76; Marsha Jean Darling, "The Growth and Decline of the Afro-American Family Farm in Warren County, North Carolina, 1910–1960," Ph.D. diss., Duke University, 1982. See also Leo McGee and Robert Boone, eds., *The Black Rural Landowner—Endangered Species: Social, Political and Economic Implications* (Westport, Conn.: Greenwood Press, 1979).

12. Schweninger, "A Vanishing Breed," 48–49. See also Jay R. Mandle, *The Roots of Black Poverty: The Southern Plantation Economy after the Civil War* (Durham: Duke University Press, 1978), 42–43; Robert McKenzie, *One South or Many?* (New York: Cambridge University Press, 1994), 144.

13. Mark Schultz, *The Rural Face of White Supremacy: Beyond Jim Crow* (Urbana: University of Illinois Press, 2005), 46. Edward Ayers, *The Promise of the New South: Life after Reconstruction* (New York: Oxford University Press, 1992); Peggy G. Hargis, "Beyond the Marginality Thesis: The Acquisition and Loss of Land by African Americans in Georgia, 1880–1930," *Agricultural History* 72, no. 2 (Spring 1998), 244.

14. Higgs, "Accumulation," 735.

15. Higgs, "Accumulation," 735. See also Margo, "Accumulation of Property," 773–75.

16. Schultz, *Rural Face,* 50.

17. Hargis, "Beyond the Marginality Thesis," 257. See also Peggy Hargis and Patrick Horan, "The 'Low-Country Advantage' for African Americans in Georgia, 1880–1930," *Journal of Interdisciplinary History* 28 (Summer 1997): 37–40.

18. Hargis, "Beyond the Marginality Thesis," 262.

19. Aldert S. Root and Lewis A. Hurst, *Soil Survey of Duplin County* (Washington, D.C.: Government Printing Office, 1905), 6–7.

20. Canaday and Reback, "Race, Literacy," 434.

21. Schultz, *Rural Face,* 51–52; Sharon Ann Holt, *Making Freedom Pay: North Carolina Freedpeople Working for Themselves, 1865–1900* (Athens: University of Georgia Press, 2000). For equally innovative treatments of antebellum property accumulation, see Dylan C. Penningroth, *The Claims of Kinfolk: African American Property and Community in the Nineteenth-Century South* (Chapel Hill: University of North Carolina Press, 2003); Melvin Patrick Ely, *Israel on the Appomattox: A Southern Experiment in Black Freedom from the 1790s through the Civil War* (New York: Alfred A. Knopf, 2004).

22. Evan Bennett, personal communication to the author, July 15, 2010; e-mail from Evan Bennett to the author, August 11, 2010.

23. Thad Sitton and James H. Conrad, *Freedom Colonies: Independent Black Texans in the Time of Jim Crow* (Austin: University of Texas Press, 2005), 7; Dianne Swann-Wright, *A Way Out of No Way: Claiming Family and Freedom in the New South* (Charlottesville: University of Virginia Press, 2002).

24. Sitton and Conrad, *Freedom Colonies,* 60, 176. For a lawyer's historic analysis of heir property, see Thomas W. Mitchell, "From Reconstruction to Deconstruction: Undermining Black Landownership, Political Independence, and Community through Partition Sales of Tenancies in Common," *Northwestern University Law Review* 95, no. 2 (Winter 2001), 505–80.

25. Robert C. Kenzer, *Enterprising Southerners: Black Economic Success in North Carolina, 1865–1915* (Charlottesville: University Press of Virginia, 1997), 127.

26. Kenzer, *Enterprising Southerners*, 10.

27. Holt, *Making Freedom Pay*, 7–24.

28. Schultz, *Rural Face*, 45.

29. Schultz, *Rural Face*, 9.

30. Schultz, *Rural Face*, 54.

31. Barbara Jeanne Fields, *Slavery and Freedom on the Middle Ground: Maryland during the Nineteenth Century* (New Haven: Yale University Press, 1985), 178–79.

32. J. William Harris, *Deep Souths: Delta, Piedmont, and Sea Island Society in the Age of Segregation* (Baltimore: Johns Hopkins University Press, 2001), 25.

33. Debra A. Reid, "African Americans, Community Building, and the Role of the State in Rural Reform in Texas, 1890s–1930s," in Catherine McNicol Stock and Robert D. Johnston, eds., *The Countryside in the Age of the Modern State: Political Histories of Rural America*, (Ithaca: Cornell University Press, 2001), 39. See also Debra A. Reid, "African Americans and Progressive Reform," *Agricultural History* 74, no. 2 (Spring 2000): 322–39.

34. Sitton and Conrad, *Freedom Colonies*, 173–78; Hargis, "Beyond the Marginality Thesis," 246; Debra A. Reid, *Reaping a Greater Harvest: African Americans, the Extension Service, and Rural Reform in Jim Crow Texas* (College Station: Texas A & M University Press, 2007), xxi.

35. Pete Daniel, "African American Farmers and Civil Rights," *Journal of Southern History* 73, no. 1 (February 2007): 3–38. Pete Daniel has expanded this analysis in his book-length manuscript "Dispossession Blues: African American Farmers in the Age of Civil Rights."

36. Valerie Grim, "The High Cost of Water: African American Farmers and the Politics of Irrigation in the Rural South, 1980–2000," *Agricultural History* 76, no. 2 (Spring 2002), 347–48.

37. Following the lead of the federal government, many historians compare all farms owned by black people with all farms owned by white people without adjusting for size. U.S. Commission on Civil Rights, *Equal Opportunity in Farm Programs: An Appraisal of Services Rendered by Agencies of the United States Department of Agriculture* (Washington, D.C.: Government Printing Office, 1965), 6n4, 10, 11. Schweninger, "A Vanishing Breed," 53; Daniel, "African American Farmers and Civil Rights," 9.

38. C. Vann Woodward, *Origins of the New South, 1877–1913* (Baton Rouge: Louisiana State University Press, 1951), 205; Harold D. Woodman, "The Political Economy of the New South: Retrospects and Prospects," *Journal of Southern History* 67, no. 4 (November 2001), 806. See also Leon F. Litwack, *Trouble in Mind: Black Southerners in the Age of Jim Crow* (New York: Alfred A. Knopf, 1998), 137.

39. Video of Shirley Sherrod, http://www.naacp.org/news/entry/video_sherrod/ (accessed July 25, 2010).

II

Farm Acquisition and Retention

2

Out of Mount Vernon's Shadow

Black Landowners in George Washington's Neighborhood, 1870–1930

SCOTT E. CASPER

Three "farmers," three life experiences: On September 24, 1894, black people lined the central streets of Alexandria, Virginia, to mark the anniversary of Lincoln's preliminary Emancipation Proclamation. As anticipated by the *Washington Post*, the "big military and industrial parade" would include representatives of the city's black-owned businesses and trades, "showing the progress made during the past thirty-one years"; military companies and other clubs from Washington, Baltimore, and Fredericksburg; and an "emancipation ship, drawn by six horses." The grand marshal would hail from neighboring Fairfax County: "Farmer Dandridge Smith, of Mount Vernon township, being the man who will ride at the head of the line, aided by a staff of farmers."[1] Thirteen Septembers later, a young couple filed a marriage license with Fairfax County's court clerk. Florence E. Ford, aged twenty, and Wilbert P. Brown, twenty-four, both lifelong residents of the county, were married in the black enclave of Gum Springs where the bride's parents lived. The Reverend Alexander Truatt, minister of Alexandria's Alfred Street Baptist Church, officiated. Where the license asked for the "Occupation of Husband," either Wilbert or Florence declared, "Farming," even though he had no work at the time and would soon take a job with the local electric railroad company.[2] Two years afterward, in the summer of 1910, the U.S. census taker visited an old, twice-widowed woman named Sarah Robinson, in childhood a slave at Mount Vernon and later a free employee there. In the enumerator's estimation, Robinson too was a "farmer." Describing her own pursuits that November, she explained what that occupation entailed: "I am very seldom home. I am a market woman."[3]

Dandridge Smith, Wilbert Brown, and Sarah Robinson all belonged to the African American community that lived along one historic nine-mile stretch: the roads between Mount Vernon, George Washington's storied home, and Alexandria, the city of about 15,000 that had been an antebellum hub of the interstate slave trade. That vicinity was in turn a small part of what federal census takers and local officials called Fairfax County's "Mount Vernon district," a spatio-legal entity that encompassed not just the eight thousand acres once owned by the "Father of his Country" but an area roughly six times that size, home also to the founding father George Mason and other Revolution-era statesman-slaveowners (map 2.1). Smith, Brown, and Robinson had probably worshiped together, attended the same celebrations, and known many of the same people all their lives. Smith (born in 1840) and Robinson (1844) had been acquainted since childhood, residing at or near Mount Vernon but on different sides of the line separating freedom from slavery. Robinson's second husband was Brown's grandfather, and she had helped raise him since he was a small boy. And Smith was distantly related to Florence Ford, Brown's bride. In some respects, the common elements of these people's life experiences grew out of the specificities of community and place: links to Mount Vernon on one side and Alexandria on the other; and changing local economic opportunities and constraints around the turn of the twentieth century.

At the same time, the divergences among these people's and their families' roads into and out of farming reveal two significant aspects of the experience of "black farmers": the economic fault lines that divided people within ostensibly the same place and a shared community, and the transformations between 1870 and 1930 that diminished the economic viability of farming for most black landowners. The differences stemmed from more than the alternative potential meanings of "farmer" and "farming" in the symbolic public space of a civic parade, the aspirational blanks on a marriage license, and the classificatory boxes of a census page. Time mattered: whether one had been born free or enslaved before the Civil War; when and under what circumstances one entered the ranks of landholders. So did gender, even though farming was at root a family's occupation, not exclusively the province of husband or wife. Class distinctions counted, too, even (perhaps especially) within a small, geographically contained community. Finally, it is crucial to take account of place, in two senses: the existence of distinct spatial enclaves even within one "community"; and

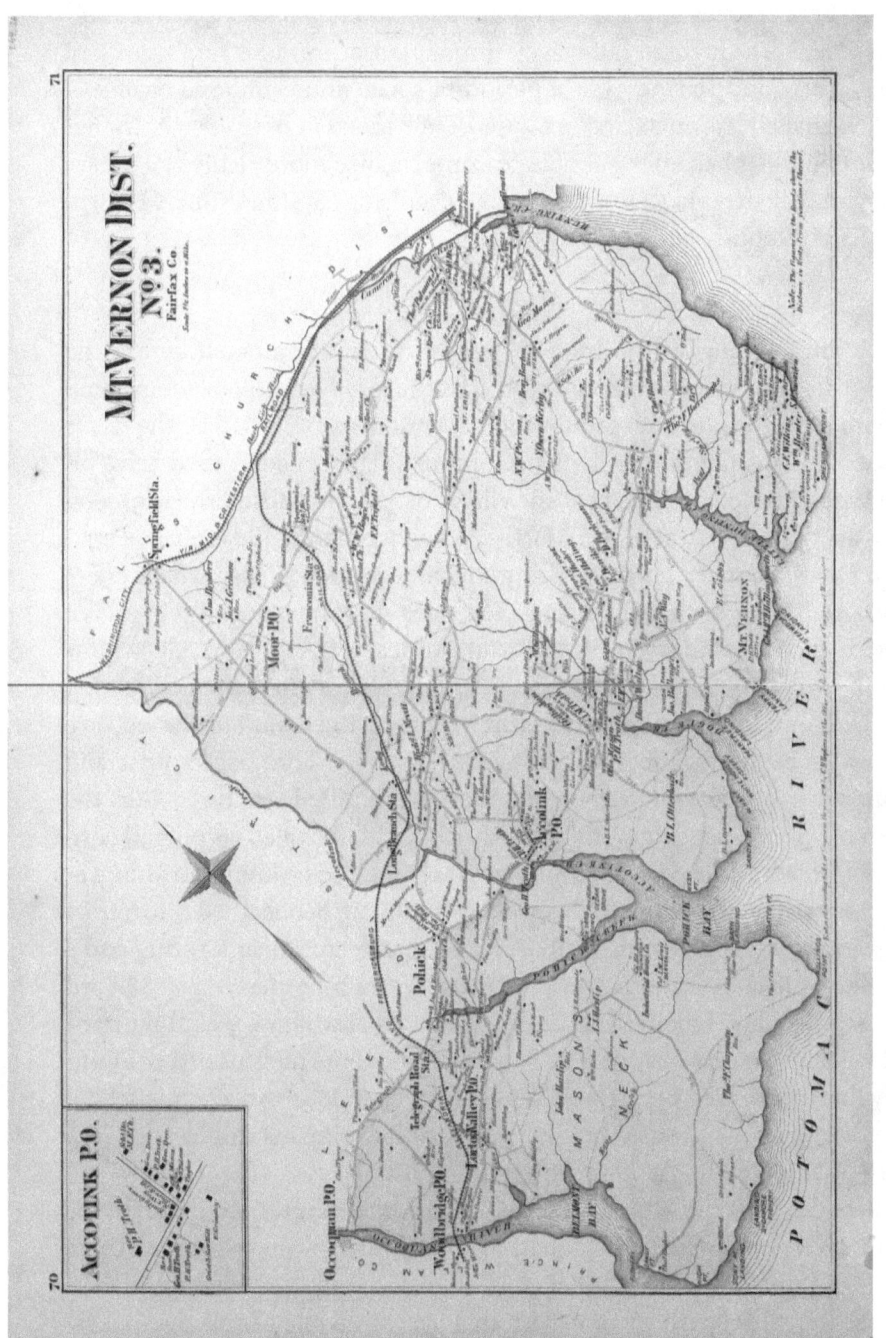

Map 2.1. Mount Vernon District No. 3. Source: *Atlas of Fifteen Miles around Washington, including the County of Montgomery, Maryland.* Compiled, drawn and published from actual surveys of G. M. Hopkins. Philadelphia: G. M. Hopkins, 1879, Library of Congress Geography and Map Division, p. 70.

the different locations, from Mount Vernon to Gum Springs to Alexandria, where people's familial, economic, and communal lives occurred and intersected. Through an intensive examination of this one community of landholders and "farmers" in a period of social and economic change—and, ultimately, through close analysis of one moment of stress within that community—it becomes possible to contextualize more richly the everyday, complex experiences of people like Dandridge Smith, Wilbert Brown, and Sarah Robinson.

* * *

Black landholding in the Mount Vernon district originated before the Civil War and typically among freed slaves favored by some white person. Members of the Quander family, their ancestors manumitted by the terms of George Washington's will, owned approximately one hundred acres on the Woodlawn plantation, near the village of Accotink, formerly belonging to Washington's nephew and Martha Washington's granddaughter. Patriarch Lewis Quander, a substantial grain and livestock farmer, left an estate appraised at more than $1,100 in 1866, including such accoutrements of wealth and status as a watch ($20) and two feather beds ($18). His widow Susan owned $4,000 in real property as of 1870, an estate divided among her own and their children in the early 1880s.[4] The Gum Springs enclave traced its beginnings to similar opportunity. West Ford, its founder and Dandridge Smith's grandfather, had been manumitted around 1806 by the terms of George Washington's sister-in-law's will. A skilled carpenter, Ford then worked for three generations of Washingtons at Mount Vernon over fifty years. The first of them, Bushrod Washington, bequeathed him a tract of land, which Ford sold to purchase a 214-acre parcel near a spring and a stand of gum trees adjacent to the Mount Vernon property. In 1857 Ford divided that land among his four children, two of whom—including Dandridge Smith's mother—stayed there and formed the nucleus of a community that established Bethlehem Baptist Church in 1863 and a public school five years later. At least eleven of West Ford's descendants still owned Gum Springs land, totaling at least 110 acres, in 1911.[5]

Between 1870 and 1910, scores of African Americans acquired land in the Mount Vernon district. Only fourteen black people owned real estate there in 1870, three of them Quanders or Fords; and only four held more than $1,000 in real property. By contrast, that year 154 white people owned real estate, 124 of those more than $1,000 (and 39 of them more than $10,000). Plantation agriculture still dominated the district: the 1870 census reveals wealthy white "farmers" employing dozens of black and white "farm laborers" or "farm hands." By 1911, more than 160 black individuals owned land, a more than tenfold increase over four decades. Blacks owned just 3 percent of the district's privately held land: 1,438 acres, as compared with 42,302 acres held by whites. And African Americans' holdings were typically small—most less than ten acres, many less than half that. Still, those small plots represented the aspirations and accomplishments of nearly one hundred families.[6]

Those who purchased real estate in the district after 1870 followed the path to land ownership most characteristic of post–Civil War black people: they worked their way from farm laborers to "farmers." In the early 1880s, Henry Randall and William Robinson bought neighboring parcels of what would become another small black enclave, about halfway between Gum Springs and Alexandria. Randall had worked as a farm hand in 1870, employed by a family of New York migrants to Fairfax County. A decade later the census recorded him as a "farm helper" in the employ of Charles Ballenger, whose substantial holdings lay less than a mile east of Gum Springs on the Accotink Turnpike. Robinson had worked in 1870 as a farm hand in a neighboring district of Fairfax County, likely for a wealthy farmer who also operated a brick works on his property. The 1880 census found Robinson and his family in the Mount Vernon district, where William worked as a farm laborer for a wealthy clock and watch maker who owned "City View" farm about two miles north of Gum Springs.[7] Randall and Robinson both purchased tracts of the "Spring Bank" estate—Randall ten acres, Robinson eventually nearly forty—from Sallie E. Mason, widow of a descendant of the Revolutionary George Mason. (She had already sold an adjacent ten acres to another black man, Griffin Johnson, who had been her late husband's attendant and nurse in his final illness.)[8] In their trajectory toward becoming "farmers," Randall and Robinson typified the district's black landowners. The 1900 census listed forty-seven black people, roughly two thirds of them landowners and four of them women, as "farmers." Of those whose occupation in 1880 can be determined, 56 percent had been farm laborers, sometimes identified as "hands" or "helps."[9] (Many black landowners were not considered farmers, and several "farmers" did not own but rented the land they worked.)[10]

Once possessed of property, William Robinson and Henry Randall disposed of it in ways designed to expand and solidify black holding. Like West Ford, Robinson distributed parcels to his adult children (his daughters and their husbands), creating a virtual family compound "on the hill" at Spring Bank. In the late 1890s Randall participated in a project to extend land ownership beyond his own family. With four other men, he contributed money to create the Joint Stock Club of Gum Springs, which purchased about twenty acres from a West Ford descendant and sold half-acre or one-acre parcels inexpensively to local citizens, including several women. Another such community took shape among black farm workers at Mason Neck, part of the Mount Vernon district that had once belonged to George Mason's Gunston Hall plantation: they established a school and a church in the 1860s, and by 1900 many of them bought small farms. Similar familial and communal approaches to property occurred elsewhere in late nineteenth-century Virginia and the South, embodying what the historian Dianne Swann-Wright has called "landholdership" rather than land ownership: "purchased lands became possessions shared with families and friends . . . not merely a manifestation of financial security but the cornerstone of their community" and "an avenue to personal and group independence." It was probably no coincidence that seven of the Joint Stock Club's first eight sales occurred on Washington's Birthday 1898, symbolizing the purchasers' own independence through landholding.[11]

Women also participated in the process of dispersing land ownership, as another Mount Vernon district family's experience revealed. In the early 1870s Lloyd Washington, a former slave (and no known relation to the white Washingtons), purchased forty acres of the "Mount Vernon estate"—the roughly one thousand acres that George Washington's descendants still owned after many antebellum subdivisions and the Mount Vernon Ladies' Association's 1858 purchase of two hundred acres for preservation. In 1889 he sold four and one-eighth acres to Mount Vernon's housekeeper Sarah Robinson, who had lived there nearly all her life. Before the Civil War, while Dandridge Smith grew up free on the neighboring Gum Springs land (and worked at Mount Vernon occasionally for wages), Sarah had been the legal property of the last Washington to own the historic estate. She returned after the war with her husband Nathan Johnson, both of them employees of the Ladies' Association, and over a quarter century she established a position of respect in the eyes of her employers and tourists alike. Although Sarah wed William Robinson in October 1888, she purchased the property under her previous married name, Johnson, probably because she and Nathan (who died in 1885) had saved their earnings for years for just such a purpose. Lloyd Washington gave her no charity, collecting $350 for the small farm (and selling her son a two-acre tract a few years later). After Lloyd Washington died, his widow and their two daughters executed a less commercial transaction. They divided his property with his two illegitimate daughters, who possessed no formal legal claim to his estate. Among black women who owned land in the Mount Vernon district, Lloyd Washington's wife and daughters were more typical than Sarah Robinson: most women landholders inherited their property from husbands or fathers, rather than buying it with their own earnings.[12]

No black people in the Mount Vernon district amassed anywhere near $20,000 in property before 1910, the standard by which historian Loren Schweninger has defined "prosperous" blacks after the Civil War. Even the district's most well-to-do African Americans fell far short of such affluence, although their neighbors with smaller holdings surely perceived the difference from themselves. Sandy Alexander accumulated forty-one acres valued at $1,435, sufficient property to be named on the published 1878 map of the district, like the Quanders and Fords (map 2.2). Lovelace Brown, the district's largest black landowner by the mid-1890s, possessed more than a hundred acres, including a seventy-two-acre parcel of the Mount Vernon estate, valued at more than $2,100. He and his son Ulysses together owned more than $600 in personal property in 1895, including six horses. By the 1890s dairying was Fairfax County's chief agricultural pursuit, and a few black landholders maintained a presence in it, perhaps to sell milk, butter, and cheese in neighborhood stores or in Alexandria. (Wealthy white dairymen with expansive farms, substantial pasturage, and large herds dominated the county's wider market, which supplied the needs of Washington, D.C., and its expanding suburbs.) Sandy Alexander owned eight cattle in 1890, and the Spring Bank farmers Griffin Johnson and William Robinson eight and seven, respectively, in 1908.[13]

The records of one Gum Springs household—that of Dandridge Smith, the "farmer" who led Alexandria's 1894 Emancipation Day parade, and his wife Annie M. Smith—revealed the pinnacle of material affluence within this community. Like Dandridge's parents and his grandfather West Ford, the Smiths were leaders within the Gum Springs community. At the same time they inhabited the broader, emerging black middle or professional class, which included also Annie's sister and brother-in-law, a schoolteacher and a physician in Petersburg, Virginia. Dandridge and Annie operated a modest dairy and produce farm, indicated by their assessment for eight cattle in 1895 and ten in 1901, by the sale of "1 Lot milk crocks and cans" after Annie's death in 1907 (Dandridge died the previous year), and by the presence of plows and harrows in Dandridge's estate. Together they owned 26 acres of land: Dandridge twelve, Annie fourteen, all formerly belonging

Map 2.2. Detail, Mount Vernon District No. 3, showing Gum Springs and the property locations of Susan Quander and Sandy Alexander in relation to Mount Vernon. Source: *Atlas of Fifteen Miles around Washington, including the County of Montgomery, Maryland*. Compiled, drawn and published from actual surveys of G. M. Hopkins. Philadelphia: G. M. Hopkins, 1879, Library of Congress Geography and Map Division.

to West Ford. The couple also operated a general store of some sort: Annie's executors sold "1 small stock of groceries and notions," two pairs of counter scales, a small coffee mill, a tobacco cutter, three tea canisters, "2 three foot (damaged) show cases," and four "Cake cases"; and her estate inventory included $41.66 in "Bills due for store account." The Smiths' inventoried possessions bespoke a measure of gentility: Dandridge's two horses (black and white) and Annie's one (gray and named "Gum"), a "buggy" and three wagons ("Farm wagon," "market wagon," and "small wagon"), two stoves rather than just one, a sideboard as well as a dining table and chairs, and lace curtains. The personal items Annie described in her last will reinforced that perception: fancywork and china (pillow shams and "my best pincushions and dinner-plates"), jewelry ("These Earrings in my ears"), and a variety of books and pictures. Annie Smith's will reflected also her appreciation of her family's and community's past and future. She bequeathed to her mother "Brother Maddens picture," a portrait or photograph of the first minister of Bethlehem Baptist Church. She left the bulk of her estate—her land, after its sale—to four nephews and nieces, to be "invested in a building association for each until they shall become 21 years of age." Half an acre of that land was to be reserved as "a graveyard for our immediate family."[14]

By contrast, the Smiths' neighbors typically wrote no last wills, buried their dead in the church cemetery, and earned their living in occupations besides farming. By the time many African Americans possessed the resources to purchase land in the 1880s and 1890s, the opportunity to subsist solely as small farmers barely existed any longer in the Mount Vernon district. Even with ten acres, Henry Randall's family made ends meet with a variety of work: the 1910 census listed Henry as "farmer and laborer," his wife Mary as a laundress, their son as a laborer on the electric railroad, and their daughter as a house servant. William Robinson's acquisition and subsequent distribution of land since the 1880s ensured that all four households of his kin in 1910 (widow Sarah, two daughters and sons-in-law, and grandson Wilbert Brown) held at least five acres. The census identified someone in three of those households as a "farmer." But two of those farmers, Wilbert and his stepfather John Bailey, were "laborers" too; and Louisa Bailey, Wilbert's mother, worked as a laundress about a third of the year. In the immediate vicinity of Wilbert Brown's house, six black men worked for the railroad company, all but one of them members of "farming" families. Among Wilbert's relatives, only Sarah Robinson was listed solely as a "farmer," presumably because she now operated her late husband's property and (at sixty-six) had no other paying job. Wilbert's land, and possibly that of his neighboring relatives at Spring Bank, was "hard," not conducive to raising crops. Perhaps, like black people elsewhere, those in the Mount Vernon district acquired some of the poorest land when they amassed the resources to buy land at all.[15]

Many black landowners in the district were not farmers, beyond possibly some household production. Personal property tax records reveal that numerous Gum Springs landowners possessed neither farming implements nor livestock. Among these were Wilbert Brown's parents-in-law, Emma and George Ford—who also had longstanding connections to Dandridge Smith and Sarah Robinson. Like Robinson, George Ford had been enslaved at Mount Vernon as a small child and had returned there in the late 1860s, when his stepfather took a job with the Mount Vernon Ladies' Association. Over the years Ford himself became a Mount Vernon employee, working on the grounds until he and his extended family resigned in 1889 to move to his stepfather's new house in Gum Springs, closer to the local school for his children. Ford and Smith were distant step-cousins: George Ford's stepfather had also been West Ford's grandson, but through an enslaved branch of the family. Thanks to that bifurcated genealogy, he inherited none of the elder Ford's property. Emma, not George, was technically the landowner: Henry Randall's niece, she became one of the first beneficiaries of the Joint Stock Club of Gum Springs in 1897. Her half-acre made her family landholders but not farmers; George remained a manual laborer most of his adult life. In 1908, the year of his daughter's marriage, he worked laying concrete for the electric railroad company.

* * *

As Wilbert Brown recollected, "I got married to settle down, accumulate a home and try to make a man of myself; that was my idea of getting married." That idea did not materialize immediately. He and Florence spent their first months of marriage shuttling from one relative's household to another: three months with Florence's parents, four months with Sarah Robinson after Wilbert's grandfather died, three months with his mother and stepfather. Unemployed at the time of the wedding—he listed "farming" as his occupation, perhaps, because he had helped William and Sarah on their farm—Wilbert got a job with the same railroad company that employed his father-in-law (figure 2.1). He earned $1.35 a day, six days a week, for working in the power house. Florence helped with the cooking and other domestic work in the households where they resided. Meanwhile Wilbert contracted with a carpenter to build them a two-story house on the five-acre plot he

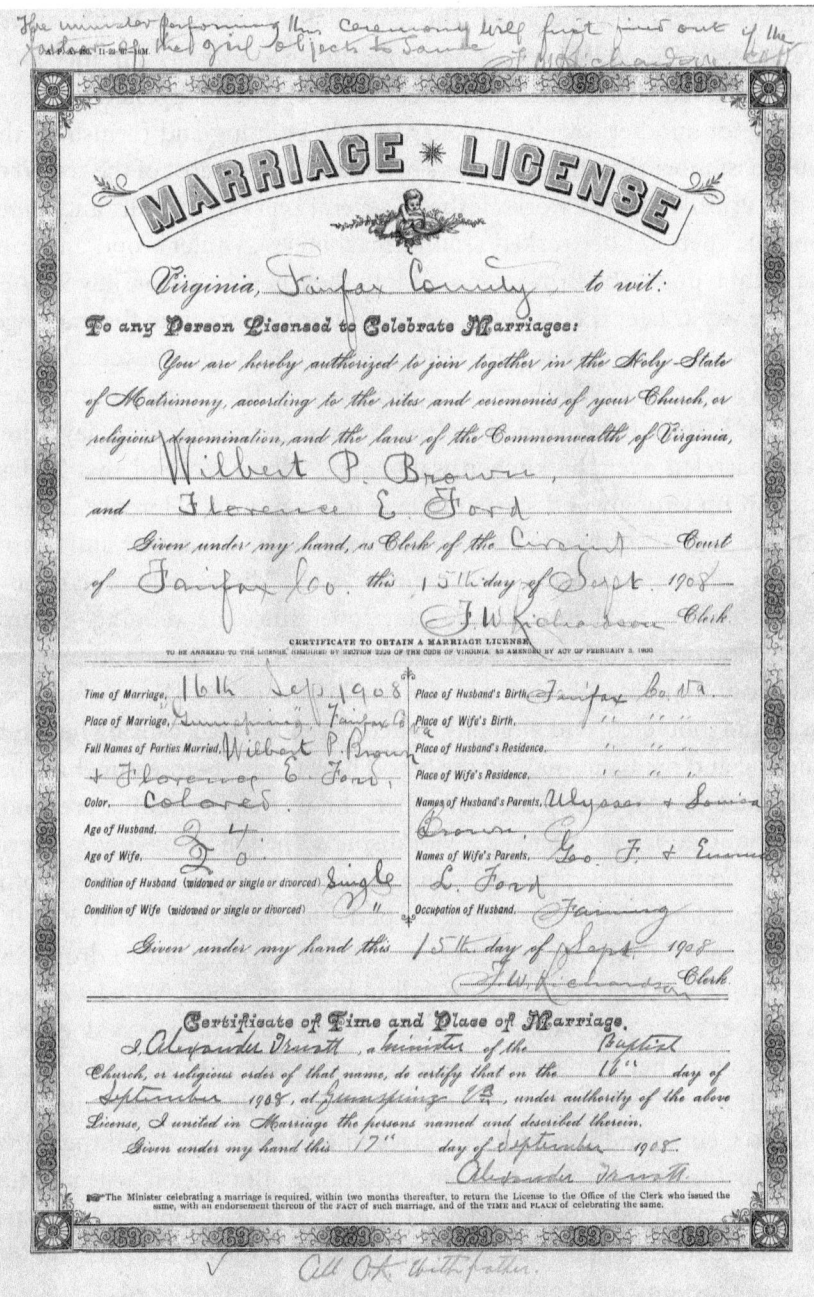

Figure 2.1. Marriage License between Wilbert Brown and Florence Ford, Fairfax County, Virginia, 1908. Courtesy of John T. Frey, Clerk, Fairfax Circuit Court, Fairfax County Court House, Fairfax, Virginia.

inherited from his grandfather. The construction cost $266.80 and furniture another $52.50. When the carpenter finished in early summer 1909, Florence asked that a closet be added; the carpenter suggested a dresser instead, for another seventeen dollars. In all, building and furnishing the house cost more than three quarters of a year's wages. Most of the rest went to groceries, Wilbert's work clothes ("several pairs of overalls and shoes a month," because he worked around machinery), winter wood and fuel, and church dues. The Browns moved into their new house on July 9, 1909, and five weeks later their son Clarence was born. A year into the marriage, Wilbert seemed to have acquired the outward trappings of success.[16]

But Florence and Wilbert were far from happy. They argued everywhere they lived. Their fights turned violent the week before moving day, when they quarreled over the kitchen wallpaper. Wilbert realized that he had tacked it up wrongly and started to take it down, when Florence came in and objected. According to him, Florence picked up a hammer and threatened to kill him with it, the latest example of the "disagreeable and ungovernable temper" he claimed she had developed since the wedding. According to Florence, Wilbert got mad, "seized her by the throat and choaked [sic] her until practically all the breath had left her body." Then he "grabbed her by the shoulders, and violently butted her in the face, causing her great suffering and pain and making the blood flow freely" before punching her in the face for good measure—all when she was eight months pregnant. Parenthood added another source for dispute. The following July, Wilbert's mother, Louisa Bailey, apparently insinuated to Florence's mother, Emma Ford, that Florence was not caring properly for the baby. On July 30, 1910, Louisa handed Clarence to Florence with the warning not to drop him. Just outside the window, his arms full of kindling wood, Wilbert echoed his mother's warning. Another argument ensued: Florence said Wilbert started toward her menacingly; he said she threatened to knock his brains out with a brick. The next morning, a Sunday, Wilbert walked the three miles to George and Emma Ford's place in Gum Springs to tell them that their daughter meant to run him out of the house. But she left instead. After Wilbert went to work on Monday morning, Florence's mother, her sister, and three of their female Randall relatives went to the house, packed Florence's possessions, and took her and the baby away to the Fords.[17]

Wilbert filed for divorce. He claimed that Florence had deserted him and that he therefore owed her no further support. Florence countersued: she wanted the divorce too, but not on his terms. Given that Wilbert owned five acres and earned a daily wage, she sought to recover her attorney's fees and to receive support for herself and Clarence. She also wanted to retrieve several articles she claimed to have left at the house: a table and chairs, a cooking stove, some bedding, and a hen and twenty-two chickens. Florence and Wilbert both hired attorneys, and the case went to Fairfax County chancery court. A chancery commissioner heard depositions in Alexandria on November 7 and 11, 1910.

Little about the Browns' case—the initial complaints, the procession of witnesses, or the resolution—was unusual for divorce proceedings around the turn of the twentieth century. Hundreds of African Americans in Virginia and Washington, D.C., sued for divorce in chancery courts between the end of the Civil War and the 1920s. Spouses deployed gendered arguments to impugn each other, much as Wilbert and Florence Brown did.[18] In the telling of Wilbert and his family, Florence was the shrew, never satisfied with his diligent providing and negligent at domestic work and child care. Wilbert's kin claimed that Florence had treated him contemptuously, complained constantly about money, and kept their households up all night with her quarreling. According to Sarah Robinson, she told Florence that "I am an old woman and have had two husbands and they are both dead, and I have never had this trouble in my house, and I am sorry and ashamed of it." In the version of Florence and her parents, she had faithfully stood by Wilbert and kept house for him even after his violence transgressed societal expectations of husbandly protection. George and Emma Ford remembered the months when the newlyweds lived with them: Wilbert, unemployed, had contributed little to support his wife or their household, and he "did not act loving" toward Florence. By July 1910, Emma and George could see that things were wrong, because their daughter looked malnourished and weak.

Each family presented their own child as blameless. Emma Ford agreed with Florence's lawyer that her daughter had been "a model wife in every particular." George characterized Florence as "an easy child," the product of her parents' firm hand: "We whipped our children to let them know right from wrong, so that when they come to be their own woman they knew." For her part, Sarah Robinson painted Wilbert as "always a very amiable child with me," and Wilbert's mother Louisa Bailey testified that he had treated Florence lovingly "and had a pet name for her." In another reflection of the deeply gendered nature of the proceedings, one of the attorneys insinuated that all might have been well if not for the interference of the mothers-in-law. In the end, Wilbert got the divorce on his legal grounds (Florence had deserted him), while Florence got her financial requests:

court costs, including $50 from Wilbert to pay her attorney, and $5 a month in child support.[19]

Beneath the "he said, she said" litany of the Browns' unhappy marriage, the depositions in their divorce hearing revealed the economic fault lines among these landholding black people as well as the geographical relationships and intersections that contoured their lives. In purely economic terms, Florence Ford married up. Wilbert Brown's grandfathers, William Robinson and Lovelace Brown, had been two of the district's wealthier black landowners, while Florence's father was a laborer whose wife had purchased their small plot of land from the joint stock company established by her uncle. In social terms, the picture was more complicated. Florence's parents both belonged to respectable local families of long standing, the Fords and the Randalls (even if Emma was a niece, not a daughter or heir). On Wilbert's side, William and Sarah Robinson possessed a degree of gentility, due in large measure to Sarah's long position of respect among her neighbors and at Mount Vernon. However, Lovelace Brown had become notorious in the neighborhood in 1898, when he murdered his son (Wilbert's father) Ulysses, apparently after a dispute over land. He dissolved his property holdings to pay for an unsuccessful legal defense and spent most of his remaining years in the state penitentiary. It is impossible to know how those events affected the neighbors' view of the Brown family. Perhaps, indeed, they sympathized with Wilbert and his widowed mother, who remarried soon thereafter. Nevertheless, economics alone likely did not determine people's standing within the community: so did the histories they had shared, the extent to which the prosperous contributed to the common weal (as Dandridge and Annie Smith had done), and their participation in church and associational life.

It is, however, possible to discern traces of class difference within the depositions in *Brown v. Brown*, particularly between the two witnesses who had shared a decades-long history at Mount Vernon, first as slaves and later as employees: Sarah Robinson and George Ford. In identifying herself as "a market woman," Robinson referred not to the historian's definition of a market culture but to the small farmer's occupation of peddling her produce. In some respects, she was a long way from her onetime role at George Washington's historic estate, where she represented the image of southern hospitality to visitors and tended to the elite women of the Ladies' Association during their annual council meetings. But at Mount Vernon she had also sold milk and guide books, and with her first husband she had operated the site's lunchroom in the 1870s and early 1880s. Even as it evoked a mythic, pre-commercial Old Dominion past, historic Mount Vernon always belonged to a contemporary world, preparing Sarah for her commercial life on William Robinson's farm and especially in town. Little wonder, then, that her testimony in her step-grandson's divorce proceedings bespoke gentility in both vocabulary and sentiment: Florence "treated [Wilbert] with rather cool contempt"; Sarah did not interfere in the newlyweds' quarrels because "it was not my motto."[20]

By contrast, George Ford's deposition suggested the lingering resentments of a laboring man, favored neither at Mount Vernon nor by his relatively prosperous kin. After describing how he and Emma had raised their children, Ford elaborated:

> Q. In other words, you made all of your children behave themselves?
> A. I did; that was the way I was brought up. I am motherless and fatherless, but that was the way I was brought up in the world.
> Q. Where were you brought up?
> A. At Mt. Vernon; worked there for eighteen years; and after I was twenty-one years old until I was able to buy this place I have got. John Augusta [sic] Washington, the last one of the Washingtons, he was my master. I wasn't half brought up in this world. I don't want to bother with a thing like this.

While Sarah Robinson's encounters with Mount Vernon's visitors and proprietors had evoked Old South gentility, George Ford had performed the menial labor of groundskeeping. Three decades later he retained the sense of himself as a working-class man—a self-perception he expressed as impatience with legal proceedings and details. "I was a slave; had little show," he told Wilbert's lawyer. "I am a man continually at work and don't take down a date," he responded when asked the span between two events. He knew what mattered: Wilbert knocked Florence around; "Every man is supposed to be the head of his own house"; he had taken in Florence and her son, at the cost of more mouths to feed, because that was what fathers did. But people's ages and the dates of events concerned him little: "To make my living I don't have no time for such things. I don't go and hunt for trouble, it comes to you, like it is now. This is your [the attorney's] trade; my trade is putting down concrete." A wage laborer, not a farmer, he followed the prospects for employment out of Gum Springs and all the way to Washington, fifteen miles north, where he worked for "the Medical Department" by the time his daughter's divorce case went to court.[21]

Just as revealing, the testimony in *Brown v. Brown* allows us to map in a preliminary way the spatial dimensions of an uncommon community's life. Most historians of southern African Americans from the Civil War to World War I have focused either on rural experience (with small towns as social and political hubs) or urban life in such places as Atlanta or Washington.[22] The women and men of Fairfax County's Mount Vernon district inhabited another sort of space: historically rural, and still somewhat so, but always connected to the city of Alexandria and beyond it to Washington; linked to the historic ground of George Washington's Mount Vernon, where many of them had ancestral roots or had worked themselves; and increasingly suburban as developers eyed the area around the nation's capital, ever more connected by electric trolley lines. Alexandria, the commercial center for the Mount Vernon neighborhood since Washington's day, was now accessible in minutes; the nation's capital, in just an hour. Prosperous dairymen reliably got their milk into the District of Columbia year-round, while wage workers like George Ford sought the best-paying work over a wider radius than they had done three decades before. With leverage provided by those opportunities as well as the construction of a U.S. Army camp near Mount Vernon, local laborers—accustomed to but not wedded to agricultural work—demanded and got higher wages from nearby employers (including the Mount Vernon Ladies' Association).[23]

The geography of such a community came into view through the depositions of Florence and Wilbert Brown and their relatives and friends.[24] First, the nine miles between Mount Vernon and Alexandria contained not one black enclave but at least two: Gum Springs, the longest-established black neighborhood in the entire Mount Vernon district; and the smaller cluster of households on the former Spring Bank estate, where Wilbert's extended family as well as the Randalls had lived since the 1880s. Florence's parents referred to the Robinsons, Baileys, and Browns as living "on the hill," a reference clearly to the higher ground at Spring Bank but possibly also to the relative prosperity of their daughter's new in-laws. Living three miles nearer to Alexandria, Sarah and William Robinson and their relatives may have forged closer ties to that city of fifteen thousand than did the residents of Gum Springs. For example, Wilbert Brown was baptized early in the twentieth century not at Bethlehem Baptist Church in Gum Springs but at Alfred Street Baptist Church in Alexandria. We cannot know why Alfred Street's minister Alexander Truatt, not Bethlehem's long-serving Reverend Samuel K. Taylor, presided at Wilbert and Florence's wedding. Conceivably, though, the Fords and the Robinsons inhabited distinct little communities. Scattered references in the depositions suggest that Florence might have been isolated in her in-laws' neighborhood: although she kept the grocery-store order book, Wilbert's mother Louisa Bailey took it into Alexandria to buy the groceries. The distance between the two enclaves was not insuperable. Wilbert walked it one Sunday morning to talk with his in-laws, and Emma Ford traveled in the opposite direction the next day to help her daughter move out. Even so, when Florence lived with Sarah, then with Wilbert's mother and stepfather, and at last in her and Wilbert's own home on the hill, the three miles may have seemed a significant separation from her own kin.[25]

The depositions also suggest these semi-rural African Americans' myriad, often gender- and class-specific links to Alexandria. Although the Washington, Alexandria, and Mount Vernon Railway carried people of both sexes, its segregated cars were particularly the conduit by which black workingmen commuted early in the morning and around 5:30 in the evening. When they both worked for the railroad company, George Ford and Wilbert Brown encountered each other every morning on the train, a commute that fell coldly silent once Wilbert and Florence split up. "Market women" like Sarah Robinson and Louisa Bailey got to town not by train but by wagon, to set up their wares on Cameron Street. In that Alexandria marketplace, where since antebellum times black women had peddled their farm goods outside the market building that housed more substantial white-owned shops, Louisa and Emma had words about Florence's care of the baby, and gossips like Martha Jenkins could overhear such conversations. Conversely, civic celebrations like the annual Emancipation Day parade were open to all, even as prosperous black "farmers" and tradesmen marching in the parade put class distinction on display to spectators lining the sidewalks. Houses of worship such as Alfred Street Baptist Church admitted women and men. So did the Alexandria circuit court office on Cameron Street, within sight of the marketplace, where Wilbert, Florence, and their witnesses assembled in November 1910. There, unlike at church or in the civic parade, a white judge and white attorneys, all men, directed the proceedings. Many more such connections between the landholders of Gum Springs and Spring Bank and the larger world of Alexandria could surely be traced. The city had a century-old tradition of African American associations and black-owned businesses, from the Odd Fellows lodge that counted William Robinson among its members (and paid Sarah Robinson a widow's benefit after he died) to the funeral parlors where those of sufficient means likely had their relatives prepared for burial in church cemeteries closer to home, such as the one adjoining Bethlehem Baptist Church (where Sarah joined William in 1920).[26] For black people living between Mount Vernon and Alexandria, the city exerted an ever-increasing pull by the early twentieth century.

* * *

The old plantation, now a national tourist site, remained a source of opportunity in only limited ways. In the mythic history of Mount Vernon, *the* "farmer" is George Washington himself, his attention to agriculture and horticulture commemorated on the historic landscape of his preserved home. Ironically, given the jaded way George Ford described his early life in his daughter's divorce proceedings, the last job in his lifetime of labor required him to reinforce that image. In 1923, aged sixty-six, he won the position of guard at George Washington's tomb, a role reserved for a local, elderly black man with some connection to historic Mount Vernon. For the next twelve years he reversed his commute—directionally, technologically, and culturally. Rather than take the electric railroad north to Washington, he now walked the much shorter distance south to his historic post. Rather than lay the concrete foundations for new buildings, he now embodied a distant past, surely evoking for some tourists the superannuated slave paying homage to his exalted master. As Mount Vernon's superintendent wrote, "George upholds the tradition of the old servants in that he was born at Mount Vernon and the blood of the old slaves is in him." If he followed the Ladies' Association's script, he never spoke of the life that had taken him and his kin away from Mount Vernon for more than three decades. In the end, the inheritance that paid off for him was precisely his family connection to Washington's home.[27]

Ford's former son-in-law Wilbert Brown never became a "farmer," notwithstanding the five acres he inherited from his grandfather, because the Mount Vernon district changed far more than Mount Vernon itself did. In 1920 the census listed Brown once again as a laborer for the railroad company. Ten years later he worked as an embalmer in a funeral parlor, likely in Alexandria, even though he still inhabited the family farm. Brown and his mother and stepfather might also have left the church and the faith of their earlier years: unlike most of their neighbors, they were buried in Alexandria, in a Methodist Episcopal Church cemetery. Generational change—inheriting one's parents' and grandparents' property, their agricultural livelihood, and their position in the community—did not work for Wilbert Brown as it had for Dandridge Smith in the 1870s and 1880s. That story was repeated throughout the Spring Bank enclave and the larger Gum Springs neighborhood. The 1930 census listed virtually every black landowner in those areas as something other than a farmer, and indeed as not living on farms at all, even people who resided on the same property where they or their parents had lived in 1910. Henry Randall's widow owned property valued at $10,000 but was described as not residing on a farm; her son George worked as a linesman for the electric light company. Next door, her son William was listed as living on a farm (perhaps the primary portion of his late father's land) but not as a farmer: he worked for the light company too. In or near Gum Springs, the census taker listed only one old man as living on a farm. Every other employed African American, including people whose families had been farming there in 1910 and who still lived on their families' property, worked at something other than agriculture, though some of them surely continued to raise crops for home consumption. According to the census taker, white people now did virtually all the "farming" in the vicinity.[28]

By 1930 the economic transformation of the Gum Springs neighborhood and the smaller Spring Bank enclave, a change clearly in view as early as 1910, was nearing completion. The district pulled its residents closer into Alexandria's orbit even as it eventually pushed many of them or their descendants off their land. Two major roads, the Mount Vernon Parkway along the old trolley route and Route 1 along the old Accotink Turnpike, would soon solidify the suburban and commercial character of what had once been the ground of African Americans' aspirations. Nevertheless, Gum Springs remains to this day a black neighborhood, with a sense of identity rooted in Bethlehem Baptist Church and in a history that stretches back not to "George Washington, Pioneer Farmer" but to the landholding pioneer West Ford.[29]

Notes

1. "Emancipation Anniversary," *Washington Post*, September 8, 1894, 7. I am grateful to Ashton Robinson for acquainting me with the chancery court divorce record that informs many of the findings here, and to Greta de Jong, C. Elizabeth Raymond, and the editors of this volume for incisive critiques of earlier versions of this essay.

2. Marriage license, Wilbert P. Brown and Florence E. Ford, September 17, 1908, in file Marriage Licenses June–October 1908, Fairfax County Circuit Court Historical Records, Fairfax County, Virginia (hereafter cited as FCHR).

3. Deposition of Sarah Robinson, November 7, 1910, in *Wilbert P. Brown v. Florence E. Brown*, p. 34, chancery case 1910-003, Circuit Court, Fairfax County, FCHR, http://www.lva.virginia.gov/chancery/default.asp#res (accessed June 8, 2010).

4. Lewis Quander estate inventory and appraisal, April 16, 1866, Will Book Z-1, pp. 460–62, FCHR; for Susan Quander's 1870 real property, see 1870 United States Federal Census (hereafter cited as Census, identified by year), Mount Vernon District, Fairfax County, Virginia, p. 44, database online at Ancestry.com (Provo, Utah: Ancestry.com Operations, accessed July 26, 2010); for the land division, see *John P. Quander etc. v. Susan Quander etc.*, chancery case 1881-028, Circuit Court, Fairfax County, FCHR, http://www.lva.virginia.gov/chancery/default.asp#res (accessed June 29, 2010). On successful families of George Washington's freedpeople, including the Quanders, see Edna Greene Medford, "Beyond Mount Vernon: George Washington's Emancipated Laborers and Their Descendants," in *Slavery at the Home of George Washington*, ed. Philip J. Schwarz (Mount Vernon, Va.: Mount Vernon Ladies' Association, 2001), 138–57.

5. On West Ford and his land purchases, see Scott E. Casper, *Sarah Johnson's Mount Vernon: The Forgotten History of an American Shrine* (New York: Hill and Wang, 2008), 24–27; for the division among his children, see John Terry Chase, *Gum Springs: The Triumph of a Black Community* (Fairfax, Va.: Heritage Resources Program of the Fairfax County Office of Comprehensive Planning, 1990), 27–31. I have calculated the acreage still owned by West Ford's descendants from the Fairfax County Land Tax Books—South, 1911: Colored/Mount Vernon District, pp. 86–90, FCHR (hereafter cited as Land Tax Books, identified by year), in conjunction with the 1870, 1880, 1900, and 1910 Censuses.

6. The data here were calculated from the 1870 Census and the 1911 Land Tax Books.

7. For Randall's employment, see 1870 Census, Mount Vernon District, p. 39, and 1880 Census, Mount Vernon District, p. 28, both at Ancestry.com (accessed June 22, 2010). The location of Charles Ballenger's farm can be found on the map "Mount Vernon Dist. No. 3," in G. M. Hopkins, *Atlas of Fifteen Miles around Washington, Including the County of Montgomery, Maryland* (Philadelphia: G. M. Hopkins, 1879), 70. For Robinson's employment, see 1870 Census, Falls Church District, Fairfax County, Va., p. 62, and 1880 Census, Mount Vernon District, p. 31, both at Ancestry.com (accessed June 22, 2010).

8. Randall's land purchase: Sallie E. Mason to Henry Randall, November 24, 1884, Deed Book D-5, p. 510, FCHR. Robinson's purchases: Sallie E. Mason to William Roberson (*sic*), January 28, 1880, Deed Book Z-4, pp. 107–8; and Sallie E. Mason to William Robinson and Elizabeth Williams (Robinson's daughter), February 26, 1887, Deed Book H-5, pp. 236–37, FCHR. Griffin Johnson's purchases, including one dictated by will: George Mason (executor), George Mason (estate), and Sallie E. Mason to Griffin Johnson, November 27, 1874, Deed Book R-4, pp. 344–45 (life tenure on five acres) and 346–47 (sale outright of five acres); Last Will of George Mason of Spring Bank, September 6, 1867, Will Book A-2, pp. 524–27, FCHR.

9. That is, fifteen out of twenty-seven. Of the other twelve, six were already farmers by 1880, three had been "farm helps" on their own fathers' land, and the remaining three included a sailor, a one-armed whitewasher, and a blacksmith. Occupations cannot be determined for thirteen, in most cases because they were not listed in the 1880 census for Fairfax County. Another five were too young in 1880 to have an occupation, and two of the women "farmers" of 1900 (typically widows or wives of farmers) had no occupation listed twenty years earlier. This information, as well as the calculation of women landowners, is based on the 1880 and 1900 Censuses and on the 1901 and 1911 Land Tax Books. Black

"farmers'" landownership in the Mount Vernon district slightly outpaced the 59 percent of Old Dominion black "farmers" listed as owning their land in the 1900 census (see Loren Schweninger, *Black Property Owners in the South, 1790–1915* [Urbana: University of Illinois Press, 1997], 174), even if the vast majority of black heads of household neither were listed as farmers nor owned real estate.

10. This information is derived from Personal Property Tax Records—Colored/Mount Vernon District, 1900–1910, FCHR, as well as the 1900 and 1910 Census (owning vs. renting land).

11. Quotation: Dianne Swann-Wright, *A Way out of No Way: Claiming Family and Freedom in the New South* (Charlottesville: University of Virginia Press, 2002), 71–72. For the Joint Stock Club of Gum Springs, see Chase, *Gum Springs*, 31. Its land sales are recorded in Deed Books A-6, p. 337 (to Nathan Webb, February 22, 1898); A-6, p. 498 (to Millie Mitchell, February 22, 1898); B-6, p. 134 (to Samuel K. Taylor, February 22, 1898); C-6, p. 332 (to Henry Randall, February 22, 1898); C-6, p. 451 (to Susan Belfield, February 22, 1898); X-6, p. 298 (to Emma Ford, August 14, 1897); J-8, p. 477 (to Fannie King, February 1, 1919); I-9, p. 237 (to Gabriel Johnson, February 22, 1898); and X-10, p. 203 (to Hamilton Grey, February 22, 1898). The sales to Webb and Randall, both trustees of the Joint Stock Club, were larger parcels from a different tract of land than the other purchases. On the Mason Neck enclave, see Paula Elsey, "The 'Willing Workers': A Black Community on Mason Neck," *Yearbook: The Historical Society of Fairfax County, Virginia* 26 (1997–98): 93–122.

12. Lloyd Washington to Sarah Johnston (*sic*), April 16, 1889, Deed Book I-5, p. 128, FCHR; *Administrator of Lloyd Washington v. Hannah Washington et al.*, chancery case 1897-002, Circuit Court, Fairfax County, Virginia, FCHR, http://www.lva.virginia.gov/chancery/default.asp#res (accessed July 26, 2010). For women's role in "transferring property among neighbors and kin," see Debra A. Reid, "Furniture Exempt from Seizure: African-American Farm Families and Their Property in Texas, 1880s–1930s," *Agricultural History* 80, no. 3 (2006): 340.

13. Schweninger, *Black Property Owners in the South*, chap. 6. Information about landowning comes from the 1891, 1901, and 1911 Land Tax Books; for personal property such as livestock and farm implements, I examined the Personal Property Tax Records for 1890, 1895, 1901, 1905, 1908, and 1910. For the agricultural transformation of Fairfax County toward dairying, see Patrick Reed, "1870–1925," in *Fairfax County: A History* (Fairfax, Va.: Fairfax County Board of Supervisors, 1978), 415–16, 515–17.

14. Annie M. Smith last will and testament, Gum Spring, April 14, 1902 (probated September Term 1907), Will Book 3, pp. 567–68, FCHR; estate inventories of William Dandridge Smith (approved October 11, 1907) and Annie M. Smith (approved October 25, 1907) and Sale List (November 7, 1907), Will Book 3, pp. 608–10, FCHR. For Annie Smith's sister and brother-in-law, see 1900 Census, Petersburg, Va., Ward 4, district 100, p. 5, at Ancestry.com (accessed July 25, 2010). Besides Lewis Quander's 1866 estate inventory, the only similar documents I have found in the FCHR for members of the Gum Springs or nearby community are William Robinson's will (which lists only his land, and leaves all possessions to his widow) and Robinson's and Lloyd Washington's estate inventories (which likewise offer no details about household belongings or farm equipment). Perhaps Annie Smith, as a woman writing her will, was more attentive to such domestic

possessions as books, pictures, and bed linens than a man would have been. But even the act of writing a will set her apart from most of her and Dandridge's neighbors, who owned far less and (more important) may not have seen fit to avail themselves of that legal process. On the development of the "black middle class" in this period, and especially its self-conscious distinction from the black working class, see Martin Summers, *Manliness and Its Discontents: The Black Middle Class and the Transformation of Masculinity, 1900-1930* (Chapel Hill: University of North Carolina Press, 2004), 6–7; Kevin K. Gaines, *Uplifting the Race: Black Leadership, Politics, and Culture in the Twentieth Century* (Chapel Hill: University of North Carolina Press, 1996).

15. Information about occupations is from 1910 Census, Mount Vernon District, Fairfax County, Va., pp. 17–18, at Ancestry.com (accessed June 30, 2010). For Wilbert Brown's "hard" land, see deposition of Louisa Bailey, November 7, 1910, in *Brown v. Brown*, p. 44.

16. Wilbert P. Brown second cross-examination, November 7, 1910, in *Brown v. Brown*, p. 37 ("I got married"); information about the Browns' residence and employment derived from various depositions in *Brown v. Brown*; for earnings and expenses, see Wilbert P. Brown deposition, *Brown v. Brown*, pp. 10, 18–20 ("overalls and shoes," p. 20). For Wilbert's land, see last will of William Robinson, Will Book 4, p. 99, FCHR.

17. Complaint of Wilbert P. Brown, c. August 11, 1910, in *Brown v. Brown*, p. 1 ("disagreeable and ungovernable temper"); Answer of Florence E. Brown, c. August 30, 1910, *Brown v. Brown*, p. 3 ("seized her by the throat"). Descriptions of their arguments, from different points of view, appear throughout the depositions in their divorce proceedings.

18. See Dylan C. Penningroth, "African American Divorce in Virginia and Washington, D.C., 1865–1930," *Journal of Family History* 33 (January 2008): 21–35. Penningroth examined 473 divorce cases in five Virginia counties (not including Fairfax), of which 312 were "brought by black plaintiffs" (23), and 156 cases in Washington, of which 31 percent were brought by African Americans. The arguments and language deployed in the Browns' case strikingly resemble the composite picture assembled by Penningroth, as well as many of his specific examples, with one exception: never in the Browns' proceedings did African American migration become an issue, as it did in many other divorce cases over the period.

19. Depositions in *Brown v. Brown* of Emma Ford, November 11, 1910, pp. 48 ("did not act loving"), 58 ("model wife"); Sarah Robinson, November 7, 1910, pp. 32 ("amiable child"), 33 ("I am an old woman"); George Ford, November 11, 1910, p. 64 ("easy child," "whipped our children"); Louisa Bailey, November 7, 1910, p. 41 ("pet name"). For the attorney's insinuation, see deposition of Emma Ford, p. 62: "A good deal of your testimony has been taken up with giving conversations back and forth between you and Wilbert's mother. Isn't it a fact that but for fusses you have been having with her, your daughter would never have left her husband?" Other details in this paragraph are drawn from these depositions as well as those of Wilbert and Florence Brown. For the resolution of their case, see "In the circuit court of Fairfax Co., Va.," November 30, 1910, handwritten, unnumbered page at end of *Brown v. Brown* transcript.

20. Deposition of Sarah Robinson, November 7, 1910, in *Brown v. Brown*, pp. 32, 34. On Robinson's work at Mount Vernon and how the site at once evoked an earlier Old

Dominion and inhabited its own contemporary world, see Casper, *Sarah Johnson's Mount Vernon*, esp. chaps. 6 and 7.

21. Deposition of George Ford, November 11, 1910, in *Brown v. Brown*, pp. 63–65, 68.

22. For an example of the former, see Steven Hahn, *A Nation under Our Feet: Black Political Struggles in the Rural South from Slavery to the Great Migration* (Cambridge, Mass.: Belknap Press of Harvard University Press, 2003); for an example of the latter, see Tera Hunter, *To 'Joy My Freedom: Black Women's Lives and Labors after the Civil War* (Cambridge, Mass.: Harvard University Press, 1997), and Sharon Harley, "For the Good of Family and Race: Gender, Work, and Domestic Roles in the Black Community, 1880–1930," in *Black Women in America: Social Science Perspectives*, ed. Micheline R. Malson et al. (Chicago: University of Chicago Press, 1990), 159–72. Fon Louise Gordon, *Caste and Class: The Black Experience in Arkansas, 1880–1920* (Athens: University of Georgia Press, 1995) takes a different approach, sketching both rural and urban experience and arguing that Arkansas' black middle class was "an urban-town phenomenon whose message was not necessarily compatible with the agricultural system of which most black Arkansans were a part" (working in sharecropping or crop lien systems) or with rural black Arkansans generally. Turn-of-the-century "farming" in the Mount Vernon district of Fairfax County, by contrast, did not typically involve sharecropping or large-plantation agriculture. "Class" differences existed among "rural" families themselves, and helped shape their urban interactions (e.g., leading the Emancipation Day parade vs. commuting to town to work for the railroad company).

23. For suburban development, see William H. Snowden, *Some Old Historic Landmarks of Virginia and Maryland* (Andalusia, Va., 1904), 29; for the challenges to the local labor market, see Casper, *Sarah Johnson's Mount Vernon*, 208–10; on the construction of Camp A. A. Humphreys (later Fort Belvoir), see Reed, "1870–1925," in *Fairfax County, Virginia: A History*, 494–95.

24. The approach here owes much to Elsa Barkley Brown and Gregg D. Kimball, "Mapping the Terrain of Black Richmond," *Journal of Urban History* 21 (March 1995): 296–346, which distinguishes between sacred, civic, and commercial space in one urban setting. While the findings in my study are based primarily on the mentions of place and space in one rich document, examined in relation to census and tax records, more extensive research into black-owned Alexandria businesses and institutions might at least suggest paths and places the rural residents of the Mount Vernon district frequented in Alexandria.

25. Depositions in *Brown v. Brown* of Louisa Bailey, November 7, 1910, p. 44 (Florence said she "didn't like it on the hill"); George Ford, November 11, 1910, p. 63 ("When they went on the hill"); Wilbert Brown, p. 20 (grocery order book). For Wilbert's baptism, see Alton S. Wallace, *I Once Was Young: History of Alfred Street Baptist Church, 1803–2003* (Littleton, Mass.: Tapestry Press, 2003), 87.

26. Deposition of George Ford, November 11, 1910, in *Brown v. Brown*, p. 64 (railroad commute); deposition of Emma Ford, November 11, 1910, in *Brown v. Brown*, p. 53 (Cameron Street Market; Martha Jenkins); R. H. Lancaster Lodge No. 1370, Grand United Order of Odd Fellows of the State of Virginia, Records, 1890–1910 (box 76, folders 2, 3, 8), Special Collections, Alexandria Public Library, Alexandria, Virginia; *Fairfax County, Virginia*

Gravestones (Merrifield, Va.: Fairfax Genealogical Society, 1998), vol. 5, pp. SA-127–40 (Snowden and Bethlehem Cemetery; Sarah and William Robinson as well as George and Emma Ford and Florence E. Brown, p. SA-135). For the Cameron Street market, see *Alexandria Gazette*, August 28, 1876, p. 2, quoted in T. Michael Miller, *Pen Portraits of Alexandria Virginia* (Bowie, Md.: Heritage Books, 1987), 281.

27. Harrison Howell Dodge, *Mount Vernon: Its Owner and Its Story* (Philadelphia: Lippincott, 1932), 97.

28. 1920 Census, Mount Vernon District, Fairfax County, Va., district 36, p. 31 (Wilbert Brown's occupation), and 1930 Census, Mount Vernon District, Fairfax County, Va., district 18, pp. 14–19 (Spring Bank and Gum Springs vicinity), both at Ancestry.com (accessed August 4, 2010). Elsewhere in the Mount Vernon district, other African Americans including several of the Quanders were still listed as farmers. For the Alexandria burial of Wilbert Brown, his mother and stepfather, and his second wife, see Wesley E. Pippenger, *Tombstone Inscriptions of Alexandria, Virginia* (Westminster, Md.: Family Line Publications, 1992), 2:19–24. Wilbert died in 1934, aged forty-nine; his mother Louisa Bailey survived him by eighteen years.

29. A contemporary example: In the summer of 2008, Bethlehem Baptist Church sponsored a summer camp for "at-risk" children from the Gum Springs neighborhood. The camp's focus was the history of the neighborhood: participants studied the lives of West Ford and other noteworthy figures and produced their own book about the community's past.

3

James E. Youngblood
Race, Family, and Farm Ownership in Jim Crow Texas

KEITH J. VOLANTO

On June 4, 2009, at a ceremony held in Austin, Texas, with state Agriculture Commissioner Todd Staples in attendance, eighty-six-year-old Eddie Lee Youngblood and her daughter Vicki Holmes joined members of seventy other families to receive recognition under the Texas Department of Agriculture's Family Land Heritage Program, honoring farms and ranches in continuous agricultural operation by the same family for more than a hundred years. In 1894 Eddie Lee's father, an African American farmer named James Edward Youngblood, had purchased forty acres of land about 2.5 miles south of Coolidge in Limestone County. This initial plot served as the basis of the family's land holdings for the next century. In this essay I chronicle the quest for information about James E. Youngblood's background, explore the factors allowing him to purchase land during the Jim Crow period, and describe how the Youngblood family was able to maintain farming operations to the present day.[1]

For decades the origins of James E. Youngblood, nicknamed "Squire" (or "Square," in the rustic Texas dialect), were unknown to his descendants beyond some basic information. Using family oral history and some census data, Lenora Youngblood Smith and Eula Williams Youngblood, two family members interested in genealogy, dutifully compiled a family history which they completed in 1998. In this work Lenora and Eula ascertained that Squire was born in either 1868 or 1869 in western Polk County (now San Jacinto County), located in the Big Thicket area of Southeast Texas. In the 1870 U.S. Census for Polk County they also discovered a mulatto man named James Youngblood, who they believed might be Squire's father, given the location and the similarity of names. The descendants surmised that Squire left the region at a young age for unknown reasons and wound up in Limestone County, where a white family known to be named the Yarbroughs raised him while he worked on their farm. Squire got married in 1894 and used his savings to finance the purchase of his first forty-acre tract of land. Beyond this outline, little else was known to the family members. Lenora and Eula speculated about possible scenarios but openly acknowledged that their labor of love was incomplete and simply the closest accounts matching the information that they had been given. They were hopeful that "some young family member will continue the search . . . will add to it . . . or will make the necessary corrections."[2]

Recent research into James Youngblood's background, using Lenora and Eula Youngblood's invaluable compilation as a basis for exploration, has allowed me to produce a slew of new insights into Squire's past. With information provided by Internet resources, modern DNA analysis, contact established with distant relatives, and traditional research with documentary sources discovered in local archives, I have been able to ascertain some basic facts about Squire's origins and determine the various factors that contributed to the man's ability to purchase land and remain moderately prosperous as a small-scale farm owner during the Jim Crow era.

In many ways the story of James E. Youngblood begins on a Lowndes County plantation in the Black Belt of Alabama several decades before he was born. There, one day in the spring of 1833, a white planter named Thomas B. Youngblood took advantage of one of his slaves sexually. Nine months later, on December 29, the unknown slave mother gave birth to a boy who was given the name James Thomas Youngblood (figure 3.1). This child remained in Alabama with the Youngblood family for the next twenty years and later accompanied the planter, his wife Matilda, their children, and eighty-six other slaves as they trekked westward to Polk County in 1853, part of the large migration into Texas that occurred in the decade before the Civil War. The allure of virgin cotton-growing lands, and access to the outside world via steamboats ascending and descending the Trinity River, contributed to Polk County's rapid population growth, soaring 253.5 percent from 2,348 (including 805 slaves) in 1850 to 8,300 (including 4,198 slaves) in 1860. Thomas B. Youngblood died a year after arriving, having just set up an operation of 3,786 acres along the San Jacinto River with sixty-one slaves (he likely sold twenty-five of the original eighty-seven slaves upon arrival to cover expenses and purchase land). His slaves constituted the bulk of his declared wealth, valued at $30,500 out of his total

Figure 3.1. James Thomas Youngblood (1833–1891), former slave of Thomas B. Youngblood and son of an unknown slave mother. Youngblood owned 188 acres of land by 1880. Source: Patrick King.

real and personal property of $36,186, according to the 1854 county tax assessment. At the time of his death Thomas Youngblood was already one of the largest planters in the county. Ownership of his slaves transferred to his widow Matilda and his son-in-law, James Watson, who had married Mary Youngblood, one of Thomas's daughters.[3]

James Thomas Youngblood remained in Polk County until emancipation, then lived in the area and maintained contact with his white relatives, the Youngbloods, and white in-laws, the Watsons. He appears on the voter registration rolls in 1867 when the U.S. Army followed guidelines laid down by Congress in the Reconstruction Act to register all eligible voters, including male freedmen. The 1870 U.S. Census listed freed slaves by name for the first time, and he is the James Youngblood whom Lenora and Eula discovered during the course of their research. He lived on a farm, though it is unclear whether he owned the land at that time. (Ten years later the 1880 federal agricultural census lists him as owning sixty acres of tilled land and 128 acres of unimproved woodland and forest, with a total value of

$900.) Living with James were his twenty-eight-year-old wife Eliza (figure 3.2), who had served as a house slave for the Watsons since being given to the couple as a wedding present when she was seven years old; his daughters Mary (age nine) and Mourning Elizabeth ("Lizzie") Youngblood (age three); plus a son listed as Ennis (age four months). Three other children were also living in the house: Adaline Erby (age eleven), Cynthia Erby (age eight), and Eli Erby (age six).[4]

African American kinship patterns were often quite complex during slavery and for many decades thereafter, flexible enough to include multiple spouses and their offspring, extended family members, and even fellow slaves with no formal blood ties at all. James Thomas Youngblood's family bible clarifies many details, though not all the mysteries with regard to his family. Very elaborate handwriting within the opening pages of the bible provides family members' birthdays and reveals that Adaline and Cynthia were Eliza's children from a relationship during slavery involving a man other than James Thomas Youngblood. Eli Erby is not mentioned; therefore it can be assumed that he was probably a cousin or nephew living with the family. We also learn that Mary Youngblood was a product of James's relationship with another woman during slavery.[5]

Which leads us to Ennis—James and Eliza's only son. Within the James T. Youngblood family bible the unknown writer noted that "James Ennis Youngblood" was a son of James Thomas and Eliza born in 1869 but that he died in 1875. The proximity in birth years, plus the fact that Ennis is listed as having the first name "James" and a middle name with an initial of "E" provides revealing possibilities that cannot be ignored. It appears that James Ennis Youngblood was the same person as James Edward (Squire) Youngblood, with the year 1875 possibly signifying when he left the family rather than a death year. Further corroborating this theory is the fact that James Thomas, Eliza, Adaline, Cynthia, and Mary are all buried in the family plot at Sandfield Cemetery in San Jacinto County, yet there is no grave for James Ennis. Patrick King, a great-great-grandson of Lizzie Youngblood, has also related the details of a recent conversation he had with her last surviving granddaughter, Blanche Washington Allen. According to Blanche, her grandmother Lizzie had a light-skinned brother named James who was not raised by the family but would occasionally visit. When informed that the family bible stated that James had died in 1875, she dismissed that notion, saying, "Then he must have been a walking ghost!" She also identified the person in a picture of Squire that I provided as "Uncle James."[6]

Figure 3.2. Eliza Youngblood (1842–1924), former house slave of Mary Youngblood and James Watson. She and James Thomas Youngblood had one son, James Ennis Youngblood, aka Squire. Source: Patrick King.

DNA evidence supports the hypothesis that James Thomas Youngblood was Squire Youngblood's father. Recently a male-line descendant of Squire's, a great-grandson, took a DNA test, the results of which showed strong matches in genetic markers between himself (and thus Squire) and several *white* male Youngblood descendants who have been proven to be related to a common ancestor named John Miles Youngblood (born in Baltimore, Maryland, in 1708). Though the exact nature of the connection between John Miles Youngblood and Thomas B. Youngblood has yet to be established, the assumption is that Thomas B. Youngblood was a great-grandson of John Miles Youngblood. In any case, one fact is undeniable—Squire not only shared the white Youngbloods' surname (as many former slaves and their descendants did); he also shared their genes.[7]

Squire Youngblood "died" at the end of Reconstruction in one record, but the 1880 U.S. Census shows him living on as a "hireling" with a white family, the Yarbroughs, revealing the complicated relationships that linked some black farm families with white kinship groups. The census states that on a farm outside Waxahachie in Ellis County, sixty-two-year-old retired Methodist minister Solomon Shaw Yarbrough lived with his wife Mattie, a twelve-year-old son named John, a twenty-eight-year-old son named William, William's wife Bettie, their two young children, and an eleven-year-old mulatto boy listed as "Squire Watson." There is no doubt that Squire Watson is James E. Youngblood. In addition to the Youngblood family oral history that connects Squire with the Yarbrough family, a San Jacinto County marriage certificate has been located showing that on February 3, 1876, William Yarbrough married Mary Elizabeth (i.e., "Bettie") Watson— the daughter of the planter James Watson (Thomas and Matilda Youngblood's son-in-law). It is likely that around this time the newlyweds moved to the Waxahachie area to live with William's father, and they arranged for Squire, whose mother had served as Mary and James Watson's house slave, to be brought along to work on the farm. When the census taker asked for Squire's surname, the Reverend Yarbrough or his son William answered "Watson," either not caring that it was really Youngblood or just assuming that Watson was correct. This information from the public records verifies the story of Squire's stay with the Yarbroughs as passed down in the Youngblood family oral history, but it establishes a much earlier point of contact between Squire and the Yarbroughs than his descendants had previously known.[8]

Due to the minister's age and failing health, his son William probably managed the farm (which had ninety-five acres of tilled land in 1880, forty of which were dedicated to raising eleven bales of cotton) and assigned various tasks for young Squire to perform. Since Reconstruction era agriculture deviated little from that of the antebellum period, his work would have been similar to that done by slaves just twenty years before—preparing the soil, planting the crop, chopping weeds, and picking the cotton, not to mention other rough work not related to cotton production. Squire was never legally a part of the Yarbrough family. No adoption records have been located among the San Jacinto and Ellis County public records. Reverend Yarbrough's wife and sons are mentioned in the minister's will, but not Squire. Given the racial climate in post-Reconstruction Texas, one would not expect to find any such acknowledgment.[9]

Youngblood family oral history supports the notion that in return for receiving the services of a hardworking farm laborer, the Yarbroughs raised Squire, treated him relatively well, and taught him to be industrious and enterprising while learning basic farm management techniques that he would apply later on his own farm. Nevertheless, one is left to ponder what kind of psychological toll this displacement took on the young child. Whether or not he knew why he left his family and wound up in many ways bound almost like a slave to the Yarbroughs, the circumstances must have been troubling to him and probably explain why he rarely spoke of his early childhood. His failure to come to grips completely with his removal may also partly explain his occasionally notorious temper as an adult.[10]

The surviving record is unclear concerning how long Squire remained in Ellis County. Reverend Yarbrough died on December 31, 1885, but Limestone County tax records indicate that his son William owned two hundred acres of land there, valued at $700, as early as 1882. (In his will Solomon Yarbrough alluded to owning land in Limestone County and that he had already "made some advancements" of this land to his sons Thomas and William.) It is unclear whether Squire accompanied William Yarbrough to Limestone County soon after the preacher's son acquired the land or only upon Solomon Yarbrough's death.[11]

Squire appears for the first time in the Limestone County public records during the 1892 tax assessment, which indicated that he owned a horse or mule valued at $40 and miscellaneous property valued at $10. Beginning with that enumeration, Squire appears regularly in the Limestone County tax records, providing evidence of his subsequent ascent as a property-owning farmer (figure 3.3).[12]

Squire lived with the Yarbrough family until he leveraged his capital during late 1894 and bought his own farm. Personal goals of love and marriage along with societal pressure—white attitudes toward free black labor—prompted him to acquire his own farm. Soon after becoming engaged to a local girl named Willie Lou Stephens, he overheard Mrs. Yarbrough express happiness over the marriage because she thought it would mean having extra help around the house. Squire became even more committed to purchasing his own land so that he and his new family could lead free and independent lives. In mid-November 1894, he completed a deal with J. H. and Octavia Heidleberg to acquire his first forty acres of land for a total of $680. The deed shows that James paid $250 up front in cash (from his savings plus possible assistance from William Yarbrough) and agreed to make payment on two notes of $135.78 due on November 15, 1895 and 1896, respectively, and one last note for $158.44 due on November 15, 1898. Each note carried a 10 percent per annum interest charge from the due date until

Figure 3.3. Portrait of James E. Youngblood (1869–1946), also known as Squire. Source: Vicki Holmes.

paid, and the Heidlebergs held a lien on the land until all notes and interest were paid. Less than four months later, on March 1, 1895, Squire married Willie Lou. In December she gave birth to their first child, Alfred.[13]

The early years of farm ownership were quite modest for Squire. For ten years he held only the original forty acres, while gradually adding a few more horses, mules, and some cattle (table 3.1). He made enough to purchase a carriage for himself and his growing family, but his miscellaneous property remained low. It is not known what specific crops Squire initially grew on the farm besides cotton. The family gained members during these years and he had many mouths to feed. From 1895 to 1907 Willie gave birth to at least one child every other year. After Alfred came Mary (1897), followed by Robert Grover (1899), Ulysses (1901), the twins Theodore Roosevelt and Booker T. (1903), Shallie (1905), and Delillian (1907).[14]

Over the next fifteen years Squire's hard work led to his ability to pay off his notes, save some earnings, and expand his holdings. As table 3.1 indicates, he acquired an additional one hundred acres in 1904, allowing him almost to quadruple the amount of land he possessed while more than doubling his total net worth to a value of $1,440. By 1910 James owned 173 acres

Table 3.1. Property of James E. Youngblood, 1893–1910

Year	Acres	Value	Horses/Mules	Cattle	Hogs	Carriages	Misc.	Total
1893	-	-	1	-	-	-	$10	$40
1894	-	-	2	-	-	-	0	$80
1895	40	$400	2	-	-	1	$20	$480
1896	40	$360	3	-	2	1	$20	$450
1897	40	$365	3	-	-	1	$27	$450
1898	40	$350	3	-	2	1	$27	$420
1899	40	$360	4	2	-	1	$25	$460
1900	40	$365	4	2	-	1	$15	$530
1901	40	$370	4	2	3	1	$10	$475
1902	40	$375	6	5	4	1	$15	$635
1903	40	$375	6	6	4	1	$10	$655
1904	147	$1,150	6	9	2	1	$10	$1,440
1905	147.5	$1,285	5	5	4	1	$15	$1,500
1906	147.5	$1,650	4	6	5	1	$20	$1,880
1907	141	$1,350	6	4	5	2	$10	$1,560
1908	174	$2,900	4	6	3	2	$25	$3,320
1909	173	$2,670	5	4	1	2	$35	$3,090
1910	173	$3,480	7	4	1	2	$40	$4,120

Source: Limestone County Tax Rolls, microfilm reels 114702–5, Baylor University, Waco, Texas.

and possessed a total net worth of $4,120, almost ten times the amount he held when he first purchased the farm. At the time, there were 1,033 black farmers in the county, but he was one of only 247 who owned their land. (By contrast, the county had 3,934 white farmers, of whom 1,563 were farm owners.)[15]

Squire accomplished this feat before his eldest children actually reached working age, but he could anticipate having their labor to assist with chores and the demanding physical labor on diversified Texas farms that inevitably included cotton as a cash crop, cattle running on pasture, and hogs and corn as food sources and sales commodities. Willie and her children tended fields as labor needs demanded, but, similar to other Texas farm women and children, they contributed to the farm family economy by also performing such tasks as preserving food, making butter, raising poultry, and tending gardens. In addition they undertook all the domestic chores, such as cooking for the family on a wood-burning stove, cleaning laundry by dousing clothes in a tub filled with hot water followed by intense scrubbing on washboards, and maintaining the cleanliness of the farmhouse (figure 3.4).[16]

Figure 3.4. Farmhouse owned by Squire Youngblood, who is pictured standing on the front porch (wearing a hat) with some members of his family, sometime between 1901 and 1915. Source: Vicki Holmes.

In 1909 Willie passed away at the young age of thirty-five. At forty-one years old, Squire became the sole head of a large brood. Alfred, Mary, and Robert Grover all served as general farm laborers while also attending school. The five younger children remained with the family. Though it is not known who took care of them while the elder children were working with their father in the fields, it is probable that such tasks were twelve-year-old Mary's responsibility. To help with farm work Squire did hire an additional laborer from outside the family, a twenty-two-year-old black man named Thomas Igleheart.[17]

The family functioned without a female head for seven years until Squire remarried. According to Eddie Lee Youngblood, James met her mother, Mattie Elizabeth Hobbs, in 1916 while visiting a local store where she worked. He was forty-seven years old; she was twenty-six. The couple's first child, a boy named Billie, died of pneumonia in 1917. A second child, Oscar, was born in 1919. By then Alfred no longer lived on the farm, and nor did Mary, but Squire had the full services of twenty-year-old Robert Grover, eighteen-year-old Ulysses, seventeen-year-old Booker T. and Theodore, fifteen-year-old Shallie, and twelve-year-old Delillian to work his land, which had expanded by an additional thirty acres in 1916.[18]

During the 1920s the Youngblood family grew further. Two daughters, Helen and Eddie Lee, and two sons, Tracy and Clarence Edward, joined the family; in 1930 they were aged ten, eight, six, and two, respectively. The sons Robert Grover, Ulysses, Theodore, and Shallie had all left the farm. Though Booker T. died of appendicitis in 1930, his widow Harriett remained with the family (they had no children).[19]

Youngblood family oral history paints a consistent picture about Squire's personality and the way he handled his children. He could be a demanding task master who often used harsh discipline with the children. Quick to use a buggy whip to get his message across, he once took out one of Theodore's eyes and almost did the same to one of his daughters. Shallie left the farm in favor of the military after one particularly harsh beating. Eddie Lee usually avoided such punishment by simply not talking back to her father, as some of the other children sometimes did. "I learned early to maneuver," she recalled. This personality trait may have derived from the fact that Squire never had a normal childhood in the traditional sense. Because all he knew was a life of discipline and hard work, he demanded the same from his children. However, Eddie Lee, a retired grammar school teacher, believes that her father simply did not know how to discipline children properly. Perhaps it was a combination of both.[20]

Despite Squire's occasional cruel side, Eddie Lee described him as a devoted family man who tried as best he could to instill in his children the values of hard work and education. While some left the farm to join the military or, in Theodore's case, simply for the sake of individual freedom, he helped them attend school and tried to maintain contact with them. After graduating with a history degree from Sam Huston College in Austin, Theodore worked day and night for several years as a bus boy and porter for the Austin Hotel and as a janitor at the Capitol Building to support himself, his wife Jewel, and his boys Ted Jr. and Alvin. Theodore remembered one time when his father visited Austin, and Squire declared proudly that his son was going to make it because he was never home and was always working.[21]

Theodore's anecdote displays much about Squire's outlook. Not only were the values of hard work and material acquisition imparted to him by the Yarbroughs; they were reinforced by Squire's acceptance of the philosophy of Booker T. Washington, who, like himself, had risen from lowly circumstances. Squire admired Washington, named a son after him, and practiced the teachings of the "Wizard of Tuskegee" by pursuing wealth, contributing to his community, and ignoring what he agreed were fruitless efforts to demand acceptance and equality from white men, given the existing racial climate.[22]

By the onset of the Great Depression, Squire Youngblood was running a diversified farming operation that enabled a strong degree of self-sufficiency and independence. Though they raised some cotton for cash, the family were not dependent upon that staple for their livelihood. The Youngbloods also harvested hay, peas, and corn on the land in addition to raising some cattle, hogs, turkeys, guineas, and chickens. Further, Squire hired a few sharecroppers to raise cotton and peas on the land. Squire's diversification reflected scientific farming goals pursued by some independent African American farmers during this era. Working with the Negro Division of the Texas Agricultural Extension Service, which urged them to break their reliance on cotton, they planted multiple crops, tended to soil fertility to keep the land productive, raised poultry to ensure a nutritious family diet, preserved food to avoid waste and save money, and often increased their marketing options by participating in cooperatives. To the delight of the local Extension Service agent, Squire engaged in many of these activities.[23]

From family sources we can glean a basic sketch about how the farm operated during this time and Squire's role in managing its affairs. Most of the work devolved upon the children, and Squire kept them busy. Eddie Lee recalls getting roused with the other children before daylight and then waiting for the sun to come up to perform the various tasks assigned to them, such as clearing land, chopping weeds, tending to the animals, and gathering crops. During cotton-picking season the children were sent out to harvest the crops of other farmers to bring in extra money for the family. Theodore described his father as being excellent with numbers, able to measure a strip of land down to the inch, a skill probably acquired from his time with the Yarbroughs, since he had little formal schooling. But as much as Squire valued hard work, Eddie Lee never remembered seeing her father performing any physical labor himself—by this time in his life (in his fifties and early sixties), he was content supervising his children and monitoring the work of his sharecroppers.[24]

The self-sufficiency of the farmstead enabled the family to weather the Great Depression. Eddie Lee recalls her mother making sure that the family never went hungry. In fact, she states that it was "the only time growing up that I remember having three square meals." She also has a recollection of her father gaining additional income as the result of his participation in the federal government's cotton plow-up and emergency cattle slaughter campaigns. Both programs were supervised by the Agricultural Adjustment Administration (AAA), which paid farmers to destroy a portion of their growing crop in 1933 and to reduce the number of cows in 1934 in order to drive up prices through the reduction of the existing surplus of cotton and cattle. In these endeavors the AAA relied upon the Extension Service to act as its foot soldiers overseeing the work. The Negro Division of the Texas Extension Service worked closely with African American farmers to publicize the programs, oversee their implementation, ensure farmer compliance, and distribute payments.[25]

Squire also earned extra income by running a small syrup mill on his farm, catering to the widespread desire among rural folk for cheap sweeteners. Neighbors cut cane in their fields, removed the leaves, and brought their cane to Squire's farm for processing. Syrup mill operators typically asked for a third of the syrup produced as compensation but provided a valuable service to poor rural communities.[26]

Though possessing an enterprising nature, Squire could be charitable and earned the respect of others as a recognized leader in the local African American community. Eddie Lee commented on her father's generosity during the Depression, often sharing surplus vegetables with hungry area children. In an article titled "This Was Coolidge in 1904" by Mrs. J. Clinton Byers in the *Coolidge Herald* of August 13, 1954, the woman (who was white) stated that the first piece of furniture her husband sold at his new store was a casket purchased by Squire Youngblood for another family's baby, something he did on more than one occasion. "Squire was one of the straightest Negroes we ever knew," she noted. "He came for caskets for most of the Sandy [land] Negroes and we never did lose any money on them. Think he held a firm hand over his race in those parts and gloried in the fact that they paid their obligations." At Comanche Crossing, the famous Limestone County meeting place (known formally as Booker T. Washington Park) where freedmen annually celebrated emancipation on June 19, or "Juneteenth," the site's historical marker lists the forty names of the park's founders. The last one listed is "Square Youngblood."[27]

By the 1940s James E. Youngblood was entering his seventies and could take pride in the establishment of a comfortable existence as a successful small farm owner. He accepted modernity—in his later years, Squire's home was wired for electricity and included a large radio, which he enjoyed while sitting in his rocking chair with his feet propped up on a table. He was especially diligent every Sunday in listening to W. Lee "Pappy" O'Daniel's weekly show. Squire also enjoyed driving his automobile, especially for jaunts to nearby Coolidge for socializing. His joy of driving, however, almost led to a premature demise. Eddie Lee vividly remembers the day her father left for town with his son Theodore's boys, Ted Jr. and Alvin, who had been visiting their grandfather for the summer. She recalls after a while seeing the wrecked car being towed back and wondering what had happened. In the days before crossing gates and lights, apparently Squire slowed down as he approached a railroad grade but failed to notice an oncoming train, which broadsided the vehicle. The event made local news for a while. A newspaper clipping titled "They Escaped Injury" contains a photograph of the boys posing in their Sunday best, the caption stating that they were unharmed in a train crash that demolished their grandfather's car. Squire was treated for severe abrasions, lacerations, and shock but was otherwise unharmed.[28]

James E. Youngblood died on February 2, 1946, and was buried in a plot next to his first wife and some of his children in Woodland Cemetery near Mexia. Two years earlier, he had initiated a deed transfer (completed in 1946) to ensure that his wife Mattie would have clear title to the land. Not long after Squire's death, another tragedy occurred when the family home was consumed by fire. Though nobody was hurt, most of the family's property, including photographs, documents, and mementos were destroyed as Mattie and Eddie Lee watched helplessly. Viewing this event as it unfolded was very traumatic for Mattie. As Eddie Lee tried to assure her mother that God would take care of them, Mattie responded: "Well, he sure seems to be messing up now!" With financial assistance from her teaching job, Eddie Lee purchased and moved a three-bedroom wood frame replacement home to the original home site, where it remains to this day.[29]

Despite her losses, Mattie persevered, maintaining the farm with the assistance of her children, Oscar and Eddie Lee, plus her stepson Robert Grover and his son J. E., who lived nearby. Vicki Holmes, Eddie Lee's daughter, visited and worked there during these years and grew to love the farm. Mattie lived on the farm until 1965, when she moved to a home next to Eddie Lee in nearby Mexia. She lived another twenty years until her death in 1985. She is buried next to Squire at Woodland Cemetery. Due to diminishing returns, cotton growing ceased on the farm by the mid-1960s and sharecropper labor was phased out. Ever since, the family has continued farm and ranch operations but has focused primarily on raising beef cattle for sale and growing hay for feed.[30]

James E. Youngblood's story demonstrates how one African American was able to overcome adversity and establish a productive family farm in East Texas during the Jim Crow era. Though hard work was important to him, it was an attribute held by many freedmen and their offspring, who were nevertheless unable to achieve landholding status. Other factors came into play as well. First, despite the trauma of being removed from his family, the circumstances of Squire's displacement ended up providing him with opportunities that others did not have due to his extended kinship relationship with the Yarbroughs. Another factor aiding Squire was no doubt his large family. Most of his fifteen children survived into adulthood, providing him with an essential labor force he utilized to maintain and expand his diversified farming operations. Finally, by adhering to Booker T. Washington's philosophy, with its inherent degrading acceptance of second-class social status, he maintained good relations with the white community, contributed economically to the tax base, and did not challenge the political status quo that protected white supremacy during his lifetime. Meanwhile, Squire frequently aided members of the black community if they needed help, which probably paid many dividends for him, financially and psychologically. Though his upbringing had distanced him from African American culture, his philanthropy (or patriarchy) gave him purpose and some authority among members of his race during an era of racial segregation.

Though he has been deceased for more than sixty-five years, James E. Youngblood's memory and the land upon which he raised his family remain the glue holding Eddie Lee and the descendants of Squire's other children together. The power of his legacy is reinforced at Youngblood family reunions held every few years since 1976. Though the family's members are now scattered around the country, with strong concentrations outside Texas in the Los Angeles and Kansas City areas, Squire's descendants still come together to rejoice, to reconnect, and to remember their roots. As Ted Youngblood III wrote in the program for the 1996 gathering held in Coolidge:

> We gather together to fellowship and celebrate what we are, where we came from, and who we are—Youngbloods. We have also come to this spot to remind ourselves that because of the strength of this family, we've been able to survive and will survive the turmoils of life.

... For those who have gone before us and with the hope and faith in those who will follow, let us take a moment to reflect, imagine and dream of the homestead—where it all started.[31]

Notes

1. My wife, Theresa Youngblood, is a great-granddaughter of James E. Youngblood. I would like to thank her, Eddie Lee Youngblood, Vicki Holmes, Alvin Youngblood Jr., Arlene Youngblood, David Youngblood, Eula Williams Youngblood, Julie Youngblood, Lenora Youngblood Smith, Stella Youngblood Marks, Ted Youngblood III, and Patrick King for all the help they provided in making this essay possible. Since 1974 the Texas Department of Agriculture has honored over 4,300 families under the Family Land Heritage Program. See "Governor's Resolution Declaring June 4, 2009 Family Land Heritage Day," http://www.agr.state.tx.us/vgn/tda/files/1848/30680_FLH%20Declaration.pdf.

2. Lenora Youngblood Smith and Eula Williams Youngblood, "The Youngblood Legacy," in possession of the author, hereafter cited as Youngblood Family History Album.

3. James Thomas Youngblood's birth date comes from his family bible (hereafter cited as James T. Youngblood Family Bible) in the possession of Patrick King, a great-great-great-grandson of James Thomas Youngblood through his daughter Mourning Elizabeth (Lizzie); I first identified Patrick through Ancestry.com. (Coincidentally, I was finally able to establish contact with Patrick because I found out that he happened to be a longtime friend of my wife's brother, David Youngblood. Though Patrick joked with David when they first met in college twenty years ago that they were probably cousins because of the Youngblood name, they had no idea at the time that it was actually true.)

According to Thomas Youngblood's tombstone located in the Youngblood Family Cemetery in San Jacinto County, Texas, the planter was born on December 31, 1805. The 1850 U.S. Census indicates that he was born in Georgia. Marriage records from Lowndes County, Alabama, indicate that Thomas had married Matilda Alexander in 1831, two years prior to exploiting James Thomas's mother. He had just inherited many of the Youngblood family's slaves after his father Jacob died in Lowndes County in 1832.

Microfilm copies of the Polk County tax rolls for 1853 (located at the Sam Houston Regional Library and Research Center in Liberty, Texas, hereafter cited as SHLRC) provided the number of slaves that Thomas B. Youngblood possessed upon his arrival in Texas. It should be noted that James Thomas Youngblood is not mentioned in the probate record of Thomas Youngblood's estate (Thomas died intestate), a copy of which is in the possession of Patrick King. Further, the 1860 U.S. Slave Schedule for Polk County does not list a mulatto male of James Youngblood's age being owned by Matilda Youngblood or any member of the Watson family. However, the schedule notes that Thomas Youngblood's brother, J. J. Youngblood, who lived in Polk County, owned a mulatto male born around 1834, along with a sixty-year-old black woman. Thus, it is quite possible that James Thomas and his mother remained with the Youngbloods but lived with his white father's brother.

4. 1867 Voter Registration Records, Microfilm Reel VR-10, Texas State Library. James Thomas Youngblood registered as Voter No. 623 on September 3, 1867, as "Jim

Youngblood." For details on the 1867 voter registration and its role in Reconstruction era Texas politics, see Carl H. Moneyhon, *Texas after the Civil War: The Struggle of Reconstruction* (College Station: Texas A&M University Press, 2004). 1870 U.S. Census for Polk County, Texas. Non-population Census Schedule for San Jacinto County, Texas, 1880. James Thomas Youngblood was the only male with the Youngblood surname listed as "mulatto" in the entire 1870 census for Texas.

5. Opening pages of the James T. Youngblood Family Bible. Because of the writing style and the fact that neither James nor Eliza could write, Patrick King surmises, and I concur, that a literate white woman (possibly Matilda Youngblood or her granddaughter Bettie Watson) inscribed the bible's initial entries. For discussions on African American family relationships during and after slavery, see John W. Blassingame, *The Slave Community: Plantation Life in the Antebellum South* (1972; rev. ed., New York: Oxford University Press, 1979), 149–91; Barry A. Crouch, *The Dance of Freedom: Texas African Americans during Reconstruction*, ed. Larry Madaras (Austin: University of Texas Press, 2007), 39–53; Herbert G. Gutman, *The Black Family in Slavery and Freedom, 1750–1925* (New York: Vintage Books, 1976); and Dylan C. Penningroth, *The Claims of Kinfolk: African American Property and Community in the Nineteenth-Century South* (Chapel Hill: University of North Carolina Press, 2003).

6. James T. Youngblood Family Bible; conversation with Patrick King. Lizzie Youngblood eventually married Norman Patten, the brother of Edward A. Patten—an African American farmer and teacher who served a term in the Texas House of Representatives upon his election in 1890 and was the maternal great-grandfather of Barbara Jordan, the first African American from Texas to be elected to the U.S. Congress. Norman and Edward's father, Silas Patten, was one of Thomas Youngblood's slaves who made the journey to East Texas from Alabama in 1853.

7. Youngblood Family DNA results in possession of the author. Youngblood family genealogists have studied their ancestry for over thirty years and have not yet accounted for many of John Miles Youngblood's descendants due to scarcity of documentation, similarity of names, and movement of many Youngbloods about the country. We know that John Miles had at least six children—Henry Miles, Mary, John Miles Jr., Thomas, Jacob, and James—but not all of their children (let alone their many grandchildren) have been identified. Some of the genealogists with whom I have communicated have theorized that Thomas B. Youngblood's father Jacob may have been a son of John Miles's son James. Thus the connection would be: John Miles Youngblood (born in 1708) to James Youngblood (born in 1740) to Jacob Youngblood (born in 1760) to Thomas B. Youngblood (born in 1805), and from there to James Thomas Youngblood to James Edward (Squire) Youngblood.

8. The 1880 U.S. Census for Ellis County, Texas; San Jacinto County Marriage Records, microfilm reel 1006955, SHLRC. For a one-page obituary of Solomon Shaw Yarbrough produced by the Methodist Church and touting his evangelical zeal and effectiveness as an energetic preacher of the gospel, see *Minutes of the Annual Conferences of the Methodist Episcopal Church, South, for the Year 1886* (Nashville, Tenn.: Southern Methodist Publishing House, 1887), 87. According to a recollection written by Velma Bohanan Harman, one of the preacher's great-granddaughters, and kindly presented to me by Beth Bradley (a

great-great-granddaughter of Solomon Yarbrough whom I was able to contact via Ancestry.com), it appears that Reverend Yarbrough married well. His wife Mattie was a daughter of Captain Thomas Hinds, a wealthy planter from a prominent early American family who came to Texas in 1840 with 130 slaves. This accounts for the several land holdings that the Yarbroughs possessed despite Solomon's meager earnings as a minister.

9. The amount of tilled soil on Solomon Yarbrough's farm is listed in the Non-population Census Schedule for Ellis County, Texas, 1880. Will of Solomon Shaw Yarbrough, Ellis County, Texas (Probate) Will Records, microfilm reel 1034624, Special Collections, University of Texas at Arlington (hereafter cited as S. S. Yarbrough Will). For a description of the rigors of cotton raising during the antebellum period, see C. Allan Jones, *Texas Roots: Agriculture and Rural Life before the Civil War* (College Station: Texas A&M University Press, 2005).

10. Examples of Youngblood family history that reiterate the view that the Yarbroughs treated Squire well and instilled industrious values within him can be found in the Youngblood Family History Album and a transcript of an October 25, 1973, oral interview by Jean Gilbert with Theodore Roosevelt Youngblood Sr. (one of Squire's sons), located in the Theodore Youngblood Biographical File, Austin Files—Biography Collection, Austin History Center, Austin, Texas (hereafter cited as Theodore Youngblood Sr. Interview Transcript, AHC).

11. S. S. Yarbrough Will; 1882 Tax Roll for Limestone County, Texas, microfilm reel 114701, Baylor University, Waco, Texas (cited hereafter as Limestone County Tax Roll).

12. 1892 Limestone County Tax Roll, microfilm reel 114702. Squire emerges as "Squire Youngblood" in the public record for the first time in 1891. In the Deed Record for San Jacinto County, the date of instrument for a land transfer between William Yarbrough and Squire Youngblood is listed as January 17, 1891, though the formal date of filing is shown to have occurred on January 3, 1900. This land had been part of the Vital Flores survey, initially acquired by James Watson and later deeded to his son-in-law, William Yarbrough. Deed Record for San Jacinto County, microfilm reel 1006957, SHLRC. The circumstances behind this land transfer are unknown, and there is no evidence that Squire ever lived on this land or farmed it. Nevertheless, it does show another connection between Squire and the Yarbroughs. The San Jacinto Deed Record also shows that Squire later transferred this land to Eli Lillie in 1914. Eddie Lee Youngblood believes that the Lillies were somehow related to Squire. It is possible that Eli Lillie was the same person living with James Thomas and Eliza Youngblood listed as Eli Erby in the 1870 U.S. Census—both were listed in the censuses as mulattos born about the same time (in 1864 and 1865, respectively.) Interview with Eddie Lee Youngblood, March 20, 2010 (cited hereafter as Eddie Lee Youngblood Interview).

13. Eddie Lee Youngblood Interview; copy of the Youngblood-Heidleberg deed provided to me by Vicki Holmes; the date of Squire's marriage to Willie is found in the Youngblood Family History Album and verified in the Limestone County Marriage Records, microfilm reel 986083, Baylor University, Waco, Texas; Alfred's birth date comes from the Youngblood Family History Album.

14. Limestone County Tax Roll, reel 114702; birth years for the Youngblood children come from the Youngblood Family History Album.

15. Limestone County Tax Roll, reel 114702. Limestone County agricultural statistics

come from the 1910 U.S. Census, *Agriculture, 1909 and 1910, Reports by States with Statistics for Counties—Nebraska to Wyoming and Territories*, volume VII.

16. For excellent coverage of Texas farm women's lives and their contributions to family economies, see Rebecca Sharpless, *Fertile Ground, Narrow Choices: Women on Texas Cotton Farms, 1900–1940* (Chapel Hill: University of North Carolina Press, 1999).

17. Willie's death year comes from the Youngblood Family History Album; I derived her age from the 1900 U.S. Census for Limestone County, Texas. The 1910 U.S. Census for Limestone County provided the family information.

18. Eddie Lee Youngblood Interview; 1920 U.S. Census for Limestone County, Texas; Youngblood Family History Album. In 1916 Alfred Youngblood's draft registration card shows him to have been living in Dallas working as a janitor. *World War I Draft Registration Cards, 1917–1918*, database online at Ancestry.com (Provo, Utah: Ancestry.com Operations, 2005). The additional thirty acres that James acquired in 1916 are noted in a copy of the Youngblood Family Land Heritage Program Application that was graciously given to me by Vicki Holmes.

19. The 1930 Census of the United States for Limestone County, Texas. The children's birth years are confirmed in the Youngblood Family History Album, which also notes that one last child, Rudolph, was born in 1931.

20. Eddie Lee Youngblood Interview; Theodore Youngblood Sr. Interview Transcript, AHC; Stella Youngblood Marks to author.

21. Eddie Lee Youngblood Interview; Theodore Youngblood Sr. Interview Transcript, AHC. Theodore eventually rose to become the longtime head waiter at the Austin Hotel and later the Driskill Hotel, where he was well known to Lyndon Johnson and other Texas establishment political figures who regularly attended the hotels for meetings and carousing. For a profile of Theodore Sr. as he prepared to oversee Austin Hotel staff for the 1950 Jefferson-Jackson Day dinner, see "Head Waiter Ready for Veep's Visit," *Austin Statesman*, May 24, 1950.

22. For the life and philosophy of Booker T. Washington, see Booker T. Washington, *Up from Slavery: An Autobiography* (Garden City, N.Y.: Doubleday and Company, 1901), and Louis R. Harlan's award-winning biographies *Booker T. Washington: The Making of a Black Leader, 1856–1901* (New York: Oxford University Press, 1972) and *Booker T. Washington: The Wizard of Tuskegee, 1901–1915* (New York: Oxford University Press, 1986).

23. Youngblood Family Land Heritage Program Application; Eddie Lee Youngblood Interview. For great coverage of the Extension Service's efforts with African American farmers in Texas, see Debra A. Reid, *Reaping a Greater Harvest: African Americans, the Extension Service, and Rural Reform in Jim Crow Texas* (College Station: Texas A&M University Press, 2007).

24. Eddie Lee Youngblood Interview; Theodore Youngblood Sr. Interview Transcript, AHC.

25. Eddie Lee Youngblood Interview. For a description of the Agricultural Adjustment Administration's cotton plow-up campaign in Texas, see Keith J. Volanto, *Texas, Cotton, and the New Deal* (College Station: Texas A&M University Press, 2005), chap. 2; for details on the cattle program, see C. Roger Lambert, "Texas Cattlemen and the AAA, 1933–1935," *Arizona and the West* 14 (Summer 1972): 137–52, and "Southwestern Cattlemen, the Federal Government, and the Depression" in Donald W. Whisenhunt, ed., *The Depression in*

the Southwest (Port Washington, N.Y.: Kennikat Press, 1980): 42–57; for coverage of the Negro Division and Roosevelt's New Deal programs, see Reid, *Reaping a Greater Harvest*, chap. 5.

26. Conversation with Ted Youngblood III. For a discussion of syrup mill operations in African American freedom colonies in Texas, see Thad Sitton and James H. Conrad, *Freedom Colonies: Independent Black Texans in the Time of Jim Crow* (Austin: University of Texas Press, 2005), 67–69.

27. Eddie Lee Youngblood Interview; *Coolidge Herald*, August 13, 1954. The excerpt from the article that I cited was a transcription written in the hand of Mattie Youngblood, Eddie Lee's mother, and provided to me by Vicki Holmes. For information on Juneteenth in Limestone County, see Doris Hollis Pemberton, *Juneteenth at Comanche Crossing* (Austin: Eakin Press, 1983).

28. Eddie Lee Youngblood Interview; undated clipping from an unknown local newspaper, probably the *Coolidge Herald*, in the possession of Theresa Youngblood. The article stated that the accident occurred as the boys were closing their summer stay at Squire's farm and that Ted Jr. (born in 1928) and Alvin (1929) were twelve and eleven years of age, respectively. Thus the accident took place sometime in July, August, or September of 1940.

29. Limestone County Deed Records, vol. 286, 577–78 (October 14, 1944), and vol. 302, 90–91 (September 19, 1946); Youngblood Family Heritage Program Application; Eddie Lee Youngblood Interview. Mattie experienced the loss of a second child in 1951 when her son Tracy was killed in an automobile accident on Highway 171 just east of Coolidge. Youngblood Family History Album.

30. Youngblood Family Land Heritage Program Application; Eddie Lee Youngblood Interview.

31. Youngblood Family History Album; 1996 Youngblood Family Reunion Program. On the power and meaning of homecomings and reunions to descendants of African American farm owners who established freedom colonies in Texas, see Sitton and Conrad, *Freedom Colonies*, chap. 7. As a result of connections made from this research, Patrick King organized the first family reunion to take place involving the descendants of Squire Youngblood and the other offspring of James Thomas and Eliza Youngblood, held in San Jacinto County during mid-November 2010. More than a hundred relatives attended to share aspects of their interesting family history.

4

Benjamin Hubert and the Association for the Advancement of Negro Country Life

MARK SCHULTZ

Could African Americans have climbed to the middle class through agriculture? Since we know that black wealth today is largely urban, we assume that the answer is no. We know that the prevailing story recounts the tragedy of African American farmers in the South, a story burdened with repeating themes of sharecropping, crop liens, exploitation, dependency, poverty, and frustration. When African Americans found a means of escape to northern industry during the great migrations that bookend the Great Depression, they embraced the opportunity. Now, as the number of farmers dwindles in the United States, the phrase "black farmer" has become almost an oxymoron.

Yet there is more to the story of southern black farmers than poverty, dependency, and flight. During the antebellum era, while most African Americans farmed as slaves, some free people of color found a pathway to land ownership between the estates of white planters. Others made their way north and purchased their own farms in Ohio, Indiana, Illinois, Michigan, and Wisconsin. After the Civil War a majority of black farmers in the South struggled in the quicksand of sharecropping, but others found ways to amass property. Thousands joined the Exoduster movement and established homesteads in Kansas and Oklahoma. Many more became landowners within the South. By 1910 a quarter of all black farmers had purchased their own land. A similar percentage held land in 1920. To put these figures in context, a million and a half African Americans trekked north between

1910 and 1940 in the traditionally defined Great Migration. Simultaneously, over 426,000 African American families lived on their own farms in the early twentieth century. Although most of these families lost their land in the long agricultural depression of the 1920s and 1930s, they nevertheless laid a foundation for their descendants. Children raised on farms owned by their parents tended to get a better education than did the children of sharecroppers. They developed self-reliant habits of mind and a sense of optimism that they could succeed, despite the barriers thrown up by white supremacy. Many of these children found their way into the urban middle class, frequently in the North. In doing so, they demonstrated that farm owning offered both immediate security and a durable path out of poverty.[1]

Well into the twentieth century, many African American leaders championed scientific agriculture based on education, stewardship of the soil, and the improvement of rural society as the most promising path to black economic independence. Before World War I opened new industrial opportunities in the North, they may have been right. Booker T. Washington was the most recognizable of these agrarians, but others shared this faith, such as Robert R. Moton of Tuskegee Institute, Kelly Miller of Howard University, and Thomas Campbell and Robert Lloyd Smith of the Alabama and Texas agricultural extension services, respectively. Moton believed that modern agricultural training in a traditional school setting could give rural African Americans the tools they needed to help themselves, while Campbell believed that the rural masses could be reached only by means of a "moveable school" that would carry information to them. Smith first organized black Texan farmers—particularly landowners—into the Farmers' Improvement Society of Texas, a private cooperative for buying and selling and providing financial services and loans to members. Later he moved to head the Negro Division of the Texas Agricultural Extension Service, disseminating scientific farming information through demonstrations, fairs, youth clubs, etc. Miller, a sociologist and the dean of the College of Arts and Sciences at Howard, called for both higher education and technical and agricultural training as complementary means for the progress of the race and the individual. Although situated in the urban North, he viewed agriculture as the best avenue of economic independence for the masses and warned against its increasing abandonment after World War I. Today these proponents of black farm ownership seem to represent a dead end, so few of them are now remembered.[2]

In the decades after Washington's death in 1915, Georgia's Benjamin Franklin Hubert rose to prominence among these agricultural spokesmen.

Most of the progress that hundreds of thousands of black farm families had previously made resulted from individual effort, or the struggles of isolated "freedom colonies," but Hubert believed he could provide institutional support for a regionwide mass movement.[3]

In 1928 Hubert organized the Association for the Advancement of Negro Country Life (AANCL) to promote an economically viable and socially attractive life for African Americans on southern farms. He established the association on the ideals of the Country Life Movement of the early twentieth century. He hoped that the increasing abandonment of the land by white farmers created an opening for African Americans to purchase it at bargain prices, and to set up a self-sustained black society based on formal cooperation and scientific farming. To demonstrate the viability of his plan, Hubert used his position as president of Georgia's black land grant college to channel funds and provide organizational oversight to nurture his childhood home in middle Georgia into a model black farming community. At its peak, his Log Cabin Community included over one hundred African American families on nearly 15,000 acres of farmland. A strong rural black middle class arose, somewhat insulated from the effects of Jim Crow laws. These farm owners educated their children in an excellent school and voted regularly throughout the twentieth century. From the late 1920s through the 1940s, black and white southern newspapers regularly featured Hubert, the AANCL, and the Log Cabin Community, but their story is now entirely lost from the historical record.[4]

Hubert's vision came from two sources: his family experience and his formal education. Having been born into a black landowning community in middle Georgia, he knew from experience that agriculture could bring economic independence. His parents, Zacharias (Zach) and Camilla Hubert owned several hundred acres, having begun with a small plot Zach had purchased in northern Hancock County in 1876 with some help from white family members.[5] One black neighbor owned a farm that may have approached two thousand acres. All around the Huberts, a dozen other families owned smaller farms. Together they organized a church and a rudimentary four-year grade school. Zach built a general store. They named their all-black community Springfield.[6]

Despite the turmoil of the late nineteenth century, a period fraught with racial violence, economic exploitation, and legal discrimination, Benjamin and his eleven siblings grew up in relative security. During the antebellum era Hancock had been staunchly Whiggish. After the Civil War it remained an essentially conservative county in which the white elite suppressed anti-black violence, and African Americans forged patronage ties with influential whites. Zach and Camilla educated their children in the conformist survival skills of Jim Crow Georgia. They taught the children Christian piety and economic self-sufficiency. They disciplined them to stay out of trouble and act humbly around whites who might be jealous of their economic success. And they promoted education. The Hubert children—all twelve of them—passed from the little Springfield school to college to careers in education.[7] Like his brothers, Benjamin attended Atlanta Baptist College (later known as Morehouse College), where he earned a high school diploma and graduated with a B.A. in 1909. Upon graduation he traveled to Amherst and enrolled in the agricultural science program at Massachusetts Agricultural College.[8]

At Massachusetts, Benjamin studied under Kenyon L. Butterfield.[9] A founder of rural sociology, Butterfield served as a member of President Theodore Roosevelt's Country Life Commission and in 1919 became the first president of the American Country Life Association. Agricultural experts of the Progressive era fretted over rural poverty and the ongoing flight of discontented rural youth to the cities. In response, they organized the Country Life Movement to improve economic and social conditions on the farms to approximate those of the urban middle class. Their solution included scientific farming (to be taught by government-sponsored agricultural extension experts), cooperatives (to achieve a competitive economy of scale), and improved rural social institutions, such as churches, schools, recreation centers, fairs, and health clinics. With these reforms, country life could be made profitable and enjoyable. This new agrarian creed was taken up by a generation of professional agricultural reformers. Beginning in 1902 the U.S. Department of Agriculture (USDA) hired white agricultural extension agents to preach it across the South. In 1915 the USDA created a separate division for black agents to take part in the work. Young Benjamin Hubert adopted this agenda as his own. Springfield, Georgia, had taught him that farm ownership offered African Americans a path to the middle class. Butterfield gave him credibility with agricultural experts and philanthropists, scientific tools, and a formal program with which he would try to build a large-scale movement. By the time of the New Deal, the USDA and most agricultural experts rejected Butterfield's small-scale, community-based, scientific approach to farming, in favor of agribusiness. Hubert, however, would never give it up.[10]

After he completed his work at Amherst in 1912, Hubert accepted a position as professor of agriculture at South Carolina State Agricultural and

Mechanical College at Orangeburg. Within a few years he had become director of the Agricultural Extension Service of the college, the supervisor of Vocational Teacher Training, superintendent of the Colored State Fair Association, and director of the college's agriculture department.[11] When World War I erupted, Hubert served on South Carolina's Food Administration Board. After the war he helped direct the agricultural reconstruction of Europe, one of the few African Americans to find federal employment during Woodrow Wilson's presidency.[12]

Hubert returned to the United States late in the summer of 1919. Perhaps he felt anger and outrage, as did so many black soldiers upon returning to a hostile, racist society. If so, he had to submerge these feelings, for within the year he accepted a position as director of the Department of Agriculture at the most celebrated black accommodationist educational institution in the country—Tuskegee Institute. Tuskegee in 1920 had passed the height of its influence. Booker T. Washington had died five years earlier, but it remained a powerful symbol of black achievement, particularly for those who hoped that real freedom and economic independence would grow in the soil of black-owned farms. Washington's successor, Robert Moton, was a capable man who maintained some of the web spun by the "Wizard of Tuskegee" and who, like Washington, played a pragmatic balancing game. Like Washington, he publicly seemed to concede political and social equality for blacks in return for some space in which to train black students in the financial stability of business and agricultural and mechanical science.

Soon, Moton began to groom Hubert to succeed him as the third president of Tuskegee. Hubert took on additional responsibilities as Tuskegee's supervisor of Vocational Teacher Training and as supervisor of the Negro Division of the Agricultural Extension Service for the state of Alabama. He quickly won the respect of the philanthropists who supported the institution. In the ensuing decades, as Hubert promoted the Association for the Advancement of Negro Country Life, Tuskegee trustees would rank among his most important financial supporters.[13] Hubert later wrote that Moton had "told [him] several times that the Trustees had [him] in mind as the next principal of Tuskegee Institute." In 1926 the offer came. He declined it. Instead, Benjamin Hubert left Tuskegee and Alabama to assume the presidency of a small, nearly insolvent black college in his home state, Georgia State Industrial College for Colored Youth, later known as Savannah State College.[14] It was not the first time Hubert had turned down the offer of an influential position. A few years earlier, his brother, James, had urged him to accept an Urban League position on Long Island. James himself was just about to become director of the Brooklyn branch of the Urban League, and soon after, executive director of the entire New York office. "I would much like to have you in these parts," James wrote. "We could divide up on the city between us and run the whole business." But the two brothers disagreed about the direction in which hope lay. James, early in the Great Migration, had placed his money on the industrial North. Benjamin drew on their own family's story of success—and its agricultural roots.[15]

A number of reasons influenced Benjamin Hubert's decision to assume the presidency of Georgia State. Zach Hubert seems to have played a key role in his son's decision. In 1910 the patriarch of the family had called his eldest, John Wesley Hubert, from a teaching position at Tuskegee back to Springfield to turn the community's privately supported black grade school into a high school. He believed that the community needed the educational instruction John Wesley could provide. In 1926 Hancock County's farmers were experiencing great hardship from the boll weevil and low cotton prices. Zach looked to Benjamin in the 1920s as he had looked to John Wesley two decades earlier. From an influential position in the state, Benjamin could better aid the Springfield community. Then on March 16, 1926, having made his will known, Zach died.[16] In addition to this private pressure, ambition may have influenced Hubert. Although Tuskegee was the most famous black agricultural institution in the country, its presidency came with liabilities. When Moton retired in 1934, Hubert was again considered for the Tuskegee position. He declined in a newspaper interview, citing his satisfaction with Georgia State Industrial College. "Here our program is in the making," he said, "and we are realizing fine results. At Tuskegee, the program is about complete, and the new appointee would have little to do other than follow an established routine." Clearly, Hubert had no intention of becoming the custodian of the program Booker T. Washington had formed. He wanted the opportunity to innovate, and a college on the verge of closing its doors offered him a free hand.[17]

Founded in Savannah in 1890, Georgia State Industrial College was Georgia's first black state-supported school. Although it was a land grant college, it had combined a liberal arts program with conventional trades and agriculture. By the 1920s it had fallen into such neglect by the state that the federal government threatened to discontinue all support of Georgia land grant colleges if the state continued to ignore its responsibilities toward black education. A reconstituted board of trustees began to search for a new president and found Hubert, a conservative, native Georgian with an

Figure 4.1. Portrait of Benjamin F. Hubert, president of Georgia State Industrial College for Colored Youth (1926–47). Source: Archives of Asa H. Gordon Library, Savannah State University.

impressive resume and a heartfelt commitment to agricultural education (figure 4.1).[18]

Hubert began his term of office by delivering a Washingtonian speech before the appropriation committee of the state legislature. He won a substantially increased budget with matching grants, which he secured with large donations from the General Education Board and the Julius Rosenwald Fund. Hubert's career as a fundraiser had begun.[19] With money in hand, Hubert began to expand the school. Before he resigned in 1947, he doubled the size of the faculty, steadily increased the student body from two hundred to nine hundred, and put up eight buildings despite the Depression, soliciting proficiently from private citizens, philanthropic organizations, and the state and federal government. He discontinued the high school and two-year normal programs and beefed up the academic and applied programs of the college. And of course, he expanded the work of the Department of Agriculture.[20]

One of the new faculty members he hired, Martha Wilson, remembered that the black colleges, as "orphans of the state college," received little supervision from the state. As a result Hubert exercised great control over the campus. According to Wilson, Georgia State was a "one man operation." Students and faculty who disagreed with their president "didn't stay long." Yet Hubert was a quiet, approachable man, who showed great personal interest in his students; he spent much time with them and was "down to earth" with them. Wilson stated that Hubert's image remained uniquely vivid in her memory. "He was short of stature, stocky, heavy-jawed, with heavy eyebrows and a beautiful head of hair. He wore a characteristic crooked grin sometimes and you'd wonder what he was thinking about." Although a moving speaker, Hubert spoke quietly, deliberately, without bombast. At social gatherings he became inconspicuous. Yet he had the "inner capacity to dominate all that he was involved in." He exercised "surreptitious control. You wouldn't always know that he was in control—but he was."[21]

Hubert recruited students actively throughout the state and helped most of them meet their tuition through a work-study program. Students cared for the college livestock and worked in construction or janitorial service. All nonagricultural students, regardless of their major, completed a program of study in a trade as a safety measure for employment. Hubert emphasized a practical education in which students learned trades and agriculture by working. He expanded the school farm, encouraged students to raise private gardens, and opened a cooperative country store to underscore the need for interdependence in the farm community. Much of this regimen had been used before at other black industrial schools like Hampton Institute and Tuskegee and Prairie View State Normal and Industrial College. Hubert added to it a passionate belief in self-directed farming, which came from his family's experience.[22]

Hubert believed that African Americans who fled from southern farms to northern cities had fallen into a trap of impoverished dependency. "In the towns and cities, we are asking for jobs that have largely been made possible and are largely held by other people." On the other hand, "when a man owns a farm and knows how to operate it, he is a little king in his own domain." The urban centers, he warned, offered only limited opportunities for economic independence in business and the professions. Most would be vulnerable blue-collar laborers in white-owned industries. Although he believed that activists like his brother James should attempt to broaden black opportunities in the city, he held little hope for their imminent success. "Under our present economic system," Hubert argued, "there is no other way out for the masses of Negroes in Georgia and the South but by way of the farm." As the bricklayer of Tuskegee had hoped that the trades presented African Americans their best option in the absence of equality, the Savannah farmer sought consolation in agriculture.[23]

Some white southerners called for a black education that would prepare African Americans, temperamentally and intellectually, for lives of useful service to whites. The Hampton model of industrial education was held as the ideal for this sort of training, with long hours spent in menial labor, little attention paid to liberal arts, a tendency to emphasize outdated trades (such as shoemaking or blacksmithing), and only rudimentary agricultural training. One historian has dubbed this approach "schooling for the new slavery."[24] According to a 1930 report to the Board of Regents of the university system of Georgia by a board of visitors to Georgia State, such a rudimentary program was expected in Savannah. According to the report, "the instruction in agriculture and home economics should be of a service character only." The curriculum Hubert designed in Savannah suggests a different orientation. Along with traditional topics such as canning and home garden care, it also covered farm management, finance, forestry, and marketing. Other courses taught students how to use government programs and how to purchase land. Hubert clearly wanted to prepare young rural men and women to become self-directed farm owners, not reliable farm laborers.[25]

The economic crisis of the 1920s and 1930s seems in retrospect an inopportune time to call for the elevation of a black middle class on the back of low agricultural commodity prices. Yet Hubert thought he saw an opportunity for black tenants to purchase devalued land as whites gave up the plow and moved away. His program of cooperative scientific farming would set them on the road to economic independence. In autonomous, prosperous communities, they could build a "civilization" for themselves, as Hubert often called it. Like the presidents of many other black land grant colleges, he blended Garveyite economic separatism, Washington's pragmatic deference, and Kenyon Butterfield's progressive, rural idealism. Blacks "should all understand that wealth originates from the earth," said Hubert, therefore, "where we have an opportunity to get hold of these farms with such potential wealth we should do so now, and make them serve us in building for ourselves a bigger and finer culture. The only hope for the masses of

Negroes under our present capitalistic order is to get hold of, man, and operate these farms here in Georgia and the South."[26]

Hubert's reverence for the yeoman paralleled the Jeffersonian agrarianism of Butterfield's Country Life Movement. Hubert viewed the farmer as the pillar of society. "Strong and vigorous races and nations have ever been people who have remained close to the soil," he claimed. "In spite of vast accumulated wealth in large urban centers, [those] that have left the soil have shown a general trend downward. It has always been necessary for a prosperous country to maintain on the farms, a large percentage of its people whose standards of living are in accord with the best that can be obtained in that civilization." Hubert linked agricultural independence with strength and virtue. "Land ownership tends to create thrift, self-respect and development of strong, dependable character." It "means not only leadership, but . . . permanent leadership in a life that is more nearly satisfying."[27]

"A more satisfying life on the farm" became Hubert's favorite phrase. At Savannah, students became accustomed to hearing the message. While Hubert used Georgia State as a base from which to work, he aimed to put into effect a regionwide movement to promote his vision of a civilization built upon black farm ownership. He intended to provide institutional support for aspiring black farm owners.

Independent black farming never had received a fair chance. It had a false start at the end of the Civil War in land confiscation and redistribution, but President Andrew Johnson's pardons ensured that the ex-slaves would not begin freedom with the means to make freedom meaningful. In the following decades, low commodity prices, debt, white violence, and a stacked legal system trapped most black farm families in cycles of dependency. When many black farmers made common cause with struggling white farmers along class lines in the Populist movement, they were ultimately betrayed and disfranchised for their efforts. Later, the New Deal—which might have aided aspiring black tenants to buy land of their own through the Farmers Home Administration—instead channeled most agricultural aid to the big farmers through the Agricultural Adjustment Administration, and so consolidated the land in the hands of the white and the well-off. These surviving white farmers then used federal subsidies and the expert advice of federal agricultural extension agents to mechanize their farms or transform them into pine forests.

Never in American history were landless African American farmers given significant institutional support to help them climb the ladder to land ownership. This is what Hubert attempted to provide. Like many black and white land grant colleges, Georgia State had an agricultural extension program and hosted agricultural workshops and short summer courses in several locations around the state. Additionally, Hubert had the ear of a number of philanthropists and had contacts with the newspapers. But to draw attention to his movement, he needed a case study, a way to demonstrate his plan's feasibility.

In 1928 Hubert founded an organization that would give him the financial and public relations backing he needed to launch his project. He modeled the Association for the Advancement of Negro Country Life after Butterfield's American Country Life Association. His connections among northeastern philanthropists and southern black educators won him an impressive first board of directors, including many of the leading presidents of black institutions of learning, such as Moton, Mary McLeod Bethune, and John Hope. The organization also listed Butterfield, and educational philanthropists like Julius Rosenwald, George Foster Peabody, and Mary Otis Willcox. Hubert himself was the executive secretary. Over the ensuing years these board members formed the core of the donors who provided loans and gifts to support the organization.[28]

The organization stated that African Americans were abandoning the farms for urban areas due to "industrial expansion, seasonal farm reverses, an indefinite system of home establishment and a general dissatisfaction with comparative social and educational advantages offered in the country." This list omits mention of the structural inequity of tenancy and the regular insult of southern Jim Crow. Yet these factors lay well beyond the influence of the new organization. To counter the forces it could attempt to deal with, the AANCL would, as stated in a 1929 pamphlet, carry an educational program "to the mass of rural people" concerning "the 'hows' of play and genuine enjoyment in the country." It stated that "rural programs must more and more emphasize a comfortable living as a farm objective, rather than mere money-making." It envisioned a "large group of intelligent and progressive small farm owners, self-supporting and happy in the opportunities offered for a full unhampered development of home and community life." The AANCL especially encouraged African Americans to work toward farm ownership and asked the major black institutions, churches, schools, civic and fraternal organizations, and newspapers for their support.[29]

In the years since Hubert had left his home in Springfield, the community had met with economic devastation. Early in the 1920s the boll weevil entered the county, devouring its wealth. Production of cotton in Hancock

County collapsed from 20,000 bales in 1919 to 710 bales in 1922. The number of active gins fell from twenty-three to six.[30] Simultaneously the price of cotton plummeted from thirty-seven cents per pound to thirteen. It finally struck bottom in the early 1930s at five cents per pound. Within four years, the taxable wealth of all African Americans in the county fell to a third of its 1920 level. In Springfield, the older generation of black farmers sold their cars, furniture, and draft animals, bought additional land at depressed prices, and tried to survive. But the young people became disgusted with the purposeless drudgery of farm life and began to move toward the hope and excitement of the cities.[31]

Tenant farmers had worked much of Zach and Camilla Hubert's 466 acres after their sons left home. Benjamin found them, like the other farmers in the community, without credit or hope, remaining in Springfield only because of the bonds of tradition. He stated many times later that he felt he owed it to his father to attempt to save the Hubert family farm and the farms of the other African Americans around it. He bought his parents' land for $4,000 and struck a deal with the six tenant families on it. Early in 1928 Hubert repaired their dilapidated houses. He then contracted with the families to support them if they followed his planned reform. Their hard work alone had produced nothing but poverty during the past eight years. They agreed to try. The farmers would plant only small plots of cotton, a slightly larger plot of corn, and all the velvet beans, cow peas, and potatoes that they could grow. They agreed to use large quantities of barnyard manure and commercial fertilizer and to cultivate the crops as rapidly as possible. They each agreed to raise chickens and a garden that would supply their table throughout the year. Additionally, they would expand their dairies in order to produce enough cream to market profitably.[32]

They gathered excellent harvests. While most farmers placed the majority of their land into cotton and fertilized it thinly, if at all, the Hubert tenants planted only three to six acres of cotton but manured it intensively. Instead of the usual bale for every three acres, they gathered a bale or more per acre. As they began to place their profits in the bank in Sparta, they attracted attention from the rest of the community. Soon the entire area was amenable to Hubert's direction. Hubert's instructions typified the scientific farming program taught at Georgia State and other agricultural colleges across the South. It was his cooperative and social agenda that broke new ground.[33]

As the farmers worked together, the sale of cream became a leading source of income for the community. By 1930 two creamery wagons passed through Springfield each morning to collect the product for markets in the county seat. In addition Hubert encouraged the farmers to raise more hogs and chickens. W. G. Washington, the head of Springfield's grade and high schools, shipped eggs, chickens, and other farm products to markets in Macon, Augusta, and Atlanta. Besides encouraging privately owned poultry, Hubert developed a large-scale community poultry plant that handled thousands of purebred birds in the first enclosed chicken houses in middle Georgia. The nearby Greensboro *Herald Journal* noticed the progress as early as 1934, when it remarked that "this community leads the county in pure bred dairy cattle and chickens." Hubert had even grander plans. He hoped to create in Springfield "the largest poultry center of its kind in the southeast."[34]

Cooperation, as exemplified by the poultry plant, gave the Log Cabin farmers a great edge in production. Most southern farmers knew about, but could not afford, the expensive farming equipment other regions of the country already possessed. The agricultural historian Gilbert Fite wrote that the 1930 value of machinery and implements in Georgia, as in several other southern states, averaged only $134 per farm, while the value of livestock averaged between $200 and $300. He contrasts these figures with those of Kansas and Iowa, which respectively averaged $1,010 and $1,259 for farm equipment and between $1,000 and $2,000 for livestock. Furthermore, as southern farms were small, averaging fifty-six acres in the 1930 plantation belt, each farmer had little access to credit with which to finance an increase in mechanization. Fite concluded that the high farmer-to-acreage ratios in the South prohibited them from competing successfully with the large midwestern farms.[35]

Some of Benjamin Hubert's contributors expressed the same concerns. One wrote in 1938 to thank Hubert for giving her a sack of flour that had been grown and ground by the community, asking if he could "see it in competition with commercial enterprise? And make it pay?" Hubert responded that they produced it for their own use but that they were able to market "to advantage" their surplus flour, vegetables, and fruit, both "locally and otherwise." Yet Hubert himself admitted in 1939 that while African Americans were losing "the so-called negro jobs" in the cities, it was also "becoming extremely difficult for people without capital to make headway" in agriculture. The situation appeared frustrating.[36]

Hubert attempted to answer the problems posed by southern agriculture in four ways. Echoing the message that black county extension and home demonstration agents had steadily preached for a generation, he encouraged black farmers to withdraw from dependency on the market by becoming self-sufficient. He then found experts to supplement the work of black farm agents in instructing African American farmers in the most productive methods of scientific farming. Additionally, he advised farmers to enlarge their acreages. He suggested a "four-horse family farm" of 100 to 150 acres in size or larger, "depending upon the managerial ability of the farm operator." Finally, although he believed that industry and security sprang from private property, he promoted a cooperative approach to the most capital-intensive aspects of farming.[37]

In a manuscript he wrote in the 1930s, Hubert stated, "in order to contend with power farming, [the small farmer] must lean heavily upon cooperative activity." This, he argued, "can most quickly be achieved in the South through community center activities where large-visioned, sane leadership may be provided in economic, civic, educational, and recreational community programs." Hubert cautioned that such a program would prove difficult without "some financial stimulation" from "outside cooperating agencies which might function in some such way as the Julius Rosenwald Fund has been able to cooperate in the betterment of rural education for Negroes in the South." He was hoping that a demonstration of success in Springfield would induce either philanthropists or the federal government to make such an investment.[38]

The practice of cooperation at Springfield embraced almost every aspect of farm life. Besides a cooperative gas station and grocery store, health care clinic, and recreation center, the farmers shared the chicken houses described earlier as well as a corn mill, wheat mill, saw mill, and sweet potato curing plant. They shared a community thresher and a creamery and were planning in the 1940s to obtain tractors and a dairy barn. These programs began in the summer of 1932, when Hubert organized the canning plant. The community purchased the cans cooperatively by the carload and preserved at cost the community's vegetables, fruit, and berries. They then saved what they wanted and shipped the surplus to colleges, restaurants, hotels, and other large dealers in cities throughout the region.[39]

As it had done with canned goods, the community made financial transactions with the outside world as a cooperative. It sent representatives to cities to sell produce in the community's one-and-a-half-ton truck. The community agents would then return with merchandise for the community store. The farmers of Log Cabin also threshed their grains, ground them, and prepared them for market cooperatively. At first, Hubert ordered the flour sacks from a commercial mill that imprinted them with the image

Figure 4.2. Camilla-Zach Log Cabin Center, 1932. Courtesy of Hargrett Rare Book and Manuscript Library, University of Georgia Libraries.

of their rustic community center, the symbol and soul of the community (figure 4.2). Later he had the sacks manufactured within the community itself. In 1934 the *Atlanta Journal* reported that "perhaps no section of the state is growing more or better wheat, than this community."[40]

As he found a way to make the community profitable, Hubert attracted African American farmers with small amounts of capital. Hubert recruited some farmers directly at agricultural education workshops Georgia State College held around the state. Others were recruited by black agricultural extension agents who worked with him and by the black and white newspapers that promoted the project. As white landowners moved out, Hubert acted as an intermediary, connecting buyers with willing Negro sellers. In addition, he and the philanthropists who supported the AANCL aided some aspiring farm owners through loans and outright gifts. They even instituted a land bank from which tenants could borrow funds to purchase land. Half of these farms were fifty acres or smaller, but some were much larger. The Springfield militia district had long contained a strong black community, but it grew wider and stronger, particularly into the 1940s. In 1930 black families owned 40 percent of the land in the district; in 1948 they owned 80 percent. The community contained about 8,700 acres in 1929. According to the *Savannah Morning News*, one hundred families connected with the community owned 12,000 acres in 1940. Later Hubert estimated that the community encompassed 15,000 acres and hoped that it would grow to 50,000. The community's influence rippled beyond its boundaries. Although black farm ownership declined steadily throughout the South in the decades after 1920, Hancock County's black farmers increased their acreage from about twenty-five thousand acres to about thirty-five thousand acres between 1930 and 1950.[41]

The community provided an economic boon for most of the families who settled there. At a time of serious deprivation, Kelly Miller, the Howard University essayist and sociologist, reported that "not one [of the farmers around Springfield] seemed in dire want or on the brim of suffering and starvation on account of the depression." While the economic aspect of the Log Cabin Community was a resounding success, Hubert believed that the crisis of rural life arose only partly from farmers' need for more money. In accord with the philosophy of his former professor, Kenyon Butterfield, and the Country Life Movement, he believed the problem equally social in nature. Rural people were leaving the farms because they wanted the purchasing power of urban people as well as a cultural and social experience that, if not the same, was equally rich. So Hubert sought to improve broadly the quality of life in Springfield.

He drew on his network of philanthropists to create the Mary Otis Willcox Health Clinic with a full-time nurse and a doctor who visited regularly. He promoted house and yard beautification. He built a massive community center out of rough-hewn logs and fitted it with a swimming pool, the only one in the northern half of the county. He added funding and teachers to the existing Rosenwald school. Hubert liked to brag that 80 percent of the graduates went on to college. Indeed, during these years he helped dozens of youths from Springfield into Georgia State College or other black colleges.

Hubert helped so many students attend college, in fact, that he ultimately undermined his goals in Springfield. Young people with degrees in business or law or engineering do not usually settle in sparsely populated rural areas. Instead, they move to town, as did young residents of Log Cabin during the 1940s through 1960s. At the turn of the twenty-first century, the farms have converted to stands of pine, and few families still live in the area. The people who grew up in the community still return regularly, bringing their children and grandchildren to annual reunions. They say their community gave them the education, confidence, and skills to launch them into lives as urban business people and professionals. So in a way, the soil of Springfield did indeed grow a black middle class, but not as Hubert had predicted.

And Hubert? He ruled Georgia State until he retired in 1947 under a cloud stirred up by his autocratic administrative style. He then returned to Springfield to oversee the work of the Log Cabin Community. A few years later he suffered a debilitating stroke and became a recluse until his death from a cerebral hemorrhage on April 30, 1958. The community slowly bled dry by the exodus of its youth, and the pine woods that cover middle Georgia reclaimed the land. And now, from a distance of sixty years, what should we make of Hubert's experiment?

Hubert never realized his vision of developing a regionwide movement. The Log Cabin Community drew thousands of visitors, both ordinary and famous, but its example was not followed. Might it have been? In 1929 Hubert joined Robert Moton and a few others in drafting a position paper on "The Economic Status of the Negro" for President Herbert Hoover. The paper articulated many of Hubert's principles, including scientific farming, cooperation, and the promotion of land ownership among black farmers.[42] Later Hubert operated on the margins of President Franklin Delano Roosevelt's kitchen cabinet and witnessed the faint gestures that the Farmers Home Administration made toward the support of black farmers. But the federal government never assumed the role regionwide that philanthropists had undertaken at Log Cabin.[43]

Could Benjamin Hubert's vision have worked if it had been more widely applied across the South? It clearly served the people of the Log Cabin Community in Springfield, Georgia. They owned their homes and farms and prospered through the longest depression in American history. Their children and grandchildren claim that during the decades in which they lived on the land, they were cushioned from the worst demoralizing effects of the Jim Crow system. They watched their parents vote, sporadically in the 1920s and 1930s, and then as a community after 1946.[44] They attended high school and frequently continued to college. Economic independence clearly gave them options, and most of these young people chose to leave the farm between the 1940s and the 1960s to take advantage of the choices their education gave them. During the expansion of American industry, they joined the urban middle class.

On the one hand, the Log Cabin Community was built on a foundation laid by a number of black families who had secured land by the 1870s, based in part on their family ties to whites. Zach Hubert and a few of his neighbors maintained close ties with influential white neighbors, showed great discipline, and made tremendous sacrifices in striving for independence. And race relations in Hancock County, Georgia, while assuredly white supremacist, were generally marked by a conservative, paternalistic ethos that frowned on white mob violence. This starting point, while far from anomalous, certainly did not exist everywhere across the rural South.

On the other hand, Georgia proved to be the most hostile state toward black farm ownership. Only 13 percent of black farmers owned land there in 1900, as opposed to 21 percent in South Carolina and 67 percent in Virginia.[45] If the Log Cabin Community experiment could succeed in Georgia, then why not elsewhere? Scholars are only now beginning to study the all-black freedom colonies that dotted the South. At least some of these developed cooperative systems with aid from county extension agents, Jeanes Teachers, and the Rosenwald Foundation, before their young people left them in the 1920s and they slid into decline. Finally, the AANCL began in 1928, close to the nadir of southern agriculture. If despite the recent and devastating arrival of the boll weevil and the imminent onset of the Great Depression, Hubert's strategy of cooperative and scientific farming transformed tenants into landowners and allowed existing black farm owners to maintain their land and develop a vibrant community, what might have happened if the experiment had been attempted in more prosperous times, or with the full support and deep pockets of the federal government? Might African Americans more broadly have used land ownership as a springboard to education, moveable resources, and the urban middle class? Hubert and the AANCL offer us an intriguing counterfactual.

Notes

I thank Carlton Morse and the editors of *Beyond Forty Acres* for their comments on this chapter. I also thank Caren Agata, information literacy coordinator, Asa H. Gordon Library, Savannah State University, for finding the photograph of Benjamin Hubert that illustrates this essay.

1. The story of black farm ownership is one of the most understudied fields in southern history. It includes only one full monographic study, Loren Schweninger's *Black Property Owners in the South, 1790–1915* (Urbana: University of Illinois Press, 1990). For two excellent studies of southern black landowning communities see Melvin Patrick Ely, *Israel on the Appomattox: A Southern Experiment in Black Freedom from the 1790s through the Civil War* (New York: Vintage Books, 2004), and Thad Sitton and James H. Conrad, *Freedom Colonies: Independent Black Texans in the Time of Jim Crow* (Austin: University of Texas

Press, 2005). For the northern context, see Stephen A. Vincent, *Southern Seed, Northern Soil: African American Farm Communities in the Mid-West, 1765–1900* (Bloomington: Indiana University Press, 1999). For the role of black agricultural extension agents in the story of black farm owning, see Debra A. Reid, *Reaping a Greater Harvest: African Americans, the Extension Service, and Rural Reform in Jim Crow Texas* (College Station: Texas A&M University Press, 2007). For the mid-twentieth-century decline of black farming, see Leo McGee and Robert Boone, eds., *The Black Rural Landowner—Endangered Species: Social, Political, and Economic Implications* (Westport, Conn: Greenwood Press, 1979). The number of black farm owners comes from Schweninger, *Black Property Owners*, 184.

2. For Moton, see Robert Russa Moton, *Finding a Way Out* (New York: Doubleday, Page, and Company, 1920); and William Hardin Hughes, ed., *Robert Russa Moton of Hampton and Tuskegee* (Chapel Hill: University of North Carolina Press, 1956). For Campbell, see Thomas M. Campbell, *The Moveable School Goes to the Negro Farmer* (Tuskegee: Tuskegee Institute Press, 1936; reprint, 1969), and Allen W. Jones, "Thomas M. Campbell: Black Agricultural Leader of the New South," *Agricultural History* 53, no. 1 (January 1979): 42–59. For Smith, see Reid, *Reaping a Greater Harvest*, 1–85; for Miller, see Miller, "The Farm—The Negro's Best Chance," *Opportunity*, January, 1935, 21; and August Meier, "The Racial and Educational Philosophy of Kelly Miller, 1895–1915," *Journal of Negro Education* 29, no. 2 (Spring 1960): 121–27. Even W.E.B. Du Bois, who is most often identified as Washington's critic, carefully tracked and celebrated the expansion of black farm ownership in the late nineteenth and early twentieth century. He wrote one of the first studies of black farm ownership in a 1901 Bulletin of the Department of Labor, *The Negro Landholder of Georgia*.

3. Frequently African American farmers clustered together to purchase land or offer one another protection. For more on all-black farming communities see Susan Eva O'Donovan, *Becoming Free in the Cotton South* (Cambridge: Harvard University Press, 2007), 147–49; Sitton and Conrad, *Freedom Colonies*; Elizabeth Rauh Bethel, *Promiseland: A Century of Life in a Negro Community* (Philadelphia: Temple University Press, 1981; rev. ed., Columbia: University of South Carolina Press, 1997); and Janet Sharp Hermann, *The Pursuit of a Dream* (New York: Vintage Press, 1983).

4. For a more extensive study of Hubert and his organization, see Mark Roman Schultz, "A More Satisfying Life on the Farm: Benjamin F. Hubert and the Log Cabin Community," M.A. thesis, University of Georgia, 1989. Hubert's personal papers and the administrative records of the Association for the Advancement of Negro Country Life and the Log Cabin Community are housed in the Hargrett Rare Book and Manuscript Library, University of Georgia, Athens (hereafter cited as BFH papers).

5. Lester F. Russell, *Profile of a Black Heritage*, (Franklin Square, N.Y.: Graphicopy, 1977), 53–54. Russell was a university professor and the husband of one of Zach and Camilla Hubert's granddaughters. He based his family history on interviews conducted with family members. Accounts differ concerning Benjamin Hubert's birth. One affidavit sworn to by one of his cousins in 1919 places it in 1883, while other records cite 1886 or 1887. Most sources, including his obituary in the *New York Times*, May 1, 1958, place the date on December 25, 1884.

6. For a discussion of Zach and Camilla Hubert's path to land ownership see Mark R. Schultz, "Interracial Kinship Ties and the Rise of the Black Middle Class," in *Georgia in Black and White* (Athens: University of Georgia Press, 1994), 147–48.

7. Schultz, "A More Satisfying Life," 28–30. Russell, *Profile*, 88–109; "A Remarkable Negro Family," *Southern Workman* (October 1925): 454–57; Willie Snow Ethridge, "An Aristocracy of Achievement," *Macon Telegraph*, September 1, 1929, also printed in pamphlet form (Savannah, Presses of Review Printing Company), 4–6, in BFH papers. The Hubert boys all attended Morehouse and the girls, Spelman. The Huberts were and still are a remarkably accomplished family. Among Benjamin Hubert's brothers, Zachary Taylor Hubert became president of Jackson College in Mississippi and Langston College in Oklahoma, while James Hubert served as executive director of the New York Urban League. Other siblings became college professors, Jeanes Supervising Teachers, agricultural extension agents, pastors, and high school principals. The term *conservative* derives from Joel Williamson's designation of three distinct white attitudes toward blacks in the late nineteenth-century South. Conservatives expressed the aristocratic view that blacks were inferior but that whites had an obligation to protect and educate them and find a secure place for them in the social hierarchy. Liberals espoused racial equality. And radicals viewed blacks as dangerous beasts and sought to drive them ever lower in society. Joel Williamson, *The Crucible of Race: Black-White Relations in the American South since Emancipation* (New York: Oxford University Press, 1984), 4–7.

8. Williamson, *Crucible*, 30–34.

9. *The Index* (yearbook of Massachusetts Agricultural College), 1912, 66, 145, 177.

10. Liberty Hyde Bailey, *The Country-Life Movement in the United States* (New York: Macmillan, 1911); William L. Bowers, *The Country Life Movement in America, 1900–1920* (Port Washington, N.Y.: Kennikat Press, 1974); David B. Danbom, *The Resisted Revolution: Urban America and the Industrialization of Agriculture, 1900–1930* (Ames: Iowa State University Press, 1979). For the evolution of the guiding philosophy of the USDA, see Reid, *Reaping a Greater Harvest,* and Pete Daniel, *Standing at the Crossroads: Southern Life since 1900* (New York: Hill and Wang, 1986). See Reid also for the role of local African American agricultural reformers in formulating scientific and cooperative strategies.

11. BFH to Rev. Richard Carroll, November 7, 1916; program of the South Carolina State Fair for Negroes, March 1917; H. O. Sargent to L. S. Hawkins, May 9, 1918, Orangeburg file, BFH papers.

12. William J. Newlin (National Educational Recruiting Secretary) to BFH, January 6, 1919; S. C. Fairley (Army Overseas Educational Commission) to BFH, January 10, 1919; untitled newspaper clipping, January 15, 1919; Oscar M. Miller (War Personnel Board, National War Work Council) to BFH, February 14, 1919; William Newlin to BFH, February 13, 1919; F. H. Cardozo (director, Department of Agriculture, Tuskegee Institute) to BFH, January 15, 1919; R. S. Wilkinson (president, South Carolina State Industrial College) to BFH, April 23, 1919; Col. Reeves (Headquarters, American Expeditionary Forces University), copy of Special Orders No. 109, to BFH, June 7, 1919, in "World War" file, BFH papers; "A Remarkable Negro Family," *Southern Workman* (October 1925): 455–56.

13. William Henry Willcox to BFH, November 28, 1921, BFH papers; "A Remarkable Negro Family," *Southern Workman* (October 1925): 455–56.

14. BFH to George Foster Peabody, December 13, 1934, Peabody file, BFH papers. When Moton stepped down in 1934, the press speculated that Hubert would replace him. It seems that he was considered the leading candidate until he publicly stated that he did not intend to leave Georgia State College.

15. James Hubert to BFH, August or September 1916, BFH papers.

16. *Sparta Ishmaelite*, March 19, 1926.

17. "Who Will Head Tuskegee?" *Savannah Morning News*, March 3, 1935; "Not Interested in Tuskegee, Hubert Tells Davis Lee," newspaper clipping, Tuskegee file, BFH papers.

18. Pamphlets describing the history of Savannah State College, compiled by Clyde Hall and Charles Elmore, Savannah State University archives; *Savannah Morning News*, June 3, 1936, BFH papers; Forty-Second Catalogue of the Georgia State Industrial College, 1931–32, 10, Hargrett Rare Book and Manuscript Library, University of Georgia, Athens; C. T. Wright, "The Development of Education for Blacks in Georgia, 1865–1900," dissertation, Boston University, 1977, 148–49.

19. Ethridge, "Aristocracy," 13–15; "Report of A. Pratt Adams" (chairman, Georgia State Industrial College) to Trustees, June 15, 1928, University of Georgia Trustees Correspondence and Reports, 1924–32, box 6, University of Georgia Archives, Athens.

20. Clyde W. Hall, *Black Vocational, Technical and Industrial Arts Education: Development and History*, (Chicago: American Technological Society, 1973), 126; pamphlets and catalogues of Georgia State Industrial College.

21. Martha Wilson, interview, Savannah, Ga., February 1989. All interviews conducted by author, and all notes in possession of author.

22. *Savannah Morning News*, June 3, 1936; Hall, *Black Vocational, Technical and Industrial Arts*, 126; Catalogue of Georgia State College, 1940–41, 22; Willis Hubert (nephew of Benjamin Hubert), interview, Springfield, Ga., February 1989. For descriptions of similarities in other programs, see Robert Francis Engs, *Freedom's First Generation: Black Hampton, Virginia, 1861–1890* (Philadelphia: University of Pennsylvania Press, 1979), 139–60, and his *Educating the Disfranchised and Disinherited: Samuel Chapman Armstrong and Hampton Institute, 1839–1893* (Knoxville: University of Tennessee Press, 1999), 98–114; and Robert J. Norrell, *Up from History: The Life of Booker T. Washington* (Cambridge: Harvard University Press, 2009), 54–55, 68–69, 95–99.

23. These quotes typified Hubert's frequent published statements through the 1930s and 1940s. *Savannah Morning News*, March 28, 1939; undated fundraising letter, clippings file, BFH papers.

24. Such traditional crafts as shoemaking, blacksmithing, and harness making had offered African Americans the opportunity to start and operate their own businesses in a pre-industrial age. But as accelerating industrialization brought cheap consumer goods and expensive tractors to the rural South, such training hemmed blacks in quaintly obsolete service sectors. For contrasting arguments on industrial education and the Hampton model, see Donald Spivey, *Schooling for the New Slavery: Black Industrial Education, 1868–1915* (Lawrenceville, N.J.: Africa World Press, 2006), and James D. Anderson, *The Education of Blacks in the South, 1860–1935* (Chapel Hill: University of North Carolina Press, 1988), who argue that this program of study intentionally blunted black students' chances for advancement in favor of a stable economy and social order. See also Eric Anderson and Alfred A. Moss Jr., *Dangerous Donations: Northern Philanthropy and Southern Black Education, 1902–1930* (Columbia: University of Missouri Press, 1999), and Engs, *Educating the Disfranchised*, who argue that this form of education was also being used with white students, and that most Hampton graduates did blaze their paths to financial independence.

25. "1930 Report to the Board of Regents of the University System of Georgia," p. 45, record group 33-1-35, unit 2, "University System Standing and Special Committee Records;" "Master Program for Apprenticeship Teaching in Vocational Agriculture conducted by GSI, January 6–March 22, 1937," p. 5, record group 33-1-51, "University System Board of Regents Chancellor's Subject Files," box 24, location #4583-09, folder "Vocational Training in Agriculture, 1934–37," Georgia State Archives, Atlanta. Prairie View Normal and Industrial Institute in Texas offered these courses by 1930, too. See Reid, *Reaping a Greater Harvest*, 33, 47–48, 53–63, 93–96.

26. Pamphlet of the Association for the Advancement of Negro Country Life for "Negro Farm and Home Ownership Week," January 28, 1929, 16–17, BFH papers. This article, although unsigned, was almost certainly written by Benjamin Hubert.

27. Ibid.

28. Various organizational tracts and papers, particularly Hubert's response to a questionnaire of the National Information Bureau, July 22, 1944, BFH papers.

29. "Negro Home and Farm Ownership Week" pamphlet, BFH papers.

30. Mark R. Schultz, *Rural Face of White Supremacy: Beyond Jim Crow* (Urbana: University of Illinois Press, 2007), 21.

31. For the boll weevil and the collapse of cotton prices in the 1920s and 1930s, see Jack Temple Kirby, *Rural Worlds Lost: The American South, 1920–1960* (Baton Rouge: Louisiana State University Press, 1987), and Gilbert C. Fite, *Cotton Fields No More: Southern Agriculture, 1865–1980* (Lexington: University Press of Kentucky, 1984), 1–22, 103–4, 120–26. Hancock County Tax Digests, 1920–24, Georgia State Archives, Atlanta. Farm prices in the Springfield area fell from $11.40 per acre in 1920 to $6.20 in 1925. Ethridge, "Aristocracy," 17.

32. Willie Snow Ethridge, "Experiment in Negro Happiness," *Macon Telegraph*, September 14, 1930 (also in pamphlet form); Kelly Miller (essayist and sociologist at Howard University), "'Log Cabin' Community Center Is Ideal Rural Project," *Washington Tribune*, September 8, 1934, (also in pamphlet form), BFH papers.

33. Ethridge, "Aristocracy" and "Experiment"; BFH to Mary Otis Willcox, November 18, 1931, Wilcox folder, BFH papers.

34. BFH to Mary Otis Willcox, November 18, 1931; BFH to David S. Baird, October 5, 1943; BFH, "5,000 for Negro Youth Camp at Log Cabin, Georgia" (manuscript); "Hens on Negro Project Make Good Records," undated newspaper clipping, BFH papers; *Herald Journal* (Greensboro, Ga.), August 17, 1934; "largest poultry center" in BFH to Robert Warren (Mayfield, Ga.), December 6, 1943; David Connely, interview, Siliom, Ga. (a white farmer who lived ten miles from Springfield), January 1989.

35. Fite, *Cotton Fields No More*, 114; Kirby, *Rural Worlds Lost*, 34.

36. Mrs. Charles Riegleman (New York) to BFH, November 20, 1938; BFH to Mrs. Charles Riegleman, November 23, 1938, Riegleman file, BFH papers; *Savannah Morning News*, April 15, 1939.

37. BFH, "The Role of the Small Southern Farm in the Future Land Utilization Program" (manuscript), undated, articles file, BFH papers, 23–25. For other studies of cooperative farming in the south, see Gilbert C. Fite, *Farm to Factory: A History of the Consumers Cooperative Association* (Columbia: University of Missouri Press, 1965), and Robert Hunt Ferguson, "Race and the Remaking of the Rural South: Delta Cooperative Farm and

Providence Farm in Jim Crow–Era Mississippi," PhD. diss., University of North Carolina at Chapel Hill, 2012.

38. "The Role of the Small Southern Farm," 19–21.

39. *Savannah Morning News*, November 3, 1940; BFH to David Baird, July 23, 1945; BFH to Mary Otis Willcox, November 18, 1931; "GA College Prexy Has a 10,000 Acre Co-op Farm Plan," untitled, undated newspaper clipping, clippings file, BFH papers.

40. "GA College Prexy Has a 10,000 Acre Co-op"; Sales Manager, Fulton Bag and Cotton Mills, to Georgia State College, July 20, 1934, and August 14, 1934; *Atlanta Journal*, April 2, 1934.

41. Hancock County Tax Digest, 1930–48, Georgia State Archives, Atlanta; Ethridge, "Aristocracy"; "Unique Rural Community Center Down in Georgia Seeks to Make Country Life More Satisfying," *Journal and Guide* (Norfolk Va.), May 21, 1932; *Washington Tribune*, September 8, 1934; BFH to Galen Stone, July 30, 1943. Undated, untitled article clipping, *Savannah Morning News*. Interviews with Wilson Hubert (nephew of Benjamin Hubert), Savannah, Ga., February 1989; Eva Andrews (Springfield native), Sparta, Ga., February 1989; Samuel Williams, Springfield, Ga., November 1988. Williams had promoted the Springfield cooperative as a black agricultural extension agent. County figures are from the Hancock County Tax Digest, 1930–1950, Georgia State Archives, Atlanta.

42. "The Economic Status of the Negro," October 20, 1930, report in clippings file, BFH papers. Since 1927 when Hoover had been secretary of commerce, he had seriously weighed Moton's proposal that the federal government aid in the establishment of a philanthropically supported land bank to aid black tenants to buy land. See Donald J. Lisio, *Hoover, Blacks, and Lilly-Whites: A Study of Southern Strategies* (Chapel Hill: University of North Carolina Press, 1985), 13–17, 187–93.

43. Although the FmHA provided a quarter of their housing to black sharecroppers, proportionate to their numbers in the rural South, it ultimately resettled only about 1,400 black families. Donald Holley, *Uncle Sam's Farmers: The New Deal Communities in the Lower Mississippi Valley* (Urbana: University of Illinois Press, 1975), 180.

44. Black landowners in Hancock County voted continuously between Reconstruction and the present. A federal district court struck down the white primary in Georgia in 1946, allowing thousands of black voters, including many Log Cabin Community residents, to vote. Schultz, *Rural Face*, 175–203.

45. Schweninger, *Black Property Owners*, 164, 174.

III

Agrarianism and Black Politics

5

Black Populism

Agrarian Politics from the Colored Alliance to the People's Party

OMAR H. ALI

Within a decade after the collapse of Reconstruction, an independent black agrarian movement—Black Populism—arose to challenge Democratic party rule in the South. Led primarily by black farmers, Black Populism was distinct from the white Populist movement of the same period, having its own organizations, leaders, and tactics to assert the economic interests and political rights of African Americans. Growing out of networks of rural black churches and mutual benefit associations that formed in the region following Reconstruction, Black Populism spanned a fourteen-year period, starting in 1886 and ending in 1900.

Among a number of the groups that helped to launch the movement was a group of farmers in Houston County in eastern Texas. There, near a cotton farm during December of 1886, sixteen black farmers and a single white farmer inaugurated what became the Colored Farmers National Alliance and Co-Operative Union (hereafter Colored Alliance), the largest of the Black Populist organizations to come. A call went out to black farmers across the state, and within three weeks several dozen delegates convened. According to one account, after "some discussion and earnest prayer . . . [the delegates] unanimously agreed that union and organization had become necessary [for] the colored race."[1] Representatives proceeded to adopt a declaration of principles:

> To promote agriculture and horticulture . . . To educate the agricultural classes in the science of economic government in a strictly nonpartisan spirit . . . To aid its members to become more skillful and

efficient workers . . . [to] protect their individual rights; [to raise] funds for the benefit of sick or disabled members, or their distressed families; [and to form] a closer union among all colored people.[2]

Jacob J. Shuffer and H. J. Spencer, two leading African American delegates, were elected president and secretary, respectively. Both Shuffer and Spencer, in addition to fellow black farmers R. M. Saddler, Willis Nichols, and Israel McGilbra, were elected to one-year terms as trustees of the new organization.[3]

In less than three years leaders of the Colored Alliance had transformed their organization into the nation's broadest network of black farm owners, tenants, sharecroppers, and agricultural laborers (largely landless workers paid wages), boasting over one million members—male and female. The southern-wide Colored Alliance's stated purpose was to promote land ownership, collective buying and selling, and improved education—all goals that could measurably improve the lives of rural black farmers, the communities in which they lived, and, in keeping with agrarian rhetoric, the nation that had granted them citizenship.[4] However, starting in 1890 leaders of the organization began to develop an independent political strategy. Working either with unaffiliated candidates for public office, the People's Party, or the Republican Party, African Americans pressed for structural political reforms—from the elimination of local poll taxes to federal oversight of southern elections—in order to gain enough electoral power to shape public policy positively.[5]

The founding and development of the Colored Alliance was part of a collective undertaking.[6] No single leader emerged to represent Black Populism as a whole; instead, dozens of leaders functioned at the local level carrying out a variety of tactics (sometimes even in opposition to each other). At times these leaders came together on a regional basis. Black organizers of the Colored Alliance, along with a handful of white leaders, consolidated existing networks of black farmers as well as sharecroppers and agricultural laborers (both wage workers and piece workers) who were affiliated with other rural-based organizations. These included the Colored Agricultural Wheels, the southern branch of the Knights of Labor, the Cooperative Workers of America, and the Farmers Union.[7] Texas alone was home to several black agrarian organizations during the mid-1880s and 1890s, including the Colored Farmers Association, the Colored Farmers Home Improvement Lodge, and the Farmers' Improvement Society of Texas. Black churches, namely, Black Baptist and African Methodist Episcopal denominations, provided platforms for communicating to black communities across the state and broader region. While the organizations were not always in agreement with one another, the range of rural black organizations and their activities in Texas, as elsewhere in the South, indicate the vibrancy of Black Populism and African American culture and politics generally during the era.[8]

The Colored Alliance's call for agrarian reform and cooperation resonated among the region's poor. It also threatened merchants and planters who opposed the more militant demands of local leaders—from higher wages for cotton picking to ending the notorious convict-lease system (measures that would directly cut into the profit making and mechanisms of control over black labor).[9] Members of the Colored Alliance attended local chapter meetings where they socialized, shared agricultural techniques and innovations, and coordinated cooperative efforts for planting and harvesting.[10]

In time, members were encouraged to enter (or reenter) the political arena. Field organizers carried out their work covertly, so as not to draw attention from employers and landlords who might be hostile to black workers and tenant farmers organizing themselves collectively. As the historian Lawrence Goodwyn notes: "Black lecturers who ranged over the South organizing state and local Alliances did not enter Southern towns behind fluttering flags and brass bands. They attempted to organize slowly and patiently, seeking out the natural leaders in rural black communities and building from there."[11]

In each state Colored Alliance members elected a superintendent, president, vice-president, treasurer, conductor, secretary, lecturer (usually with the additional title of "organizer"), and sometimes an assistant lecturer.[12] All superintendents bore responsibility for expanding the organization and reported to the general superintendent, who was elected by a board of national trustees.[13] Meetings were formalized with secret passwords and greetings; seating was assigned for the various elected positions, including a doorkeeper and a chaplain. Guidelines were formulated for opening and closing of sections of the meeting, while other rituals were adhered to, down to dress code of members when one of their own passed away: "black crape rosette, with a sprig of evergreen pinned above it on the left lapel of the coat—the rosette to be worn thirty days."[14]

Black farmers and laborers provided the Colored Alliance's natural base, and by 1891, the Colored Alliance had established dozens of chapters across every state in the South, prompting its national spokesperson, Richard M.

Humphrey, to claim a "total membership [of] nearly 1,200,000, of whom 300,000 are females, and 150,000 males under twenty-one years of age."[15] With the exception of several local female leaders, such as Phoebe Cobb of the Knights of Labor and Lutie Lytle of the People's Party, the names and specific activities of Black Populist women leaders in the movement are little known. No doubt women helped to build the movement, as their critical roles within the black churches and their visibility at rallies attest.[16] The extraordinary membership figures of the Colored Alliance may have been inflated to bolster delegate apportionment at regionwide meetings with other organizations. Exactly how many African Americans joined the Colored Alliance is unknown because most records were either destroyed for fear of reprisal or were never kept. With the exception of a few local chapters, declarations by the organization's leaders in the press are the only figures through which an approximation of the Colored Alliance total membership can be made. Detailed reports do not exist; more typical is a brief mention such as one that appeared in the *Southern Mercury* in December of 1888: Alex John, a leader of the Ebenezer Colored Alliance No. 195 in Texas, reported that his chapter comprised "10 male and 6 female members."[17]

The Colored Alliance communicated directly with members via several newspapers, including the *National Alliance* in Texas, the *Midland Express* in Virginia, and the *Alliance Advocate* in North Carolina.[18] The newspapers informed readers about the working of transportation and storage monopolies, issues of taxation, and the constriction of currency flows. They explained how all this affected African Americans through price fixing and inflated interest rates, driving up costs for farmers and keeping wages low for agricultural workers.[19] Members also learned about the Colored Alliance's latest initiatives: cooperative exchanges, lobbying efforts, and credit programs. In addition to these initiatives the organization established "Colored Homestead Companies" to assist African Americans trying to purchase their own homes and, in some areas, raised money to extend public school terms and provide financial assistance to families.[20]

While the Colored Alliance began as a strictly "nonpartisan" mutual benefit association focused inwardly on economic cooperation and education, it quickly developed into one of the most radical southern-based organizations of the era, carrying out boycotts and strikes and ultimately helping to fuel the People's Party. As the membership of the Colored Alliance increasingly asserted itself it also came under attack by white planters and merchants, who used local militia to suppress the organization.

External attacks exacerbated tension within the Colored Alliance as leaders disagreed over strategies to pursue. Problems came to a head in 1891. By the summer of that year one faction of the Colored Alliance attempted a regionwide strike of cotton pickers; another vehemently opposed the strike, while yet another faction moved fully into the electoral arena.

Within a year, virtually all traces of the organization disappeared from newspapers and other contemporary accounts. Still, the Colored Alliance's political influence continued. Certain leaders, having organized a base of support through the black alliance, redirected African Americans to focus their efforts on either building the People's Party or participating in other independent political coalitions via the Republican Party or individual candidates. By the fall of 1891, not only were major Colored Alliance leaders openly declaring their support for federal supervision of elections and lobbying Republicans to have its members nominated for office, but they were taking the lead in meetings to create a new national political party—a significant departure from the organization's "nonpartisan" stance some five years earlier.

From the outset black leaders of the Colored Alliance chose a white Baptist minister and cotton farmer, Richard M. Humphrey, as general superintendent, to serve as the organization's chief spokesperson. They also charged him with the official task of expanding the Colored Alliance nationally. Humphrey, a South Carolinian of Irish stock (second generation to the United States) and a Confederate veteran who had moved to Texas after the Civil War, was described at the time as "an elderly man . . . with plain speech and a free blunt manner."[21] His black peers acknowledged his skills as an organizer and propagandist. His commitment to the economic and political interests of African American farmers, as well as to the region's most marginalized—landless black tenant farmers and agricultural laborers—seemed above reproach, though his social views at times reflected the racist ideology of the time.[22]

Humphrey, more than any other Colored Alliance member, documented the organization's character and composition.[23] Like other agrarian clubs and mutual benefit associations of the era, the Colored Alliance encouraged its members to purchase land, improve their homes, and learn new farming techniques. Ownership of land could facilitate equal protection under the law for African Americans because poll taxes could more likely be paid by landowners. The Colored Alliance also sponsored a number of cooperative stores where local members could pool their crops for bulk sales. With price gouging for the transportation of goods to market and economies of scale not favoring the average black farmer (usually an owner of smaller amounts of land, and therefore a producer of more limited agricultural output), economic cooperation was a crucial strategy for rural black farmers' improvement. White farmers had been engaged in similar practices through their own Farmers' Alliances. Given the various forms of institutionalized racism toward African Americans in the South (affording them little if any credit, charging them particularly high interest rates, and extending almost no legal recourse) black farmers could—at least, theoretically—benefit from such cooperation.[24]

A convention of Colored Alliance chapters was called in Lovelady in March of 1888 to establish the order as a national body, to be called the Colored Farmers National Alliance and Co-Operative Union. During the summer of 1888 the Colored Alliance set ambitious goals. On July 20, President Shuffer and Secretary Spencer assigned Humphrey the task of leading the effort to "establish . . . trading posts, or exchanges, for the use and benefit of our order."[25] Humphrey spent the next two and a half years attempting to create exchanges in Norfolk, Charleston, Mobile, New Orleans, and Houston for the purchase and sale of staple crops and produce. Ideally, members would be able to buy goods at reduced prices and secure loans to pay off their mortgages.[26] Despite such projects being met with enthusiasm by members, most of the exchanges faltered as capital was difficult to raise among the organization's debt-ridden and cash-poor rank and file.[27] One Colored Alliance lecturer from Tennessee remarked: "The colored people show an eagerness for information for our cause and principles, which is unsurpassed by any audience I have ever addressed."[28]

The enthusiasm generated a rush of support for the agrarian movement, leading to African Americans creating or joining competing black associations. Around the same time that the Colored Alliance was established in Houston County, a "National Colored Alliance" was formed in the state. Headed by Andrew J. Carothers, a Confederate veteran and the son of a planter, the organization claimed a membership of 250,000 within three years of its founding, with chapters in every southern state. The National Colored Alliance likely inflated its membership figures as well.[29] In 1890, following a series of negotiations, the two organizations merged.[30] In December 1890 the consolidated Colored Alliance claimed substantial state memberships: Alabama, 100,000; Arkansas, 20,000; Georgia, 84,000; Kentucky, 25,000; Louisiana, 50,000; Mississippi, 90,000; North Carolina, 55,000; South Carolina, 90,000; Tennessee, 60,000; Texas, 90,000; and Virginia, 50,000 (714,000 of 1.2 million in thirty states).[31] Over the next six months the national body issued some fifty-six county charters, and two thousand subcharters, indicating extensive local infrastructure.[32]

Class divisions proved to be a far greater source of tension among movement leaders than their given race.[33] While the vast majority of the Colored Alliance's presidents, secretaries, and state lecturers were black, there were several white state superintendents, including Harry G. McCall of Alabama and Joseph J. Rogers of North Carolina and Virginia.[34] The role of such white organizers in the Colored Alliance as social and political brokers was crucial for the movement's development. White leaders were more easily able to establish ties with segregated white agrarian and labor organizations that shared common interests with black organizations than were their black counterparts, given the racial discrimination that infused the dominant institutions of American society. Similarly, white leaders did not face the kinds of barriers that African American leaders confronted when attempting to speak with the white press (although white leaders were not always shielded from discrimination or physical attacks). From the outset, then, Black Populism was an integrated movement, unlike the parallel white Populist movement with its segregated organizations, including the Southern Farmers Alliance and the Florida Farmers Union—both of which had provisions in their bylaws explicitly excluding African Americans; the former from its inception, the latter beginning in 1889.

One's race could be understood in other ways: just as there had been "Black Republicans" during Reconstruction who were white (the term *Black Republican* having been principally used by Democrats to deride their opponents), so had white leaders emerged as Black Populists—their defining characteristic not being their race but their participation in activities that would help to empower black farmers and agricultural workers. In other words, "Black Populist" designates an activity rather than a racial identity. Under this definition, white men such as Humphrey, McCall, and Rogers of the Colored Alliance, along with Hiram Hover of the South Carolina Cooperative Workers of America and Nicholas Stack of the North Carolina Knights of Labor, were Black Populists. Other white leaders followed them: J. W. Allen of the Alabama Colored Wheel, Vincent St. Cloud of the Georgia Knights of Labor, and Garrett Scott of the Texas People's Party. These men constituted a minority, albeit an effective one, for the movement. But it was African Americans who dominated both Black Populism's leadership and the rank and file membership. These African Americans were principally responsible for expanding the movement on the ground by recruiting new adherents, maintaining morale, and communicating on a day-to-day basis. Chief among these organizers was a former slave turned teacher and minister, Rev. Walter A. Pattillo, who led North Carolina's Colored Alliance and helped to steer Black Populism toward third-party politics.[35]

Even before the rise of the black agrarian movement, Pattillo was known as an exceptional organizer in black Baptist circles and as an accomplished community leader (figure 5.1).[36] Born into slavery in North Carolina on November 9, 1850, Pattillo taught himself how to read and write; in the late 1860s he drove wagons and worked in a sawmill; by the early 1870s he worked on a farm, which augmented his income. It also gave him credibility later as he organized the black farmers' movement, having become a stable landowner through marriage and his own efforts. In 1876 he entered Shaw University in Raleigh to study theology.[37]

Pattillo, like others of his generation, flourished in the black Baptist church. His home county, Granville, was the only county outside eastern North Carolina where the majority of the population was black.[38] There, as in other counties with high concentrations of African Americans, black Baptist and Methodist churches dotted the landscape, serving as important centers for the recruitment and cultivation of black leaders in the years following the Civil War.[39] Local black churches brought together young and old members of the community. Junior members took their lead from senior and more experienced members, assuming greater levels of responsibility. At seventeen years of age Pattillo joined the General Association of the Colored Baptists of North Carolina to promote the newly established statewide religious body. Within a few years he gained a reputation as a "convention stalwart" for strengthening ties between churches across the state.[40] His studies in theology at Shaw University brought him into even greater contact with other black leaders in the region, further raising his public profile, especially in the tobacco-growing regions of the state. Pattillo's ministry would grow so large that, as one of his sons recalled, he delivered "nearly three thousand sermons, including funerals, and baptized about 3,100" people over the course of his lifetime.[41]

Pattillo attempted to organize and serve the African American community in a variety of ways. In 1883 he ran for register of deeds as a Republican in Oxford, the seat of Granville County.[42] Attacks on his candidacy quickly mounted. His white opponent launched a campaign warning voters that if elected, the "sleek, oily, negro" would have the authority to issue marriage licenses to white couples—thereby violating, presumably, the sanctity of their unions.[43] Pattillo lost the election but continued his ministry while promoting education among African Americans as superintendent

Figure 5.1. Walter A. Pattillo. Courtesy of the Richard H. Thornton Granville County Public Library, Oxford, North Carolina.

of schools. He joined existing efforts to address other needed public services in the black community, such as helping to establish the state's first black orphanage, the Colored Orphanage Asylum. In this way, Pattillo's work may be understood as pragmatic with a moral basis, not unlike that of other reformers of the day, black and white.[44]

In the late 1880s, with growing rural economic instability—the result of falling crop prices, rising debt, and lower wages—Pattillo turned his attention to the agrarian movement sweeping the countryside. He joined the Colored Alliance, which had recently been established in North Carolina. Soon the minister was spreading the Colored Alliance's gospel of agrarian reform. In 1890 he was elected as the organization's state lecturer and began editing the *Alliance Advocate*.[45] Pattillo took care in fostering cooperation between black and white people. His son recalled: "Aside from his ministerial work, [his strength lay] in the middle ground he occupied . . . in bringing about peace and goodwill between the colored and white races."[46] According to H. H. Perry, the business agent of the Craven County Alliance in North Carolina and president of the Riverdale suballiance in James City (an all-black town), by May 1890 over three hundred Colored Alliance chapters had been established in the state.[47] Pattillo helped expand North Carolina's Colored Alliance, which by 1891 claimed a membership of 55,000 men and women.[48]

The Colored Alliance's entry into North Carolina was part of a general upsurge in the national organization's membership following the black and white Alliances' conventions in Meridian, Mississippi, in 1888. There the Colored Alliance and the two principal white Alliances (the Northern and Southern Farmers Alliances) began to cooperate with each other formally, albeit briefly. Meeting separately from the white organizations, the Colored Alliance sent representatives to the white convention to determine areas of cooperation. The black and white Alliances were united against railroad and banking monopolies. With virtually no oversight or regulation, railroad companies charged excessive prices for transporting goods to market, while banks and local merchants charged exorbitant fees and interest rates—in some instances, up to 200 percent. The Alliances were particularly careful to avoid the adoption of positions likely to create further divisions between them, especially on economic issues, given the landless and laboring membership of the Colored Alliance and the high percentage of white Alliancemen (especially at the leadership level within the Southern Farmers Alliance) who were either employers or landlords. Despite this fundamental and ultimately irreconcilable difference between the black and white Alliances, occasional cooperation took place.[49]

It had been one thing for African Americans to form organizations of their own that were devoted to education and "self-help"; lobbying for reforms under the guise of paternalistic white leadership was even acceptable. But it was quite another for black people to carry out boycotts or organize their own cooperatives and make demands that directly cut into the profits of white merchants and planters. Under the leadership of Oliver

Cromwell, a black farmer from Leflore County, Mississippi, the Colored Alliance pushed the boundaries of acceptable action, ultimately provoking a deadly reaction from white authorities.[50]

During the summer of 1889 Leflore was the scene of one of Black Populism's bloodiest fights with the white planter and merchant class. Located in the Yazoo-Mississippi Delta, Leflore was "blessed with miles and miles of dark, rich soil—soil so rich that its cotton yield per acre exceeded that of all other regions in the United States," as the historian William Holmes describes it.[51] As was typical of the Cotton Belt, local white landlords held the majority black population in an economic vise. During the early summer Cromwell began encouraging black farmers from the region to trade with a white Alliance store in Durant instead of with local white shop owners, who had been price gouging.[52] The boycott was designed to break, or at least loosen, the grip of the white merchants on the local African American community.[53]

Described by the *New Mississippian* as a "notoriously bad negro," Cromwell gained a reputation as an outspoken black leader.[54] He was soon targeted for retribution and received multiple death threats. In response to these threats, a group of seventy-five Colored Alliance members marched in "regular military style" and delivered a bold message to local white authorities: "Three Thousand Armed Men" were prepared to protect Cromwell if need be. Tensions quickly escalated, and a white posse gathered as the Colored Alliance paraded with a show of righteousness reminiscent of a parade some fourteen years earlier in Clinton, in which Cromwell himself led a cavalry column.[55] Incensed by the Colored Alliance's audacity, the white posse launched an attack on them and African Americans in the surrounding area.

With few arms or trained combatants, Colored Alliance leaders were unprepared for the onslaught. A battle broke out that left dozens of African Americans dead or seriously wounded. Mississippi's Democratic governor Robert Lowry summoned three companies of the National Guard while white vigilantes went on a rampage. Black men, women, and children in neighboring areas were indiscriminately killed, with scores fleeing into the swamps. Among those murdered were Colored Alliance leaders Adolph Horton, Scott Morris, Jack Dial, and J. M. Dial. Cromwell narrowly escaped, only to be tracked down. On the run for a week, he was trapped and then killed, but not before he "took down" five of his assailants, members of the Ku Klux Klan.[56]

After the massacre, the store was ordered by its white Alliance leadership to break all ties with the Colored Alliance and its surviving members. The murder of key Colored Alliance leaders and the accompanying trauma inflicted on African Americans in the area destroyed the local organization. The decentralized structure of the Colored Alliance, however, allowed the organization to continue functioning in other areas of the state.[57] While the white press and Democratic officials were quick to bury reports of the massacre, news of the brutality traveled among networks of African Americans. For black men and women, Leflore would serve as a difficult reminder of the lengths to which the Democratic Party in the South would go on behalf of the planter elite to maintain control over black labor.

African Americans challenged southern Democrats on the legislative front as well, principally regarding the Lodge Bill—a bill that centered on federal supervision of elections. The proposed bill would strike a deep chord among African Americans, as it would among white southerners, as it was reminiscent of federal measures taken during Reconstruction. The controversy surrounding the Lodge Bill united African Americans in opposition to the Democratic Party's use of intimidation and fraud to maintain their rule. On June 26, 1890, U.S. Representative Henry Cabot Lodge of Massachusetts introduced into Congress what detractors quickly dubbed the "Force Bill." Lodge's legislation would have allowed federal authorities to oversee national elections if, in a district with at least five hundred people, fifty voters signed a petition attesting to electoral fraud.[58] Although technically applicable only to federal elections, the bill would likely impinge upon state and local elections and therefore the degree to which black farmers could exercise political power.

Democrats strongly denounced the proposed legislation because it bore an unwelcome resemblance to laws passed during Reconstruction by calling for federal intervention in the South. Indeed, the overwhelming majority of white southerners opposed the bill. The Southern Farmers Alliance was particularly vehement in its opposition to the Lodge Bill, while, in sharp contrast, the bill was unanimously supported by Colored Alliance delegates to a national convention in Ocala in December of 1890.[59] As the unanimous black vote on the Lodge Bill suggests, African Americans spoke with a resounding voice when it came to federal protection of voting rights. The erosion of civil rights, like voting rights, was equally cause of concern among African Americans, prompting local actions by Colored Alliance leaders. In the fall of 1890 the Georgia Colored Alliance made an appeal to the state's jury commissioners that black jurors be included in cases involving black defendants. Likewise, the state's Colored Alliance lecturer, J. W. Carter, urged Georgia's state legislature to vote down a bill under consideration for a separate-coach law.[60] Unity, however, was not always operative within the ranks of the Colored Alliance. The divide between landholders and nonlandholders (sharecroppers, farm laborers, and cotton pickers), which existed at both rank and file and leadership levels, grew wider as the movement itself grew. Such differences became manifest as the Colored Alliance's nonlandholding members faced ever-harsher economic pressures, leading to a call for a regionwide strike of cotton pickers in 1891.

As material conditions grew worse across the South—with falling crop prices and plummeting wages—one faction of agricultural workers within the Colored Alliance resorted to striking. In a desperate act to secure higher wages for cotton pickers, a group of Colored Alliance leaders pushed for a strike across the entire Cotton Belt.[61] Some black farmers, who stood to lose if their crops were not harvested, opposed the strike. Others, such as E. Richardson, president of Georgia's Colored Alliance, objected to the strike for other reasons: neither should the Colored Alliance be involved in such labor strikes in the first place (which was not part of its original principles), nor for that matter, had the strike been planned carefully enough. Black farm laborers were nevertheless compelled to strike, even if their prospects for a successful outcome were dim. They did so officially through an offshoot of the Colored Alliance, called the Cotton Pickers' League.

Cotton prices had fallen precipitously—from approximately thirty-one cents in 1866, to nine cents in 1886, and then down to six cents by 1893. The fall in prices had a ripple effect: small farmers demanded fair prices for their crops; workers, fair wages for their labor—the specific amounts depended upon where they were in the cotton-growing region, as both prices and wages varied.[62] With over 67 percent of white Alliance officers listing their occupation in 1890 as farmers or planters (as opposed to only 2 percent who were listed as laborers), white Populist leaders tended to be hostile to agricultural labor strikes.[63] White Alliance leaders had little in common with the majority of African Americans, many of whom were poor landless or small landholding farmers (figure 5.2). The economic interests of African Americans in the Colored Alliance and the white planters who dominated the Alliance leadership were therefore structurally at odds. Non-landholding wage laborers demanded higher wages. Additionally, many farm families picked cotton for pay during harvest—that is, on top of tending their own crop. They too would benefit from higher wages.

Figure 5.2. Picking cotton in Mississippi, 1890s. J. C. Coovert Photograph Collection, Mississippi Department of Archives and History, Jackson, Mississippi.

In contrast, landowning employers sought not only higher prices and lower transportation costs for their crops, but the lowest wages possible for their workers, because lower wages translated into higher margins of profit.

The president of the Southern Farmers Alliance, Leonidas Polk, best expressed the white Alliance leadership's perspective when it came to labor strikes in general and the proposed cotton pickers' strike in particular. Not for one moment, he declared, did he "hesitate to advise our farmers to leave their cotton in the field rather than pay more than fifty cents per hundred to have it picked." He went on to accuse the organizers of the strike of trying "to better their condition at the expense of their white brethren." "Reforms," he stated, "should not be in the interest of one portion of our farmers at the expense of another."[64] The double standard on which Polk's statement rested reveals the extent to which white landowners were divorced from—indeed in direct opposition to—African American farmers and agricultural laborers.[65] In line with this, in their editorial pages, the *Progressive Farmer* and the *Caucasian*, both white Alliance newspapers (the former being under Polk's editorship), sternly opposed the Colored Alliance's strike.[66]

White planters in Charleston and Memphis who refused to pay their workers anything more than fifty cents per hundred pounds of cotton picked were to be the first targets of the strike. Fueling reports of a widespread strike amassing in the Cotton Belt, on September 26, 1891, the *Cleveland Gazette* warned that a circular had been mailed out from Texas to "every colored sub-alliance throughout the country, fixing the date when the strike of the pickers [would] be simultaneously inaugurated, and how it [should] be conducted."[67] Coordination of such a massive strike, however, would prove difficult.

The task of organizing the regionwide strike began in the summer of 1891 and ultimately fell on the shoulders of local leaders. The action itself was to take place in mid-September, although the launching date varied by as much as ten days across the South. Pickers in South Carolina and East Texas, for instance, walked out on September 12, while elsewhere pickers held off for another week. The staggering of the strike reflected the variation in peak harvesting times but also the lack of coordination on the part of leaders. The combination of factors led to disastrous results: local leaders were summarily fired, while pickers were threatened with force if they did not return to work. Despite the planters' swift retaliation, outbreaks continued. The most notable took place in Lee County, Arkansas, where Ben Patterson, a thirty-year-old black agricultural worker, led the effort.[68]

Patterson, originally from Memphis, Tennessee, traveled in late August to Lee County to mobilize cotton pickers in the Delta. For three weeks, with temperatures soaring, Patterson plied the cotton fields, recruiting workers for the strike. Gaining the support of a group of twenty-five black workers, he called for the local strike to begin on September 20. Assuming that many more pickers would join in the protest once it was under way, he both underestimated the strength of planters' control of the black labor force and overestimated the willingness of black workers to follow his lead. The strike, which began on the plantation of a Colonel H. P. Rodgers, fell short of Patterson's and other organizers' expectations.[69] In calculating the prospects of their success, most pickers, despite their low wages, saw the possibility of better wages as hardly worth the very real risks involved in striking: the loss of current and future earnings (meager as they might be), imprisonment, physical harm, even death. As had been the case in East Texas and South Carolina, dozens of strikers were summarily fired in Arkansas. The adamant few who persisted in their efforts were rounded up and punished. When groups of black strikers under Patterson's lead began scouring neighboring areas in search of recruits, planter militias came after them with a vengeance.

After five days of on-again, off-again battling between planters and strikers—most of the latter armed only with hoes, sticks, and knives—the cotton pickers' strike was defeated. Planters were aided by the chaos of the fighting that broke out. Apparently many workers decided to keep picking, viewing the prospects of a successful strike as dim and unwilling to risk their wages and jobs. So frenzied did the fighting between the different groups become that during one melee a white posse inadvertently burned a white-owned cotton gin. In the end, at least fifteen people—including two black workers who had refused to strike and a white plantation manager—were killed. At least six strikers were imprisoned. Of those killed, nine were lynched by white vigilantes at the instigation of local planters.[70] Patterson, who had been wounded during one of the gunfights, was arrested by a deputy and taken on board the *James Lee*. He was transported upriver to be jailed, but at Hackney's Landing, before he arrived to the town where he was to be incarcerated, a group of white hooded men took Patterson off the boat, tortured and then executed him.[71]

In the aftermath of the strike the white Alliance's main newspaper, the *National Economist*, stopped printing excerpts from the *National Alliance*, the principal newspaper of the Colored Alliance. Factionalism severely weakened the Colored Alliance because black farmers and workers opposed to the strike could not come to terms with strikers and their sympathizers who had joined the Cotton Pickers' League, the organization formed by leaders of the Colored Alliance to launch the strike. The failure of the strike had regional consequences, and with few exceptions, the Colored Alliance soon collapsed. Leaders of the organization who had been moving toward electoral politics over the previous eighteen months nevertheless carried forward the work of Black Populism.[72]

The tactical failures of the Colored Alliance and the Cotton Pickers' League, the inability to sustain cooperative stores, and the limitations involved in lobbying elected officials for agrarian reforms had convinced increasing numbers of African Americans of the need to engage the Democratic Party directly at the ballot box.[73] Several Colored Alliance leaders representing black farming interests had already begun running for public office as Republicans in the late 1880s. Lecturer Crawford of Georgia's Colored Alliance was elected to his state assembly as a Republican; the Rev. George W. Lowe of the Arkansas Colored Agricultural Wheel was elected to his state assembly and then reelected on the Union Labor ticket; W. A.

Grant, president of South Carolina's Colored Alliance, sought the Republican Party's congressional nomination in the First District, and South Carolina's principal lecturer, George Washington Murray, known as "the Black Eagle," was elected to Congress as an insurgent Republican.[74] Absent a larger political strategy, however, these forays into electoral politics that depended almost exclusively on the Republican Party were limited.

Some Black Populists recognized that if they were going to defeat the Democrats at the polls and gain majorities in local or state government, they would have to work with white independents to combine their votes. Drawing on previous Republican-Greenback fusion experience, African Americans, most of whom were Republicans, began working with white independents (and disaffected Democrats) along a new trajectory, establishing a string of local and statewide third parties in the early 1890s. By building independent electoral alternatives, African Americans would no longer rely on the Republican Party as their primary electoral vehicle. The inside-outside tactic of establishing third parties while making use of existing Republican organizations not only set Black Populism on a new course but targeted the Democrats' control of the electoral process by leveraging the political power of black farmers with white independents. As the *Cleveland Gazette* made plain, "The Afro-American Farmers Alliance [is] going into politics."[75]

The formation of the national People's Party signaled a major turning point in both black and white Populism. Between 1889 and 1891, operating through a series of parallel national conventions that brought together delegates of the black and white Alliances and several other organizations (including members of the Knights of Labor and the Women's Christian Temperance Union), African American and white third party advocates established a new independent political party. Walter Pattillo, among other Colored Alliance leaders, emerged as a key organizer in the conventions leading to the formation of the national People's Party in 1891.[76] Thus, despite the regional dissolution of the Colored Alliance in the fall of 1891, the organization continued to have influence. In both Georgia and Texas, chapters of the Colored Alliance would directly feed the growth of the People's Party in the mid-1890s.[77] The People's Party—and the electoral tactic of running fusion campaigns with the Republican Party—would become the new means through which African Americans attempted to advance their interests. During the spring of 1891 Rev. John L. Moore, the superintendent of Florida's Colored Alliance and a state executive committee member of the new People's Party, expressed the agrarian politics of the movement when he asserted, "As members of the Colored Farmers Alliance [we are] going to vote with and for the man or party that will secure for the farmer or laboring man his just rights."[78]

The Colored Alliance leadership's growing attention to the electoral process, and the subsequent shift in Black Populism toward independent politics, presented a new challenge to the Democratic Party's monopoly in the South. For African Americans, new possibilities were in the process of being created to exert what numeric strength they had in the electoral arena. After consolidating Black Populism as a regional force by activating and then linking networks of black agrarian organizations across the South, Colored Alliance leaders positioned themselves to shape what would become the national People's Party and its local affiliates. The rise of the new party, including its fusion with the Republican Party in selected states, not only continued the development of Black populism but would come to pose the most powerful threat yet to Democratic Party rule in the South.

Notes

1. Richard M. Humphrey, "History of the Colored Farmers' National Alliance and Co-Operative Union," in *The Farmer's Alliance History and Agricultural Digest*, ed. Nelson A. Dunning (Washington D.C.: Alliance Publishing Company, 1891), 288.

2. Ibid.

3. Charter of the Alliance of Colored Farmers of Texas, filed in the Department of State, February 28, 1887, microfilm accessed at Corporations Section, Secretary of State, Austin, Tex.; Patrick J. Dickson, "Out of the Lion's Mouth," M.P.S. thesis, Cornell University, 2000, 58, n8.

4. Humphrey, "History," 288.

5. Studies of Black Populism include Omar H. Ali, *In the Lion's Mouth: Black Populism in the New South, 1886–1900* (Jackson: University Press of Mississippi, 2010); Gerald Gaither, *Blacks and the Populist Revolt: Ballots and Bigotry in the New South* (Tuscaloosa: University of Alabama Press, 1977; rev. ed. published as *Blacks and the Populist Movement: Ballots and Bigotry in the New South*, 2005); and Steven Hahn, *A Nation under Our Feet: Black Political Struggles in the Rural South from Slavery to the Great Migration* (Cambridge, Mass.: Harvard University Press, 2003), 414–40.

6. African Americans comprised approximately 33 percent of all farmers in the South, a far greater percentage than in either the North or West; Girard T. Bryant, "The Populist Movement and the Negro," M.A. thesis, University of Kansas, Lawrence, 1938, 122; Bureau of the Census, *Report on the Productions of Agriculture*, Department of the Interior, 11th Census (Washington, D.C.: Government Printing Office, 1895), 118–19.

7. William Edward Spriggs, "The Virginia Colored Farmers Alliance: A Case Study of Race and Class Identity," *Journal of Negro History* 64, no. 3 (Summer 1979): 203–4. Law-

rence D. Rice gives a brief description of the Colored Farmers Association in *The Negro in Texas, 1874–1900* (Baton Rouge: Louisiana State University Press, 1971), 179.

8. Debra A. Reid, *Reaping a Greater Harvest: African Americans, the Extension Service, and Rural Reform in Jim Crow Texas* (College Station: Texas A&M University Press, 2007), 1–21; Bernice R. Fine, "Agrarian Reform and the Texas Negro Farmers, 1886–1896," M.A. thesis, North Texas State University, 1971, 81–82; Robert Carroll, "Robert Lloyd Smith and the Farmers' Improvement Society of Texas," M.A. thesis, Baylor University, 1974.

9. Edward L. Ayers, *The Promise of the New South: Life after Reconstruction* (New York: Oxford University Press, 1993), 154–55.

10. One report came from Macon, Georgia, where the Rev. E. F. Love offered a resolution for the formation of cooperative associations, cooperative farms, and storehouses. He said, at a meeting of 350 African Americans, "There is no reason why the Negro should not control the Negro trade and handle the money the Negro has to spend." *Atlanta Constitution*, April 3, 1888; Bryant, "Populist Movement," 23.

11. Goodwyn, *The Populist Moment: A Short History of the Agrarian Revolt in America* (New York: Oxford University Press, 1978) 122.

12. Colored Farmers' National Alliance and Co-Operative Union, *Ritual of the Colored Farmers' National Alliance and Co-Operative Union of the United States* (Houston: Culmore Brothers, c. 1889).

13. Humphrey, "History," 288–92; Spriggs, "Virginia Colored Farmers," 194–95; Gaither, *Blacks and the Populist Revolt* (1977), 1–16.

14. *Ritual of the Colored Farmers' National Alliance*, 9.

15. Humphrey, "History," 290.

16. See Ali, *In the Lion's Mouth*, 160–64.

17. *Southern Mercury*, December 13, 1888; Bryant, "Populist Movement," 23.

18. The *National Alliance* was published in Houston from 1889 through 1891 and served as the national publishing organ of the Colored Alliance; the *Midland Express* was published in Boydton as the official Virginia Colored Alliance publishing organ, beginning in 1891 and continuing through 1893; and the *Alliance Advocate* was published in Oxford around 1890 for the North Carolina Colored Alliance. In addition to these newspapers, there is a reference made by the Colored Alliance superintendent for North Carolina, J. J. Rogers, in a letter he wrote to the *Progressive Farmer*, that the order launched an official newspaper called the *Colored Alliance* in Dallas in July of 1888. See *Progressive Farmer*, July 31, 1888, noted in Dickson, "Out of the Lion's Mouth," 84–85.

19. Spriggs, "Virginia Colored Farmers," 194.

20. William F. Holmes, "The Demise of the Colored Farmers' Alliance," *Journal of Southern History* 41, no. 2 (May 1975): 187–200; Dickson, "Out of the Lion's Mouth," 140.

21. Philip S. Foner and Ronald L. Lewis, *The Black Worker during the Era of the Knights of Labor* (Philadelphia, Pa.: Temple University Press, 1978), 423.

22. As was the case with most Black Populists, Humphrey died in obscurity, in his case in Texas in 1906; Ellis A. Davis and Edwin H. Grobe, eds., *The New Encyclopedia of Texas*, 2 vols. (Dallas: Texas Development Bureau, 1925), 648. Dickson, "Out of the Lion's Mouth," 76. Floyd J. Miller, "Black Protest and White Leadership: A Note on the Colored Farmers Alliance," *Phylon* 33, no. 2 (2nd Qtr., 1972), 170. William Warren Rogers, *The One-Gallused*

Rebellion: Agrarianism in Alabama, 1865–1896 (Baton Rouge: Louisiana State University Press, 1970). Yanosky, "The Colored Farmers' Alliance and the Single Tax," 1–13.

23. Humphrey, "History," 288–92; Humphrey published *The Farmer's Alliance History and Agricultural Digest* (1891), edited the weekly *National Alliance* newspaper for two years beginning in 1889; made occasional press statements; and provided testimony to the Senate Committee on Agriculture and Forestry in 1890; see the *National Economist,* June 7, 1890. See letters in the *Southern Mercury* and the *National Economist* for names of newly appointed business agents, reports from the organization's cooperative efforts in Virginia and South Carolina, and its public political activities—such as those at the Ocala convention of black and white Alliances in December of 1890 and at the People's Party meeting in St. Louis in February of 1892.

24. Robert Lloyd Smith, founder of the Farmers' Improvement Society of Texas, was one among a number of black leaders who urged economic cooperation for the betterment of black farmers. See Debra A. Reid, "African Americans, Community Building, and the Role of the State in Rural Reform in Texas, 1890s–1930s, in *The Countryside in the Age of the Modern State,* Catherine McNichol Stock and Robert D. Johnston, eds. (Ithaca, N.Y.: Cornell University Press, 2001), 43–45.

25. Ibid., 289.

26. Holmes, "Demise," 187.

27. The issue of black agricultural indebtedness, or "debt peonage," is outlined in a number of southern histories, including Ayers's *The Promise of the New South* and C. Vann Woodward's *The Origins of the New South, 1877–1913* (Baton Rouge, Louisiana State University Press, 1951; rev. ed., 1972).

28. *Weekly Toiler,* July 1, 1888; Gaither, *Blacks and the Populist Revolt* (1977), 7.

29. Holmes, "Demise," 188.

30. *National Economist,* January 25, 1890.

31. *Atlanta Constitution,* December 4, 1890; *Raleigh Progressive Farmer,* December 23, 1890. The other 486,000 claimed members lived in nineteen states.

32. *Cleveland Gazette,* July 18, 1891; Jack Abramowitz, "Accommodation and Militancy in Negro Life, 1876–1916," Ph.D. diss., Columbia University, 1950, 30.

33. For a critical discussion about the limitations of the concept of race in U.S. history see Barbara J. Fields, "Ideology and Race in American History," in *Region, Race, and Reconstruction: Essays in Honor of C. Vann Woodward,* ed. J. Morgan Kousser and James M. McPherson (New York: Oxford University Press, 1982), 143–77.

34. Miller, "Black Protest," 172.

35. Omar H. Ali, "The Making of a Black Populist: A Tribute to the Rev. Walter A. Pattillo," *Oxford Public Ledger* 121, no. 25 (March 28, 2002).

36. Pattillo is listed in the 1880 U.S. Census (Tenth Census) as a "mulatto," a minister and teacher, twenty-nine years old, married, and the head of his household; Sassafras Town, Granville, NC Film 1254965, T9-0965, 483C. Personal communication from Pattillo's great-grandson, Dr. Walter H. Pattillo at his home in Durham, North Carolina, July 14, 2001.

37. According to the 1870 Granville County Census, Pattillo worked on a farm. See Moses W. Williams and George W. Watkins, *Who's Who Among North Carolina Negro Baptists* (Alexandria, Va.: Chadwyck-Healey, 1940), 344.

38. LaRue P. Cunningham, "The Negro in Granville County, North Carolina, as Reflected in the Oxford Public Ledger and Other Related Sources, 1880–1900," M.A. thesis, Atlanta University, 1972, xi. The 1850 Granville County Census lists 10,975 "Slaves" and "Free Blacks & Mulattoes," compared to 10,383 "Whites"; Barnetta McGhee White's *In Search of Kith and Kin: The History of a Southern Black Family* (Baltimore: Gateway Press, 1986), 11.

39. C. Eric Lincoln and Lawrence H. Mamiya, *The Black Church in the African American Experience* (Durham, N.C.: Duke University Press, 1990), 20–75.

40. Claude R. Trotter et al., *A Splendid Enterprise: History of the General Baptist State Convention of North Carolina* (Raleigh, N.C.: Irving-Swain, 1999), 257.

41. Williams and Watkins, *Who's Who*, 345. In 1870 Pattillo married Mary Ida Hart, and they had twelve children. The information is from a copy of the Pattillo family album of marriages, births, and deaths shown to me by Dr. Walter H. Pattillo Jr. at his home in Durham, North Carolina, on July 14, 2001.

42. *Oxford Torchlight*, June 26, 1883.

43. Robert W. Winston, *It's a Far Cry* (New York: Henry Holt, 1937), 160–61; William A. Mabry, *The Negro in North Carolina Politics since Reconstruction* (Durham, N.C.: Duke University Press, 1940), 22–28.

44. Alan Keith-Lucas, *A Monument to Black Initiative and Courage: Central Children's Home, 1883–1990* (Lexington, N.C.: Wooten, 1991); Williams and Watkins, *Who's Who*, 345; Ali, "Making of a Black Populist"; *Raleigh News and Observer*, September 18, 1886.

45. In addition to editing the *Alliance Advocate*, Pattillo is said to have edited the *Baptist Pilot*; see Williams and Watkins, *Who's Who*, 345.

46. Ibid.

47. Craig Thurtell, "The Fusion Insurgency in North Carolina: Origins to Ascendency, 1876–1896," Ph.D. diss., Columbia University, 1998, 82, 165. Craven County was itself 65 percent African American; Bureau of the Census, *Negro Population 1790–1915* (Washington, D.C.: Government Printing Office, 1918); Thurtell, "Fusion Insurgency," 165, n15.

48. Gaither, *Blacks and the Populist Revolt* (1977), 12; Abramowitz, "Accommodation and Militancy," 30.

49. William W. Rogers, "The Negro Alliance in Alabama," *Journal of Negro History* 45, no. 1 (January 1960): 39–40; *National Economist*, March 14, 1889; Dickson, "Out of the Lion's Mouth," 111–12.

50. Barbara Jeanne Williams, the great-great-granddaughter of Oliver Cromwell, generously shared with me her family stories and documents. In 2001, at the time that I interviewed her, she was a Ph.D. candidate in African history at the University of Chicago.

51. William F. Holmes, "The Leflore County Massacre and the Demise of the Colored Farmers Alliance," *Phylon* 34, no. 3 (3rd. Qtr., 1973), 270.

52. Cromwell is said to have been the "main instigator of the whole affair . . . an ex-convict, formerly of Jackson"; *St. Louis Post-Dispatch*, September 7, 1889.

53. Holmes, "Leflore County Massacre," 267–74.

54. *New Mississippian*, September 4, 1889. The newspaper describes him as a leader of the September 4, 1875, riot in Clinton, Mississippi.

55. Charles Hillman Brough, "The Clinton Riot," in *Publications of the Mississippi Historical Society*, vol. 4, ed. Franklin L. Riley (Oxford, Miss.: Mississippi Historical Society,

1906), 53–63; *Mississippi in 1875: Report of the U.S. Congressional Committee to Inquire into the Mississippi Election of 1876 with Testimony and Evidence* (Washington, D.C.: Government Printing Office, 1876), 2 vols., 1:466–68. The report is also known as the "Boutwell Report," named after the committee's chair, U.S. Senator George S. Boutwell of Massachusetts.

56. On August 15, 2001, Barbara Jeanne Williams shared with me the family story of Cromwell's final days, which her great-aunt had told her in the late 1970s.

57. News reports subsequent to the Leflore County massacre indicate that the Colored Alliance continued to operate in other parts of Mississippi. See the April 11, 1891, *National Economist* report of Mississippi Colored Alliance assistant lecturer "Mr. McAllister"; Herbert Aptheker, ed., *A Documentary History of the Negro People in the United States*. 4 vols. (New York: Carol Press, Citadel, 1989–90), 2:809–10.

58. *Congressional Record*, 51st Congress, Session 1, 5,789–93, 6,538–45, 6,851, 6,869.

59. *Boston Journal*, December 1890.

60. *National Economist*, August 2, 1890; William F. Holmes, "The Southern Farmers' Alliance: The Georgia Experience," *Georgia Historical Quarterly* 72, vo. 4 (Winter 1988): 649.

61. Ayers, *Promise of the New South*, 258.

62. *Kansas City American Citizen*, September 11, 1891; *New York Age*, October 3, 1891; William Gnatz, "The Negro and the Populist Movement in the South," M.A. thesis, University of Chicago, 1961, 114. Abramowitz, "Accommodation and Militancy," 26. See *Prices of Farm Products Received by Producers* (Statistical Bulletin 16, U.S. Department of Agriculture, Annual Report for South and Atlantic and Middle South States, Washington, D.C., 1927) 46, 77, 91, 106, 119, 150, 165, 179, 194, 207, 238.

63. Robert C. McMath Jr. lists the following occupations among white officers of the Farmers Alliances in the South in 1890: "Farmer (undifferentiated)" (35.78 percent), "Small farmer" (8.42 percent), and "Planter" (23.15 percent). See Robert C. McMath, Jr., *Populist Vanguard: A History of the Southern Farmers Alliance* (Chapel Hill: University of North Carolina Press, 1975): 163; Robert C. McMath Jr., "Southern White Farmers and the Organization of Black Farm Workers: A North Carolina Document," *Labor History* 18, no. 1 (Winter 1977): 115–19.

64. C. Vann Woodward, *Tom Watson, Agrarian Rebel* (1938; repr., New York: Oxford University Press, 1969), 219; *Raleigh Progressive Farmer*, September 15, 1891; Jack Abramowitz, "Accommodation and Militancy," 44.

65. That the white Alliance leadership never objected to the Landlord-Tenant Act, which discriminated against those without property, underscores their bias against agricultural laborers, black and white; Thurtell, "Fusion Insurgency," 85.

66. Raleigh *Progressive Farmer*, September 15, 1891; *Caucasian*, September 17, 1891.

67. *Cleveland Gazette*, September 26, 1891; Aptheker, *Documentary History*, 810.

68. William F. Holmes, "The Arkansas Cotton Pickers Strike of 1891 and the Demise of the Colored Farmers' Alliance," *Arkansas Historical Quarterly* 32, no. 2 (Summer 1973), 114. Ali, *In the Lion's Mouth*, 99.

69. *Arkansas Gazette*, October 3, 1891, reprinted in Philip S. Foner and Ronald L. Lewis, eds., *The Black Worker: A Documentary History from Colonial Times to the Present*, vol. 3:

The Black Worker during the Era of the Knights of Labor (Philadelphia: Temple University Press, 1978), 361–62.

70. George B. Tindall, *South Carolina Negroes, 1877–1900* (Columbia: University of South Carolina Press, 1952), 119; McMath, "Southern White Farmers," 117; Holmes, "Arkansas," 115–17.

71. Dickson, "Out of the Lion's Mouth," 158; Holmes, "Arkansas," 117.

72. Holmes, "Demise."

73. Omar H. Ali, "Colored Farmers Alliance," in *The Encyclopedia of African American Culture and History*, ed. Jack Salzman et. al. (New York: Macmillan, 2001), 57.

74. "Standing Guard at the Door of Liberty: Black Populism in South Carolina, 1886–1897," *South Carolina Historical Magazine* 107, no. 3 (July 2006): 190–203; *Atlanta Constitution*, September 1 and 12, 1890, and October 6, 1892; Jack Abramowitz, "The Negro in the Populist Movement," *Journal of Negro History* 38, no. 3 (July 1953): 259; James C. Bonner, "The Alliance Legislature of 1890," in *Studies in Georgia History and Government*, ed. James C. Bonner and Lucien E. Roberts (Athens: University of Georgia Press, 1940), 163.

75. *Cleveland Gazette*, September 20, 1890.

76. The black delegate L. D. Laurent, for instance, appeared on the call that was issued at the end of the St. Louis convention in February of 1892 for a People's Party convention in Omaha; *National Economist*, March 5, 1892.

77. Miller, "Black Protest," 173.

78. *National Economist*, March 7, 1891; Omar H. Ali, "John L. Moore's 'In the Lion's Mouth'" in *Milestone Documents in African American History: Exploring the Essential Primary Sources*, vol. 2: *1853–1900*, ed. Paul Finkelman (Dallas, Tex.: Schlager Group, 2010), 803–13.

6

"The Lazarus of American Farmers"

The Politics of Black Agrarianism in the Jim Crow South, 1921–1938

JAROD ROLL

"Farmers skilled and trained at the calling" was the way a group of African American settlers in Kingfisher County, Oklahoma, described themselves in 1894. Claiming to be leaders of "that class of energetic, enthusiastic, frugal, industrious, and hard-working farming talent," they had moved to Oklahoma "to populate and settle this vast, vacant, invaluable and productive soil."[1] Thirty years later, black farmers in that area and throughout the South would cast their allegiances almost exclusively with Marcus Garvey's Universal Negro Improvement Association (UNIA), an organization that believed, according to an editorial in its newspaper *Negro World*, "in the farmer and in ownership in the soil as the most independent life."[2] By the 1930s many of them would join the National Federation of Colored Farmers (NFCF), an organization that promoted land ownership, cooperative purchase and marketing schemes, and general economic independence among rural African Americans.[3] "You farmers are producers," the NFCF assured its members in 1933. "As such, you are constantly adding to the wealth of the nation . . . making America a better country, a richer country, a happier country."[4] Well after 1900, then, tens of thousands of African American farmers in the South shared and invested in a faith that farming offered a means to autonomy and prosperity, for individuals and for the commonwealth, whether defined as the United States or a black nation. Their ideas about the meaning and role of rural work—for individuals, for families, for communities, and ultimately for the race—defined the shape and direction of their politics in the first three and a half decades of the twentieth century.

Recent scholarly explorations into the social, economic, and cultural aspects of rural black life after 1900 have provided a nuanced rejoinder to the narrow view that the history of African American farmers in the South was a "depressing story of degradation, poverty, and hopelessness for the men, women, and children who lived in desperation and without alternatives."[5] This essay builds on that new work by examining the political manifestations of black agrarianism in the period between the Great Migration and the Great Depression. Despite all of the limiting factors that confronted them, black farmers sustained well into the 1930s an idealized agrarian vision, rooted in the rural black movements of the late nineteenth century, which held sacred the right of small producers to independent livelihoods on the land they worked, a way of life that "shaped a core of common values of hard work, self-sufficiency, and mutual aid," as historian Melissa Walker put it. This producerist belief system, shared in many respects by white farmers in this period, gave ideological structure to black farmers' sense of individual and collective purpose that, in turn, linked the present and future to the past by means of "a sense of identity, a sense of historical and religious tradition."[6]

According to the rural black version of this tradition, it was the faithful performance of productive labor, and the value of that production to the nation, that would enable African Americans to overcome the injustices that constrained their lives. Black farmers across the South, but particularly in the region's western half, believed that if they worked hard enough they could become self-sufficient, purchase property, and ultimately free themselves from white interference. As was the case for many Americans, work legitimated citizenship and rights but it also promised the redemption of individuals and ultimately of the race from a history of oppression. Although this was a common belief, it was also an ideal one that only a small minority of black farmers ever actually achieved. Most remained landless and poor but nevertheless committed to the potential power of productive work on the land to transform their lives. As the way to either full American citizenship or an independent nation, an idealized black agrarianism fixed the imaginations of the majority—landowners and landless alike— and dominated rural black politics well into the 1930s as southern farmers threw support behind Garvey's UNIA and later the NFCF.

In the 1920s thousands of African Americans in the rural and small town South sought their future in the UNIA. Of the 1,176 UNIA divisions in the world, more than 500 were found in southern states; that is, the old Confederacy plus southern Missouri, Oklahoma, and West Virginia. The majority of these—354 divisions—took root in farming communities, with the largest concentration of Garveyite sentiment located in the Mississippi River Valley; in southwestern Georgia; in the coastal communities of Virginia and the Carolinas; and in the all-black settlements of Oklahoma and Texas (map 6.1). While most of these divisions were small—anywhere from seven to fifty members willing to pay the requisite monthly dues of sixty cents—those who joined carried considerable influence in their communities. Rural Garveyites came from the elite of rural black life; they were prosperous men (and some women), usually over thirty-five years of age, who were small landowners, successful renters, aspiring sharecroppers, teachers, and preachers who headed family, work, and religious groups. Younger farmers who were less well-off also attended UNIA meetings but without becoming official members.[7]

As Garveyites, these farmers saw themselves as key actors in a collective movement that promised the autonomy of black people worldwide. Founded in Jamaica in 1914, the UNIA attracted wide support after Garvey arrived in Harlem in 1916. From there he transformed the UNIA into a global movement to realize an independent nation that would promote and defend the rights and livelihoods of all black people, in Africa and the diaspora. This message captured a sense of urgency among African Americans after World War I. "Whatsoever my future is to be is my own creation," Garvey and his followers concluded, and "as of the individual so of the race." As noted in *Negro World*, they perceived themselves as "the leaders in the social, the civil and the business life of" their communities.[8]

The UNIA reinforced and reinvigorated efforts to find freedom working the land. Although it attracted farmers of all tenures, from sharecroppers on up, Garveyism was strongest in communities anchored by significant numbers of landowners, places like Beaufort and Georgetown, South Carolina, Pike County, Mississippi, and Okfuskee County, Oklahoma. Farmers in these areas were part of the mass migration of black people who between 1880 and 1920 sought new land to settle and claim as their own. The sense of individual and collective mission that Garveyism celebrated was especially resonant with black farmers in the cotton southwest—Arkansas, Mississippi, Missouri, and Oklahoma—where there were 134 UNIA divisions.[9] These divisions were among the largest, most active of all those in the rural South. As historian Mary Rolinson has noted, the Garveyites in these places also "showed more outward signs of upward economic mobility"

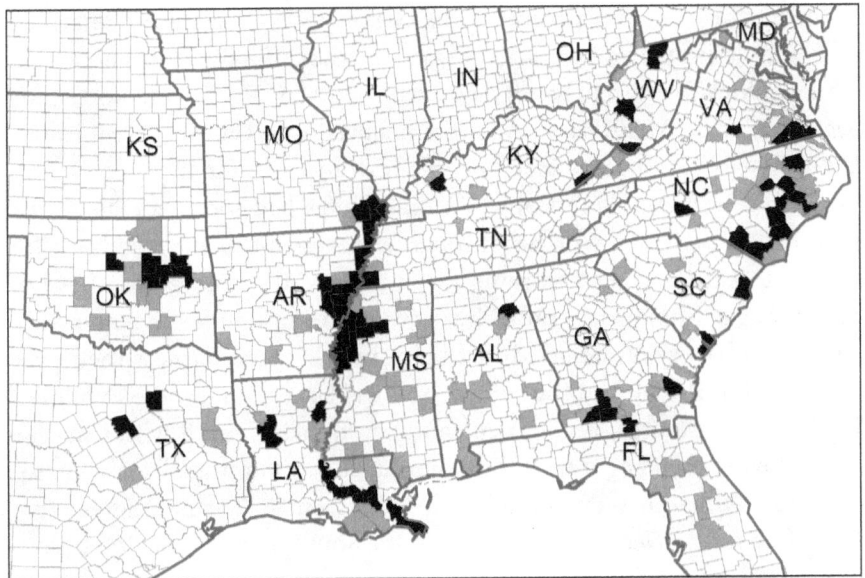

Map 6.1. County distribution of UNIA divisions in the rural South, 1920–35. Counties shaded black had two or more divisions, while those shaded gray had one division. Source: Robert A Hill et al., eds., *The Marcus Garvey and Universal Negro Improvement Association Papers*, 10 vols. (Berkeley: University of California Press, 1983–2006), 7:986–96; and the Membership Records Card File, 1925–27, UNIA Central Division Records, box 22B, MSS 20, Schomburg Center for Research in Black Culture, New York Public Library, Harlem. Map drawn by David C. Viertel, Department of Geography and Geology, Eastern Illinois University.

than those in eastern states.[10] They had initially marked out homesteads in the wooded backcountry of Mississippi's Yazoo Delta in the 1880s. The all-black community of Mound Bayou in Bolivar County, for example, achieved considerable self-reliance and prosperity. By 1907 it consisted of over 800 families that together owned more than 30,000 acres of land.[11] In the 1920s farmers in Bolivar County created nineteen separate UNIA divisions, the most of any county anywhere in the United States. The community of Mound Bayou had two.[12]

Adhering to the logic of producerism, rural Garveyites stressed the centrality of individual work to the quest for the collective independence of the race. The tradition of producerism was a strong one among southern African Americans, particularly associated with support for the Colored Farmers Alliance and Booker T. Washington. "Self-reliance is the key to human progress," wrote a Garveyite from Plantersville, Alabama. "The Negro is learning to stand upon his own feet and fight his way to the top by his own efforts," he concluded.[13] Rural Garveyites almost always described their activities using a language of work or labor. "Blytheville is up and at work, looking forward to better days," reported M. L. Poole from northeastern Arkansas.[14] Many rural followers believed that Garvey's significance lay in his ability to show black people how to work for themselves. The problem of African Americans was that whites had too often stolen the products of their toil, whether through enslavement or the frauds of Jim Crow. "It is time to start working for ourselves," declared Louisa Love of Hermondale, Missouri, because "we have been working for the other race so long."[15] Garveyites believed that black people could harness their productive labor if they had the correct political education. Mollie Bynum of Blytheville, Arkansas, urged inculcating rural black youth with Garvey's ideas "before they begin to work in jobs at starvation wages" for whites.[16] Precocious thirteen-year-old Robert Jones of Acmar, Alabama, agreed that it "is time for we Negroes down here in the South to get on the job to save our race."[17]

In the Garveyite interpretation of agrarianism, work on behalf of the race was not just a practical means to achieve autonomy but a religious duty that God would reward. "Faith without works," Arkansan Bennie Bember said, quoting the Epistle of James, "is dead."[18] This was in line with Garvey's own thinking as well as the producerist tradition. "God is not going to save you," Garvey preached. "He has given you a life to live, and if you do not exercise your own will in your own behalf you will be lost."[19] A better world for black people would come only through the faithful toil of black people. God had made it this way, and there could be no alternative. A Rev. Johnson preached to the members of the Wyatt, Missouri, division "in strong terms of the Negro depending upon God to do for them that which they themselves can do."[20] He argued that if they wanted more, they would have to get it themselves. Fellow Missourian E. W. Pinkard concurred. "A man who thinks that he is fitted for something better and is willing to work and suffer to get it," he told readers of the *Negro World*, "will eventually reach a higher plane."[21] Such an interpretation of the outcome of Garveyism stoked a sense of empowerment as well as responsibility. A three-day UNIA convention in Pine City, Arkansas, included two talks that hammered this point home: "Faithful to Duty" and "Get out of the Rut of Slothfulness and Shiftiness and Look to a Higher Thing."[22] Black tenant farmers in the Jim Crow South were telling themselves, not simply *being* told, that only they could save themselves. Neither God nor Garvey would do it for them. "Praying alone for justice won't get justice, and praying alone for a government won't get you a government," Bember wrote. "It makes no difference how much faith you have in God," he concluded, "if you make no effort to get it you will never get justice. . . . You must put forth some effort."[23]

As opposed to earlier iterations in the programs of Booker T. Washington and Black Populism, Garveyite agrarianism lent new world-changing significance to the struggles of farmers to acquire property and establish family and community autonomy. This was especially important and appealing to those who held on to a rural way of life despite the Great Migration of black people to urban areas, and despite the injustices of Jim Crow and the continuation of white racial violence. The *Negro World* emphatically endorsed this position in 1925 when it quoted the black editor of the *Cotton Farmer*, who denounced "Negro agitators," such as members of the National Association for the Advancement of Colored People (NAACP), who protested for political equality and encouraged southern blacks to leave "their manner born homes, where we have priority to many lines of endeavor, especially the production of cotton and yes, oftimes their own lands." "We believe in the farmer and in ownership in the soil as the most independent life," read another *Negro World* editorial. "The readers of The Negro World everywhere are advised to own land wherever they can and to raise their own home supplies, and thus become independent of the country storekeeper and the credit system." In other words, Garveyites in Harlem argued that the best thing for race leaders worldwide to do for the collective independence of black people was the same thing that tens of thousands of southern black farmers were doing: trying to acquire property and land. Aspiring farmers who either owned land or believed that it was within their reach would no doubt have read in this message powerful validation of their own efforts; in their minds, farmers were model race leaders, model Garveyites. As a result, Garveyite agrarianism promised solutions far more fundamental than those offered by Washington or the Colored Farmers Alliance. "The example set by Mound Bayou," a lead editorial stated in 1929, "is more far-reaching than the mere proving of the right to American citizenship" because it exemplified the one virtue that the UNIA, and countless farmers, heralded most: "self-reliance, which not only develops strength of character and power of achievement, but safeguards ownership." If members of the race would follow the example set forth by the farmers around Mound Bayou, "Africans 'at home and abroad' are bound to come into their own some day."[24]

As a result, rural Garveyites eschewed direct political protest. The NAACP could claim almost no presence in areas of UNIA strength in the

1920s, not because people were afraid to join but because they did not believe in its aims and tactics. The UNIA lauded the work of aspiring farmers, who invested their money, always in short supply, and their political effort in the cause. Confident, like Garvey, that the United States would always remain a white man's country, Garveyite farmers often looked to secure the endorsement of leading whites for their efforts to achieve racial separation. In 1925, for example, Garveyites near Blytheville, Arkansas, gained the "sympathetic consideration of the town authorities" who praised Garveyism "as being very good for the race."[25] There is evidence that some leading whites extended more than words to rural Garveyites. In 1923 white landowners in southeast Missouri, some of whom were Klan members, successfully petitioned Governor Arthur Hyde to deploy the state guard to protect black farmers from violent assaults by poor whites. He did, and the attacks stopped. The rural black communities the state defended were home to three UNIA divisions. While the motives behind this episode remain murky, it is not hard to imagine why white landowners would aid black farmers who were eager to work hard and belonged to an organization that preached the importance of productive labor.[26] An agrarian faith in the redemptive power of productive work encouraged rural Garveyites to seek détente with leading whites in order to build self-sufficient economic strength that they hoped would one day lead to political independence.

Still, the UNIA collapsed in the late 1920s. Garvey's imprisonment in 1925 and ultimate deportation in 1927 decapitated the organization, which devolved into sectarian strife. At the same time, southern farmers reeled from a succession of disasters: the collapse of commodity prices in 1926, the Mississippi River flood of 1927, the water-logged years of 1928–29, and the stock market crash of 1929. Most rural UNIA divisions failed as members stopped paying dues, moved away, or simply quit.[27]

The demise of the UNIA, however, did not mean the death of black agrarianism. As the UNIA collapsed, farmers looked to a relatively new organization, the NFCF, to advocate their beliefs in hard work, economic independence, and self-reliance. Founded in 1922 in Chicago and granted a corporate charter by the state of Illinois in 1930, the black-led NFCF promoted cooperative marketing and purchase schemes, diversified agriculture, and the values of land ownership. Although limited primarily to farmers on the midwestern prairies until 1929, the organization attracted thousands of members across the South when it began publishing a newsletter, the *Modern Farmer*, and receiving regular coverage in the *Chicago Defender*. By August 1930, when members of the NFCF's fifty local units in

Mississippi hosted their first state convention, the group boasted of units in Alabama, Arkansas, Georgia, and Tennessee. By early 1932 the NFCF had added local units in Louisiana and in southeast Missouri, where "150 Race farmers" organized their unit that February. Like the members of the UNIA, these farmers were ambitious for prosperity on the land and carried influence in their communities disproportionate to their numbers.[28]

The NFCF achieved broad regional support because it gave new political focus to the idealized black agrarianism that Garveyism had strengthened and sharpened in the 1920s. As the NFCF's primary goals suggest, it was a selective organization largely of and for successful farmers. The organization's corporate charter committed it to "devote itself to the problems of diversified production, grading, packing, shipping and marketing of farm products" and to enable black farmers to "purchase farm supplies through cooperative methods ... and to own, manage and direct farms."[29] These were strategies for landowners, or perhaps propertied renters, who made profit and controlled the product of their labor at a time when most black farmers were sharecroppers who did not. State leaders of the NFCF did not necessarily farm, but they represented rural business and cultural interests with a stake in farmers' success. Among the state leaders of the NFCF in Louisiana, for example, J. L. Chinn served as president of the local Colored Civic League, Rev. H. M. Madison was a preacher in the African Methodist Episcopal Church (AME), and R. Jones led the "Afro-Americans," a local fraternal organization. Although the Depression had shackled leading farmers with debts, some believed they could retain or regain their autonomy as independent landowners or property-owning tenant farmers. Rev. M. T. Ghess, a founder of the unit in Parma, Missouri, reported that black farmers in his vicinity had raised "excellent crops this season and [predicted] that they will be able to liquidate many old debts and in some instances have a surplus to begin the next season with." They hoped to supplement these efforts by creating "an agricultural credit organization that will enable them to finance themselves."[30]

The emphasis on self-sufficiency and cooperation resembled Garveyite calls for racial solidarity and self-possession. An Alabama member reported how his neighbors preferred NFCF membership to any association with the county extension service of the U.S. Department of Agriculture (USDA), even though it employed a black extension agent. Local whites were "saying things to harm the federation," he reported, because they feared "the organization of our farmers for their advancement and thrift." This farmer assured the federation that his neighbors would not join the

"'Jim Crow' organization" proposed by the extension service because they were happy with the savings they could achieve by organizing their own cooperative purchases and negotiating cooperative sales.[31]

While cooperative schemes were in large part the privilege of only the most secure black farmers, the NFCF also maintained that its objectives would help less fortunate black farmers, even sharecroppers mired in debt. Louisiana members, for example, declared that "when the majority of . . . Colored farmers organize" they would "in a few years free themselves from debt slavery" through the power of cooperative buying and selling based on the Garveyite principle of racial solidarity.[32] The *Negro World* reported favorably on the NFCF strategy in late 1930, declaring that the savings black farmers would achieve through cooperation came "out of the pocket of the local white wholesale or retail merchant from whom the colored farmers have hitherto been purchasing."[33] The NFCF hoped that race-conscious people in cities who had cash would provide an independent market for race-conscious farmers in the South, a scheme that would first help the most independent farmers but would gradually lift all boats. As early as 1930, NFCF-run cooperatives in Georgia began shipping their produce to black buyers in Chicago and reported that "the Colored Merchants association chain stores in New York city are negotiating to purchase several cars of melons."[34]

In some places NFCF units maintained direct links with remaining UNIA divisions. Parma, Missouri, had been home to a resilient UNIA division in the 1920s before members of that community joined the NFCF. The same was true of Mound Bayou, Mississippi, a Garveyite stronghold in the 1920s and host to the NFCF's annual convention in 1931. The *Negro World*'s praise in 1929 for the ethic of racial independence that supported Mound Bayou could just as easily have come from an NFCF official: Mound Bayou was a shining example of the one virtue that black agrarians stressed most, "self-reliance, which not only develops strength of character and power of achievement, but safeguards ownership."[35] The Depression, however, complicated this view of the world because low commodity prices, expensive debt, and bad weather made land ownership harder than ever to sustain, let alone achieve. In 1933, UNIA division 441 in Tylertown, Mississippi, held a joint meeting with the town's NFCF unit to discuss how they should respond to events. The gathering showed not only the connections between the two groups but also how agrarians were struggling to cope with the unfolding economic crisis. Jef Ellzey, a sixty-two-year-old Pike County landowner and head of the local NFCF unit, presided over the meeting, which featured the officers of both groups, all of whom owned land. They were the authorities in their community and their families and all faced the difficult responsibilities of leadership during the Great Depression. According to the report of the meeting in the *Negro World*, Mrs. Jessie Ellzey declared "to the Farmers and the U.N.I.A. People that it is time for you to think hard, and do something for the up-building of this black race of Ours." They concluded that the programs of both the UNIA and the NFCF were essential to the solution, which all present believed lay in cooperation. Rev. E. D. Cain, a local UNIA officer, then preached a sermon to the group to assure them "that if we stick together, and build up our treasures, we can build manufactories and stores." Whether members belonged to both groups was not recorded, but what is clear is that the UNIA and the NFCF together shared a firm belief in the power of hardworking, thrifty, and sober individuals to meet the needs of the race. For UNIA members like R. L. Ginn, president of division 441, the ultimate solution remained "the cause Africa." For NFCF members like Ellzey, Africa was less important so long as black people who had means did something to enhance the autonomy of the race.[36]

As the Depression worsened, however, NFCF members broke from the UNIA belief in racial separatism by calling on national agencies to ensure that rural blacks received the same aid as white farmers. The drought of 1930–31, the worst in living memory, heaped fresh misery upon farmers in Arkansas, Louisiana, Mississippi, Missouri, and Tennessee who were already reeling from the disasters of the late 1920s. When the Red Cross sent relief provisions to Leflore County, Mississippi, local NFCF members protested that county officials denied access to African Americans, explaining "this organization is here to help white only." In a daring step away from UNIA strategy, J. P. Davis, the Georgia-born president of the NFCF, encouraged farmers who had their local applications for assistance rejected to complain to the Red Cross's national office. He promised that "the persons in charge of that branch will be dismissed." Davis did more in the direction of political engagement by applying to the USDA "for further relief." He declared that Secretary of Agriculture Arthur Hyde promised "that no discrimination would be practiced by the government" in the distribution of drought assistance.[37] The reliance on personal assurances from white officials, rather than rights, suggests that although some NFCF members were beginning to look to the government for help, they did so in faith that the governing Republicans would reward their loyalty. Hyde, for one, had helped black farmers as the governor of Missouri in the early 1920s.

Still, elite white southerners answered these rather deferential NFCF efforts with acts of intimidation. Relations between the members of the UNIA and the NFCF and white leaders had been surprisingly peaceful since 1920, mainly because both organizations encouraged black farmers to continue working the land, to focus on the dignity of labor, and, until 1931, not to challenge white political power. In response to the NFCF's claims to Red Cross relief, however, whites in Leflore County arrested a federation leader and warned all blacks that this "pernicious" group would invite "serious trouble" if it persisted. The editor of the Greenwood *Commonwealth*, meanwhile, attacked the main tenets of the federation, asserting that "the Delta Negro farmer is a tenant who must buy and sell as his landlord directs."[38] The *Negro Star*, published in Wichita, Kansas, interpreted this attack as a plain attempt to terrorize "the Negro tenant farmers who had organized into the National Federation of Colored Farmers" and argued that whites sought nothing less than "the enslavement of the Negroes in southern plantations."[39]

Such a public denunciation of the idea of black agrarianism prompted the NFCF to embolden its efforts. In August 1931 the group held its annual convention in Mound Bayou, fifty miles northwest of Greenwood, with "promises to be the biggest meeting of Colored farmers ever held in the United States." Defying threats from whites, the convention was designed to reinforce both the real and the imagined aspects of black agrarianism. In advance of the gathering, "fifty red-blooded Negro farmers of Jeff Davis County, Mississippi," joined the organization "to aid them in marketing of their crops and also to make their purchases co-operatively."[40] Lest there be any confusion about their defiant stance, Rev. B. W. Byram, president of the Bolivar County unit and owner of 160 acres, reaffirmed that "organization is the only salvation" for black farmers. Here and there the NFCF's cooperative plans were working. A unit in Holmes County, Mississippi, for example, bought their groceries collectively in 1931 and saved nearly $500 as a group. To celebrate and honor leading farmers like these, the NFCF created an annual holiday called "Farmers' Sunday," when NFCF members would encourage their preachers to "devote their services on that day to discussions and sermons on farm subjects." "Surely but slowly the Race farmers are waking up to the fact that in union there is strength," one member reported. The NFCF was still very much an organization of the farming elite, but claims like this reflected a growing realization that its members needed government help in addition to their own productive labor in order to achieve their independence.[41]

The convention in Mound Bayou gave the NFCF new national political visibility. In addition to familiar discussion on the benefits of cooperation, delegates debated the possibility of securing farm loans from the federal government. Arthur B. LaCour, field representative of the Federal Farm Board, a price-stabilization agency that President Herbert Hoover created in 1929, delivered a keynote address that spoke directly to how farmers could get more federal help. LaCour voiced support for the aims of the NFCF when he stressed "the importance of the farmer growing enough food to feed his family and stock," the essence of the idea of autonomy that lay at the heart of black agrarian thought.[42] Apparent government sympathy toward the federation seemed to invite greater faith that the Hoover administration would actually provide assistance. At the annual convention the following year in Memphis, the NFCF boasted that "every courtesy and every aid is being extended the organization by some of the highest authorities." The NFCF now believed, president Davis stated, "that united action will give the federation authority to approach the government and business world . . . to justify and obtain recognition, respect and satisfactory returns upon our industry and endeavors." In Memphis the NFCF "pledged itself to work for President Hoover," the same kind of appeal to the patronage of elite whites that Garveyites had often pursued (figure 6.1).[43]

Storming to victory in the November election, Franklin D. Roosevelt rendered this allegiance obsolete but also created new opportunities to advance the cause of black farmers. The flurry of New Deal legislation during Roosevelt's first year encouraged the NFCF to make new demands on the federal government. In June 1933 Leon R. Harris, secretary of the organization, wrote to the USDA in support of the provisions for raising commodity prices contained in the Agricultural Adjustment Act (AAA) passed in May but argued that the government should encourage black farmers, particularly tenants, "to produce their own living" as part of the crop reduction. Harris suggested "that Negro tenants and lessees be given proper encouragement to remain on the farms and eventually become land and home owners." Anticipating later New Deal efforts to house landless farmers on unused land, he also announced that the NFCF was "now planning for development and colonization of some large tracts of land in Arkansas, Louisiana, Mississippi, Texas, and other states" for the benefit of "Race farmers," in this case particularly those without land of their own.[44]

Harris gave fuller shape to the NFCF's developing vision of black agrarian politics in his keynote address to the group's convention in Memphis in

144 · Jarod Roll

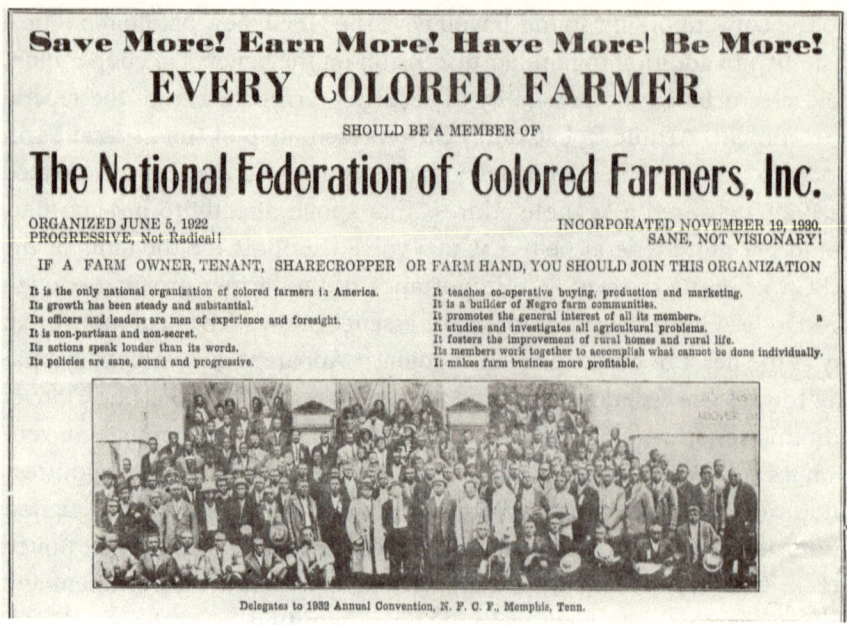

Figure 6.1. The National Federation of Colored Farmers encouraged all black farmers and farm laborers to join the "PROGRESSIVE, Not Radical!; SANE, NOT VISIONARY!" organization, as evidenced by this 1933 promotional broadside. Source: Gov. Guy B. Park Collection, State Historical Society of Missouri, Columbia.

October 1933. "You farmers are producers," he told the delegates. Whereas Garveyites emphasized the role of black production in the creation of a black nation, NFCF members now heard about how their work contributed to the United States. "You are constantly adding to the wealth of the nation. You are making America a better country, a richer country, a happier country." But the logic of agrarian producerism was no longer working. As citizens who engaged in productive labor, Harris asked, "What are you getting?" "You are getting very little from your labor," he answered. The reason, as he saw it, was that black farmers were not working collectively. "You will remain the Lazarus of American farmers and continue getting only the crumbs from the table until you become well organized." The NFCF could not "afford to fail" in its attempts to remedy this since "the destiny of one-half of our Race group in this nation depends on the success and fortune of organized Colored farmers." Harris preached more than just a call for work, however. "We must let the whole nation know what we think about these problems" facing black farmers, he declared, particularly the "evil" of tenancy and the "misery and unhappiness" of men who watched their wives and children toil as "cotton-patch slaves." To fix these things, the NFCF had to "tell all the powers that be, both in government and out of government, that the American Race farmer wants to be a real farmer." In short, Harris's address enunciated a new agrarian protest politics that was based on a claim to citizenship rights legitimated by productive labor.[45]

More important, Harris now argued that the government should not only assist the best farmers but also those who worked hard but suffered crushing dependence as landless farmers due to the injustices of the sharecropping system. The NFCF, like the UNIA before it, had to this point proffered top-down solutions to the problems of black farmers. Harris's statement in late 1933, however, gave forceful new voice to the problems of the poorest among them. It was as bold as any political demand made on behalf of black farmers since the Colored Farmers Alliance in the 1890s and marked a clear break from the politics of the UNIA.

As the economic crisis worsened, the NFCF sharpened calls for government assistance. In October 1934 the Charleston, Missouri, unit of the NFCF, which claimed over two hundred members, "some of whom are progressive owners of good farms," hosted the organization's annual meeting.[46] More than a thousand delegates from twenty-one states gathered at the city's all-black Lincoln High School to discuss the convention theme, whether the New Deal "has been a curse or a blessing to Race farmers."[47] This was not necessarily an idle exercise, since Henry A. Hunt, the assistant to the governor of the Farm Credit Administration (FCA), was in attendance. As a member of Roosevelt's "black cabinet," Hunt could give the NFCF a strong voice in the New Deal administration, but as an official of the FCA, an agency set up to prevent farm foreclosures, Hunt's real power might only benefit farm owners.[48]

Not yet ready to condemn the Roosevelt administration outright, the NFCF was nevertheless developing a more robust stance on racial equality in public policy to go alongside its more forceful calls for government support of black farmers. In the run-up to the 1934 convention, secretary Harris announced that "the organization fights debt-slavery, injustice, and persecution. It is the only national farm organization," he declared, "in which the Race farmer has a voice and a vote."[49] The resolutions of the Charleston convention called on the government to reinforce the goals of black agrarians by establishing "at least one model Race farm community in each southern and border state," a demand that resembled proposals, albeit not race specific, then circulating in the Federal Emergency Relief Administration. While they praised the government for appointing people like Hunt, the delegates demanded wholesale change in New Deal farm policy, beginning with the "repeal or important revision of the Bankhead Act," the 1934 iteration of the AAA that mandated a 40 percent reduction in cotton production on all farms. The crop reduction hurt landowners, as did the abuses of white planters, who manipulated the law to deprive tenants and sharecroppers of their share of the subsidy the government awarded as compensation for reducing acreages. Finally, and most succinctly, the NFCF "requested that every effort be made by the government to widen land ownership by Race farmers."[50]

Despite its adoption of more forthright political demands that were sensitive to class differences among black farmers, the NFCF lost strength as the Depression wore on. Its continued insistence on land ownership and cooperative schemes as the primary solution to the ills of black farmers provided an increasingly unconvincing answer to the poor and landless, despite the government's creation of the Resettlement Administration (RA) in early 1935 with the power to build model communities to resettle impoverished farm families, something the NFCF had advocated. Apparent successes like the RA or the sympathy of Hunt and the FCA proved too little, too limited, and too late for the NFCF. The organization's meetings became smaller after 1934 and finally stopped altogether in 1939.[51]

By late 1934 a range of other farmer's organizations offered far more militant solutions aimed directly at landless farmers and casual farm wage workers. The communist-led Share Croppers' Union (SCU) had boasted strong support in several Alabama counties since 1931 but achieved a greater regional presence in 1935 when it facilitated the creation of the Louisiana Farmers' Union (LFU). Locally these two unions built robust support almost solely among tenant farmers and sharecroppers around strident demands, made through collective action, for the reform of the government's AAA legislation, higher wages for casual field labor, and greater government attention to the living conditions and physical health of the rural poor.[52] At the same time, the Southern Tenant Farmers' Union (STFU), formed in 1934 in eastern Arkansas at the instigation of white socialists, grew quickly into the most consequential rural labor union in the South. With tens of thousands of members, African American and white, across Arkansas, Mississippi, Oklahoma, Tennessee, and Missouri, the STFU took direct and indirect action to demand better wages and living conditions and new reform legislation. The STFU's strikes and lobbying campaigns placed the plight of the rural poor at the forefront of national political discussions by the summer of 1935 and, among other things, led to the 1937 transformation of the RA into the Farm Security Administration (FSA), with a far more expansive brief to improve the lives of landless farmers, including programs to encourage scientific farming, land ownership, self-sufficiency, cooperative ventures, and community government. The NFCF had called for something similar to the FSA since 1933, but it was the direct protest tactics of groups like the STFU that made it happen. The STFU, SCU, and LFU bypassed the NFCF as the political voice of black farmers because they spoke to the needs of the vast majority who were tenants, sharecroppers, and wage hands rather than the minority who owned land or property.[53]

Outflanked by rural working-class groups on the left, the NFCF also lost ground to the NAACP as the leader on racial issues among rural blacks. The federation's calls for cooperative farming and self-sufficiency had always rested on a black nationalist premise that African American communities could achieve and sustain their own autonomy by the diligent husbandry of their own resources. While the group amended that view as the Depression worsened, the NFCF remained self-consciously a black-led organization serving the interests of the most prosperous black farmers. It was willing to deal with leading whites but always as an agent of people who desired their independence.

As nationalist sentiment drained away in the mid-1930s, however, the NAACP experienced renewed membership growth throughout the rural South among landed and landless farmers because of its direct demands for government action on a range of issues, from civil rights to economic rights. At the NAACP's Southern Regional Conference in Mobile, Alabama, in early 1936, delegates from local branches in Alabama, Florida, Georgia, Louisiana, and Mississippi publicly pledged themselves to fight for "full citizenship, better living conditions and equal rights" for all African Americans, particularly in the South. The NAACP attacked Jim Crow on the one hand and poverty on the other. "We encourage farm ownership, scientific farming and cooperative marketing among Negroes. We endorse and pledge our support to the tenant farmers, white and black, in their efforts to organize for mutual protection and raise the standard of living among farmers in the South [and] urgently request the Federal Government to investigate conditions of tenant farming, and the failure of the sharecroppers and tenants to receive their fair share of benefits under the New Deal agricultural program."[54] Neither the UNIA nor the NFCF had ever gone so far, but the NFCF had signposted the paths that the unions and the NAACP now traveled at its expense.

Rather than embrace the more militant mood, the leaders of the federation turned more cautious in the mid-1930s by seeking not the support of poor blacks but rather the favor of rich whites. The federation held its 1935 convention in Little Rock, Arkansas, where Mayor R. E. Overman "assured his support" and was invited to give the welcoming address. The following year, when the federation returned its annual convention to Charleston, Missouri, only five hundred people attended, half as many as in 1934. The delegates condemned tenancy and sharecropping but reveled in a telegram from Secretary of Agriculture Henry Wallace, who wrote that the NFCF's "cooperative efforts for the common good deserve the commendation of all who are interested in the welfare of agriculture." Wallace went on to express admiration for black farmers "whose whole-hearted cooperation" in the AAA had made it so "successful." That most black farmers were forced to participate and that only a very few considered the AAA to be anything other than a travesty seemed lost on both Wallace and the NFCF. If delegates thought otherwise, they kept it quiet, no doubt because there were so many leading white people in attendance. E. E. Oliver, the mayor of Charleston, gave the welcoming address. Other speakers included official representatives from Governor Junius M. Futrell of Arkansas, Governor Eugene Talmadge of Georgia, and the AAA, including a message from Cully Cobb, who headed the Cotton Section. None of these were thought to be friends to the landless farmers who joined groups like the STFU.[55]

Once considered a dangerous threat, the NFCF, and to some extent the UNIA, now appeared to be safe representatives for white politicians to endorse. The NFCF's embrace of government crop reduction schemes and dedication to encourage landless people "to purchase farms and to build better homes" made a welcome contrast to combative, grassroots demands for justice from rural unions on behalf of sharecroppers. White elites also heaped praise on the vestiges of southern Garveyism. In March 1936 Joseph Gray, a leading Garveyite in Charleston, Missouri, went before the all-white city council and "presented the program so intelligently that the Mayor [E. E. Oliver] and officials endorsed his work there with the UNIA."[56] The problem, of course, was that by the end of 1936 neither the UNIA nor the NFCF could boast of any support whatsoever among the majority of black farmers. By the summer of 1936 the STFU had the political momentum after it forced Governor Futrell of Arkansas, through protest and strikes, to set up a state commission to study and remedy the problem of landlessness. No wonder Futrell fawned over the NFCF.[57]

The agrarian certainties of Garveyites and NFCF supporters failed in the end, but that should not reduce our appraisal of the appeal or power of those certainties in their own time. As the agricultural economy underwent intense centralization and mechanization in the late 1930s, black farmers of all classes and tenure levels would find in the wreckage of their agrarian beliefs the resources with which to meet new political realities and opportunities. Determined to work but unable to because of structural change in agriculture, black farmers articulated a new demand that they, as American citizens, had the right to earn a living wage and that the government had a duty to help them exercise that right. If the government ensured them a fair chance, black farmers argued, they could contribute their best efforts to the nation, as workers and citizens.

Notes

1. Daniel F. Littlefield Jr. and Lonnie E. Underhill, "Black Dreams and 'Free' Homes: The Oklahoma Territory, 1891–1894," *Phylon* 34 (1973): 354–55 (quote).

2. "Our Farmers Should Raise Their Home Supplies," *Negro World*, January 23, 1926.

3. "Charleston Gets 1934 National N.F.C.F. Convention," *Charleston Spokesman*, August 25, 1934.

4. "What This Country Needs Is New Blood in Our Biggest Business: Help the Farmer and the Race Problems Will Pass Out," *Chicago Defender*, November 11, 1933.

5. These important works include Mary G. Rolinson, *Grassroots Garveyism: The Universal Negro Improvement Association in the Rural South, 1920–1927* (Chapel Hill: University of North Carolina Press, 2007); Debra A. Reid, *Reaping a Greater Harvest: African Americans, the Extension Service, and Rural Reform in Jim Crow Texas* (College Station: Texas A&M Press, 2007); Melissa Walker, *Southern Farmers and Their Stories: Memory and Meaning in Oral History* (Lexington: University Press of Kentucky, 2006); Steven Hahn, *A Nation under Our Feet: Black Political Struggles in the Rural South from Slavery to the Great Migration* (Cambridge: Belknap Press of Harvard University Press, 2003), 457–76; Valerie Grim, "African American Landlords in the Rural South, 1870–1950," *Agricultural History* 72 (Spring 1998): 405–16; and Loren Schweninger, *Black Property Owners in the South, 1790–1915* (Urbana: University of Illinois Press, 1990), 162–64, 208. For the "depressing story," see R. Douglas Hurt, "Introduction," in Hurt, ed., *African American Life in the Rural South, 1900–1950* (Columbia: University of Missouri Press, 2003), 1 (quote).

6. Walker, *Southern Farmers and Their Stories*, 216 (first quote); M. Thomas Inge, ed., *Agrarianism in American Literature* (New York: Odyssey, 1969), xiv (second quote). See also Reid, *Reaping a Greater Harvest*, xxi–xxii; Bruce Palmer, *"Man over Money": The Southern Populist Critique of American Capitalism* (Chapel Hill: University of North Carolina Press, 1980), 3–8; and Jarod Roll, *Spirit of Rebellion: Labor and Religion in the New Cotton South* (Urbana: University of Illinois Press, 2010), 1–10.

7. "Locations of UNIA Divisions and Chapters," in Robert A. Hill, ed., *The Marcus*

Garvey and Universal Negro Improvement Association Papers, vol. 7 (Berkeley: University of California Press, 1991), 986–96; Roll, *Spirit of Rebellion*, 52–75 (for younger farmers who attended meetings, see p. 65).

8. "U.N.I.A., Nearing the Greatest World Conference of Race, Calls upon Negroes Everywhere to Rise Up and Be Men," *Negro World*, April 27, 1929 (first quote); "Preach the Gospel of Conservation of Race Resources," *Negro World*, August 13, 1927 (second quote).

9. "Locations of UNIA Divisions and Chapters," in Hill, *Marcus Garvey*, 7:986–96.

10. Rolinson, *Grassroots Garveyism*, 109.

11. Janet Sharp Hermann, *The Pursuit of a Dream* (New York: Oxford University Press, 1981), 221–23. On rural black migration westward, see William Cohen, *At Freedom's Edge: Black Mobility and the Southern White Quest for Racial Control, 1861–1915* (Baton Rouge: Louisiana State University Press, 1991), 252–58; Schweninger, *Black Property Owners in the South*, 143–84; and John C. Willis, *Forgotten Time: The Yazoo-Mississippi Delta after the Civil War* (Charlottesville: University Press of Virginia, 2000), 41–75.

12. "Locations of UNIA Divisions and Chapters," in Hill, *Marcus Garvey*, 7:990–91.

13. "Self Reliance Is the Mainspring of Success," *Negro World*, February 6, 1926.

14. "North Arkansas Alive in the Good Work," *Negro World*, June 7, 1924.

15. "A Well Wisher Who Reads the Negro World," *Negro World*, June 7, 1924.

16. "Mollie Bynum Prays for the Redemption of Africa," *Negro World*, June 7, 1924.

17. "Thirteen-Year-Old Boy Who Thinks Far Ahead," *Negro World*, December 20, 1924.

18. Bennie Bember, Tuckermann, Arkansas, to the Editor, *Negro World*, February 16, 1929.

19. Marcus Garvey quoted in Randall K. Burkett, *Garveyism as a Religious Movement: The Institutionalization of a Black Civil Religion* (Metuchen, N.J.: Scarecrow Press, 1978), 49.

20. "Wyatt, Mo.," *Negro World*, December 8, 1928.

21. E. W. Pinkard, Hermondale, Missouri, to the Editor, *Negro World*, September 5, 1925.

22. "Pine City Div., Arkansas Holds 3-Day Convention," *Negro World*, October 6, 1923.

23. Bennie Bember, Tuckerman, Arkansas, to the Editor, *Negro World*, February 16, 1929.

24. All from *Negro World*: "America Will Escape Blot on Fair Escutcheon by Granting Pardon to Marcus Garvey, Says 'Cotton Farmer' of Mississippi," April 18, 1925 (first quote); "Our Farmers Should Raise Their Home Supplies," January 23, 1926 (second and third quotes); "The Lesson of Mound Bayou," March 30, 1929 (remaining quotes).

25. "Convention Report," August 4, 1924, in Hill, *Marcus Garvey*, 5:652; Roll, *Spirit of Rebellion*, 70–74.

26. Roll, *Spirit of Rebellion*, 56–63.

27. Rolinson, *Grassroots Garveyism*, 161–91.

28. All *Chicago Defender*: "The Week," December 28, 1929; "Mississippi Farmers Save by Co-Operative Marketing," July 19, 1930; "Federation of Farmers Granted Corporate Charter," December 6, 1930; and "The Farmers' Column," February 13, 1932 (quote). See also Neil R. McMillen, *Dark Journey: Black Mississippians in the Age of Jim Crow* (Urbana: University of Illinois Press, 1990), 135.

29. "Federation of Farmers Granted Corporate Charter," *Chicago Defender*, December 6, 1930.

30. All "The Farmers' Column," *Chicago Defender*: January 10, 1931 (first quote); July 9, 1932 (second quote); and February 27, 1932 (third quote).

31. "Mississippi Farmers Save by Co-Operative Marketing," *Chicago Defender*, July 19, 1930 (quotes).

32. "The Farmers' Column," *Chicago Defender*, January 10, 1931.

33. "Colored Farmers Getting Together," *Negro World*, October 18, 1930.

34. "Mississippi Farmers Save by Co-Operative Marketing," *Chicago Defender*, July 19, 1930.

35. Roll, *Spirit of Rebellion*, 62, 72, 82; "The Lesson of Mound Bayou," *Negro World*, March 30, 1929 (quote).

36. "Tylertown, Miss.," *Negro World*, July 1, 1933 (first two quotes); "Tylertown, Miss.," *Negro World*, May 20, 1933 (final quote); U.S. Census Bureau, Manuscript Census, 1930, Mississippi: "Jef Ellzey," Beat 1, Pike County; "Jacob Ellzey," Beat 1, Walthall County; "Edward D. Cain," Beat 2, Walthall County; "Gain Rimes," Beat 2, Walthall County; "Lizzie Ellzey," Beat 1, Pike County; and "Dan Weary," Beat 3, Walthall County.

37. Both in *Chicago Defender*: "Red Cross to Aid All Stricken Farmers," January 17, 1931 (first three quotes); and "Tell of Methods to Get Farm Loans," January 24, 1931 (final quote). For more on the drought of 1930–31, see Nan E. Woodruff, "The Failure of Relief during the Arkansas Drought of 1930–31," *Arkansas Historical Quarterly* 39 (1980): 301–13, and Roll, *Spirit of Rebellion*, 78–85. On Davis, see "Georgia Man Wins Highest Federal Department of Agriculture Award," *Chicago Defender*, April 28, 1951.

38. Quotes in McMillen, *Dark Journey*, 135.

39. "Mississippi Paper Terrorizes Negro Farmers," *Negro Star*, April 3, 1931.

40. "The Farmers' Column," *Chicago Defender*, June 20, 1931 (all quotes).

41. "The Farmers' Column," *Chicago Defender*, August 15, 1931 and August 29, 1931 (first quote); "World's Flashlight," *Negro Star*, April 6, 1934 (second quote); "The Farmers' Column," *Chicago Defender*, April 18, 1931 (third quote).

42. "Farmers End Three-Day Meeting in Mound Bayou," *Chicago Defender*, September 5, 1931.

43. "Farmers to Hold Confab in Memphis," *Chicago Defender*, September 17, 1932 (first and second quotes); "Notes of the Campaign," *Chicago Daily Tribune*, November 1, 1932 (final quote).

44. "Urges 'Square Deal' for Race Farmers: Department of Agriculture Asked to Take Hand in Rural Situation," *Chicago Defender*, June 24, 1933. For the effect of the AAA, see Pete Daniel, *Breaking the Land: The Transformation of Cotton, Tobacco and Rice Cultures since 1880* (Urbana: University of Illinois Press, 1985), 92, 100–101; and David E. Conrad, *The Forgotten Farmers: The Story of Sharecroppers in the New Deal* (Urbana: University of Illinois Press, 1965), 55–58.

45. "What This Country Needs Is New Blood in Our Biggest Business: Help the Farmer and the Race Problems Will Pass Out," *Chicago Defender*, November 11, 1933 (all quotes).

46. "Charleston Gets 1934 National N.F.C.F. Convention," *Charleston Spokesman*, August 25, 1934 (quote); "Farmers Close Best Confab in Charleston, Mo.," *Chicago Defender*, November 17, 1934.

47. Both *Chicago Defender*: "Farmers Close Best Confab in Charleston, Mo.," November 17, 1934; and "New Deal Will Get Real Hearing at Farmers' Meet," October 20, 1934 (quote).

48. Donnie D. Bellamy, "Henry A. Hunt and Black Agricultural Leadership in the New South," *Journal of Negro History* 60 (October 1975): 474–75; "Farmers Close Best Confab in Charleston, Mo.," *Chicago Defender*, November 17, 1934; William E. Leuchtenburg, *Franklin D. Roosevelt and the New Deal* (New York: Harper and Row, 1963), 52.

49. "Expect Big Delegation at Farmers' Annual Convention," *Chicago Defender*, September 15, 1934.

50. "Farmers Close Best Confab in Charleston, Mo.," *Chicago Defender*, November 17, 1934 (all quotes).

51. Sidney Baldwin, *Poverty and Politics: The Rise and Decline of the Farm Security Administration* (Chapel Hill: University of North Carolina Press, 1968), 106–7; Paul E. Mertz, *New Deal Policy and Southern Rural Poverty* (Baton Rouge: Louisiana State University Press, 1978), 125–26. The final NFCF conference seems to have been held at Lincoln University in Jefferson City, Missouri, in 1939: "12 States Represented at Farmers' Convention," *Chicago Defender*, November 4, 1939.

52. Robin D. G. Kelley, *Hammer and Hoe: Alabama Communists during the Great Depression* (Chapel Hill: University of North Carolina Press, 1990), 159–75; Greta de Jong, *A Different Day: African American Struggles for Justice in Rural Louisiana, 1900–1970* (Chapel Hill: University of North Carolina Press, 2002), 99–115.

53. For more on the STFU, see Donald G. Grubbs, *Cry from the Cotton: The Southern Tenant Farmers' Union and the New Deal* (Chapel Hill: University of North Carolina Press, 1971); and Roll, *Spirit of Rebellion*. For more on the FSA, see Baldwin, *Poverty and Politics*, 191–201.

54. "Resolutions," April 26, 1936, folder "Southern Regional Conference, Alabama, Florida, Georgia, Louisiana, Mississippi, 1936," container 1, series G: Branch Files, Part 1: 1919–1939, Papers of the National Association for the Advancement of Colored People, Library of Congress.

55. "Federation of Race Farmers in Meet Soon," *Chicago Defender*, September 28, 1935 (first quote); "Organized Race Farmers Close Meeting," *Chicago Defender*, November 14, 1936 (all other quotes).

56. "Organized Race Farmers Close Meeting," *Chicago Defender*, November 14, 1936 (first quote); "Report of Activities in UNIA Divisions and Garvey Clubs," March 1936, in Hill, *Marcus Garvey*, 7:673 (second quote).

57. Grubbs, *Cry from the Cotton*, 118–24.

IV

Farm Families at Work

7

Land Ownership and the Color Line

African American Farmers in the Heartland, 1870s–1920s

DEBRA A. REID

John and his wife, Lillie, and their family ran away from a prominent slave-owning family in St. Charles, Missouri, in 1863. The fugitives boarded a northbound train that took them to East Dubuque, Illinois, a town at the juncture of three states, Wisconsin, Illinois, and Iowa. John and Lillie did not stop in Illinois, likely because of racially restrictive ordinances that deterred permanent settlement by blacks. Nor did they stop in Iowa, though other fugitives and free slaves had done so. Instead they traveled overland to Grant County, Wisconsin, and spent one winter farming near Bloomington, before moving into an area where freed slaves from Virginia owned land. Freedmen and Civil War veterans moved to Pleasant Ridge, as the community came to be called, and by 1900 one hundred folk attended school there and worshiped in the United Brethren church, eventually finding eternal rest in the cemetery. Descendants praised "these sturdy ambitious folks [who] set about in this densly wooded county to establish homes and grasp the oppertunities [*sic*] they had hense forth been denied." They worked and worshiped with their white neighbors, and they "bought land and built homes, their number being on the tax roll from 1856."[1]

Back in Missouri, Daniel A. Griffith and his family suffered the loss of approximately one-third of their personal property when John, Lillie, and at least seven additional family members fled. Griffith, a county court judge, farmer, and miller, managed a substantial property that included thirty-six slaves in 1860, some owned by him, others by his unmarried sister, Eliza, and still others owned in common by two of Griffiths' children, aged two and four years. John and Lillie may have moved their family because they feared being sold following the division of an estate, though the Griffiths apparently never sold any members of the Green family.[2]

Correspondence between the Griffiths and Thomas, a son of John and Lillie, implied a cordial relationship (figure 7.1). Newsy letters from St. Charles contained details about farm operations and gossip concerning old friends and family. Mrs. Fannie F. Griffith recounted how her son, Hunter, "plows the whole season, drives the reaper and drills in all the wheat; he raised sixteen hundred bushels wheat this year, and has eighty acres in wheat this fall." The letters traversed up and down the Mississippi River corridor documenting a migration pattern and crop culture rarely associated with black farmers but one that warrants more analysis.[3]

Wisconsin became the thirtieth state in May of 1848. It gained notoriety as the new wheat frontier and drew farmers from leading wheat-producing areas including New York, Pennsylvania, Virginia, Ohio, and Prussia. The cash crop offered economic opportunity to black migrants, including the freed Shepard family, who purchased land around which Pleasant Ridge developed, and more lenient legislation offered them hope for racial equality. Wisconsin exhibited more legal tolerance toward African Americans than did free-states bordering the upland South, specifically Ohio, Indiana, and Illinois. Approximately one-third of the residents in Wisconsin had supported a provision to the territorial constitution in 1846. An 1849 referendum on black suffrage received more "yes" than "no" votes but did not pass because most voters did not mark either choice. Wisconsinites gave more support to black suffrage in 1857 (41 percent) and 1865 (46 percent). In 1866 the Wisconsin Supreme Court ruled in favor of black suffrage in *Gillespie v. Palmer*.[4] Wisconsin thus seemed like a good choice to blacks seeking citizenship; not only was Wisconsin known as the birthplace of the Republican Party, but it became one of the first states to make black suffrage legal. Only a small number of black families, however, purchased land in Wisconsin. Why did so few black farmers follow the Mississippi River north, as the Green family did, to realize their freedom?

This paper argues that wheat, combined with supportive legislation and tolerant neighbors, provided the means by which black landowning families created a short-lived (mid-nineteenth to early twentieth century) and exclusive farm utopia. Some migrants established themselves in Pleasant Ridge after accompanying kin of their former owners to the new state, as did the Shepard family, but others came on their own volition, as did the Green family. Those few who came adopted farming methods similar to

Figure 7.1. Thomas Green, farmer from Pleasant Ridge, a black farming community in southwestern Wisconsin. Photograph c. 1936. Source: Original in the Cunningham Museum, Platteville, Wisconsin. Digitized version, courtesy of Grant County Historical Society, WHi-44862, Wisconsin Historical Society.

those of their white native-born and foreign neighbors. In rural southwest Wisconsin this required clearing land and diversifying production with a concentration on wheat as the cash crop. Cultural geographer Carville Earle has argued that "wheat farmers and their urban neighbors mobilized their forces" and contributed to "the rise of the Republican party—their last, best hope for preserving 'unnatural limits' on the extension of slave society." This boded well for black landowners, but white support for causes such as anti-slavery and free labor did not translate into extension of equal rights for their black neighbors. White settlers considered themselves entitled to inexpensive public land that agrarian policies guaranteed to settlers in the expanding nation. William Horner, a nephew of the Shepard family's former owner, came to Wisconsin to invest in lead mining initially, but he bought public land during the mid-1850s. The Shepard family purchased their land not from public sale at low prices but from a private owner who could charge higher prices. Countless white settlers acquired land through the same means. After Reconstruction, when Republicans lost their radicalism, a combination of state and local laws created barriers that excluded blacks completely from areas of the upper Midwest not already inhabited by blacks; but communities such as Pleasant Ridge, established before the Civil War, already existed within a majority white rural milieu and continued to do so, as did similar communities throughout the Midwest, despite repressive local and state laws.[5]

Migration studies often confirm an east-to-west movement in keeping with the pattern envisioned by Frederick Jackson Turner as part of his frontier thesis. Cultural geographers affirm east-to-west routes as part of cultural hearth theory. For African Americans, the most distinct westward migrations followed paths that remained on the latitude of the majority of the population, so freedmen from eastern upland southern states interested in farming the frontier were more likely to move into Kansas rather than Wisconsin during the 1870s, and land-rush settlers in Oklahoma found a climate conducive to cotton cultivation during the first years of the twentieth century. Much less attention has been paid to anomalous migration patterns that could have populated the northern wheat belt with African American landowners. Sociologist George Hesslink has described the trend to settle in comparable geographic areas as a consequence of "a friction of space": "usually [blacks] did not originate from a strongly dissimilar section of the country, but rather from states bordering the free North." Hesslink's theory can help explain patterns; for example, lighter skinned, educated African Americans from the upland South tended to move into midwestern states, while field slaves with no white ancestry from the geographically distant deep South did not. Based on this theory, low slave densities in states adjoining free states would result in a low number of black farmers seeking freedom in the wheat belt of the Midwest. In fact, too few African Americans migrated into the area to generate a movement, but enough arrived to affirm their right to landownership and autonomy, and they attested to the importance of wheat as a cash crop that could sustain rural farm communities in general, including those of black farmers.[6]

Wheat, an important cash crop grown in a broad band from the Atlantic throughout the northern plains, offered opportunities for property accumulation and independence. Farmers in black settlements in Ohio, Michigan, Indiana, and Illinois had been raising wheat since they broke the sod, and milling and transporting it required an infrastructure that helped communities grow. Wheat, if considered as a variable acting within the "friction of space" theory, could explain why black farmers from wheat-producing areas in Virginia, Tennessee, Kentucky, and Missouri sought wheat-producing areas in the northern Midwest, far from their locus of enslavement.[7]

Wheat not only played a significant role in both southern and northern agriculture; it also played a central role in the antebellum freedom debate. A lucrative wheat market in the Atlantic world prompted Chesapeake colonists to produce the grain. Chesapeake exports soon rivaled Pennsylvania shipments of wheat and flour to British and even non-British ports of call in defiance of mercantile legislation known as corn laws. The wheat zone that lay within the river valleys of Pennsylvania, Maryland, and northern Virginia developed as the breadbasket of the colonies. Settlers moving west with the wheat belt took the crop with them into Ohio, Michigan, Tennessee, and Kentucky. Wheat farmers did not need bound labor to produce a crop. In fact, they found it more profitable to hire folk to drill and harvest the grain rather than retaining slaves. Owners often expanded operations by building mills and training slaves as coopers and wagon makers to get flour to market. Blacks freed by wheat farmers started their own small farms, and, in turn, raised wheat as part of their diversified operations. A series of events in 1831, including abolition debates in the Virginia congress, Nat Turner's rebellion, and the McCormick reaper demonstration, indicate the uneasy tension between slavery, freedom, and wheat.[8]

The reaper offered the potential to reduce the need for hired labor at harvest time. The McCormicks developed their reaper in Rockbridge County, Virginia, in the state's wheat belt, but relocated into the expanding northern wheat belt, eventually establishing the McCormick Harvesting Machine Company in Chicago in 1847, coincident with the migration of intense wheat production to the upper Midwest and northern plains. The reaper, which could be modified to mow hay before and after cutting the grain crops, facilitated diversified crop and stock farming that could result in financially stable farms owned by black and white alike.[9]

William Horner and his family had relocated from Warren County, Virginia, a wheat-producing area near the Pennsylvania border. Pleasant Ridge offered a similar topography, and the former Virginians, again white and black alike, understood the infrastructure necessary for wheat production and marketing.[10] The "sturdy ambitious folks" who cleared the hillsides and created the wheat (and corn) fields became midwestern farmers. They operated more capital-intensive farms. Higher improved-land values made this possible. They used the collateral to invest in the machinery essential to cultivating wheat and a variety of other crops for sale and for feed for their stock.[11]

Only fifty-eight blacks farmed in Wisconsin in 1900, and they accounted for only 0.3 percent of all farmers. But more than three-quarters of this miniscule number owned their land (77.6 percent), a rate of ownership exceeded only by black farmers in South Dakota (88.2 percent) and white farmers in the West (80.1 percent; table 7.1). In fact, black landowners

Table 7.1. African American Farms, North-Central States, with Comparative Data for African American–Operated Farms in Other Regions and for White-Operated Farms in the United States, 1900

	African American Operated	Owner (%) Operated[a]	Tenant (%) Operated[b]	Manager (%) Operated	Total Acreage (Average per Farm)	Value per Farm[c]	Product Value per acre[d]
Illinois	1,486	724 (48.7)	757 (50.9)	5 (0.3)	83,107 (55.9)	$2,238	$5.97
Indiana	1,043	587 (56.3)	447 (42.9)	9 (0.86)	52,251 (50.1)	$2,240	$7.48
Iowa	200	107 (53.5)	89 (44.5)	4 (2.0)	15,359 (76.8)	$3,917	$7.95
Kansas	1,782	1,053 (59.1)	712 (40.0)	17 (1.0)	173,614 (97.4)	$2,109	$4.06
Michigan	626	472 (75.4)	151 (24.1)	3 (0.5)	38,259 (61.1)	$2,303	$5.96
Minnesota	31	18 (58.1)	11 (35.5)	2 (6.5)	4,493 (144.9)	$3,218	$3.43
Missouri	4,950	2,657 (53.7)	2,256 (45.6)	37 (0.7)	271,333 (54.8)	$1,610	$5.14
Nebraska	78	45 (57.7)	29 (37.2)	4 (5.1)	15,067 (193.2)	$3,565	$2.83
No. Dakota	18	13 (72.2)	5 (27.8)	0 (0)	13,572 (754.0)	$5,277	$1.29
Ohio	1,966	1,236 (62.9)	702 (35.7)	28 (14.2)	105,494 (53.7)	$2,186	$7.50
So. Dakota	17	15 (88.2)	2 (11.8)	0 (0)	9,027 (531.0)	$5,264	$1.45
Wisconsin	58	45 (77.6)	13 (22.4)	0 (0)	5495 (94.7)	$2,284	$3.72
Bl. North Central	12,255	6,972 (56.9)	5,174 (42.2)	109 (0.9)	787,071 (64.2)	$2,008	$5.39
Wh. North Central	2,179,667	1,552,712 (71.2)	607,456 (27.9)	19,499 (0.9)	815,138,136 (373.9)	$5,268	$5.67
Bl. North Atlantic	1,761	1,150 (65.3)	544 (30.9)	67 (3.8)	84,407 (47.9)	$2,712	$8.10
Wh. North Atlantic	675,366	522,109 (77.3)	140,206 (20.8)	13,051 (1.9)	65,301,850 (96.7)	$4,361	$7.56
Bl. South Atlantic	287,933	84,389 (29.3)	202,578 (70.4)	966 (0.3)	15,573,561 (54.1)	$566	$5.08
Wh. South Atlantic	673,354	442,396 (65.7)	222,813 (33.1)	8,145 (1.2)	88,660,241 (131.7)	$1,917	$3.66
Bl. South Central	444,429	95,029 (21.4)	348,805 (78.5)	595 (0.1)	21,712,876 (48.9)	$690	$6.71
Wh. South Central	1,206,867	741,910 (61.5)	455,930 (37.8)	9,027 (0.7)	234,764,064 (194.5)	$2,065	$2.62
Bl. Western	337	257 (76.3)	73 (21.7)	7 (2.0)	76,005 (225.5)	$3,117	$2.26
Wh. Western	234,854	188,179 (80.1)	39,136 (16.7)	7,539 (3.2)	92,961,460 (395.8)	$7,221	$3.06

TOTAL U.S. (Black)	746,717	187,799 (25.2)	557,174 (74.6)	1,744 (0.2)	38,233,933 (51.2)	$669	$6.01
TOTAL U.S. (White)	4,970,129	3,447,130 (69.4)	1,465,646 (29.5)	57,353 (1.1)	798,908,187 (160.7)	$4,016	$4.41

Sources: For African American farms, W. E. Burghardt Du Bois, "The Negro Farmer," *Negroes in the United States*, Bureau of the Census, Bulletin 8 (Washington: Government Printing Office, 1904), 69–98: Table II: Number and Acreage of Farms Operated by Negroes, Value of Farms of Negro Farmers, 1900; Table V: Value of Property on Farms of Negro Farmers, 1900; Table XLV: Number and Acreage of Farms Operated by Negroes, Value of Specified Classes of Farm Products, June 1, 1900, with Value of Products of 1899, and Expenditures in 1899 for Labor and Fertilizers, with Averages, by State and Territories; and Table XLVI: Number of Farms Operated by Negroes, Classified by Tenure, By States and Territories, 1900. Reissued in Special Reports: Supplementary Analysis and Derivative Tales. *Twelfth Census of the United States*, 1900 (Washington, D.C.: Government Printing Office, 1906), 511–79; reprinted in Herbert Aptheker, compiler and editor, *Contributions by W. E. B. Du Bois in Government Publications and Proceedings* (Millwood, N.Y.: Kraus-Thomson, 1980): 229–346.

For comparative data from other regions, Twelfth Census of the United States, 1900 (Washington, D.C.: U.S. Government Printing Office, 1902), Census Reports, Volume V, *Agriculture Part I: Farms, Livestock, and Animal Products*, pp. cx, 4–5, 158–59: Table CVII: Average Number of Acres of Land, Percent of Land Improved, and Average Value Per Farm of All Farm Property, For Farms of White and Negro Farmers, June 1, 1900, By States and Territories; Table 2: Farms, June 1, 1900, White and Colored Farmers, and of Specified Area, Principal Source of Income, and Value of Products of 1899, Not Fed to Livestock, Classified by Tenure, by States, and by Territories; and Table 13: Classification by Tenure, for Farms of White Farmers, of the Number and Acreage of Farms, Value of Specified Classes of Farm Property, Value of Products, and Expenditures for Labor and Fertilizers, with Averages by States and Territories.

a. Owners include full owners, part owners, and owner-tenants (i.e., owning land that they farmed as well as farming other land as tenants).
b. Tenants include both cash and share tenants.
c. Value per farm is an average and includes land, improvements, buildings, implements and machinery, and livestock.
d. Product values are averages for 1899, not including products fed to livestock.

accounted for more than 50 percent of all black farmers in all Midwestern states except Illinois (48.7 percent) in 1900. Only in the West and North-Atlantic regions did the rate of ownership among black farmers exceed the Midwest, but ownership among white farmers in these regions outpaced that realized by black farmers. By 1900, thirty-five years after emancipation, African Americans had not attained the dream of private land ownership indelibly linked to being American to the same degree as white farmers.[12]

Instead, as W.E.B. Du Bois wrote in 1901, the process of property accumulation represented "the widespread accumulation of small sums in many hands rather than the advance of a few captains of industry." Du Bois realized the precarious nature of rural blacks, explaining that even though one-third owned fewer than ten acres, this "indicat[ed] the narrow margin for accumulation between present income and expense among colored people." But Du Bois believed that the data also confirmed that blacks were "in the midst of an unfinished cycle of property accumulation." That process continued through the 1910s. By 1920 nearly 220,000 black farmers owned nearly six million acres of land across the United States, but the small number and acreage of those owning land in Wisconsin supported Du Bois' claim of incremental change. Yet other opportunities replaced farming as the occupation of choice for those seeking full citizenship rights, and rural African Americans, particularly the rural youth, no longer believed the agrarian rhetoric that acquiring land and property could free them. The potential of black land ownership peaked during the early twentieth century. After World War I rural youth, white and black alike, turned to the cities for employment and cultural outlets.[13]

During the period of growth between Reconstruction and World War I, the potential that property ownership represented for blacks nevertheless caught the attention of reformers. Du Bois and others commented on the importance of class differentiation and what it could mean for community development. Du Bois concluded his 1898 study of Farmville, Virginia, by noting that a "clear differentiation of classes among Negroes, even in small communities was emerging." He believed that farm owners occupied the highest social class, along with teachers, grocers, and artisans. Du Bois believed that most did not recognize this potential, but some whites did, and interpreted the class division in a positive light. Orra Langhorne, a white Virginia woman, believed that "the best sign for the Negroes of our land is that they are fast separating into classes, a fact to which their white fellow-citizens often fail to attach the importance it deserves." Reformer Lily H.

Hammond from Augusta, Georgia, argued that middle-class blacks and whites had much in common. This certainly applied to the black and white farmers in Pleasant Ridge who interacted in work and social situations. White neighbors asked black farmers to help stack hay; children went to school together and played together; they fought and made up; they cooperated to get work done. Shared responsibilities generated a cooperative spirit.[14]

Yet race consciousness affected the relations of wheat farmers of southwestern Wisconsin despite shared class status as landowners and despite mutual dependency to sustain the rural infrastructure. Residents did not encourage miscegenation. Descendents recalled that "chances for intermarriage within the Pleasant Ridge community were sometimes slim . . . and young men and women migrated toward more populous centers to find mates." Toleration more than integration prescribed race relations within Pleasant Ridge and other rural communities.[15]

Republican newspapers editorialized about the connections between land ownership and black citizenship rights during Reconstruction, but most, including the *Chicago Tribune*, looked South for inspiration, rather than to examples in the Midwest. "The Negro as Landowner" appeared in 1875, more than twenty years after Pleasant Ridge began. The *Chicago Tribune* editor waxed optimistic about prospects for former slaves in Arkansas. Of 40,000 who had voted, 2,000 owned their own farms or houses on lots in town. They had made themselves into "good citizens" by binding themselves to the soil, and this promised "a safe solution of that sectional monstrosity known as the Southern question." Blacks in Arkansas had purchased their property despite "political strife and domestic insecurity." The *Chicago Tribune* posited that if landowning whites, such as the "old-time planters" who hoped to settle black landowners permanently on their farmlands, could ally with landowning blacks then "the odious 'color-line'" could be overcome. This belief that land ownership could unite the races in pursuit of common goals emerged from rhetoric nearly as old as the nation: Jeffersonian agrarianism. It linked to farming the Lockean ideals of inalienable rights, specifically liberty and property, and claimed that farming provided the best foundation for public morality, independent decision making, and political activism. For the nation to exist, it needed citizen farmers; but tellingly, the *Chicago Tribune's* reporting removed the black citizen farmer physically from the readership by reporting on the situation in Arkansas. Reporters apparently did not investigate the black landowners growing wheat in the Midwest, some of whom may have purchased McCormick reapers or hired reaper crews, a technology that helped create the wealth that the McCormick family, which owned the *Tribune*, enjoyed.[16]

The radical Republicans who championed the agrarian ideal during Reconstruction believed that "Negro land-owning [could] be a powerful factor in taking the Negro, as such, out of color-line politics." In other words, it could integrate freedmen into "political communities" in keeping with "progressive and conservative part[ies]." Farm families in Pleasant Ridge well understood the relationship between land and political involvement and influence. The families had interacted with owners such as the Griffith family in Missouri, who provided lessons of how real estate, wealth, business acumen, and political influence went hand in hand. Daniel A. Griffith served as a judge on the St. Charles County Court, following in his father's footsteps, and operated the family's flour mill, Griffith's Mill, in addition to the large farm with at least eighty acres planted in wheat in a given year. The Green family exercised their right to acquire land as part of the process toward securing economic stability and political influence. They paid their taxes and developed their community as white farm families did.[17]

But newspapers, including the *Chicago Tribune,* often pitted black farmers against whites in a battle, rhetorical and real, over which race would retain authority over local, state, and national decisions. Most southern newspapers championed race-based conflict more than mutual dependency. Articles emphasized separation rather than cooperation. Yet settlers, regardless of race, argued that agricultural settlements could help them enjoy personal liberty and ultimately equality. Despite the separatist rhetoric, interracial contact occurred on the ground, even if infrequently and in the context of mutual exchange of labor that defined farm families' relations in sparsely settled areas. Black migrants established farming settlements, freedom colonies and even all-black towns such as Nicodemus, but white settlers in Dunlap, Kansas, a town named for the first white settler in the area, encountered Exodusters in 1879. Dunlap drew migrants because of its proximity to the Missouri, Kansas and Texas Railroad, the Neosho River, and rich agricultural land (figure 7.2). The town became an important transportation hub for three counties, which certainly benefited farmers of both races who lived around the community.[18]

Other migrations occurred during the late nineteenth and early twentieth century, with each race protecting their property interests but interacting as necessity dictated. Black homesteaders entered the Dakotas synchronous to the Exodusters entering Kansas, during 1879 and 1880, but the

Figure 7.2. John Summer and family displaying their possessions in front of their home near Dunlap, Kansas, 1880 to 1885. Source: Kansas Historical Society.

Dakota migration has received less attention. Northern urban interest in the venture, particularly from Mr. Watkins, chief engineer with a Chicago fire department, financed land purchases and recruited thirty families to settle thousands of acres. Migrants to the Dakotas left from different departure points than the Kansas migrants and included fewer destitute settlers. They followed paths that explorers and Buffalo soldiers had trodden. They purchased large farms and followed market forces that made wheat and cattle ranching relatively profitable pursuits. Sometimes migrants moved on, as Kansans did into Oklahoma and Dakotans did into Wyoming, in pursuit of all-black utopias. In 1890 black Kansans urged migrants to head to Oklahoma "to found a Negro state in which the white man will be tolerated as a necessary evil, but to whom no political honors will be given." They planned to work with whites only if whites asked to be included. The separatists expected "full social equality; you must compel the white man to accept you at his table in his home and in his bed." They would not "permit a white man to be elected to any office whatever. We will rule." Residents of Langston City, Oklahoma, were ready to die to protect their all-black town from white encroachment. They saw the town lots that they had purchased and improved as critical to their being able to get quick access to farm land when the Indian land opened for settlement on September 22, 1891.[19]

Not all African Americans believed in colonization. Some found its association with separation threatening and called for assimilation instead. Frederick Douglass, in 1883, delivered an address to a congregation in Washington, D.C. He argued that "assimilation and not isolation is our true policy and our natural destiny. Unification for us is life: separation is death. We cannot afford to set up for ourselves a separate political party, or adopt for ourselves a political creed apart from the rest of our fellow citizens. Our own interests will be subserved by a generous care for the interests of the Nation at large. All the political, social and literary forces around us tend to unification." Douglass conveyed these sentiments during a period of intense independent party formation, at a time when the Republicans marginalized black and pro-black members and when the Democrats followed suit by limiting black suffrage.[20]

Separatist actions emphasized race difference and in comparison, stories about biracial cooperation seemed imaginative. Yet separatist communities did not exist in a vacuum; they did not flourish in isolation. Pleasant Ridge residents used their economic clout to secure their real and personal property and thus their economic independence. Then as a minority population, they participated in local marketing networks, sustained rural community social and cultural infrastructure by attending school and church with their neighbors, and exercised a distinctly American goal, the agrarian ideal of independent land ownership, apace with their white neighbors and peers.

Black and white farm families responded similarly to challenges they faced within their agricultural region in response to localized or regional market forces. Yet different pressures arose when local, state, and national decisions distinguished between the farmers, regardless of their capabilities, because of their color, and determined that one farmer deserved more than the other because of race. White farmers of a certain class shared governance and economic influence with their peers. They took advantage of farmers of both races who did not have similar clout. By isolating themselves emotionally if not physically from their white peers, black farm families could cultivate their own crops to sell to meet their needs, regulate their separate society, establish moral parameters, and thus secure the race's future. They often criticized blacks who chose city life over the country or who appeared not to care about land ownership as a means to independence, and they justified this because of their belief that land ownership could help eliminate the color line.

Agrarians, both white and black, renewed their efforts to draw rural and urban youth to farming at the turn of the twentieth century. Land rushes created waves of community building on former Indian land on the plains, and agrarian rhetoric sounded a celebratory refrain to lure migrants. Oscar Micheaux, a native of Murphysboro, Illinois, took this approach when he asked, "What is the northern Negro doing as a self-supporter? . . . All the Negro produces in the northwest would not feed the colored population of Chicago three days, still he boasts of what the race is accomplishing." Micheaux believed that "farm lands are the bosses of wealth," and he urged young men to take advantage of homesteading opportunities. He based his comments on his own experiences homesteading in South Dakota starting in 1905. He dramatized these experiences in his first and third novels, *The Conquest* (1913) and *The Homesteader* (1917). He made *The Homesteader* into a movie in 1919. Yet the more he reworked his message, the fewer blacks listened.[21]

Black agrarians developed a back-to-the-land movement contemporaneous to the formation of the Country Life Commission in 1908 and synonymous with the so-called Golden Age of Agriculture of 1909 to 1914, a period when prices for farm products exceeded the cost of production. Landowning black farmers could support early twentieth-century agrarian-led colonization efforts because organizers expressed traditional separatist values that resonated with them, and black farm owners would strengthen the class's cause. The most visible colonization effort, the Universal Negro Improvement Association (UNIA), began in 1914 and pursued extreme separation through its Back-to-Africa campaign. Scholarly attention to that development has obscured more localized colonization efforts. Oscar Micheaux, the author and film maker, continued advocating for homesteading, as did other reformers who hoped to settle urban blacks on farms in the country. Joseph Elward Clayton—a Texan who maintained at least three residences, one in rural Littig, Texas, east of Austin, another in Houston, Texas, and a third in Chicago—promoted rural life from these bases sporadically during the early 1920s and into the 1930s under the auspices of the National Self-Help Association. Clayton had initially used the Texas Department of Agriculture to generate visibility for his schemes, and when his association with that agency ended he worked with different local entities to establish black communities on acreage in Arkansas and Mississippi. A black cooperative, the National Federation of Colored Farmers, founded by businessmen in northern cities, sought to sustain rural black communities across the nation by coordinating marketing and supply systems during the 1920s and 1930s. Educator Benjamin F. Hubert, president of Georgia State Industrial College for Colored Youth and executive secretary of the Association for the Advancement of Negro Country Life, promoted development of the Log Cabin Community, a 15,000-acre resettlement project near Springfield, Georgia, from the late 1920s through the 1940s. These projects indicate the traction that agrarian values held for a few while the many turned toward the city for their livelihood.[22]

Agrarians implied that farmers never suffered from glutted markets or depressed prices. Pests, floods, disease, or fire never destroyed their crops. They never faced retribution for delivering the first wheat to the elevator or bale to the gin or having the best hog in the sale pen. Reality proved quite different, but the agrarians remained committed to diversity as the key to success even as specialized production of cotton or tobacco increased and southern agriculture became plantation monoculture.

Success stories attest to the importance of diversification to economic solvency and indicate the hard work required to sustain it. Black farmers who planted different crops had visible, tangible evidence that they controlled decision making on their farm. The acreage mattered less than the autonomy that went with real property ownership. In 1896 Nathan Pointer, a farmer in Halifax, Virginia, had tobacco growing on his hillsides and several large straw stacks near his granary, evidence of his investment in two traditional cash crops in the state. But he also had corn in the field and 125 fruit trees in his orchard. The acreage would not have impressed many at the time; he had purchased six acres in 1880 for $500, but after sixteen years of improving the soil, planting the orchard and building a house, barn, and outbuildings, his property was worth $2,000. At fifty years of age he lived within a community of black and white farmers and farm laborers; his wife, son, and three daughters were all of an age to help with the constant demands of a small but diversified farm. He invested his profit into another farm and improved it, doubling its value.[23]

Nathan Pointer conveyed the potential for black landowners to function independently from white authority and success depended on diversification. In Pleasant Ridge, farm families raised wheat, horses, corn, and hogs and kept cattle and chickens. They raised vegetables for themselves and fodder for their stock. In this they likewise followed the patterns of their white peers. They learned about diversity in an agricultural setting with ready markets for a variety of products. Farmers in other parts of the midwestern wheat belt did the same. Thomas Jefferson, a mulatto farmer in St. Ferdinand Township in St. Louis County, Missouri, lived not too far from St. Charles County, where the Greens had lived before fleeing to Wisconsin. Jefferson owned twelve acres of land, all tillable and valued at $720.

He was only thirty-one years old in 1880 and had four children under the age of ten. A black servant and laborer from Virginia, Mathias Patton, lived with the family. They farmed in proximity to white native-born and foreign families. Jefferson had agricultural machinery worth $50 at his disposal and two horses and one hundred barnyard fowl worth $80. The family collected 300 dozen eggs and devoted all twelve acres to raising Indian corn; they produced $240 worth of agricultural products. Seventy-year-old Harry Boyed of Carondelet Township, more than twice Jefferson's age, owned land, machinery, and livestock of a comparable value to Jefferson's, but Boyed reported more diversification, as could be expected of a man with a mature extended family sharing his household. Boyed and his wife, four sons, two daughters, and two grandsons produced $300 in farm products, predominantly potatoes and apples, to which he dedicated half of his acreage. He hayed two acres and he also had a hog and barnyard fowl. Farmers from Darmstadt, Hessen and Prussia, Ireland, New York, and Ohio lived around him. He had no black neighbors, judging from the route the census enumerator took based on the return.[24]

Black farmers in the St. Louis area did not raise cotton because the growing season was too short. Instead, black and white farmers alike raised a cash crop that had defined agriculture in the Mississippi River Valley since French settlers arrived in the late 1600s: wheat. Yields were not large; the Norman Watkins family planted four of their ten tillable acres in wheat and harvested thirty bushels. But the crop, in conjunction with other crops and livestock, could provide the economic stability critical to purchasing and maintaining a farm.[25]

In St. Louis County, Missouri, wheat apparently provided a crop option that returned adequate income for labor expended, even during the volatile years when midwestern farmers challenged the exorbitant freight and storage rates charged by railroad and grain elevator operators. Landless black farmers appear to have negotiated reasonable fixed rates for their leases because they had the resources to leverage the landlord. The more a tenant provided for himself, the greater the return on his lease. These tenants, however, did not invest their profits into real estate. Some chose leasing rather than ownership as a strategy. At least in St. Louis County, families who rented for a fixed rate operated larger farms than owners, perhaps because the tenants invested earnings into new machinery and in farm labor, which allowed them to expand their production as new land became available to lease. Owners of few acres may have found themselves constrained with no access to additional acreage. More must be done to

Figure 7.3. Owners and laborers performed menial labor on farms, regardless of their race. In this image, men wield grain cradles while women and children gather the sheaves, and nothing can distinguish laborers from landowners. But the image also conveys the persistence of white supremacy, with a white man in a suit coat overseeing all laborers. Location unknown, c. 1899. Source: McCormick-International Harvester Collection, Whi-9207, Wisconsin Historical Society.

document whether these fixed-rate tenants transitioned to farm ownership or not and to analyze the factors that affected their choices.

A cluster of ambitious fixed-rate tenants farmed in Bonhomme Township, St. Louis County. There several black and mulatto tenant farmers rented land, apparently from German immigrants with large land holdings who lived nearby. Each tenant paid agricultural laborers for several weeks of work. Nelson Hubbard, a twenty-six-year-old black farmer born in Missouri, of parents from Virginia, rented forty acres of tillable land, which he divided equally between corn and wheat. He paid $100 for fifty weeks of labor. Henry Jackson, a forty-year-old Virginian with five children, tilled ten acres of wheat and thirty acres of corn and paid $70 for the equivalent of twelve weeks of labor. John Morris, a forty-six-year-old black farmer from Virginia with two sons who worked on the farm, cultivated twenty-five acres of corn and fifty acres of wheat and paid $60 in wages for six weeks of work. Those who hired six weeks of labor likely did so just during the harvest season and threshing season; longer periods of labor indicated that farmers needed year-round help because they could not manage the workload with family members alone (figure 7.3).[26]

An extensive transportation infrastructure provided ready market access for these farmers when the time came for them to sell their wheat. Newspapers, specifically the *St. Louis County Watchman*, a Republican paper published every Friday starting September 29, 1881, in Clayton, Missouri, incorporated market information in every issue. It had the largest circulation of any newspaper in the county, and in its pages was information on crop outlooks, St. Louis markets in comparison to Chicago markets, machinery, fertilizers, pests, and other items of interest to local farmers. Not all black farmers, however, used diversification to secure their own land. Instead, fixed-rate tenants, or cash tenants, invested in personal property rather than real estate, specifically machinery and draft animals. The community of black tenants farming for German landowners in Bonhomme either hired reapers to harvest their grain or pooled their resources and invested in reapers to facilitate harvest. African Americans followed threshing crews, as did Bill Black in 1870. Black farmers used modern harvesting equipment, and the technology would have appealed to black and white tenants and owners alike if it hastened the harvest and saved grain. Investment in machinery may have displaced agricultural laborers, but urban jobs offered steadier wages, which gave agricultural laborers in proximity to cities options not available to many rural laborers. Machinery, particularly reapers, allowed farmers to remain viable in the face of inadequate numbers of laborers and of laborers accustomed to earning higher wages than farmers could pay.[27]

Numerous manufacturers experimented with harvesting technology during the late nineteenth and early twentieth century as the wheat belt spread farther west through the northern plains and into the Pacific Northwest. The companies' attention to southern wheat states, however, indicates the continued viability of wheat as a cash crop in areas with long histories of cultivating the crop. International Harvester made machinery promotion an educational undertaking through the agricultural extension staff that the company employed and sent into the field. They documented trials photographically and described them in the company newspaper (figure 7.4). Wheat farmers in vicinity of the trials could see for themselves; otherwise, farmers as far afield as Virginia, Tennessee, Wisconsin, Kansas, and South Dakota could read about the demonstrations or contemplate ads in farmers' journals such as the *Prairie Farmer*.

Farm life required hard work and diligence, and owners and tenants of both races who could mechanize did so. Imagine the labor required to operate a forty-acre farm as diverse as that owned by John Martin in

Figure 7.4. African Americans near Columbia, Tennessee, harvest wheat on the W. P. Ridley farm with an International 8–16 HP kerosene tractor and two Deering binders. The three farm hands cut eighty acres in thirty hours using thirty gallons of kerosene and five quarts of cylinder oil. Photograph taken June 14, 1921. Source: McCormick-International Harvester Collection, WHi-8526, Wisconsin Historical Society.

Bonhomme Township, Missouri. Martin, forty-two years old, and his wife and father-in-law had to supplement their labor by paying $75 in wages to hired help. They estimated the value of their agricultural products at $1,200. They dedicated the majority of their tillable acreage to wheat in 1879, and harvested 500 bushels. They planted two acres in oats, much of which likely went to feed their horse and three mules. They raised corn, which fed their ten hogs, as of June 1880. Their milk cow produced enough cream-rich milk that the family processed 175 pounds of butter. In addition to these more typical midwestern farm crops, however, they raised market garden or truck farming produce. The census enumerator listed three acres of Irish potatoes raised and also reported $400 worth of "market garden produce," likely peas, lettuce, cabbage, beets, okra, and other vegetables sold at city markets. The family also sold 6,000 pounds of grapes raised on two acres of vines, and $150 worth of forest products in the form of 100 cords of wood. Firewood markets helped farmers supplement their income, and farmers in the wooded hills and river bottoms around St. Louis realized significant extra income through their woodcutting, nearly $1.50 per cord on average.[28]

The census data may indicate more what farmers wanted rather than what they had, and the evidence may not be as precise as its copious statistics suggest. Regardless, the variety of crops and stock on many midwestern farms required constant labor, year-round. Farm families dedicated winter months to woodcutting and stock care, spring to soil preparation and planting, summer to wheat harvest and corn cultivation, and fall to corn harvest and wheat planting and meat processing. It is easy to see how farmers wore out, and even though they may still have owned land, their work-worn bodies could not keep up with the daily routines. Their retirement meant the passing of an era defined by land ownership and community development.

The patriarch of the Green family, John, died during October 1890; two of his farmer sons, Thomas and Hardy, remained in the community. But the Green and Shepard families and their peers in Pleasant Ridge all recognized that the education they had provided now offered opportunities off the farm. No family member took over the Green farm when Thomas died in 1937, and the community ceased to exist by the 1950s. The land that the families had worked to clear, and which testified to their having secured freedom, remained in production but not by African American farmers. Rural youth had embraced new careers through which they could express their autonomy, and farming no longer seemed the most visible way to gain economic independence and local influence.

Notes

I received a Council on Faculty Research grant during the 2008–2009 academic year from Eastern Illinois University, which supported research on farmers in Missouri. Staff at several institutions made this article possible, including Michael Everman, Missouri State Archives, St. Louis; Gary Kremer, State Historical Society of Missouri, and staff at the University of Missouri–Columbia Archives and the Western Historical Manuscript Collection, Columbia; the Missouri State Archives and Lincoln University Archives in Jefferson City; and at the St. Louis County Library. The Booth Library staff at Eastern Illinois University processed countless interlibrary loan requests and provided trial access to several digitized newspaper collections that gave this essay depth and breadth. I thank Shawn Hale for suggestions that improved this chapter.

1. Quotes from "History of the Negro Pioneer Settlers of Grant County [Wisconsin]," handwritten manuscript, n.d., 2, in Charles Shepard Papers, 1850–1958, Wisconsin Historical Society, Madison (hereafter cited as Shepard Papers, WHS). This history indicates that John and Lillie and family bought the farm from Thomas Greene's estate, which may have caused some of the fugitives from Missouri to adopt the spelling Greene. Note that Green appears as Green and Greene in historic sources, most commonly Green in the early years. The Prussian farmer Thomas Greene appears in the 1870 census in proximity to the black farm families. His household included five children and he owned $3,000 in real estate and $500 in personal property: Dwelling 159, Household 162, Schedule 1: Free Inhabitants in Town of Beetown, Grant County, Wisconsin, *U.S. Federal Census, 1870*, 23. For additional family memories see "First Negro settlers," [c. 1958], handwritten manuscript, and Dave Stevens, "Only One Survivor of Negro Colony," *Telegraph-Herald* (Dubuque, Iowa),

June 1, 1958, both in Shepard Papers, WHS. See also Zachary L. Cooper, *Black Settlers in Rural Wisconsin* (Madison: State Historical Society of Wisconsin, 1977; repr., Madison: Wisconsin Historical Society Press, 1994); Robert R. Dykstra, *Bright Radical Star: Black Freedom and White Supremacy on the Hawkeye Frontier* (Cambridge: Harvard University Press, 1993); Valerie Grim, "African Americans in Iowa Agriculture," in *Outside In: African American History in Iowa, 1838–2000*, ed. Bill Silag (Des Moines: State Historical Society of Iowa, 2001): 166–89.

2. Letter to John Green, n.p., from Handy Fuller, c/o Mr. E. Fielkerson, St. Charles, Missouri, May 28, 1879, Shepard Papers, WHS, indicates that the Griffith family left St. Charles and moved to Texas. Also consulted in Shepard Papers, WHS: "History of the Negro Pioneer Settlers," 3; letter to Thomas from Miss Fannie [Griffith], St. Charles, Missouri, January 25, [c. 1854]; letter to Thomas from F. Griffith, St. Charles, Missouri, January 21, [c. 1864]; and letter to Thomas Green, Lancaster, Grant County, Wisconsin, from Fannie F. Griffith, St. Charles, Missouri, November 4, 1870. In *U.S. Federal Census, 1860*, see p. 25, Daniel A. Griffith, Dwelling 180, Household 179, Schedule I: Free Inhabitants in St. Charles Township, St. Charles County, Missouri; and p. 2, Daniel A. Griffith Jr., Eliza A. Griffith, and Daniel A. Griffith, individually and as agent for Eliza A. Griffith, Schedule 2: Slave Inhabitants in St. Charles Township, St. Charles County, Missouri.

3. Letter to Thomas from Miss Fannie, St. Charles, Missouri, January 25, [c. 1854], 1–2. Someone penciled in [c. 1854] at a later date, and it is likely inaccurate because "Hunter," aka John Hunter Griffith, would have been only two in 1854 and not old enough to plow, drill grain, or drive the reaper. Daniel A. Griffith married Fanny F. Fielder/Fedder on December 9, 1850, in St. Charles, Missouri; see Missouri Marriage Records, 1805–2002, database online at Ancestry.com (Provo, Utah: Ancestry.com Operations, 2007); original data (microfilm), Missouri Marriage Records, Missouri State Archives, Jefferson City.

4. John G. Gregory, "Negro Suffrage in Wisconsin," *Transactions of the Wisconsin Academy of Sciences, Art and Letters* 11 (1898): 94–101.

5. Carville Earle, "To Enslave or Not to Enslave: Crop Seasonality, Labor Choice, and the Urgency of the Civil War," in *Geographical Inquiry and American Historical Problems* (Stanford, Calif.: Stanford University Press, 1992), 226–57, quote at 252–53. James W. Loewen, *Sundown Towns: A Hidden Dimension of American Racism* (New York: New Press, 2005). William Horner purchased public land in 1854 and 1855. His purchase complied with the Land Act of 1820. See Certificate No. 15,433, to William Horner, Grant County, Wisconsin, 40 acres, October 2, 1854; and Certificate No. 18414, to William Horner, Grant County, Wisconsin, 40 acres, November 10, 1855, both digitized and available via "Search Land Patents," General Land Office Records, Bureau of Land Management, http://www.glorecords.blm.gov/ (accessed August 19, 2010).

6. For antebellum migration into the Midwest and on to Canada, see William H. Pease and Jane H. Pease, *Black Utopia: Negro Communal Experiments in America* (Madison: State Historical Society of Wisconsin, 1963); for postbellum migration see Nell Irvin Painter, *Exodusters: Black Migration to Kansas after Reconstruction* (New York: Alfred A. Knopf, 1976; 2nd ed., University of Kansas Press, 1986). Robert G. Athearn, *In Search of Canaan: Black Migration to Kansas, 1879–1880* (Lawrence: Regents Press of Kansas, 1978). For statistics on migrations that challenge the east-west model and link separatist movements to black nationalism see Selena Ronshaye Sandefer, "For Land and Liberty:

Black Territorial Separatism in the South, 1776–1904," Ph.D. diss., Vanderbilt University, 2010. George K. Hesslink, *Black Neighbors in a Northern Rural Community* (Indianapolis: Bobbs-Merrill Company, 1968), 39.

7. Juliet E. K. Walker, *Free Frank: A Black Pioneer on the Antebellum Frontier* (Lexington: University Press of Kentucky, 1983), 83–89. Stephen A. Vincent, *Southern Seed, Northern Soil: African American Farm Communities in the Midwest, 1765–1900* (Bloomington: Indiana University Press, 2002), 86. The Confederate States of America used the term Trans-Mississippi West to define the theatre of war west of the Mississippi River in Arkansas, Louisiana, Missouri, Texas, and the Indian Territory. I use it to reconsider the centric idea of east-to-west migration patterns and the Turnerian idea of a frontier always on the western fringe of settlement. Could African Americans have become wheat farmers in a northern trans-Mississippi region encompassing parts of Wisconsin, Illinois, Iowa, and Minnesota, and extending into the northern Plains of the Dakotas, Nebraska, and western Kansas, if more cultural support had existed for migrants?

8. Lewis C. Gray, *History of Agriculture in the Southern United States to 1860*. 2 vols. (Gloucester, Mass.: Peter Smith, 1958); Earle, "To Enslave or Not to Enslave," 226–57, and "Why Tobacco Stunted the Growth of Towns and Wheat Built Them into Small Cities: Urbanization South of the Mason-Dixon Line, 1650–1790," in *Geographical Inquiry*, 88–152. Debra A. Reid, "Wheat," in *The World of a Slave: Encyclopedia of Material Slave Life in the United States*, ed. Martha Katz-Hyman and Kym Rice, 2 vols. (Westport, Conn.: Greenwood Press/ABC-CLIO, 2010), 2:526–32.

9. Alan L. Olmstead and Paul W. Rhode, "Beyond the Threshold: An Analysis of the Characteristics and Behavior of Early Reaper Adopters," *Journal of Economic History* 55, no. 1 (March 1995): 27–57.

10. "History of the Negro Pioneer Settlers," 1; Pease and Pease, *Black Utopia*, 2–3; Hesslink, *Black Neighbors*, 29–56; Vincent, *Southern Seed*. Other black farmers relied less on former masters and financed their own way. Free Frank McWhorter used funds he had earned in Kentucky to purchase his own land in Pike County, Illinois, in 1830, and he lived in the rural community he developed, New Philadelphia, until he died in 1854. McWhorter and his sons planted wheat as soon as they could prepare the soil. The family hauled that crop and other diverse agricultural products to the ferry on the Mississippi River for sale to St. Louis markets. Walker, *Free Frank*, 83–89.

11. Descendents of settlers wrote down their memories during the 1930s, when a reporter for the Plattville, Wisconsin, newspaper interviewed Thomas Greene, a son of John and Lillie, and during the 1950s when they handwrote two brief histories of the black settlement. The former reflected increased interest in former slaves documented by the Works Progress Administration and the oral histories collected by WPA staff. The latter indicated growing consciousness of race relations in the aftermath of the *Brown v. Board of Education* decisions. Statistics in decennial agricultural census returns document the higher land values for midwestern states.

12. Table 10: Farms, June 1, 1900, Classified by Acreage, Tenure, and Color of Farmer, with Averages and Percentages, by Counties, in Statistics of Agriculture, General Tables, *Census Reports*, Volume V, *Agriculture* Part I, *Farms, Livestock, and Animal Products, Twelfth Census of the United States, 1900* (Washington, D.C.: U.S. Government Printing Office, 1902), 138–39.

13. In Wisconsin 58 farmers operated 5,495 acres; 45 owned their land in 1900. W.E.B. Du Bois, *The Negro Landowner in Georgia*, U.S. Department of Labor, Bulletin 6, no. 25 (Washington, D.C.: Government Printing Office, July 1901), 647–777, reprinted in Herbert Aptheker, ed., *Contributions by W.E.B. Du Bois in Government Publications and Proceedings* (Millwood, N.Y.: Kraus-Thomson, 1980), 95–227, "widespread accumulation" on 121, "unfinished cycle" on 227. W. E. Burghardt Du Bois, "The Negro Farmer," in *Negroes in the United States*, Bureau of the Census, Bulletin 8 (Washington, D.C.: Government Printing Office, 1904), 69–98; reissued in *Special Reports: Supplementary Analysis and Derivative Tables, Twelfth Census of the United States, 1900* (Washington, D.C.: Government Printing Office, 1906), 511–79; reprinted in Aptheker, *Contributions by W.E.B. Du Bois*, 229–346. The number of black farmers (owners, tenants, and sharecroppers) held relatively stable based on 1910 and 1920 census returns. An average of 909,539 black farmers; an average of 218,792 black farm owners; an average of nearly 15.7 million acres owned nationwide; an average of 9,172 black farmers in the Midwest; and an average of 5,663 black owners in the Midwest. For 1910 census statistics see *Negro Population in the United States, 1790–1915* (Washington, D.C.: Government Printing Office, 1918; repr., New York: Arno Press and New York Times, 1968). For 1920 and 1930 see Charles E. Hall, *Negro Farmer in the United States*, Census of Agriculture, Fifteenth Census of the United States: 1930 (Washington, D.C.: U.S. Government Printing Office, 1933).

14. W. E. Burghardt Du Bois, *The Negroes of Farmville, Virginia: A Social Study*, U.S. Department of Labor Bulletin 3, no. 14 (Washington, D.C.: Government Printing Office, January 1898), 1–38, reprinted in Aptheker, *Contributions by W.E.B. Du Bois*, 7–44, quote on 44. Orra Langhorne, *Southern Sketches from Virginia, 1881–1901*, ed. Charles E. Wynes (Charlottesville: University of Virginia Press, 1964), 135, quoted in Edward L. Ayers, *The Promise of the New South: Life after Reconstruction* (New York: Oxford University Press, 1992), 16–17, n29. Stevens, "Only One Survivor of Negro Colony."

15. Stevens, "Only One Survivor of Negro Colony."

16. "The Negro as a Landowner," *Chicago Tribune*, April 23, 1875, 4.

17. Ibid.; E. M. Beck and Stewart E. Tolnay, "The Killing Fields of the Deep South: The Market for Cotton and the Lynching of Blacks, 1882–1930," *American Sociological Review* 55, no. 4 (August 1990): 526–39. Daniel A. Griffith served as county court judge in 1858–60 and 1860–62 and operated Griffith's Mill, a family business. See *History of St. Charles County, Missouri, 1765–1885* (National Historical Company, 1885); see "County Court Judges," in chap. 6 (186–204) and chap. 12 (298–447), transcribed by Deborah Heimann, St. Charles County, Missouri USGenWeb pages (2003) and available at http://www.rootsweb.ancestry.com/~mostchar/history6.htm and http://www.rootsweb.ancestry.com/~mostchar/history12.htm (accessed August 18, 2010).

18. Nell Irvin Painter, *Exodusters: Black Migration to Kansas after Reconstruction: The First Major Migration to the North of Ex-Slaves* (New York: Alfred A Knopf, 1976); see 116 for Dunlap as the site of the second colony established by Benjamin "Pap" Singleton in 1879. Quintard Taylor, *In Search of the Racial Frontier: African Americans in the American West* (New York: W. W. Norton and Company, 1998). Glen Schwendemann, "Nicodemus: Negro Haven on the Solomon," *Kansas Historical Quarterly* (Spring 1968). "Dunlap," *Kansas: A Cyclopedia of State History, Embracing Events, Institutions, Industries, Counties,*

Cities, Towns, Prominent Persons, etc., ed. Frank W. Blackmar, 2 vols. (Chicago: Standard Publishing Company, 1912), 1:553.

19. "The Dakota Colored Colony," *Cleveland Gazette* 1, no. 12 (December 29, 1883): 2. Beti VanEpps-Taylor, *Forgotten Lives: African Americans in South Dakota* (Pierre: South Dakota State Historical Society, 2008); Michelle C. Saxman, "To Better Oneself: Sully County's African American 'Colony,'" *South Dakota History* 34, no. 4 (Winter 2004): 319–28. William H. Pease and Jane H. Pease, *Black Utopia: Negro Communal Experiments in America* (Madison: State Historical Society of Wisconsin, 1963), 46–62. A. G. Stacey, "[Topeka byline]," *American Citizen* (Kansas City, Kansas), February 28, 1890, quoted in Martin Dann, "From Sodom to the Promised Land: E. P. McCabe and the Movement for Oklahoma Colonization," *Kansas Historical Quarterly* 40, no. 3 (Autumn 1974): 370–78; Daniel Littlefield and Lonnie Underhill, "Black Dreams and 'Free' Homes: The Oklahoma Territory, 1891–1894," *Phylon* 34, no. 4 (December 1973): 342–57, esp. 346; "Blood Likely to Flow: Negro Settlers and Cowboys May Meet in Battle in Oklahoma," *Chicago Daily Tribune*, September 22, 1891, 1. Steven Hahn, *A Nation under Our Feet: Black Political Struggles in the Rural South from Slavery to the Great Migration* (Cambridge: Belknap Press of Harvard University Press, 2003), landowners and strategies to secure land, 454–61.

20. "Address by Hon. Frederick Douglass, Delivered in the Congregational Church, Washington, D.C., April 16, 1883, on the Twenty-First Anniversary of Emancipation in the District of Columbia, Washington, D.C., 1883," 16, digitized by the Antislavery Literature Project, http://antislavery.eserver.org/legacies/the-lessons-of-the-hour/the-lessons-of-the-hour.pdf (accessed July 6, 2010).

21. Oscar Micheaux, "Where the Negro Fails . . . There Aren't 300 Negro Farmers in the Ten States of the Northwest—More Opportunities than Young Men to Grasp Them," *Chicago Defender*, March 19, 1910, quote on 1; Janis Hebert, "Oscar Micheaux: Black Pioneer," *South Dakota Review* 11, no. 4 (Winter 1973–74): 62–65. Learthen Dorsey, "Introduction," in Oscar Micheaux, *The Conquest: The Story of a Negro Pioneer Family* (Lincoln, Neb.: Woodruff Press, 1913; repr., Lincoln: University of Nebraska Press, 1994): xi–xxi. Micheaux revisited his comments about non-ambitious black men: "they seem to lack the 'guts' to get into the northwest and 'do things.' In seven or eight of the great agricultural states there were not enough colored farmers to fill a township of thirty-six sections," *The Conquest*, 146. Learthen Dorsey, "Introduction," in Oscar Micheaux, *The Homesteader: A Novel* (Sioux City, Iowa: Western Book Supply Company, 1917; repr., Lincoln: University of Nebraska Press, 1994): 1–8. VanEpps-Taylor, *Forgotten Lives*, 150. Micheaux reworked *The Homesteader* again in 1931 into a feature-length film, becoming the first African American feature film director. Micheaux continued to try to convince blacks of the potential that homesteading offered them, reworking *The Conquest* and *The Homesteader* yet again into the 1944 novel *The Wind from Nowhere*.

22. For selected studies of the Universal Negro Improvement Association and its founder, Marcus Garvey, in relation to rural and agricultural history, see Jarod Roll's essay in this volume. For Clayton see Debra A. Reid, "African Americans, Community Building, and the Role of the State in Rural Reform in Texas, 1890s–1930s," in *The Countryside in the Age of the Modern State: Political Histories of Rural America*, ed. Catherine McNicol Stock and Robert D. Johnston (Ithaca: Cornell University Press, 2001): 38–65, esp. 55–59; for the

NFCF see Debra A. Reid, "The National Federation of Colored Farmers: Constructing Separatist Networks during the 1920s and 1930s," paper presented at Rural History 2010, University of Sussex, England, available at http://www.ruralhistory2010.org/Papers/Reid.pdf (accessed February 24, 2011). For more on Benjamin Hubert and the Association for the Advancement of Negro Country Life, see Mark Schultz's essay in this volume.

23. "Pointer Makes It Pay: An Afro-American Halifax [Virginia] Farmer Near South Boston Who Does Well," reprinted from the correspondence by Rev. C. C. Penick, *Southern Churchman* (n.d.), in *Cleveland Gazette* 13, no. 52 (August 1, 1896): 1. Nathan Pointer and family, *Twelfth Census of the United States, 1900*, Schedule 1: Population, Banister Magisterial (part of E. Dist.), Halifax County, Virginia, Sheet no. 6, Supervisor's Dist. no. 6, Enumeration Dist. no. 40 (hereafter SD and ED).

24. Loren Schweninger explains the time-consuming research process using manuscript census records for 1850, 1860, and 1870 in *Black Property Owners in the South, 1790–1915* (Urbana: University of Illinois Press, 1990), 2–3, 371–91. Thomas Jefferson, *Tenth Census of the United States, 1880*, Schedule 1: Population, St. Ferdinand, St. Louis County, Missouri, sheet 37, SD 1, ED 181; Schedule 2: Agriculture, sheet 19, SD 1, ED 181, line 2. Harry Boyed, *Tenth Census of the United States, 1880*, Schedule 1: Population, Carondelet Township, St. Louis County, Missouri, sheet 26, SD 1, ED 171; Schedule 2: Agriculture, sheet 20, SD 1, ED 171 line 8. Boyed reported 15 tillable acres valued at $1,000, $40 in machinery, and $75 in livestock. For general statistics, compilations by state departments of agriculture or agencies such as the Missouri Negro Industrial Commission can be useful. "State's Negro Population Centers in 25 Counties," *St. Louis Post-Dispatch*, January 22, 1922, 10.

25. Carl J. Ekberg, *French Roots in the Illinois Country: The Mississippi Frontier in Colonial Times* (Urbana: University of Illinois Press, 1998); Reid, "Wheat." Hawkins, *Tenth Census of the United States, 1880*, Schedule 2: Agriculture, sheet 6, SD 1, ED 188, line 6.

26. For Nelson Hubbard, Henry Jackson, and John Morris, see *Tenth Census of the United States, 1880*, Schedule 1: Population, Bonhomme Township, St. Louis County, Missouri, SD 1, ED 186, sheets 24 (Hubbard) and 25 (Jackson and Morris); and Schedule 2: Agriculture, SD 1, ED 186, sheet 16, lines 1 (Hubbard), 7 (Jackson), and 8 (Morris).

27. For mention of Bill Black, see letter from Hardy Fuller, St. Charles, Missouri, to John Green, May 28, 1879, Shepard Papers, WHS. Carville Earle, "The Industrial Revolution as a Response to Cheap Labor and Agricultural Seasonality, 1790–1860: A Reexamination of the Habakkuk Thesis," in *Geographical Inquiry*, 173–225.

28. John Martin, *Tenth Census of the United States, 1880*, Schedule 1: Population, Bonhomme Township, St. Louis County, Missouri, sheet 1, SD 1, ED 183; Schedule 2: Agriculture, sheet 1, SD 1, ED 183, line 1.

8

Of the Quest of the Golden Leaf
Black Farmers and Bright Tobacco in the Piedmont South

EVAN P. BENNETT

In the early autumn of 1939, photographer Marion Post and sociologist Margaret Jarman Hagood, rambling around the back roads of Orange County, North Carolina, stopped to talk to black farmers in Cedar Grove Township, northwest of Chapel Hill. No record of the conversation exists, but the farmers allowed Post to photograph their farms and even posed for a few shots. The meeting no doubt was steeped in the complex racial mores of the day. The presence of two unaccompanied white women on their property could cause Burrie C. "Doc" Corbett, his cousin Wesley Crisp, and their neighbors no small amount of trouble if misinterpreted in the Jim Crow South. Risking offense by turning them away perhaps presented hazards, too, however, especially once Post, in the employ of the Photographic Division of the Farm Security Administration (FSA), revealed her position as an agent of the state. What of the inevitable questions about their everyday lives almost certainly asked by Hagood, author of the then soon-to-be-released (and now classic) study of white tenant farm women, *Mothers of the South* (1939)? The questions of strangers—Do you own or rent this farm? How many acres do you own? How many of your children are in school?—test the limits of hospitality enough; how much more when the questions cross the era's ever-present gendered color line? And what of Post's requests to photograph their farmsteads? Prosperous black farmers sometimes found themselves the target of white farmers' anger and therefore often acted with discretion.

The extent to which the farmers Post and Hagood met were willing to open their lives to outsiders' eyes suggests much about both the farmers and the larger black community of Cedar Grove. A significant number of black landowners called the township home. In 1930 at least forty-seven black farm families, or roughly 35 percent of black families living on farms, owned the land on which they lived. By 1939 the number of black owner-operators had increased by nearly a fifth countywide, so the number of black landowning farm families in Cedar Grove had also likely grown by the time the women landed at Doc Corbett's doorstep.[1] Sixty-year-old Corbett, the son of former slaves, owned more than six hundred acres of land in a county where the average farm measured just over eighty-six acres. He was a prosperous farmer and local community leader. Just two years before Post and Hagood's visit, Governor Clyde Hoey had chosen Corbett to represent North Carolina at the meeting of the National Federation of Colored Farmers. His parents, Richard and Teash Corbett, had also been landowners before their deaths (in 1914 and 1924, respectively), as had his brother, Charlie, who died in 1923. Another brother, forty-five-year-old Bennie, owned his own land just up the road. Richard and Teash bought their farm in the first decade of the twentieth century; all of the Corbett brothers purchased their first farmlands in the boom years of World War I. Nearly a generation younger than Doc Corbett, thirty-nine-year-old Wesley Crisp, also the child of parents born in slavery, owned 165 acres in the same neighborhood (figure 8.1). Like the Corbett brothers, he also had a landowning brother, Eddie, who also lived just up the road. Unlike the Corbetts, however, Wesley and Eddie were first generation landowners. Both began buying land in the 1920s.[2]

What she saw in Cedar Grove piqued Post's interest. "[W]e came across a very interesting settlement of negro *owners* with well equipped large farms, some of the 'grown' children going to college, etc.," she wrote to Roy Stryker, her boss at the FSA. "We want to do much more photography around there.... At least spend a good deal more time & make a more thorough study of that situation." Familiar with shooting the South's deepest pockets of rural poverty—indeed, charged by Stryker to seek them out in defense of the FSA—Post knew that the prosperous black farm community of Cedar Grove, where even many of the sharecroppers worked for black landowners, was unique. Sociologist Howard Odum's wonder at what Post and Hagood reported validated her surprise. The famed scholar, then leading the charge to study and correct the South's endemic poverty from his post at the University of North Carolina, "was particularly interested to set up a special project to concentrate & work on just that group."[3]

What Post and Hagood saw in Cedar Grove was in fact not the norm for

Figure 8.1. Negro-owned farm of about 165 acres and tobacco barns belonging to Wes Cris[p], cousin of B. C. Corbett, in a very prosperous settlement near Carr, in Orange County, North Carolina, September 1939. Source: Library of Congress, Prints & Photographs Division, FSA/OWI Collection, LC-USF34–052049-D.

the rural South. Focused on the plight of the rural South's poorest people, Post, Hagood, and even Odum can be forgiven for overlooking communities like Cedar Grove. And they were not alone. For at least a generation, assessments of the lives of black rural southerners had found little but blight. Even the most sensitive studies could not escape the general poverty that shaped life for millions of black rural southerners. In his classic *The Souls of Black Folk* (1903), W.E.B. Du Bois indicted cotton, the crop lien, and conniving white elites for the deep poverty of black rural people in Dougherty County, Georgia. Alluding to the object of mythic Jason's quest in a chapter titled "Of the Quest of the Golden Fleece," Du Bois posited that "one might frame a pretty and not far-fetched analogy of witchery and dragon's teeth, and blood and armed men, between the ancient and modern quest of the Golden Fleece," between the travails of the Argonauts and those of the landless black cotton farmers of the Black Belt. Du Bois' characterization of the link between cotton, credit, and black rural poverty has remained a touchstone for historians of the rural South, who have found that the conditions Du Bois described were not limited to Georgia or even to the Cotton South.[4]

Yet the Corbetts, the Crisps, and the several dozen other landowning families of Cedar Grove call into question depictions of the unrelenting bleakness of the lives of black rural southerners. Despite their poverty and the continuing obstacles of racism, black rural people built bonds of community and the institutions that nurtured them. While there is no denying the difficulties black farmers faced, not all lived under the heel of a landlord and/or time merchant. Black landowners, while few in number regionwide, nevertheless built stable foundations not only for their own families but for their communities as well.

No region illustrates this better than the bright tobacco–growing region straddling the Virginia–North Carolina border where Doc Corbett and his neighbors lived. Known in tobacco circles as the Old Bright Belt, the region was not immune to tenancy and the crop lien, but it nevertheless boasted of some of the highest levels of black land ownership anywhere in the nation in the late nineteenth and early twentieth centuries. This was the result of a number of factors, including the large-scale division of plantation lands after the Civil War, but the rise of bright tobacco for cigarettes in the late nineteenth century played a critical role. True, for many, tobacco promised prosperity but delivered poverty. However, the growing demand for bright leaf tobacco offered both black and white farmers the opportunity to turn even a few marginal acres into a profitable farm. In good years, it paid well enough to give even poor farmers a foothold. Black farmers like Doc Corbett used their tobacco money to buy their own farms, establish their families on the land, and build rural communities.

For many of these farmers, growing tobacco was more than a means to make money. The demands of tobacco agriculture shaped their human culture. Their work and their folkways, their society and their lives revolved around its seasons, just as was the case for white farmers. For African American farmers, of course, tobacco had a special resonance: working in and around the fields, curing barns, and strip houses could not but stir memories of slavery and subjugation. Yet many, like Doc Corbett's cousin Charlie Wells, who specifically reported to census enumerators in 1930 that his farm was a tobacco farm, claimed tobacco culture as their own.

Sadly, much of this legacy has been forgotten. Like other tobacco farmers, especially those at the margins, black tobacco farmers faced the pressures of population outmigration, changing global trade patterns, and the economic pressures to adopt machines and other technologies, in addition to the complexities of generational succession common to rural people, and their numbers fell precipitously after 1960. Discrimination by local and national agricultural agencies only compounded the challenges they faced. Denied or delayed in receiving loans and shut out of the county committees that distributed tobacco allotments, black tobacco farmers regularly found themselves with little access to the many federal mechanisms that kept many small white tobacco farmers afloat in the decades after the creation of the federal tobacco program in the 1930s. Numbering in the tens of thousands as late as the 1950s, black tobacco farmers have nearly disappeared. The 2002 agricultural census counted just over 900 black tobacco farm operators nationwide; these accounted for 2.5 percent of all tobacco farm operators. In 2007, only 227 remained, largely as a result of the 2004 "buyout" legislation that ended the federal tobacco program.[5]

As powerful as demography, popular memory is also culpable for the forgotten legacy of black tobacco farmers. Beginning in the wake of emancipation in the late nineteenth century, southern and national agricultural leaders described black rural life largely in terms of the labor African Americans were expected to provide on southern farms. Despite the reality of thousands of black farm families staking their claim on the land, leading farm voices and policy makers failed to conceive of African Americans as agriculturalists or agrarians. Only white men were truly farmers; all others were the help. Until only recently, much of the scholarship on black rural southerners failed to escape this framework. Reducing black rural life to its economic constraints, scholars of southern agriculture long underestimated black southerners' connection to the land and instead depicted the rural South as a place to be escaped. More recent scholarship has corrected this deterministic approach in important ways, focusing on the dynamics of black farm family life, rural African Americans' relationships with the natural world, and the nuances of black-white interaction in the rural countryside, among other things. These works, with some exceptions, by turning their gaze away from the fields, have missed the extent to which black farm families, especially black landowning farm families, enmeshed themselves into the South's crop cultures.[6]

This applies especially to tobacco. One might be forgiven if one surmised, based on recent films, popular books, and museum displays, that tobacco farmers were overwhelmingly white men.[7] Partly a result of the recent dearth of black tobacco farmers, but also a product of assumptions about just who qualifies to be a rural southerner, black tobacco farmers (men and women) have disappeared from the popular memory of Tobacco Road. Examining the lives of families like the Corbetts, the Crisps, and their neighbors helps to restore them to their proper place.

Acquiring land was never easy for African Americans, but by the early twentieth century, black farmers across the upper South had made rapid gains in land ownership. The increasing willingness of white landowners to sell to African Americans, the increasing availability of credit through black-owned financial institutions, and broad encouragement from leading voices made land ownership a goal for thousands of black rural families. By 1910, historian Loren Schweninger has found, nearly half of black farmers in the upper South owned their land. The highest rates of black farm ownership were in Virginia, where "former slaves and their children became almost obsessed with the idea of acquiring their own land." Much of the growth of black land ownership occurred in the Virginia Tidewater, where white depopulation coupled with the rise of truck farming gave black farmers the opportunity to establish themselves economically.[8]

A second region of growth was in the former Southside plantation belt. Here, plantation slavery had been the hallmark of what historian Joseph C. Robert called the "Tobacco Kingdom," a roughly rectangular region in the Piedmont centered at Danville, Virginia, extending from the Piedmont's fall line in the east to the foothills of the Blue Ridge in the west, and roughly two counties north and south from the Virginia–North Carolina state line.[9] In the decades following the Civil War, this region underwent a revolution in land tenure. Overall, the number of farms in the region grew by more than three-quarters between 1870 and 1890, and then grew again by more than half by 1920. Sharecroppers and other tenants operated a large number of these farms, but both black and white farmers purchased much of the land. In 1900 landowners operated just under half of the region's farms; by 1920 they worked three-fifths. In that time the number of owner-operated farms increased by half, as more than 18,000 new landowners plowed their own ground. The majority of these farmers, like Richard and Teash Corbett, bought land in the first decade of the century, when low tobacco prices sent land prices downward. The boom years accompanying World War I also provided many farmers the opportunity to buy land for the first time.

Two trends supported expanded land ownership. First, the subdivision of former plantation lands brought many formerly unimproved acres into cultivation. Unable or unwilling (or both) to recreate the plantation system, many former planters and their heirs opted to sell their lands and move on in the decades following the Civil War.[10] "Mr. Overby . . . was busy all the time," a planter in Mecklenburg County, Virginia, complained in 1891, "cutting up and selling land to negroes at $10 per acre which cost $2."[11] According to census figures, Mr. Overby was obviously not the only one doing so. Between 1860 and 1920 the number of Mecklenburg County farms rose by an astonishing 500 percent. The amount of improved acreage increased by only 16 percent during the same period, indicating that many of the new farms resulted from the division of existing farmlands rather than the clearing of unimproved or forest land. Tenant farms accounted for much of the growth, but the number of landowner-operated farms more than doubled during these years. Figures from neighboring plantation counties bear out a similar pattern.[12]

The clearing and farming of once sparsely populated but not necessarily marginal lands at the edges of the plantation belt also propelled the expansion of landownership in the late nineteenth and early twentieth centuries. Beginning in the 1870s, small farmers took advantage of low land prices in both untapped and former cotton regions in the central and western North Carolina Piedmont and opened it to tobacco agriculture. The process continued well into the first decades of the twentieth century. As in former plantation districts, sharecropping and tenancy rose in many of these areas, but so did landowning. As late as 1919 the extension agent in Randolph County, North Carolina, noted the increasing number of farmers pouring into the county to grow tobacco. "Up until two years ago we hardly knew that tobacco could be grown here," he claimed. "The industry is making such progress that land that was selling for $20 an acre is now selling for $50. Some land has sold for over $100 an acre to tobacco growers from the mountainous counties who are seeking more level land."[13] Indeed, by 1920 the number of owner-operated farms had increased by roughly two-fifths since 1880. Neighboring counties reported similar and even greater increases.[14]

The growth in black landownership mirrored the broader expansion of land ownership in the Virginia–North Carolina Piedmont in the half century after the Civil War. In the Virginia Southside counties, where plantation slavery had been strongest and black populations the largest, black land ownership grew steadily in the late nineteenth century and exploded in the first two decades of the twentieth century. By 1900 just over a third of Southside black farmers owned their farms; by 1910 nearly half did. Black landowners by 1910, in fact, outnumbered black tenants in six Southside Virginia counties and nearly equaled them in two others (table 8.1). Between 1900 and 1920 the number of black landowners in Southside Virginia rose by 84 percent.[15]

Across the state line in North Carolina, the rate of black land ownership grew even faster. In 1900 just over one-fifth of black farmers owned their

Table 8.1. Rates of Black Ownership, Virginia–North Carolina Piedmont, 1900–1950

County	1900 %	1910 %	1920 %	1930 %	1940 %	1950 %
VIRGINIA						
Brunswick	40.8	58.9	58.3	44.5	48.9	41.7
Campbell	46.4	68.0	52.7	52.4	58.2	56.9
Charlotte	37.8	59.1	67.2	46.6	43.7	43.7
Franklin	37.5	56.7	58.6	51.5	46.2	53.7
Halifax	36.5	38.8	41.5	29.4	29.4	27.4
Henry	15.6	33.2	39.4	45.8	62.4	68.2
Lunenburg	50.1	66.4	58.6	47.7	53.9	42.8
Mecklenburg	33.5	49.5	43.9	31.0	34.3	30.5
Nottoway	44.0	71.4	68.2	68.1	66.9	71.2
Patrick	25.7	49.2	59.5	31.3	37.4	45.0
Pittsylvania	17.3	31.4	33.8	20.9	22.9	27.6
Virginia Total	**35.2**	**49.6**	**48.6**	**37.4**	**40.2**	**37.6**
NORTH CAROLINA						
Alamance	25.5	47.1	47.2	30.7	34.9	32.9
Caswell	9.3	21.1	27.4	19.0	23.4	19.9
Chatham	20.1	37.5	40.6	29.4	34.7	42.3
Davidson	20.6	39.2	41.8	17.4	29.2	46.1
Durham	8.6	20.5	25.6	19.7	22.7	28.6
Forsyth	43.0	56.8	58.5	24.8	37.0	43.4
Granville	13.6	24.4	30.9	19.2	18.4	16.8
Guilford	40.1	53.4	57.5	34.1	46.3	37.0
Orange	25.0	39.2	40.5	34.2	37.0	37.0
Person	13.3	18.7	39.8	15.6	15.3	13.1
Randolph	58.9	68.8	78.9	44.8	55.6	62.0
Rockingham	14.0	24.3	30.2	20.5	24.1	21.0
Stokes	16.4	27.1	35.7	26.4	27.0	24.2
Surry	48.8	57.6	63.7	26.2	38.0	33.3
Vance	13.3	30.8	33.6	15.8	20.5	17.1
Wake	16.7	26.8	26.2	18.0	28.6	17.6
Warren	19.2	36.5	38.2	24.8	33.4	29.3
Yadkin	34.2	58.2	56.3	14.9	37.0	47.0
North Carolina Total	**20.0**	**33.1**	**36.7**	**23.0**	**28.1**	**24.6**
Overall	26.7	41.1	42.9	29.2	34.0	30.3

Source: Historical Census Browser, University of Virginia, Geospatial and Statistical Data Center, http://fisher.lib.virginia.edu/collections/stats/histcensus/index.html (accessed June 29, 2010).

land; by 1910 roughly one-third did so. By 1920 the number of black landowners had more than doubled since 1900. As in Virginia, the number of black landowners grew fastest in the region's former plantation counties— the line of counties abutting Virginia, stretching from Warren County in the east to Rockingham County in the west. There, the number of farms operated by black landowners tripled between 1900 and 1920; the number of sharecropped farms grew by less than a third in those counties during the same period. Unlike in Virginia, however, the highest rates of black land ownership came not in former plantation counties but in those counties where white yeoman farmers had once predominated. In Randolph County, at the fringes of the traditional plantation belt, African Americans were only 11.5 percent of the population and operated only 7.6 percent of the county's farms in 1920. Yet of these, more than three-quarters owned their land. In other peripheral counties, like Yadkin and Surry in the foothills of the Blue Ridge, where the black population was traditionally small, a similar pattern prevailed.[16]

There was no simple path to landownership. As in other parts of the South, African Americans hoping to buy land had to convince sometimes reluctant whites to sell to them. Many relied on the connections patronage offered, but this often could not protect them from hostile whites. In 1915 Vance County whites killed a black farm family and burned their house to the ground "for the new crime of landowning."[17] Nevertheless a few factors helped black farm families in their search for land. For one, the widespread availability of land for sale reduced the competitive pressure on land prices. While prices for the best land could skyrocket in periods of intense demand, as the Randolph County agent suggested, prices for average land remained fairly low. In 1887, according to one report, excellent tobacco land in Granville County could fetch upward of $40 per acre, but less desirable lands could be had for $5 to $7 per acre.[18] While a rough measure, the average farm values of owner-operated farms suggest that prices continued to remain low at least until the boom years accompanying World War I. In 1910, a year of depressed tobacco prices but also the end of a decade of growing land acquisition by African Americans, the median average value of owner-operated farms was just over $17 per acre.[19]

For poor, landless farmers even low prices could often prove too high, of course, but in the Piedmont some found opportunities to earn additional incomes largely denied poor black farmers in other parts of the South. Seasonal peaks in demand for workers offered many tenants opportunities to earn additional income. Skilled field hands often earned a premium over other workers because of their ability to manage the complexities of growing and curing bright tobacco. "Skillful tobacco hands command from $15 to $24 per annum more than ordinary farm laborers," one observer noted of conditions in Rockingham County, "and double what they could get in the shipping-tobacco regions."[20] At the same time, many black women found seasonal work in the Piedmont's many tobacco factories as stemmers; some black men found work on the floors of the region's auction houses.[21] Often, to pool their resources, families drew on the income children could earn working either for neighbors or in town.

The better availability of credit regionally also helped black farmers. The crop lien was a common tool used by both black and white small farmers to obtain seasonal credit, but its use was not widespread in the Piedmont. Instead, landowners usually secured lines of credit from local banks. Many more banks existed for white farmers, of course, but the savings banks and credit unions operated by and for African Americans in Richmond, Durham, and other towns expanded opportunities for black farmers in the Piedmont to obtain loans for purchasing land.[22] Some black farmers also found warehousemen to be willing lenders, provided they agreed to sell their tobacco on the warehousemen's floors. "The average negro farmer has no trouble getting loans," one white Extension Service agent complained in 1919, "so he will not work for the white man."[23] As with land prices, these arrangements often cost black farmers more than white farmers, but for the growing number of landowners they proved invaluable.

None of these opportunities existed in an agricultural vacuum, of course. Instead, they were in part the product of the expansion of bright tobacco agriculture across the Piedmont in the late nineteenth and early twentieth century. Planters in Caswell County perfected the means for curing tobacco into a bright yellow color (as opposed to the dark color of the traditional Virginia "shipping" tobacco) in the middle of the nineteenth century; by the 1880s the popularity of the yellow leaves among chewing tobacco manufacturers and, increasingly, cigarette makers drove up prices for the leaf. Hoping to break out of the agricultural and economic doldrums that had settled in over much of the Piedmont, farmers across the region began growing bright tobacco. Prices fell in the 1890s as a result of a national depression, the market dominance of the American Tobacco Company, and increased production in eastern North Carolina, but farmers across the Old Bright Belt (as the Piedmont came to be called to distinguish it from the New Bright Belt in the east) continued to find it more profitable than any other crop they could grow. Bright tobacco seemed to thrive in the region's largely infertile soils, and while the cultivation techniques it required limited the amount of acres a family could grow (as well as the amount of time they could devote to other crops), the prices good tobacco could bring at auction could make even a small farm profitable.[24]

Tobacco agriculture often brought little of the material wealth it promised, especially to the landless. Nevertheless it could provide the way off the treadmill of rural poverty. Late nineteenth-century stories of upward mobility proffered by boosters interested in promoting the tobacco trade must be taken with a grain of salt, but they nevertheless reveal something about the changes bright tobacco wrought. In 1880 a Granville County editor wrote encouragingly of a farmer equipped with little more than "two eyes, two hands, and two feet" who worked four years on shares before buying an unimproved 120-acre farm at $7.50 an acre. Since then, the editor continued, he had "not only paid for his land, but [had] built a fine dwelling and every necessary out-house, all the most convenient and substantial model." The once landless tenant now had a farm that was "all paid for and [he] could sell the place of $25 an acre."[25] During the World War I era, the return of high prices fueled similar stories. "Most of the farmers are getting out of debt, in many cases buying new homes," one Extension Service agent reported in 1918.[26] "The calls ... for help in the selection of water and light systems for the farm home have come largely from the tobacco section," another reported the following year.[27]

Like their white neighbors, many black farm families in the Old Bright Belt used bright tobacco as a means of improving their economic status. Not all succeeded, of course, but given just the right conditions, some could turn a few acres of tobacco land into a foothold. "The farmers ... have made good in growing tobacco," a black Extension Service agent reported from Mecklenburg County in 1917; "it has sold extremely well and many have paid some of their debts which have been standing for years." "Anthony Jones bought 40 acres of land and finished paying for it out of his crop of tobacco," he noted the following year. "Junius Jones, Charlie Ogburn, Ebert Feggins, Joseph Feggins, and John Goode ... bought land this year for the first time. Sandy Russell sold $12,000 worth of tobacco."[28] Small wonder a contemporary told his superiors that it was "not at all necessary to urge tobacco growing" among the black farmers of Vance County.[29]

Black landowners' reliance on, even eagerness for, tobacco agriculture calls into question popular depictions of black-owned farms as invariably small, subsistence-oriented, and situated on the most marginal of lands. Certainly this image has a basis in reality, but in the Old Bright Belt, black land ownership was far more complex. Bright tobacco seemed to thrive on infertile soil, but it would not grow just anywhere and instead required soils containing a certain range of chemical and morphological qualities. The complex soil patterns of the Piedmont, shaped by a long geological history of chemical decomposition and erosion, meant that good tobacco land was often broken into small patches. A given tract of land might have only a small percentage of good tobacco land. Black and white farmers alike adjusted their land tenure to this reality, piecing together the best tobacco lands they could get and blurring the lines between owner and tenant in the process. Pittsylvania County farmer Sampson White's description of his farming activities in late nineteenth century is suggestive of the range of possibilities in land tenure the Old Bright Belt presented. "I have been renting land for ¼ rent," he explained, "I also work a farm of my own and has been [sic] for 9 years. I work men for a part of the crop and they pay ½ the fertilizer bill and gets ½ of the crop. I work land of my own and rent land and rent land to others."[30] White was hardly the average landowner, of course, but his farm practices were not unique. Like him, thousands of black landowners, like their white neighbors, embraced the complexity of farming in the larger tobacco economy. "Tobacco is an important crop," one Extension Service agent wrote of the region around Doc Corbett's farm. "You can not interest Negro farmers in this section unless one wants to talk about tobacco."[31] In their quest for survival, even prosperity, black farm families in much of the Piedmont looked for more than just their own vines and fig trees, understanding that a good tobacco patch could help them more.

The lives of black tobacco farmers in the Piedmont also require us to explore the relationship between African Americans and the crop cultures of the South more deeply. American agricultural history, especially that of the South, and black history are indivisibly linked. Indeed, African American history stretches back to the tobacco fields that encircled the Chesapeake in the seventeenth century. Yet, while historians have explored how the labor regimens of the South's crops shaped the lives of Africans and their descendents, and have paid attention to how age, sex, and skill in working these crops could make life in the fields different for various individuals, the questions of what black farmers (broadly defined to include any who worked the fields) thought of the crops they grew, or how communities of black farmers imposed meaning on the crops remain less developed. Not so with the experiences of white farmers. Much has been written, much of it by white farm families themselves, of tobacco's role as a cultural touchstone, of its power to evoke visceral memories of smell, touch, and sound, of the sense of community and family that the rituals of its seasons could imbue in those who labored among the leaves.[32] While black voices have been recorded, their experiences in the fields and barns have largely been cast (with some merit) as examples of the continuation of racial subjugation beyond slavery or lumped together with white farmers based on the assumption that the cultural values rooted in tobacco must have been the same regardless of race (or class, for that matter). Black farmers' relationship to tobacco, in other words, has either been cast in overwhelmingly negative terms or left unexplored.[33]

Evidence suggests that black farm families afforded tobacco a place in their lives that ranged far beyond its economic value. Tobacco agriculture shaped life and labor, culture and custom among black farmers much as it did for their white neighbors. Black farmers and their families expressed similar appreciation for the rhythms of tobacco's seasons, the sensual experience of growing tobacco, and the opportunities for renewing family and community connections that shared labor in busy seasons presented. Farm families in Cedar Grove, for example, found tobacco harvest time to be a perfect occasion for holding community dances that drew revelers from as far away as neighboring counties. Music scholar Kip Lornell has argued that these dances nurtured musical styles that reflected a deep appreciation for rural life and tradition.[34]

Tobacco auction season proved as enticing to black farm families as white farm families. Black farmers paid attention to the news of the markets, following prices as auctions began in Georgia and openings progressed northward. (National black newspapers carried market news, indicating that interest in the goings-on likely extended far beyond the farms.) Marion Post's photographs of auctions in Durham, made during the same fall she met Doc Corbett, reveal a world in which black farmers participated not only in auctions but in the social events surrounding them as well. Like white farmers, they attended Brunswick stew fundraisers, listened to itinerant preachers, bought goods from peddlers, sold livestock, and shopped for the best deals at local stores (figures 8.2, 8.3) This world was highly segregated: black and white farmers slept in segregated bunk rooms as they awaited the opening of the auction, and stores and restaurants also enforced the color line, but auction warehousemen arranged tobacco on the floors without regard to the color of its producer, and the enclosed spaces necessitated black and white interactions that mirrored those sometimes found in the fields.

Figure 8.2. Negro farmer talking with warehouse man about price he received at auction for his tobacco, Durham, North Carolina, November 1939. Source: Library of Congress, Prints & Photographs Division, FSA/OWI Collection, LC-USF33–030673-M4.

Figure 8.3. Farmer buying patent medicine from salesman outside tobacco warehouse during auction sale, Durham, North Carolina, November 1939. Source: Library of Congress, Prints & Photographs Division, FSA/OWI Collection, LC-USF33–030702-M4.

Like their white neighbors, black farmers also earned social prestige on the warehouse floors, where, in the highly public ritual of auctioning tobacco, their abilities in growing and handling the leaf were exhibited to the community. In 1937 black farmer Harvey Wagstaff, a landless tenant, moved to southern Alamance County, where he found "people . . . growing very little tobacco, and that of a poor quality." "Determined to show his neighbors how to produce good quality tobacco," he set himself as an example. After caring for his plants and fields carefully, he "cured and sold the best tobacco crop ever grown in his community this year." In the end, his crop brought him more than $1,200 in profit. "I intended to do a good job of it this year as I had just moved over here," he told the black county extension agent. "I wanted Mr. Foster, my landlord, to see that I was a good farmer."[35] As Wagstaff's account suggests, skill could sometimes earn esteem for black farmers across racial lines as well. Certainly this was true of Doc Corbett, whose skill as a farmer earned praise from a white Extension Service agent. "Some of our most respected and substantial farmers are negroes," he explained to his superiors in 1942. "B.C. Corbett, who is one of the largest tobacco farmers in the county and will probably sell about $20,000.00 worth of tobacco this year, is a negro. He is one of the Neighborhood Leaders and has taken an active part in supporting all war programs."[36] For many black farm families, their tobacco crops served as points not only of individual pride but of race pride as well. Their finely arranged piles of tobacco offered at the auction and their neatly ordered farms were proof that white people's long-held claims that African Americans could never succeed as farmers were completely wrong (figure 8.4).

The extent to which we can speak of a unique black tobacco culture is limited, of course. Farm families developed idiosyncratic and tangled attachments to the crop about which it is difficult to generalize. Like much of the southern cultural landscape, Piedmont tobacco agriculture was made by whites and blacks together. Nevertheless the experiences of each group (not to mention the various subsets of each group) were distinct. Black farmers were, on average, poorer than white farmers and thus often had less ability to diversify their production or add acreage. Black landowners often toiled on smaller farms and more often worked on other people's land in addition to their own. In addition, no matter their success or abilities, they still faced walls of discrimination that left them outside leadership roles in the larger tobacco economy. No black farmer, no matter how well he knew the crop or how much land he owned, could hope to become a buyer for a tobacco company, an auctioneer, or a warehouse owner, paths open for

Figure 8.4. Stock barn with wagon and truck of hay on a very prosperous farm of over 600 acres belonging to B. C. Corbett in a black settlement near Carr in Orange County, North Carolina, September 1939. Source: Library of Congress, Prints & Photographs Division, FSA/OWI Collection, LC-USF34-052050-D.

white farmers and their sons. Black and white farm women alike found these paths blocked, too, but racism shaped landowning women's experiences as well; the wives and daughters of black landowners, for example, were much more likely to work in the fields or at off-farm seasonal jobs than were those of white farmers.

Such limitations led farmers to redouble their efforts on their farms in support of the black community. In 1942 Doc Corbett parlayed his position into an opportunity to tell a national radio audience of the hard work the black farmers in his and other communities were doing for the war effort.[37] The leaders of the White Oak Grove Baptist Church, the cultural center of the Cedar Grove black community, were all prominent farmers. Doc Corbett's father Richard Corbett established the church on a corner of his farm not long after purchasing the land so that, according to family lore, his wife Teash would not have to walk so far to worship services. His son-in-law Lawson Pinnix, also a landowner, served as an elder, as did Charlie Wells, another landowner and the husband of Teash's niece. Anderson "Bud" Yarborough, another landowning farmer, served as minister.[38] Much the same story could be told of neighboring churches like Mt. Zion A.M.E., which landowner Bedford Corbett (no relation) helped to establish in the late nineteenth century, and Lee's Chapel Baptist Church, where tobacco farmer Currie Ellison served as an elder.[39] Numerous institutions of higher education across the Piedmont, from tiny St. Paul's College in rural Brunswick County to what is now North Carolina A&T University in Greensboro, received much of their material support from the region's tobacco farmers, who found in these places levers with which to lift up the black community (and their own children).

Sadly, the importance of black-owned farms to Piedmont black rural communities was matched only by their precariousness. Living by tobacco often meant dying by tobacco. Low prices followed a bust in the market in 1920. The setback hurt all across the Tobacco South. In response, farmers from Virginia through the Carolinas answered the call of organizer Aaron Sapiro, the legal mind behind a number of successful agricultural cooperatives, to create a cooperative marketing organization. Modeled after cooperatives like California's Sun-Maid Raisin Cooperative, the Tri-State Tobacco Growers' Cooperative sought to raise prices by controlling the flow of tobacco to the market by having the majority of tobacco growers agree to market their crops through the cooperative.[40] With the help of the Extension Service, thousands joined the Tri-State in 1920 and after. The cooperative's leaders, looking back on the failures of earlier attempts to create cooperatives, actively sought the support of black tobacco growers. Hoping to hold onto their farms, black farmers rushed to join. "Charlotte co. is the banner co. in 'sign-ups,'" the county's black Extension Service agent proclaimed.[41] Black farmers organized local meetings and became some of the most vocal supporters of the cooperative. "We, the negroes of Warren County, are getting busy to do what we can for the organization," one farmer wrote to the *Tri-State Tobacco Grower*, the cooperative's official organ, in 1923.[42] For the first few years, things appeared to be working. Across the Piedmont, black Extension Service agents reported that the farmers with whom they worked were seeing higher prices from cooperation.

Unfortunately, the high prices were fleeting, and the cooperative was failing. By 1923 its problems were becoming apparent; in 1926 it failed entirely, taking with it a large number of black farms. In Guilford County the black Extension Service agent reported that members of the cooperative had been "forced to abandon their club for other occupations because the association had not made its payments promptly."[43] Things only got worse as the decade progressed. By 1930 tobacco prices had fallen to pre–World

War I levels. Thousands lost or abandoned their farms. Between 1920 and 1930, the number of Old Bright Belt farms operated by black landowners fell by more than a third.[44]

By 1933 many farmers, white and black, were desperate for a solution to chronically low prices. Like their white neighbors, perhaps even to a greater extent, black farmers rushed to support the tobacco program created by Franklin Roosevelt's Agricultural Adjustment Act (AAA). The program required that two-thirds of farmers agree to the production limits it mandated in order for the price supports it offered to be available.[45] "We are successful in getting 93% sign up," Durham County's black Extension Service agent reported in 1933.[46] His experience was typical. Support from black farmers continued, too, beyond 1933 because the program successfully raised prices and allowed many to survive on the land. One Extension Service agent reported that higher tobacco prices had allowed black farmers in his county to buy better livestock, grow better gardens, and improve their poor acreage. "Since the AAA has been into effect," he bragged in 1935, "more than three hundred different farmers have been to see the county agent with reference to making improvements on their farms and around their homes."[47] "I had given mortgage against my place and I got a loan from the government to pay it off and to build me a house," one Durham County black farmer exulted. "The whole thing is $1600.00. In a few years I expect to pay the entire thing off for I am going to hit it a big blow this year."[48]

The program was not perfect, however. Black landowners benefited more than tenants, who, without land, could not control the all-important acreage allotments necessary to market tobacco without penalty. By 1940 the percentage of landowning black farmers had risen, but only because of a sharp decline in the number of tenants. Across the Old Bright Belt, the number of farms operated by black landowners increased by only six farms during the 1930s; more than 7,000 new farms operated by white owners appeared during the same period.[49] By 1950 the number of black landowning farmers in the Old Bright Belt fell by 5 percent, and things only got worse in subsequent decades.

A number of factors contributed to the decline in black landowning farmers over the second half of the twentieth century. Like other farmers, they faced the pressures of urbanization, mechanization, and generational change. Millions of acres of farmland across the nation fell under the bulldozer in the twentieth century. This was especially pronounced in the Piedmont, where industrialization and urbanization skyrocketed after World

War II. At the same time, keeping farms together proved challenging, as many black landowners who purchased farms in the early twentieth century tried to hand them to their children. After Doc Corbett died in 1963, his heirs divided his farmland multiple times. Much the same occurred to his brother Benjamin's estate following his death in 1968. Wes Crisp's farm, meanwhile, became the subject of much dispute after his death in 1950; it ultimately fell to his son, who lived in town and did not farm.[50]

Federal farm programs, especially the federal tobacco program, were most responsible for the massive decline in black landowning farmers in the late twentieth century. Not intended to dispossess black farmers, the program's operation nevertheless placed far greater pressure on black farmers than white ones. Part of the problem was structural, a result of the program's design and implementation. While Congress modified the program's particulars over the years, the tobacco program essentially was one of carrots and sticks. Landholders on whose land tobacco was produced in the years between 1930 and 1932 received allotments based on historical production during those years. (Allotments followed the land, not the family that farmed it, meaning that tenants had no claims on allotments, no matter how much tobacco they produced in those years.) Each year, Department of Agriculture forecasters examined trends in demand and then determined how much tobacco would be needed to meet this demand. Each spring, landowners received notice of how much of their allotments could be grown in order to be eligible for participation in the program. Those who agreed to abide by the specifications received price supports if their tobacco failed to sell at what were called "parity" prices; those who refused to abide by them had to pay a prohibitive 50 percent tax on all tobacco they marketed. Every three years, farmers decided through referenda whether the program would be in effect. They voted it down only once—in 1938. Overall, the program raised farm families' incomes and helped to keep small tobacco farms profitable in an era of farm growth and consolidation.[51]

Many small farmers bore the burden of the program's production controls, however. To keep production in line with demand even as foreign leaf production soared, tobacco program managers regularly had to reduce domestic production. When made, allotment reductions took effect across the board, meaning that small farmers continued to divide what were already small slices of the pie. Made too small, tobacco farms became unprofitable, since many fixed costs did not decline in proportion to acreage reductions. A curing barn cost just as much for a farmer with a one-acre allotment as for one with a five-acre allotment. By the 1960s many of the smallest tobacco farms in the Piedmont had been abandoned, and their allotments were either leased or redistributed to larger growers. By the 1980s thousands more had disappeared or their owners had taken off-farm jobs to make ends meet.[52]

Black farmers' experiences with the operation of the tobacco program were somewhat contradictory. For many, a tobacco allotment proved to be a saving grace. Studies of black Piedmont farmers made in the 1970s and 1980s found that allotments were a key determinant in whether black farmers remained on the land.[53] Yet, because black-owned tobacco farms tended to be smaller and dependent almost entirely on their tobacco crops, black farmers experienced dispossession disproportionately. "Tobacco allotment too small," an activist working among black farmers in southern Virginia in 1968 noted briefly. "Afraid of the future. Picture looks worse and worse."[54] Between 1950 and 1992 the number of black-owned farms in the Old Bright Belt declined by more than 90 percent; by 1997 there were less than five hundred black-owned farms in the region.[55]

Broader economic and demographic changes cannot fully explain such a precipitous decline, however. Instead, outright discrimination proved to be most destructive to black farmers. Informed by what rural sociologist Jess Gilbert has called "low modernist" thinking that wedded a desire for centralized, expert planning with the need for participatory democracy sensitive to local knowledge, the developers of the tobacco program created a system in which the power to wield federal authority fell into the hands of local elites.[56] Acting through elected local committees, white elites adjudicated questions about allotments, deciding how they were distributed and enforced. Racism, as Pete Daniel has shown, shaped how many county committees made their decisions.[57] "I own 232½ acres of land," one black farmer from eastern North Carolina wrote to the Secretary of Agriculture in 1959. "My *tobacco acreage allotment* however is 4⁵⁄₁₀₀ [4.05] acres. I definitely feel I am being discriminated against by the local office of the commodity stabilization in this matter because I am a negro."[58] Many black landowners in the Old Bright Belt would no doubt have shared his complaint. Brunswick County farmer Linwood Brown, for example, sued the U.S. Department of Agriculture in the early 1990s because of ill-treatment at the hands of USDA officials and later joined with Mecklenburg County farmer John Boyd Jr. in the creation of the National Black Farmers Association. He was also a litigant in the landmark 1999 lawsuit *Pigford v. Glickman*, in which the federal district judge found a widespread pattern of discrimination by the U.S. Department of Agriculture against black farmers.⁵⁹

Determining the exact cause of such discrimination is difficult, of course. The general white racism of the region explains part of it, but the failure of federal authorities to provide the same services to black farmers as to white ones also likely reflected a broader attitude of white elites about the abilities of African Americans as farmers. Continuing a pattern extending back to the end of slavery at least, white officials denigrated the abilities of black farmers and refused to see their goals and aspirations as landowners as legitimate. Through their land ownership and efforts to build black rural communities, black tobacco farmers like Doc Corbett and his neighbors across the Old Bright Belt challenged this narrow range of vision. That a victory (however incomplete) over the white racism of federal authorities began in the region is not especially surprising. That it might owe something to tobacco is.

Notes

1. 1930 United States Federal Census, Manuscript Census Returns, Cedar Grove Township, Orange County, North Carolina, database online at Ancestry.com (Provo, Utah: Ancestry.com Operations, 2002). U.S. Census Bureau, *Sixteenth Census of the United States: 1940, Agriculture*, vol. 1: *State Reports*, Part 3: Statistics for Counties (Washington D.C.: Government Printing Office, 1942), 325.

2. Information about familial relationships and land acquisition for B. C. Corbett, Richard Corbett, Teash Corbett, Charlie Corbett, Benjamin Corbett, Wesley Crisp, and Eddie Crisp come from the 1900, 1910, 1920, and 1930 United States Federal Censuses, Manuscript Census Returns, Cedar Grove Township, Orange County, North Carolina, Ancestry.com. Ages and name spellings for B. C. Corbett, Benjamin Corbett, Wesley Crisp, and Richard Corbett come from their death certificates: North Carolina Death Certificates, 1909–1975, database online at Ancestry.com (Provo, Utah: Ancestry.com Operations, 2007). Death date and name spellings for Teash Corbett and Charlie Corbett come from their grave markers; transcriptions available at Cemetery Census, http://cemeterycensus.com/nc/orng/cem072.htm.

3. Marion Post to Roy Stryker, October 2, 1939, Roy Stryker Papers, University of Louisville (microfilm), series 1, reel 2, Library of Congress.

4. W. E. B. Du Bois, *The Souls of Black Folk* (1903; repr. with introduction by Randall Kenan, New York: Penguin, 1995), 163. The scholarship on the poverty of post–Civil War southern agriculture is voluminous. Classic studies include Arthur Raper, *Preface to Peasantry: A Tale of Two Black Belt Counties* (1936; repr. with introduction by Louis Mazzari, Columbia: University of South Carolina Press, 2005), and Thomas J. Woofter, *The Plight of Cigarette Tobacco* (Chapel Hill: University of North Carolina Press, 1931). See also Harold D. Woodman, *King Cotton and His Retainers: Financing and Marketing of the Cotton Crop*

of the South, 1800–1925 (Lexington: University of Kentucky Press, 1968); Jay R. Mandle, *The Roots of Black Poverty: The Southern Plantation Economy after the Civil War* (Durham: Duke University Press, 1978); Pete Daniel, *Breaking the Land: The Transformation of Cotton, Tobacco and Rice Cultures since 1880* (Urbana: University of Illinois Press, 1985); Gavin Wright, *Old South, New South: Revolutions in the Southern Economy since the Civil War* (New York: Basic Books, 1986), esp. chaps. 2–4; J. William Harris, *Deep Souths: Delta, Piedmont, and Sea Island Society in the Age of Segregation* (Baltimore: Johns Hopkins University Press, 2001).

5. U.S. Department of Agriculture, *2007 Census of Agriculture*, vol. 1, table 54, p. 58, available at http://www.agcensus.usda.gov/Publications/2007/Full_Report/usv1.pdf.

6. Stewart Tolnay, *The Bottom Rung: African American Life on Southern Farms* (Urbana: University of Illinois Press, 1999), does the best job of linking crop cultures to black family life. Other important works that have explored black rural life include Mark Schultz, *The Rural Face of White Supremacy: Beyond Jim Crow* (Urbana: University of Illinois Press, 2007), and Chad Montrie, *Making a Living: Work and Environment in the United States* (Chapel Hill: University of North Carolina Press, 2008), chap. 2.

7. See, for example, Billy Yeargin, *North Carolina Tobacco: A History* (Charleston, S.C.: History Books, 2008), and *Remembering North Carolina Tobacco* (Charleston, S.C.: History Books, 2008). Recent films on tobacco farmers, most notably Cynthia Hill, *Tobacco Money Feeds My Family* (Durham, N.C.: Markay Media, 2003), DVD, and Jim Crawford, *Down in the Old Belt: Voices from the Tobacco South* (Roanoke, Va.: Swinging Gate Productions, 2005), DVD, include interviews with black farmers. For the treatment of black farmers in tobacco museums, see Adrienne Petty, "History and Myth at the Tobacco Farm Life Museum," paper presented at the annual meeting of the Southern Historical Association, Birmingham, Ala., November 2006, in author's possession.

8. Loren Schweninger, *Black Property Owners in the South, 1790–1915* (Urbana: University of Illinois Press, 1990), 171–76, quote on 173.

9. Joseph C. Robert, *The Tobacco Kingdom: Plantation, Market, and Factory in Virginia and North Carolina, 1800–1860* (Durham: Duke University Press, 1938). A number of recent historians have explored the late nineteenth-century expansion in land ownership among black farmers in the antebellum tobacco plantation regions of Virginia and North Carolina. See Lynda J. Morgan, *Emancipation in Virginia's Tobacco Belt, 1850–1870* (Athens: University of Georgia Press, 1992); Laura F. Edwards, *Gendered Strife and Confusion: The Political Culture of Reconstruction* (Urbana: University of Illinois Press, 1997), esp. chap. 2; Jeffrey R. Kerr-Ritchie, *Freedpeople in the Tobacco South: Virginia, 1860–1900* (Chapel Hill: University of North Carolina Press, 1999); and Sharon Ann Holt, *Making Freedom Pay: North Carolina Freedpeople Working for Themselves, 1865–1900* (Athens: University of Georgia Press, 2000).

10. Jane Turner Censer, *The Reconstruction of White Southern Womanhood, 1865–1895* (Baton Rouge: Louisiana State University Press, 2003), 128–45.

11. Armistead Burwell to Edward Bouldin Burwell, October 20, 1891, Burwell Family Papers, Section 9, Virginia Historical Society, Richmond.

12. Not all former plantation counties experienced growth in the same way, but general patterns are discernible. These counties formed the core of the antebellum tobacco plantation belt of the Virginia–North Carolina Piedmont (table 8.2). Census takers did

Table 8.2. Plantation Counties in the Virginia–North Carolina Piedmont, 1860–1920

County	Total Farms 1860–1920 % Change	Improved Acreage 1860–1920 % Change	Owner-Operated Farms (All Races) 1880–1920[a] % Change	Tenant-Operated Farms (All Races; All Classes) 1880–1920[a] % Change
VIRGINIA				
Brunswick	340.6	-35.6	116.5	68.5
Mecklenburg	502.8	16.0	104.5	266.9
Lunenburg	243.3	-31.3	105.1	59.3
Nottoway	214.9	-44.2	39.4	-30.7
Charlotte	373.8	-32.1	218.1	92.4
Halifax	458.3	-18.4	115.2	153.1
Pittsylvania	318.2	9.1	77.4	128.7
NORTH CAROLINA				
Warren Vance Granville[b]	353.3	-20.6	69.0	70.7
Person	338.9	-8.1	77.2	174.9
Caswell	269.7	-42.9	44.3	168.5
Rockingham	332.6	0.3%	43.9	108.0

Sources: Compiled from 1860, 1870, 1890, 1900, 1910 and 1920 census returns, Historical Census Browser, University of Virginia.
Notes: a. Census takers did not enumerate farms by tenure until 1880, so data include returns from 1880 to 1920 only.
b. These counties shared historical boundaries. Vance County was created in 1881 out of portions of Warren, Granville, and a small portion of Franklin County.

not enumerate farms by tenure until 1880, so the final two columns consider the period from 1880 to 1920 alone.

13. "Report of the County Agent, 1919: Randolph County, North Carolina," Extension Service Annual Reports, North Carolina, reel 8, Record Group 33, National Archives, College Park, Md. (hereafter cited as RG 33, NA).

14. As in the plantation counties, not all peripheral counties experienced growth in the same way, but general patterns are discernible. These peripheral counties formed the core of the antebellum tobacco plantation belt of the Virginia–North Carolina Piedmont. Census takers did not enumerate farms by tenure until 1880, so the final two columns consider the period from 1880 to 1920 alone (table 8.3).

15. In 1900 there were 3,541 black landowners in the Virginia counties listed in table 8.1. In 1920 there were 6,501. During this same period, the number of non-landowning farmers rose by 15.5 percent, from 5,929 to 6,845. Compiled from 1900 and 1920 census returns, Historical Census Browser, University of Virginia, http://mapserver.lib.virginia.edu/.

16. Compiled from 1920 census returns, Historical Census Browser, University of Virginia, http://mapserver.lib.virginia.edu/.

17. Untitled article, The Crisis, 10:1 (May 1915): 21–22, quote on 21.

Table 8.3. Peripheral Counties in the Virginia–North Carolina Piedmont, 1860–1920

County	Total Farms 1860–1920 % Change	Improved Acreage 1860–1920 % Change	Owner-Operated Farms (All Races) 1880–1920[a] % Change	Tenant-Operated Farms (All Races; All Classes) 1880–1920[a] % Change
VIRGINIA				
Patrick	285.9	68.4	9.5	-7.1
NORTH CAROLINA				
Chatham	115.0	-26.7	10.0	-2.8
Randolph	127.7	0.6	40.5	0.8
Davidson	135.0	6.2	27.1	5.7
Forsyth	137.2	30.2	32.8	144.4
Yadkin	212.0	28.8	63.7	52.0
Surry	355.2	91.9	78.9	111.8

Sources: Compiled from 1860, 1870, 1890, 1900, 1910 and 1920 census returns, Historical Census Browser, University of Virginia.

Note: a. Census takers did not enumerate farms by tenure until 1880, so data include returns from 1880 to 1920 only.

18. Address by Col. William H. Burgwyn, Henderson (N.C.) *Gold Leaf*, November 3, 1887.

19. To arrive at this figure, I divided the total value of lands and buildings on owner-operated farms by the total number of acres under the control of owner-operated farmers for each county in table 8.1 to arrive at an average value per county. I then took the median of these values. Compiled from 1910 census returns, Historical Census Browser, University of Virginia, http://mapserver.lib.virginia.edu/.

20. J. B. Killebrew, "Report on the Culture and Curing of Tobacco in the United States," in U.S. Census Bureau, *Report of the Productions of Agriculture as Returned in the Tenth Census* (Washington, D.C.: Government Printing Office, 1883), 120.

21. Dolores Janiewski, *Sisterhood Denied: Race, Gender and Class in a New South Community* (Philadelphia: Temple University Press, 1985).

22. Charles E. Landon, "The Tobacco Growing Industry of North Carolina," *Economic Geography* 10, no. 3 (July 1934): 252. Schweninger, *Black Property Owners in the South*, 171. Troy Kickler, "Credit Unions," North Carolina History Project Encyclopedia, available online at http://www.northcarolinahistory.org/encyclopedia/49/entry/. (accessed August 3, 2010).

23. "Report of the County Agent, 1919: Mecklenburg County, Virginia," Extension Service Annual Reports, Virginia, reel 4, RG 33, NA.

24. A number of works have explored the history of bright tobacco in detail. The most exhaustive is Nannie May Tilley, *The Bright-Tobacco Industry, 1860–1929* (Chapel Hill: University of North Carolina Press, 1947), while Pete Daniel's *Breaking the Land* provides a more recent account.

25. J. B. Hunter, *Useful Information Concerning Yellow Tobacco, and Other Crops, as Told by Fifty of the Most Successful Farmers of Granville County, N.C.* (Oxford, N.C.: W. A. Davis, 1880), 19.

26. "Report of the County Agent, 1918: Surry County, N.C.," Extension Service Annual Reports, North Carolina, reel 6, RG 33, NA.

27. "Report of the County Agent, 1919: Davidson County, N.C.," Extension Service Annual Reports, North Carolina, reel 7, RG 33, NA.

28. "Report of Ned D. Morse, Mecklenburg County, Virginia, 1917," "Report of the Work of the Negro County Agents, Calendar Year 1919," Extension Service Annual Reports, Virginia, reel 3, RG 33 NA.

29. "Report of the County Agent (Negro), 1918: Vance County, N.C.," Extension Service Annual Reports, North Carolina, reel 6, RG 33, NA.

30. Sampson White to E. Dana Durand, September 1910, reprinted in Kerr-Ritchie, *Freedpeople in the Tobacco South*, 255.

31. "Report of the County Agent (Negro), 1937: Orange County, N.C.," Extension Service Annual Reports, North Carolina, reel 81, RG 33, NA.

32. Numerous examples of this literature have been produced in recent decades. For examples, see Pamela Barefoot with Burt Kornegay, *Mules and Memories: A Photo Documentary of the Tobacco Farmer* (Winston-Salem, N.C.: J. F. Blair, 1978); Wendell Berry, "Our Tobacco Problem," *Progressive* 56, no. 5 (May 1992): 17–19. Billy Yeargin, *Remembering North Carolina Tobacco*.

33. One excellent exception to this trend is Adrienne Petty, "Standing Their Ground: Small Farm Owners in North Carolina's Tobacco Belt, 1920–1982," Ph.D. diss., Columbia University, 2004.

34. Kip Lornell, "Banjoes and Blues," in *Arts in Earnest: North Carolina Folklore*, ed. Daniel W. Patterson and Charles G. Zug (Durham: Duke University Press, 1990), 221–24.

35. "Report of the County Agent (Negro), 1937: Alamance County, N.C.," Extension Service Annual Reports, North Carolina, reel 77, RG 33, NA.

36. "Report of the County Agent, 1942: Orange County, N.C.," Extension Service Annual Reports, North Carolina, reel 127, RG 33, NA.

37. *Pittsburgh Courier*, September 26, 1942.

38. Relationships and land tenure from 1920 and 1930 Manuscript Census Returns and genealogical resources, Ancestry.com. Church offices taken from gravestone transcriptions, Cemetery Census, http://cemeterycensus.com.

39. Church offices taken from gravestone transcriptions, Cemetery Census, http://cemeterycensus.com.

40. For background on the Tri-State Cooperative, see Tilley, *The Bright-Tobacco Industry*, 449–80. For Sapiro, see Victoria Saker Woeste, *The Farmer's Benevolent Trust: Law and Agricultural Cooperation in Industrial America, 1865–1945* (Chapel Hill: University of North Carolina Press, 1998).

41. "Report of the County Agent (Negro), 1922: Charlotte County, Virginia," Extension Service Annual Reports, Virginia, reel 9, RG 33, NA.

42. Letter from J. L. Bolden, *Tri-State Tobacco Grower*, July 1923.

43. "Narrative Report of the County Agent (Negro), 1926: Guilford County, N.C.," Extension Service Annual Reports, North Carolina, reel 28, RG 33, NA.

44. Compiled from 1920 and 1930 census returns for counties listed in table 8.1. Historical Census Browser, University of Virginia.

45. The best work on the creation of the federal tobacco program remains Anthony

Badger, *Prosperity Road: The New Deal, Tobacco, and North Carolina* (Chapel Hill: University of North Carolina Press, 1980).

46. "Narrative Report of the County Agent (Negro), 1933: Durham County, N.C.," Extension Service Annual Reports, North Carolina, reel 58, RG 33, NA.

47. "Narrative Report of the County Agent (Negro), 1935: Campbell County, Va.," Extension Service Annual Reports, Virginia, reel 46, RG 33, NA.

48. "Narrative Report of the County Agent (Negro), 1934: Durham County, N.C.," Extension Service Annual Reports, North Carolina, reel 63, RG 33, NA.

49. Compiled from 1930 and 1940 Census Returns.

50. Death dates come from gravestones, transcriptions at http://cemeterycensus.com/nc/orng/cem072.htm. Land records come from searches of Orange County Land Records, available at http://server2.co.orange.nc.us/OrangeNCGIS/default.aspx. Court records indicate there was a familial challenge to the title to Wes Crisp's property following his wife's remarriage after his death. His son, Lacy Crisp, ultimately inherited the property. He died in 1973. His death certificate recorded that he lived in Mebane and worked as a laborer. Death records from Ancestry.com.

51. This is of necessity a brief description of a far more complex program. Numerous works relate how the program has functioned over the years. Anthony Badger's *Prosperity Road* and Pete Daniel's *Breaking the Land* provide the best historical accounts of the program's development and operation, but both limit their discussion of the technical details in favor of broader narratives. For the details of the program's everyday operation, see Charles Pugh, "The Federal Tobacco Program: How It Works and Alternatives for Change," in *The Tobacco Industry in Transition: Policies for the 1980s*, ed. William R. Finger (Lexington, Mass.: Lexington Books, 1982), and Jasper Womach, "Tobacco Price Support: An Overview of the Program," Congressional Research Service Report, June 25, 2004, available online at http://ncseonline.org/NLE/CRSreports/04Jun/95-129.pdf.

52. For the effects of change on small Piedmont farms, see Evan P. Bennett, "King Bacca's Throne: Land, Labor, and Life in the Old Bright Belt since 1880," Ph.D. diss., College of William & Mary, 2005, esp. chap. 5.

53. Janet K. Wadley and Everett S. Lee, "The Disappearance of the Black Farmer," *Phylon* 35, no. 3 (1974): 280–81. Michael D. Schulman and Barbara A. Newman, "The Survival of the Black Tobacco Farmer: Empirical Results and Policy Dilemmas," *Agriculture and Human Values* 8, no. 3 (Summer 1991): 46–52.

54. VISTA Report from Halifax County, Virginia, August 5, 1968, folder 42, box 63, National Sharecroppers Fund Papers, Walter P. Reuther Library, Wayne State University, Detroit, Michigan.

55. The 1992 and 1997 Censuses of Agriculture.

56. Jess Gilbert, "Low Modernism and the Agrarian New Deal: A Different Kind of State," in *Fighting for the Farm: Rural America Transformed*, ed. Jane Adams (Philadelphia: University of Pennsylvania Press, 2003), 131–46.

57. Pete Daniel, "African American Farmers and Civil Rights," *Journal of Southern History* 73, no. 1 (February 2007): 3–38.

58. Bryant Miller to Secretary of Agriculture, September 16, 1959, Tobacco Division Correspondence and Other Records, 1956–59, Records of the ASCS, RG 145, NA.

59. Pigford consent decree approved, 185 F.R.D. 82. For Brown's background, see *Richmond Times-Dispatch*, February 23, 2006.

9

"Justifiable Pride"

Negotiation and Collaboration in Florida African American Extension

KELLY A. MINOR

Amanda Parrish, Leon County's African American home demonstration agent, recalled "Community Problems Handled" in her 1920 annual report. "The people wanted to know at first what was the use of joining the clubs," she explained. That question was common where home extension was new. But the women also wondered "what would become of the goods after they had canned them and how is it that the government would send an agent to them if it did not expect some pay in return."[1] In Florida during the height of legalized segregation it is not surprising that rural African Americans were cautious about, even suspicious of, outsiders sent into their county by the state and national government claiming they wanted to help local families without compensation or condition. But Parrish was genuine; extension agents offered free, voluntary programs to aid rural communities, the benefits theirs to keep. Parrish knew that, but until she could prove it to local families, they had little reason to accept or trust her. At first glance, Parrish and other black extension agents fit right into the local communities to which they were assigned. All were African American women, most were from rural backgrounds, and many were middle aged. But they also were university trained and government appointed. Armed with scientific expertise and enthusiasm for improved living, they nevertheless were strangers explaining to grown women how to run their homes and raise their children. Local women, however, came to accept home demonstration agents because the agents let the women choose what the service would become in their communities.

Together, agents and families negotiated a program of reform and then collaborated to carry it out. They were not, however, unfettered in their negotiations. African American home demonstration work faced endemic obstacles to success. On a regional scale, the southern extension apparatus was segregated and inequitable. In Florida, as elsewhere, the extension reflected race and gender bias. This segregation created a hierarchy that facilitated close scrutiny of black programs. Until the 1960s, Agricultural Extension for white men was headquartered at University of Florida (UF) in Gainesville, while its black counterpart, both Agricultural and Home Extension, operated from Florida Agricultural and Mechanical University (FAMU) in Tallahassee. White female extension was based at Florida State College for Women (FSCW) in Tallahassee.[2]

Male authority over female reform likewise existed early in Florida Extension. Until 1925, African American agricultural agent A. A. Turner directly supervised all black extension workers in Florida, and male agricultural agents taught rural women basic Home Extension practices. As extension work expanded, however, it became clear that a female district agent, akin to the white district agents who coordinated county agents and answered to the state home demonstration supervisor, would be an asset. Though county agents were scattered across the panhandle, the creation of the "Negro" District Home Demonstration position unified their work into a more comprehensive system that reached more families, put women directly in charge of the work, and tailored the programs more closely to women's needs.[3] Once black women gained home demonstration positions at the county level they organized clubs for farm women and picked local club leaders, clubwomen who demonstrated a clear grasp of program principles and who could successfully teach others. These adult positions were replicated for girls, who staffed a Junior Home Demonstration Council and served as 4-H club leaders. Club leaders served as linchpins in local home demonstration, acting as liaisons between farm families and agents.[4]

The "Negro" division in Florida and other Jim Crow states employed fewer agents in the field, controlled fewer resources for education, and reported to white supervisors who exercised varying degrees of influence on local programs. Certainly racism and sexism shaped and frequently hindered extension work among black farm families. But bias did not totally define the services that "Negro" division home demonstration agents delivered. Overcoming racism and sexism did not dominate agents' and farm families' objectives, nor did racism and sexism undermine the goals that agents and rural families pursued. In fact, fifty years of segregation caused black agents and clubwomen to turn extension's shortcomings to their advantage. By selectively adapting the standard home demonstration agenda, clubwomen could reinforce their farm communities' autonomy, consequently heightening their influence within those same rural communities.

Black farm women's personal interests and immediate goals defined the programs that agents offered. State or national prescriptions for rural reform (modified by contemporary bias) yielded to practical, customized improvements chosen by farm women and implemented in their own backyards and kitchens. Indeed, relationships between families and agents *on the ground*, within distinctive rural communities, shaped extension work more than standardized national programs, state-level bureaucracy, or even federal legislation or political activism. Despite its shortcomings, home demonstration accomplished substantive good among families, largely because agents respected farm women's abilities to define their own reform and implement it, as they had been doing for generations. A tenuous dynamic existed between agents, who acted as educators and guides about new scientific methods, and women and girls, who adapted the advice to address their own needs. If an agent could not befriend farm women and girls, she would have no audience.[5] She targeted farm owners knowing that they could decide for themselves whether to participate and could direct resources toward the project undertaken without securing permission from their landlord. Thus agents could convince farm women to devote labor to tending a garden and canning the produce to increase the variety and nutritional value of the food their families consumed (figure 9.1).

Histories of home demonstration often concentrate on the extension program's influence *on* rural families and less on how it functioned *for* rural families. They rarely consider home demonstration within the context of the rural communities in which it functioned. Home demonstration agents are either depicted as judgmental bullies who expected farm women to participate in superficial programs without addressing the endemic racism and sexism that constrained farm women's lives; or as well-meaning but highly ineffectual busybodies. In Florida, neither is true. Agents worked *with* rural women, helping many local families allay the inadequacy of their daily lives by offering diverse programs from which women chose what they wanted to pursue. Even if race and gender limitations could be swept aside, there still was no progress without local support, but earning it was neither assured nor simple. Farm women did not have an inexhaustible supply of time or resources, nor were they particularly welcoming of

Figure 9.1. Canning demonstration, Washington County, 1919. Source: A. A. Turner, "Farm and Home Makers' Clubs Bulletin." Gainesville: University of Florida, Division of Agricultural Extension, 1919, University of Florida Digital Collections.

outsiders in their close-knit communities. The farm women had to value the programs as worthy of their time and had to trust the agents to act in the best interest of their families.[6]

At the same time, black home demonstration agents could act locally in a way that black men or white women could not. All agents found that they could exploit women's association with caregiving to promote certain reforms, such as nutrition, childcare, and even sanitation. But whereas white agents might rely on their male colleagues to promote the extension cause before local governments, it was less acceptable for black men to do so. An agricultural agent seeming to take charge was likely to raise eyebrows, potentially jeopardizing local funding for his work. Black male extension agents had to appear at once competent in their own right and subordinate to a white supervisor. And initially, black farm agents resisted surrendering authority over some of extension work to women. They found, however, that sharing authority with black home demonstration agents helped the "Negro" division more than the males could on their own. For wary white taxpayers or bureaucrats, black men and women working together appeared to save costs and to be something distinct, rather than a mere duplicate of white extension.[7]

Black home demonstration agents, however, threatened local white communities and black constituents less because they appeared to be respectable women extending their knowledge about caregiving and homemaking to other women. This sense of propriety in the black agents' role in rural domestic reform has been documented in other states, and extension agents shared this credibility with other African American female reformers.[8] As long as black women did not appear to encourage black families to rise above their economic station, demand political independence, challenge white supremacy, or assume other controversial positions, the very public roles they adopted as reformers raised few objections. As Glenda Gilmore argues, "In a nonpolitical guise, black women became the black community's diplomats to the white community."[9]

Black home demonstration programs also operated within acceptable domestic reform parameters. The agents could apply their training, often gained through 1890 land grant institutions that served African American students, specifically Florida A&M in Tallahassee, in programs that focused on traditional homemaking skills. The club leaders and members, predominantly the wives of farm owners, in turn, translated this to their own communities. The farm women generated the funds they needed to implement the programs; they paid their own way. Moreover, white supervisors had final authority over the programs the black agents and club leaders implemented, but generally programs within the needs of the farm families' domestic economy proved acceptable. Rural farm women used the programs to elevate their own status within their communities, even dressing in caregiver-white uniforms to indicate their compliance with mainstream scientific reform. The attire also indicated the disposable income that black farm-owning families had. This helped them win the support of white agents and supervisors, particularly men, within the chauvinistic system. This image of black home demonstration as respectable, competent, and mainstream was part of the larger diplomatic process of earning acceptance.

Home demonstration was a constant process of negotiation and diplomacy. Together, African American home demonstration agents and farm women navigated myriad hazards en route to their goals for a more comfortable, equitable life in rural Florida. Like her white counterparts, a black agent ran a gauntlet of demands and obstacles to please each of the overlapping communities to which she belonged. Perhaps because she knew her client families were doing the same, she focused less on social and political changes that would meet resistance, and more on the tangible improvements in daily life that would raise fewer eyebrows yet still empower farm women. Even extant extension records reflect that sort of symbolic empowerment hidden by practical improvement.

Figure 9.2. Newspaper clipping of Mrs. Ethel M. Powell, Duval County home demonstration agent, and Mrs. Royal at a home pantry display in 1946, a consequence of three decades of home demonstration work in Duval County. Source: "Home Demonstration Scrapbook," University of Florida Archives.

Extension sources are both illuminating and tedious. Though official records are voluminous, most are standardized forms and repetitive narrative accounts of a year's work. Nevertheless, they are rich in subtle detail about African American farm owners. A home demonstration agent reported on discussions during meetings, programs that she and her clients tackled, and specific challenges or successes. Agents also used the reports to protect their jobs by chronicling their relevance in a poorly funded program. Consequently, controversy or complaint rarely appeared in the annual reports, and statistics about women's involvement could easily be exaggerated for effect. The narratives nonetheless reflected agents' personalities and offer insight into the agent-family relationship. A variety of photographers, from club women and agents to professionals employed by the Florida and the Federal Extension Service, documented home demonstration, and the photographs vary in quality, but not in subject. Photographs documented stories of success and tended to feature measurable evidence of accomplishment. Unofficial records, such as correspondence and newspaper articles, often illustrated, offer less filtered portraits of club women (figure 9.2). Together this mix of sources generated by and about home demonstration agents sketch out a sometimes testy, often rewarding, and always delicate balancing act between women defending their own brand of pride in rural Florida.[10]

Generally, historical criticism of home demonstration outweighs accolades, particularly regarding agents seemingly ignoring, even tolerating, institutionalized racism and sexism. For example, Carmen Harris catalogues the impact of race bias on the prolonged segregation of 4-H camps for children as well as the detriment of assumptions about racial inferiority on the larger extension program for agricultural education. Extension worker and historian R. Grant Seals agrees with Harris that the persistent shortfall of funding and resources for black extension degraded its potential to the extent that most African Americans left agriculture and agricultural extension, the reverse of its stated goals.[11]

Other historians, however, find that black agents and families made the most of the home demonstration that was available to them, specifically because it followed the separatist model that they had used to establish rural communities and secure farm land since the Civil War. Indeed, how they did so reinforces local determinism's resiliency over national and regional racism. Dianne Glave explores one way that African American women shaped home demonstration and their own lives within a segregated world. In home gardens Glave finds evidence of women consciously melding inherited traditions and selectively adopted extension recommendations. Whereas Progressive reformers (part of the milieu that launched home demonstration) "envisioned national agricultural reforms that subjugated the discrete and nuanced expertise of local actors to models of bureaucratic efficiency and skill," local women decided what programs they wanted and needed, which they chose to participate in, and how much authority agents would have. A case in point is the home garden. Glave notes that some women chose to adopt the traditional "imitation of nature" they learned from mothers and grandmothers, a seemingly chaotic cottage garden of native plants "borrowed" from nearby woods. Despite agents' critiques of such designs as disorderly signs of poverty and ignorance, the women persisted in their preference for the garden that evoked memories of their childhood and served a practical purpose.[12] In 1952 Mrs. Rosa Walker in Leon County showed off her garden, a traditional vegetable garden likely similar to those she grew up enjoying, and on which her family still depended for a diverse diet. Such a garden was distinctly rural, utilitarian,

Figure 9.3. Okra patch at home garden of Rosa Walker, Rock Hill Community, 1952. Source: University of Florida Digital Collections.

and distinctly old-fashioned in its function. It was not designed for recreation or aesthetics. For Mrs. Walker, such a garden represented a wise use of space and a reminder of tradition rather than a harbinger of modernity (figure 9.3).[13]

In contrast, some women chose to adopt extension-recommended symmetrical gardens, including a tidy lawn bisected by a sidewalk. Farm women who did this helped introduce different aesthetics into their rural communities. Mrs. Smith and her friend chose to remake the Smiths' front-yard landscape into the image of a more contemporary suburban yard with distinct lawn and shrubs (figure 9.4). It differed radically from Rosa Walker's kitchen-garden-style landscape because it was not utilitarian but purely ornamental and more urban than rural in aesthetics. Glave suspects that the design rural farm women imposed on their front yards reflected an order rooted in a row-crop tradition inherited from ancestors' slave-cabin gardens. The same is true of the women's penchant for organic gardening methods, such as composting and natural fertilizers. Home demonstration agents recommended these techniques as money-saving choices, but women had inherited them from generations stretching back to slaves who used these methods in their dooryard gardens. The net

Figure 9.4. Mrs. Smith and a friend installing foundation shrubbery in the planned style that home demonstration agents recommended, 1952. Her home, too, reflects improvements, including fresh paint and a screened porch for the family to enjoy the outdoors without worrying about mosquitoes. Source: University of Florida Digital Collections.

result was that African American women maintained traditions important to them, choosing to build on them with agent-supplied updates.[14] In both cases the agents who worked with Mrs. Smith and Mrs. Walker respected each woman's personal preferences and needs by helping them to establish successfully the kind of garden each wanted.

Black home demonstration clubs replicated these variations in garden design across the state as agents worked with clients to craft the home demonstration agenda on the local level. African American farm women's deep suspicion of outsiders, even if they were black women, made it absolutely necessary for home demonstration agents to accommodate their wishes. An agent who refused to do so simply did not last. First, local support and funding were necessary for home demonstration, and no one would spend money on programs and agents that local families did not want. Second, the structure of home demonstration meant that agents really were more facilitators than dictators. So it was that local rural women were ultimately the ones who defined their home demonstration agenda.

Losing local support tolled the end of extension, especially where taxpayers contributed to agents' salaries in a segregated system with little to spare for any female extension work, much less among black families. Home demonstration was funded on three levels; the U.S. Department of Agriculture (USDA) supplied national resources, state land grant colleges appointed and funded agents, and local governments provided the rest of an agent's salary, office space, supplies, and travel. County support varied widely; long-time "Negro" district home demonstration agent Floy Britt noted in 1952 that county funding for black female agents ranged from as little as $100 to as much as $3,000.[15] Even white agents fought for continued financing, but a black home demonstration agent regularly found that a county was unwilling to pay for her services if there were white agents, or even a black agricultural agent, to be secured instead. Because so many counties were cash poor and less likely to subsidize a black agent, black home demonstration agents often received pay almost entirely derived from state and federal funds. Though this shortchanged an agent in her salary, it facilitated putting home demonstration into counties where it could reach black residents whom county commissioners would not willingly support any other way.

Home demonstration agents learned to play gracefully whatever hand their county and clubwomen dealt. In fact, a number of black agents served a county because local support came from other sources, such as churches and civic clubs. An agent, then, who could win friends and build trust stood the best chance of working in a county because she could count on aid from outside the official extension circle. Rule one, above all else and despite what the official national extension plan might be, was to listen, plan, and act locally. Rule two was to be mindful that farm women's perceptions did not automatically match home demonstration's reality. Ironically, despite Florida Extension's inequitable policies, Florida's state Home Extension leaders encouraged, even fought for, home demonstration by and for rural African Americans. In fact, State Home Demonstration Director Flavia Gleason was one of the people most instrumental in creating, securing, and funding (from the white home demonstration budget if necessary) the "Negro" district agent position. Gleason was convinced that home agents, including black agents, had to be free of direct male control and that black home demonstration work needed to expand to more counties and families. But most farm women never met Gleason, and her office in Tallahassee was far removed from their world. Black women perceived the home demonstration apparatus as divorced from, even hostile to, their interests.

Consequently, agents had to place women's my-backyard-first concerns above national extension goals. Farm wives in Leon County, Florida, did not care what interested farm wives in North Dakota. They cared almost as little for what the USDA identified as its annual goals. They cared, instead, about their own farm economy and their family's needs. Agents who responded to this interest earned local trust and could better affect local improvements.

Consider 1920 Leon County, where Amanda Parrish collaborated with local families to customize home demonstration based on their preferences. Much of rural Florida, particularly in impoverished areas, sorely needed the kinds of improvements that home demonstration agents facilitated: sanitary toilets, home pantries, vaccinations, and screened windows. And Parrish tackled these areas. But in her annual report, she recalled as the "best pieces of demonstration work done in the county this year" the "building of a new church at Bradfordville and the repairing of several others." Certainly the church needed renovation; "the old church . . . was in a dangerous condition and had to be propped on every side in order to have services in it." So, "the clubs [that Parrish formed] set to work to build a new one in April and by the middle of Sept. had it all complete and ready for worship." Parrish had facilitated a community goal because a church that had fallen into ruin had been rebuilt by the efforts of newly formed home demonstration clubs. Church building may not have been part of the official demonstration agenda, but the project fulfilled the community goal, and as a community member, she honored the farm women's desire to devote their energies and resources to rebuilding their church. The Bradfordville church was a community focal point, and because it mattered most to the club members, it mattered most to Parrish. To her delight, "all this has aroused great interest in club work."[16]

In reality most home demonstration agents significantly adapted each year's national agenda to match clubwomen's expressed interests. Melissa Walker finds this pattern prevailing in eastern Tennessee, where black and white women's annual programs of work might differ significantly, each attuned to the resources and desires of local clubwomen.[17] Like Glave's gardeners, rural women molded their home demonstration experience by suggesting projects, asking questions, or simply refusing to join any club that did not interest them.

A successful home demonstration agent nimbly directed the flow of interest by offering her updated knowledge without demanding that clubwomen do something meaningless or impossible. Consider home

Figure 9.5. The Stewart family of Micanopy and their guests, 1951. Source: University of Florida Digital Collections.

improvement projects, which could involve great expense and labor. By the 1950s, agents would have preferred to replicate in rural communities the neat, modern suburban homes springing up across the nation. And some farm-owning families had both the means and the desire to create such homes. Others adopted improvements piecemeal, or not at all, depending on their resources and interests.

Selected accomplishments of farm-owning families provide evidence of tangible change that home demonstration agents advocated and rural families adopted in post–World War II Florida. In 1951 in Alachua County the Stewart family revamped their home into a model of home demonstration–inspired improvements. Indeed, extension publications featured their home in a photo spread capturing them at leisure and entertaining guests. The Stewarts' home reflects contemporary middle-class comforts and is not overtly rural. It embodied the ideal that home demonstration agents advocated, a modern home in a traditional rural community, the best of both worlds (figure 9.5).

Not all families, however, could reproduce or necessarily wanted to reproduce what the Stewarts achieved. Usually, home improvement results

Figure 9.6. Mrs. Rosa Walker bakes in her kitchen, Leon County, 1952. Source: University of Florida Digital Collections.

were mixed and reflected both the rural setting of a member's home and the agents' emphasis on using readily available resources. Home demonstration club members might simply clear away trash, whitewash, or rake a walk. Others built furniture from available materials such as citrus packing crates, sewed curtains and tablecloths with flour and seed sacks, and recycled old clothing into many smaller articles to decorate their living space.

Any adaptations that improved rural living caught the attention of home demonstration agents. For instance, Leon County home demonstration agent Irie Mae Clark photographed Mrs. Rosa Walker baking a cake in her own kitchen in 1952 (figure 9.6). Clark wanted to demonstrate that Walker was using the baking techniques Clark had taught her, but the photo says much more. Walker's kitchen, though tidy, was decidedly not modern. Her simple curtains were clearly homemade, the walls of her kitchen indicate that she lived in an older home modified to meet changing needs, and her stove was a relic. In fact, thirty years before, Walker's kitchen would have been the ideal of home improvement in rural Leon County. But her home was not ideal by the time Clark photographed her. Yet Clark set aside that ideal in favor of what Mrs. Walker could afford and did not feature her baking in a community kitchen or outside at a demonstration table. Her kitchen reflected the reality of her life, so Clark chose instead to emphasize that improvement was possible in any circumstance.

To some extent, Florida's climate allowed even more flexibility in home improvement and community beautification because virtually anyone could plant flowers to improve a home's outdoor appeal. Though such simple touches as bulbs or a flower planted in a coffee can had been part of home demonstration recommendations for decades, by the end of World War II flowers took on significance beyond beautification. They did not further farm family productivity but represented the shift in the postwar era away from women as productive units of the farmstead. Farm women who planted flowers had the leisure time to do so. As with Glave's gardeners, home demonstration club members chose what their home would look like to passersby. Moreover, their choices often conveyed their status as wives of farm owners whose adoption of modern technology freed their wives to do things other than cook, clean, and care for children.

Landscaping and exterior home improvement projects varied widely from farm family to farm family, as did interior improvements. Home demonstration agents featured those who simply created more comfortable homes, rather than model homes unattainable by most. Most homes featured in home improvement success stories were created by families modifying their farm home, as Mrs. Estelle Jenkins did during 1956 when she repainted, landscaped her yard, and undertook other repairs. The rehabilitated home, clad in traditional board-and-batten siding, served as a model for families in similar ubiquitous buildings (figure 9.7). As time passed, and even as resources increased, farm families continued to adapt home demonstration ideas to their own circumstances and choices. By the 1950s the handmade or self-improved strategy was still the norm. And the whole-family approach common before World War II continued; a home demonstration agent often featured family members working together on long-term home improvement.

Why, though, did home demonstration agents continue to feature homes that, though better, were not the best? In their efforts to introduce and extend contemporary models of comfort and beauty to rural black families in Florida, why did they continue to accept, even promote, homemade over commercial? First, black agents shared the extension mission to preserve rural populations by making a more comfortable rural life attainable and attractive to as many families as possible. The whole premise of home

Figure 9.7. Estelle Jenkins improved her home as part of her home demonstration work. She repainted the house, landscaped, installed a fence, and decorated the front porch with potted plants and chairs. Once her home was completed, she opened it to her neighbors during a local Better Homes tour in 1956. Source: University of Florida Digital Collections.

demonstration was to empower rural women by giving them choices and teaching them the skills necessary to improve their own lot, no matter how disadvantaged they were. Second, demanding that home demonstration club members adhere to a standard established nationally and forced on them locally by a stranger was a surefire way to drive women away from home demonstration entirely. Home demonstration agents were educators and guides, not dictators. They organized interested women into groups and gave them as many resources, including sheer encouragement, as possible. Both because they could not literally force women to do anything and because they *wanted* the women to be as self-sufficient as possible, agents took their cues from local farm women.

As a result, those most responsible for ensuring that home demonstration matched the needs of its clients were clubwomen. Their very decision to join a home demonstration club—or allow their daughters to join—most directly influenced home demonstration. Even home demonstration's structure depended on strong local participation; the program's existence only made sense if clubwomen existed to turn ideas into reality. From the start, clubwomen learned to craft their own home demonstration agenda, not only because they wanted a program that interested them but because they had less institutional support to do it for them.

Consider club leaders' role in setting a home demonstration agenda. They gathered input from clubwomen, met to condense it into clear recommendations, then collaborated with their county home demonstration agent to determine what the next year's program would include. For instance, Volusia County agent Ida Pemberton opened her 1948 annual report by detailing the goals she had set with clubwomen, based on an agenda "set up [in 1947] to include the subjects which the people thought were most needed by them." Their broad objectives were similar to those found in most home demonstration clubs: food production and conservation, low-cost clothing, and better health. But Pemberton also listed the specific remedies they developed, discrete reflections of the concerns her clubwomen had about their own families and communities. For example, one of the five major problems clubwomen wanted to address was "Negro delinquent problems." Among the several remedies listed were clues about what prompted women to make this a feature of their extension agenda, including "more supervised recreation" and "keep out of juke joints."[18] Though their general concerns were similar to most home demonstration clubwomen's, the details were unique to those women in that county. The result was a custom program of reform based on clubwomen's expressed desires. Clearly, clubwomen's interests rather than formal agendas served as keystones uniting the various elements in a county home demonstration program. This applied especially where either home demonstration was very new, and women might be put off by intrusiveness, or where it was well established and long-time members held sway.

Though there were quite a few black agents who served one county for more than a decade, it was more typical that long-time home demonstration members were community women. In fact, it was not uncommon for a subject specialist, county home demonstration agent, or even a state officer once to have been a 4-H member and then a clubwoman. Some women never became staff members but served home demonstration for decades. Duval County agent Ethel Powell noted such women in 1951. As part of National Home Demonstration Week, Florida home demonstration staff recognized clubwomen with more than a decade of involvement—the briefest tenure was twenty-five years. The woman with the longest record of service was Mrs. Ethel Anderson of Jacksonville. By 1951 she had been with home demonstration for thirty-two years. In fact, Anderson had been active in home demonstration clubs since they began in Duval County in

1919.[19] Committed club members like Anderson provided stability in home demonstration's continuing projects and credibility for agents trying to win over potential club members. But most clubwomen were not Anderson, and most black farm women were not club members.

What difference, then, did home demonstration make in the lives of Florida's farm-owning families? What significance did local acceptance of, influence on, or rejection of extension programs really mean? By its very nature—a program for and by rural women dependent on their voluntary participation—home demonstration was a venue for black farm women to exert a kind of authority they otherwise lacked. In marked contrast to most other reform programs, farm women were encouraged to take charge because the very success of home demonstration depended on their goodwill and continued interest. And it was not all for show—extension's purpose was to equip women with skills they could use in their everyday life, even without an agent's guidance, to gain control over their families' well-being.

The net effect of negotiation and adaptation in cooperative home demonstration work was significant improvement in many black rural families' quality of life. The most important examples are in health reforms. The need was real. Leon County's black agent, Alice Poole, expressed her frustration that two decades into Florida Home Extension, the state of rural health was alarmingly poor. "It is regretted that as important as Health, Home and Sanitation is, it should be so sadly neglected in the rural districts," she wrote in 1931.[20] Poor drainage around homes, for example, created breeding grounds for parasites like hookworms and mosquitoes. Florida's rate of malaria was six times higher than the national average in 1939, and the death rate per 100,000 African Americans was double, sometimes triple, the death rate for whites.[21] Every woman who joined a home demonstration club could protect herself and her family from debilitating diseases.

Agents could not force these programs on women, so the improvements they recorded over the years were the results of women choosing to accept agents' help, often through children within the farming community. For example, agents helped coordinate health clinics for local families, focusing on providing checkups and preventive care for their children. Immunizations against smallpox, typhoid, and diphtheria protected hundreds from these illnesses, widespread in rural areas and in unsanitary schools. In 1931 alone, nearly a thousand rural African Americans reported being immunized at clinics assisted by home demonstration club activities. In fact, immunizations were more common among black families than among their white neighbors.[22] Working with agents they came to trust conditioned

African American families to accept aid from other organizations, both public and private, such as the State Board of Health, the Rockefeller Foundation, and the Red Cross. Likewise, black farm families worked with their county agents to coordinate new school lunch programs that provided their children with at least one filling and nutritious meal each day—nutritious examples they brought home to their parents. And schools were among the first places in a county to receive a sanitary makeover, usually by adding sanitary privies to replace makeshift pits that contaminated the area with hookworm.

In addition, schools became vehicles for extensive health initiatives, such as National Negro Health Week (NNHW). Booker T. Washington began the movement in 1915 to galvanize health care by and for black Americans, and though men steered it nationally, women powered it on the ground.[23] Black home demonstration agents actively encouraged their clients to participate in NNHW for both its practical and social value. Mary Todd Mackenzie, Alachua County agent, reported with pride her county's work toward health in 1934. She applauded schoolchildren's involvement in the NNHW, noting the various projects they undertook to put the health cause before the public, including poster contests, a health honor roll, and a door-to-door canvas led by 4-H members and teachers.[24] The combination of Mackenzie's guidance and local women's participation extended better health into more rural homes than would have been possible without such collaboration.

During her tenure as Florida's Negro District home demonstration agent, Rosa Ballard articulated the agent's position in her adopted community. Ballard explained that "unlike the school teacher, whose groups are already organized, the demonstration agent works with voluntary groups organized by herself and maintained in proportion to her ability to interest them in her program."[25] When historians examine home demonstration from above, they see the broad strokes of a national agenda, a massive, segregated system that shorted its female and black members and families with little access to agents who understood or respected them. Certainly examples existed, but the more closely historians examine home demonstration locally, the more obvious is the great variety that existed. Nationally, agents were trained reformers, outsiders sent into strangers' homes to better their lives. But locally, home demonstration agents were community members who attended the same churches, sat around the same kitchen tables, and shopped in the same markets as the clubwomen they served. The key to casting off the burden of being a stranger was letting local women customize home demonstration. The net effect was crucial.

Home demonstration made a significant difference in the lives of rural families even though it neither radically altered social and economic situations for black farm families nor solved the inadequacies of daily life for all the families who needed it. Black Floridians who lived in the state's farm communities found that extension provided them an ally and an autonomous outlet to improve their standard of living. The home demonstration agent, even if she began as a stranger, gave families an acceptable, practical, and often enjoyable means of realizing goals. Ballard understood, as most successful agents did, that everything outside the local community mattered, but how well she related to people in their own backyards decided how much they accomplished together. Home demonstration's enduring legacy for black rural women was not only in substantive improvements in their health and comfort but in their prolonged commitment to the program that catered to what they wanted for themselves.

Home demonstration lasted because these women chose to join it in the first place, and many chose to remain active participants even as their agents and their community's needs changed. The Jacksonville newspaper featuring Ethel Anderson, the Duval County long-time home demonstration member, called her efforts, and those of other clubwomen, cause for "justifiable pride." Indeed, despite the numerous hardships and the marked diversity in local resources that made achieving maximum reform impossible, the degree to which agents and local women cooperated to accomplish what they did was a source of justifiable pride for both. Studying home demonstration, even locally, has a serious pitfall—focusing on either agents or clubwomen to the exclusion of the other. Yet the reality is that home demonstration was a mutually dependent relationship. As much as black farm women may have wanted to develop an authority of their own within a separatist community, they needed the skills an agent could offer them to gain practical independence. As much as they knew, as much support as they might have had from supervisors, agents were useless without clubwomen to teach. Ironically, perhaps, home demonstration acted as a vehicle for integrating worlds wedged apart by both official and self-segregation. White rural reformers could not so easily ignore the needs of black farm families in separate communities once they were a discrete part of the extension system. And black farm women could not so easily bar their world against the influence of whites when they joined clubs and became leaders within extension. Home demonstration programs reflected the people who created them, but they did not exist as radically different versions. The various communities to which agents and clubwomen belonged increasingly overlapped, and their members increasingly mingled, even as official policies of segregation persisted. The lines in rural communities hardened by decades of discrimination and suspicion softened when strangers became confidantes, and locals became leaders. Most important for the black farm women who joined home demonstration clubs, participation gave them two paths to empowerment and greater self-determination. First were the skills necessary to control their well-being and lessen their dependence on outsiders; second was the opportunity to exert active control over an outside program. The means to make home demonstration a success lay with the clubwomen who deliberately and selectively crafted home demonstration into something meaningful for them and their communities.

The relationship between an agent and rural black women was delicate, but it could become strong if the agent was patient and respectful. In 1922 Leon County's Amanda Parrish reinforced local women's responsibility for home demonstration's success. She could finally report that "the present outlook for the work is very bright and encouraging. Years of hard work and patience have convinced the patrons of the truthfulness and sincerity of the agents and they are gaining confidence in them." It is reasonable to expect that locals would be wary of home demonstration in its early years, when every aspect of the work was still new. But in 1922 Parrish already had been in Leon County for *five* years; it had taken her that long to win the confidence of local women. By letting them set the pace, Parrish managed to prove that home demonstration could help them. A sigh of relief is audible between the lines when she wrote that "women and girls are asking to join the clubs another year."[26]

Local women shaped home demonstration. Clubwomen's approval was so important that Duval County agent Ida Pemberton included several letters from them in her 1948 annual report. Gertrude Smith asked that Pemberton "read [my letter] to all the communities you go in" to promote 4-H club work for girls. "I wish all the mothers felt like I do," she concluded, "and I hope there will be double the number of girls next time at camp." Ruby Mills praised Pemberton as a friend, calling her "a blessing to our Community." "I thank God," Mrs. Mills wrote, "for sending to us such a fine person." Mills was particularly glad to have "learned so many things that are useful in the home that can be made into many things." Ruth Haywood told Pemberton that her home demonstration club "was one of the best clubs anywhere. Anyone would want to become a member of it." And Estella Nelson articulated her approval of both Pemberton and home demonstration most simply: "I like my club just fine."[27]

Participating in home demonstration was not something for which all black farm women had the time or inclination, but those who did choose to become involved not only benefited by it; they made it their own. Certainly all who joined a club or two did not stay involved the way Ethel Anderson did. And many who joined would not have agreed with the praise clubwomen shared with Ida Pemberton. The women suspicious of Amanda Parrish grew to trust her, but many never did find any use for the home demonstration agent in their midst. That so many rural women did not participate in home demonstration reminds historians that rather than being a formulaic, intrusive juggernaut, home demonstration was a collection of reform possibilities offered by its agents but judged by its audience. Among the myriad factors influencing whether home demonstration agents succeeded as reformers and educators, including racism and sexism, the decision really lay with community women. They chose to become involved by joining voluntary clubs. They could bring an agent to their county, or have her removed, by lobbying local governments. They influenced enrollment by spreading praise or criticism. They created annual agendas by voicing their concerns. In those places where black farm women embraced home demonstration, they not only reaped the rewards for themselves but defined what home demonstration meant and ensured its continued relevance for their unique communities.

Notes

1. Amanda W. Parrish, Leon County, Annual Narrative and Statistical Reports of State Offices and County Agents 1920–21, Florida State Library, microfilm reel 5, p. 3 (hereafter cited as ANSR with year and page and, if applicable, location [FSL] with reel number). Suspicion toward extension agents was common across the South; Carmen Harris found the same wariness among potential clubwomen in South Carolina, who were not at all certain about whether agents had some ulterior motive. See Harris's "'Well I just generally bes the president of everything': Rural Black Women's Empowerment through South Carolina Home Demonstration Activities," *Black Women, Gender & Families* 3 (Spring 2009): 96–97.

2. *Florida Extension Association of Family and Consumer Sciences Handbook 2002–2003*, http://www.feafcs.ifas.ufl.edu/pdf-docs/FEAFCSHandbook.pdf (15 September 2005).

3. A. A. Turner to Flavia Gleason, July 16, 1928; A. P. Spencer [APS] to Flavia Gleason, July 19, 1928, University of Florida Special Collections, box 21, folder 5 (hereafter cited as UFSC).

4. The "Negro" District Home Demonstration agent's position began informally with A. A. Turner's wife in 1925. Her position became official when Florida Extension hired Julia Miller in 1928. A. A. Turner to T. M Campbell, October 18, 1928; Flavia Gleason to Wilmon Newell, November 24, 1928, UFSC, box 21, folder 5.

5. See Harris, "Well I just generally bes the president of everything," for details of how South Carolina agents and clubwomen formed this same dynamic of cooperation based on the clubwomen's needs.

6. See, for example, Marilyn Irvin Holt, *Linoleum, Better Babies and the Modern Farm Woman, 1890–1930* (Albuquerque: University of New Mexico Press, 1995). For the "busybody" argument, see Deborah Fink, *Agrarian Women: Wives and Mothers in Rural Nebraska, 1880–1940* (Chapel Hill: University of North Carolina Press, 1992), 11–26; Rebecca Sharpless's study of cotton-growing farm families including their interaction with the Texas Agricultural Extension Service, *Fertile Ground, Narrow Choices: Women on Texas Cotton Farms, 1900–1940* (Chapel Hill: University of North Carolina Press, 1999), is typical of the well-intentioned failure argument. The pattern of agent-bullying or program irrelevance is most apparent in assessments of home extension and technology, specifically electrification. See Katherine Jellison, *Entitled to Power: Farm Women and Technology, 1913–1963* (Chapel Hill: University of North Carolina Press, 1993). On the struggle between farm women's productive and consumptive roles, see Kathleen R. Babbitt, "The Productive Farm Woman and the Extension Home Economist in New York State, 1920–1940," *Agricultural History* 67 (Spring 1993): 83–101.

7. See the same phenomenon in Texas extension in Debra A. Reid, *Reaping a Greater Harvest: African Americans, the Extension Service, and Rural Reform in Jim Crow Texas* (College Station: Texas A&M University Press, 2007).

8. Glenda Gilmore explores this method of black women exerting themselves publicly in a way that seemed a mere extension of their private role in her essay, "Diplomatic Women," in *Who Were the Progressives?*, ed. Glenda Elizabeth Gilmore (Boston: Bedford–St. Martin's, 2002): 223–60. Reid, *Reaping a Greater Harvest*; see, too, Melissa Walker, *All We Knew Was to Work: Rural Women in the Upcountry South, 1919–1941* (Baltimore: Johns Hopkins University Press, 2000); LuAnn Jones, *Mama Learned Us to Work: Farm Women in the New South* (Chapel Hill: University of North Carolina Press, 2002); Evan P. Bennett, "'A Responsibility on Women that Cannot Be Delegated to Father, Husband, or Son': Farm Women and Cooperation in the Tobacco South," and Ann E. McCleary, "'Seizing the Opportunity': Home Demonstration Curb Markets in Virginia," both in *Work, Family, and Faith: Rural Southern Women in the Twentieth Century*, ed. Melissa Walker and Rebecca Sharpless (Columbia: University of Missouri Press, 2006): 67–96, 97–134; Lynne Rieff, "'Go Ahead and Do All You Can': Southern Progressives and Alabama Home Demonstration Clubs, 1914–1940," in *Hidden Histories of Women in the New South*, ed. Virginia Berhard, Betty Brandon, Elizabeth Fox-Genovese, Theda Perdue, and Elisabeth Hayes Turner (Columbia: University of Missouri Press, 1994): 134–49. For home demonstration in the context of larger reforms, see Mary S. Hoffschwelle, *Rebuilding the Rural Southern Community: Reformers, Schools, and Homes in Tennessee, 1900–1930* (Knoxville: University of Tennessee Press, 1998). On home demonstration specific to Florida, see Barbara R. Cotton, *The Lamplighters: Black Farm and Home Demonstration Agents in Florida, 1915–1965* (Tallahassee: Florida Agricultural and Mechanical University, 1982); Kelly A. Minor,

"The Price of Longevity: Home Demonstration and Rural Reform in Modern Florida," in *Migration and the Transformation of the Southern Workplace since 1945*, ed. Robert Cassanello and Colin J. Davis (Gainesville: University Press of Florida, 2009), 34–63; Kelly A. Minor, "Consumed with a Ghastly Wasting: Home Demonstration Confronts Disease in Rural Florida, 1920–1945," in *Entering the Fray: Gender Politics and Culture in the New South*, ed. Jonathan Daniel Wells and Sheila R. Phipps (Columbia: University of Missouri Press, 2010), 68–95; Kelly A. Minor, "Power in the Land: Home Demonstration in Florida, 1915–1960," Ph.D. diss., University of Florida, 2005; Lynne Anderson Rieff, "'Rousing the People of the Land': Home Demonstration Work in the Deep South, 1914–1950," Ph.D. diss., Auburn University, 1995.

9. Gilmore, "Diplomatic Women," 223.

10. Extension sources for Florida are archived at the University of Florida's Special Collections, Florida State University's Strozier Library, the Florida State Library, Florida A&M University's Library, and the National Archives and Records Administration. Many photographs have been digitized in the University of Florida's Digital Collection, the Florida Memory Project, and the National Archives.

11. See Carmen Harris, "'The Extension Service Is Not an Integration Agency': The Idea of Race in the Cooperative Extension Service," *Agricultural History* 82 (Spring 2008): 193–219; Carmen Harris, "States' Rights, Federal Bureaucrats and Segregated 4-H Camps in the United States, 1927–1969," *Journal of African American History* 93 (2008): 362–88; R. Grant Seals, "The Formation of Agricultural and Rural Development Policy with Emphasis on African-Americans, II: The Hatch-George and Smith Lever Acts," *Agricultural History* 65 (Spring 1991): 12–34.

12. Dianne D. Glave, "'A garden so brilliant with colors, so original in its design': Rural African American Women, Gardening, Progressive Reform and the Foundation of an African American Environmental Perspective," *Environmental History* 8 (July 2003): 395–96, 400.

13. Okra patch at the home of Rosa Walker, Rock Hill Community, 1952. University of Florida Archives, Special Collections, George A. Smathers Libraries Digital Collections, www.uflib.ufl.edu/ufdc/?b=UF00045848&v=00001.

14. Glave, "A garden so brilliant," 395–96, 400.

15. Floy Britt, Negro District ANSR 1952, 3–5.

16. Parrish, Leon County ANSR 1920–21, 1. Carmen Harris discovered the same emphasis on making an emotional connection with clubwomen in South Carolina; one agent reported that she focused on "an efficient satisfied rural State" as an aim for agents. Harris argues that such statements, backed by action, are evidence that agents made farm women's "happiness . . . the core of their professional purpose." See Harris, "Well I just generally bes the president of everything," 98.

17. Melissa Walker, "Home Extension Work among African-American Farm Women in East Tennessee, 1920–1939," *Agricultural History* 70 (Summer 1996): 487–501.

18. Ida Pemberton, Volusia ANSR 1948, National Archives and Records Administration, Records of the Federal Extension Service, Record Group 33.6, box 67, 2 (hereafter cited as NARA, RG 33.6).

19. Ethel M. Powell, Duval ANSR 1951, NARA RG 33.6, box 52, 7; "Thirty Years of Service" in Home Demonstration Scrapbook, UFSC, box 158, folder 6.

20. Alice W. Poole, Leon ANSR 1931 (FSL 21), 7.

21. Frederick L. Hoffman, LL.D., *Malaria in Florida, Georgia, and Alabama* (Newark, N.J.: Prudential Press, 1932).

22. Julia A. Miller, "Negro Home Demonstration Work," 1931 Report Cooperative Extension Work in Agriculture and Home Economics (Gainesville: University of Florida, 1932), 141–45, esp. 144.

23. NNHW was headquartered at Tuskegee Institute from 1915 until 1930, when the U.S. Public Health Service took over and made the week into a year-long program. See Susan L. Smith, *Sick and Tired of Being Sick and Tired: Black Women's Health Activism in America, 1890–1950* (Philadelphia: University of Pennsylvania Press, 1990), 33–39.

24. Mary Todd Mackenzie, Alachua ANSR 1934 (FSL-25), 6.

25. Rosa Ballard, "Some Facts about Home Demonstration Work," *Quarterly Journal, Florida Agricultural and Mechanical University, Tallahassee,* University of Florida Digital Collections, http://ufdcweb1.uflib.ufl.edu/ufdc (April 2010).

26. Amanda W. Parrish, Leon County ANSR 1922 (FSL-6), 3, 1.

27. Ida Pemberton, Duval County ANSR 1948, NARA, RG 33.6, box 67.

V

Legal Activism and Civil Rights Expansion

10

Black Power in the Alabama Black Belt to the 1970s

VERONICA L. WOMACK

The Black Belt includes most of five Old South states, South Carolina, Georgia, Alabama, Mississippi, and Louisiana. In 1900 nearly one-half of the entire U.S. African American population lived in this area. A concentration on one of these states, Alabama, and an analysis of African American farmer demographics in Black Belt counties in the state, can help explain the relationship between cash-crop agriculture, African American land tenancy, and political activism between the 1930s and the 1970s. An exploitive labor system emerged in Alabama, as it did across the Cotton South, in the immediate aftermath of the Civil War. In tandem with sharecropping and the crop lien emerged black separatist movements that allowed black farmers to cluster in insulated farming communities. Separatism is relative in the Black Belt, where African Americans constituted 45 to 60 percent of the population and black farmers operated between 35 and 60 percent of all farms. Nonetheless, varying strategies of Black Power developed, grounded in agricultural pursuits and tenuous connections to the land. This work argues that black farmers cultivated a unique rural Black Nationalist ideology during the 1930s; a predecessor to Black Power activities within the state. Lower class, rural blacks expanded this ideology during the 1960s as Black Muslims acquired property.[1]

Hasan Jeffries posits that the root of contemporary Black Power can be found in rural Alabama, and that it emerged during the 1960s through the work of the Student Nonviolent Coordinating Committee (SNCC). Yet the components of the ideology of contemporary Black Power emerged even earlier in rural Alabama, during the 1930s, and through the work of the Share Croppers' Union of Alabama (SCU), in connection with the Communist Party. SNCC's work helped the ideology mature. A rural Black Nationalist ideology existed in the context of agricultural activities and processes that had traditionally been associated with socioeconomic and political advancement, independence, and a distinctive and separatist black identity. Black Nationalism in rural Alabama preceded Black Power in the Black Belt but was a key influencing factor in developing its unique rural character. Black Power expressed itself in the Alabama Black Belt through land acquisition and ownership, labor negotiations, and political participation with the goal of dealing with racial hostility. Circumstances created distinctive Black Nationalism that helped shape Black Power in Alabama.[2]

The Black Belt is a crescent-shaped region that includes 623 counties in eleven states from eastern Texas to the eastern shore of Virginia and constitutes the bulk of the old plantation South. The term gained some visibility after Reconstruction when the *New York Times* reported on "Alabama's 'Black Belt': A Region Where Colored Men Are Contented and Prosperous." Booker T. Washington emphasized factors that undermined the idea of a contented and prosperous black population in 1901 when he made connections between the rich black soil, majority African American population, history of enslavement, and extreme racial politics often perpetrated through violent attacks on blacks. He observed this firsthand from Tuskegee Institute in the heart of the Alabama Black Belt. Scholars have devoted considerable attention to the region because of its biracial demographic, cash crop agriculture, extreme and persistent poverty, low education levels, poor quality of health, and high economic dependence. It has also gained attention because of its checkered history of civil rights infractions and activism. Some of the activism can be traced as far back as the post–Civil War agricultural pursuits of African Americans that linked the Republican Party and African American agricultural workers in the Alabama Black Belt, including the political and self-defense activities of the Union League in Alabama.[3]

A unique form of Black Power developed out of black farmers' contradictory relationships to the Alabama soil. Black farmers in the area experienced some of the highest rates of tenancy and lowest rates of land ownership in the United States during the early twentieth century. This sets the context for considering theories related to Black Power. According to Walton and Smith, power is analyzed in terms of (1) its base, (2) its exercise, and (3) the skill of its exercise in particular circumstances, situations, or contexts. Black Power as an ideology is as adaptable and varied as the experiences, geographies, and socioeconomic and political circumstances of people of African descent. Walton and Smith also found that Black Power increased black group identification and solidarity, and within this solidarity, black decision making and participation occurs as a result of the implementation of Black Power ideology. Stokely Carmichael and Charles Hamilton in their seminal work *Black Power* state that "black people must lead and run their own organizations. . . . Black Power is full participation in the decision-making processes affecting the lives of black people, and recognition of the virtues in themselves as black people." This general definition has been used by many scholars and activists as the basis for explaining most Black Power strategies. There is often little consensus, however, on a specific definition of Black Power; in fact, some works suggest that the term is confusing, "perhaps inevitable given the extraordinary controversy occasioned by the initial debate."[4]

Black Power as a concept has been most linked to activist race politics. "Black Power . . . is often a militant extension of race politics, a form of Black Nationalism (separatism), or a use of revolutionary tactics." In addition, some definitions even expand Black Power beyond simply organizing black groups as it has also been linked to co-racial efforts that allow for races to work together on common interests as long as the races maintain the interest of their respective group. Black Power is against coalition politics but is open to co-racial politics, which would result in groups organizing separately and working together jointly around common interests and issues. Stokely Carmichael explains this effort by stating, "Where Negroes lack a Majority, black power means *proper representation* and sharing of control."[5]

Rural areas offer different contexts for the development of Black Power. Rural blacks living in areas dominated by whites theoretically found less opposition to their separatist quest to develop a farming community, or even an all-black town. Thus, some of the first Black Power approaches in the South revolved around land acquisition and community development. Yet blacks did not readily gain access to land in the Black Belt, and in some Black Belt states, laws prohibited blacks from forming independent communities. African Americans, even though they constituted the majority population in some Black Belt Alabama counties, still could not gain proper representation, let alone share control with the minority white population.[6]

White landlords in Alabama entered into exploitive labor contracts with freedmen immediately after the Civil War. The case of Shade Moore provides an example. In a contract dated December 29, 1866, Moore and his family signed a one-year commitment to W. G. McCondichie of Snow Hill, Alabama (Wilcox County), in the Black Belt. The contract furnished land, stock, and half the necessary feed and supplies, with the advanced provisions and the rest of the supplies to be repaid at the end of the year. In addition, the contract stated, "We [the Moores] further agree to give the party of the first part a lien upon our interests in the crop until all advances are full paid." This type of arrangement made it difficult for black farmers to realize self-sustainability and economic independence. Minority white landowners used such tactics to maintain authority over the black landless majority. Some contracts also restricted the ability of tenants to make additional money beyond the initial contract. A contract for B. Wilson, who worked for P. J. Weaver in Dallas County, Alabama, paid six dollars a month and room and board. In addition, Wilson's contract, dated May 22, 1865, restricted the ability to sell poultry or produce. These efforts were used throughout the South to control black labor, limit black economic independence, and impede the labor opportunities for African Americans. However, there were some blacks in the Alabama Black Belt who had achieved some economic success. The *New York Times*, in 1879, revealed black success in securing property and assets in the region: "In all these counties the colored people are every year increasing their possessions. Many now own valuable farms, have them well stocked, and are absolutely independent." Most African Americans were not landowners, however, and were economically beholden to the whites who held the majority of property.[7]

Many whites and emigrants took advantage of legislation such as the Homestead Act of 1862 and the Land Act of 1866 to relocate, but no more than four thousand blacks participated in these settlement programs. This indicates that most blacks remained in the South, and most Alabamans stayed in Alabama, including African American residents. They did not quickly realize their dream of land ownership, but thousands of black Alabamans purchased land by 1900, and they acquired it in traditional ways. According to James S. Fisher, most initial land acquisition was achieved through confiscation and redistribution, inheritance, or direct purchase. In fact, Thomas Mitchell has found that land was overwhelmingly acquired through private purchases between emancipation and the early twentieth century. In many instances, the process proved more complicated than direct or private purchase might imply. W.E.B. Du Bois found that black farmers in the South bought land after emancipation through "a composite form of tenure," being both owner and tenant of the land farmed. In 1890, 21.7 percent of African Americans across the nation (120,738) owned property. By 1900, 21 percent of black-operated farms were entirely owned and 4.2 percent were owned in part by African Americans, leaving three-fourths of black farmers as tenants or sharecroppers. Alabama ranked sixth in the nation in 1900 in the number of black owner-operated farms, with 14,110 farms, including 11,123 owned fully, 2,871 owned partially or through other ownership arrangements, and 116 owned by an operator who also rented the land. Yet Alabama ranked seventeenth in the nation in 1900 in the proportion of black farmers in the state (15 percent) who owned their farms. Of eighteen southern states, only Georgia ranked lower, with 13.7 percent of all its black farmers owning land. Du Bois explained that while "the largest proportion of ownership is often outside the black belt ... the larger number of owners is usually in that region ... [because] the proportion of negro to all farmers rises to 75 per cent or more in eleven [Black Belt] counties. Here, the relative number of owners among the black farmers is usually smaller than elsewhere in the state. The absolute number of negro owners is, however, largest in this belt."[8]

As Du Bois explained, in 1900 "the proportion of owners among negro farmers is largest in those counties where two-thirds or more of the farmers are white, and smallest in the counties where two-thirds or more of the famers are black." He identified three factors that contributed to the uneven distribution: "the profitableness of tenant farming in the cotton belt, the concentration of land ownership there, and the general lack of any inspiring or uplifting influences." In other words, the areas with white minority populations and land consolidated into large plantations proved less conducive to black land acquisition. This meant that in the Alabama Black Belt, in the area in closest proximity to the influence of Tuskegee Institute and the separatist philosophy associated with Booker T. Washington, the fewest black farmers, proportionately, owned their land. Georgia was the only other state with a smaller proportion of black owners. In 1900, 59.7 percent (56,212) of Alabama's black farmers were cash tenants, while 25.2 percent (23,089) were sharecroppers (table 10.1).[9]

The number of farms owned by Alabama's black farmers fluctuated between 1900 and 1930, indicating the continued interest in land ownership and associated economic independence, but owning land did not free black farmers from debt. The number of farms owned by blacks increased from 11,123 in 1900 to 17,201 in 1920, and then fell to 15,920 in 1930. This included 7,801 owners in the Black Belt, 49 percent of all black owners in the state

Table 10.1. Farmers in Selected Alabama Black Belt Counties, 1930

County	Total Number of Farms	Number of Farms under Black operation
Barbour	3,690	2,262
Butler	3,512	1,695
Choctaw	2,637	1,611
Clarke	2,996	1,772
Conecuh	3,431	1,476
Crenshaw	3,534	1,030
Dallas	6,803	6,405
Greene	3,376	3,168
Lowndes	3,906	3,527
Macon	3,606	3,114
Marengo	6,141	5,314
Monroe	3,823	2,091
Perry	4,199	3,435
Pike	3,558	1,506
Russell	2,414	2,243
Sumter	4,208	3,812
Black Belt Counties Total	**61,834**	**44,461**
Alabama Total	**247,995**	**93,795**

Sources: Fifteenth Census of the United States: 1930, Census of Agriculture, 1933, 14–30. Charles E. Hall, *Negro Farmer in the United States,* Census of Agriculture, Fifteenth Census of the United States: 1930 (Washington, D.C.: U.S. Government Printing Office, 1933), Table 38: Farms Operated by Negroes—Number, Acreage, and Value of Specified Classes of Farm Property, By States and Counties, 1930, 56–57 (includes full and part owners).

in 1930. In 1930, 6,140 or 53.8 percent of all the farms blacks owned in Alabama were mortgage free, but this left 46.2 percent encumbered. That represented an increase in the number of black-owned farms in the state, but a large number operated at financial risk. The land owned declined slowly as a result. In Alabama alone, blacks owned 1.2 million acres in 1910. This included those who owned their farms, shared ownership of their farms, or rented and owned their farms. In 1920 the number of acres had increased to 1.3 million, but by 1930 the number had decreased back to 1.2 million acres. Obviously between 1900 and 1930 Black Belt farmers had managed to purchase land, thus overcoming some of the obstacles that Du Bois had identified in 1900 (table 10.2).[10]

The number of farms and acreage represented a significant property accumulation for a small percentage of black farmers in Alabama by 1930. The black landowners accounted for only 6.4 percent of all farmers in the state, 17 percent of all black farmers in the state, and 17.5 percent of all black farm operators in the Black Belt. But the vast majority of black farm

Table 10.2. Black Owners, Tenants, and Sharecroppers in the Alabama Black Belt, 1930

Area	Black Full Owner	Black Part Owners	Black Tenants	Black Cash Tenants	Black Sharecroppers
Alabama	11,417	4,514	88,454	32,055	27,572
Barbour	269	34	1,956	475	1,059
Butler	202	55	1,436	367	855
Choctaw	338	205	1,068	413	334
Clarke	499	300	973	477	223
Conecuh	409	170	897	445	349
Crenshaw	136	38	856	148	553
Dallas	343	141	5,921	5,322	476
Escambia	173	25	230	76	108
Greene	263	63	2,842	1,006	294
Lowndes	157	87	3,193	2,611	383
Macon	407	66	2,639	719	819
Marengo	395	256	4,662	2,765	1,221
Monroe	371	215	1,511	793	337
Perry	326	154	2,955	1,889	773
Pike	94	16	1,396	257	915
Russell	298	59	1,886	97	401
Sumter	340	104	3,368	1,549	871
Washington	337	40	299	151	87
Wilcox	299	117	3,202	2,384	441
Black Belt Total	5,656	2,145	41,290	21,944	10,499

Source: Fifteenth Census of the United States: 1930, Census of Agriculture, 1933, 978–83, County Table I Supplemental for the Southern States Farm Operators and Acreage. "Other tenants" accounted for in the census are not included in this table.

operators and all black agricultural laborers had little independence in their economic decision making. They remained dependent on the minority white population who owned the majority of the land. Nelson compared tenancy to "peonage, a condition that did not markedly differ from their former status under slavery . . . the underrepresentation of blacks in southern landownership is, in large measure a reflection of the powerlessness of blacks in southern politics." The majority cash and share tenant population desired change, and black farm owners sought security.[11]

African Americans in Alabama had little recourse through the normal political process to address their grievances after the era of Reconstruction. The Constitutional Convention of 1901 ended any real African American political participation in the state until the passage of the Voting Rights Act of 1965. It was crafted by powerful whites in the Black Belt and proved very controversial. Results of the election suggest that African Americans in the

Black Belt were instrumental in their own disfranchisement because election results showed overwhelming black support for the constitution. The constitution also established property qualifications that required ownership of 40 acres of land or land worth $300 to participate in elections. This allowed for the disenfranchisement of blacks working the land as tenants and sharecroppers, virtually rendering them politically powerless, lacking any political remedy and dependent on the land barons of the Black Belt.[12]

This devastated African American political participation as only fifteen hundred blacks in the state met the property qualification by 1930. The Alabama political system was not a viable solution for African Americans. The combination of a lack of political solutions and dire economic conditions required extraordinary approaches, and out of necessity blacks adopted various Black Power strategies. In turn, white landowners reacted defensively and violently against people they perceived as threatening to their socioeconomic and political power and/or land.[13]

Blacks in Alabama began to implement Black Nationalist strategies through the development and promotion of all-black towns and communities during the early twentieth century. These opportunities appealed to African Americans who had little chance in other communities for self-advancement. Most all-black towns and communities tended to be farming communities or service centers for farming communities. Between 1865 and 1915 all-black settlements proliferated in the United States. More than fifty have been documented in Oklahoma; hundreds in Texas. Residents clustered together in an effort to address challenges they faced. White southerners recognized the threat they posed and legislated against their incorporation, but blacks continued to buy land and form their communities. Most remained unincorporated and outside of public scrutiny, and thus nearly invisible to those seeking to document their existence. These all-black towns became the embodiment of Black Power, as they allowed black leadership and black economic opportunity, while promoting black consciousness and identity.[14]

One of Alabama's first all-black towns, Hobson City, incorporated in 1899, began as an all-black section of Oxford called Mooree Quarter. After a racially contentious election, blacks incorporated the new city, and by the 1900 census the population included 292 people. The development of Hobson City served as an example of an alternative approach by blacks to dealing with Alabama's racial discord. Yet this strategy was limited because, due to factors such as poverty, racial dominance, violence, and a lack of resources and land, few African Americans were able to develop all-black towns or communities. For sharecroppers and tenants, these opportunities were limited, so they developed other approaches to dealing with the socioeconomic and racial climate in Alabama.[15]

One effort in the heart of the Alabama Black Belt linked black educational pursuits and black land ownership. The Calhoun Colored School (located in Lowndes County) began with a meeting between three hundred African American Lowndes County residents and white teachers Mabel W. Dillingham and Charlotte Thorn, from Hampton Institute. Blacks raised $250 for education in the community and so began the creation of the Calhoun Colored School, which would educate blacks in industrial education. This effort was touted in a fundraising solicitation letter in the *New York Times* as a "big step in helping share-croppers."[16]

The most significant program of the school, however, was the development of a land bank with the help of Tuskegee Institute. Most of the land for the land bank was secured reputedly for an experiment by Dr. George Washington Carver. When the experiment did not occur, the property was designated for individual farms, and in 1894 a land company was organized to spearhead the effort. Eventually the land bank contained over 4,081 acres. With the help of Booker T. Washington and northern philanthropists, this property was then sold in forty- to sixty-acre tracts to promote black land ownership in the Alabama Black Belt. Reverend Pitt Dillingham, the brother of Mabel, who had died, described the project in the *New York Times* as much more than a school, calling it "a settlement among the plantation Negroes of the Black Belt." Within the article, another description by George Holms suggests it was "to teach the Negro how he may get out of debt to the merchant, to whom his crops are annually mortgaged, how he may obtain a farm on his own, how he may educate his children and become an intelligent citizen of the United States that Calhoun School was established." By 1896 the school boasted 100 acres, stocks and tools, eleven buildings, and two school houses, worth approximately $30,000, with 300 students.[17]

This was the beginning of many endeavors to promote African American land ownership by Booker T. Washington, using Tuskegee Institute as his base. Additional Tuskegee-led projects included the Home Seekers Land Company (1912) with 1,146 acres and the Tuskegee Farm and Improvement Company (1914) with 1,800 acres. These projects prescribed land ownership for black advancement, and efforts were centered on making land available for purchase by blacks. Yet many of these efforts proved largely ineffective due to economic hardships, poor land quality, and the boll weevil. Unfortunately, opportunities for land trusts and land companies were limited, and so most black residents continued to linger in a landless condition.[18]

Most blacks in the Black Belt actually worked for someone else as laborers, working seasonally chopping or picking cotton or tending to daily chores as permanent farm laborers (table 10.3). With an overall black population of 944,834 in 1930 Alabama, 320,457 lived in the Black Belt. Blacks comprised 59.3 percent of the population in the Black Belt in comparison to 35.7 percent in the whole state. Astonishingly, around 250,000 of them were black agricultural workers. They, along with sharecroppers, had the most to gain from more equitable economic and civil rights policies and practices.

Tenants had much to gain as well from more equitable rights. The 1930 census revealed that the value of land reflected the unenviable economic position of black farmers in Alabama. In 1930 the U.S. average value of land owned by blacks per farm was $1,263, while the tenant-operated land per farm was valued at $1,174. In contrast, in Alabama, land owned by blacks per farm was valued at $1,092, while tenant-operated land per farm was valued at only $764. This black tenant land value in the state was the lowest in the South, which supports Fisher's theory that valuable land was least available to black farmers, who therefore suffered economically. Owners also faced uncertainty. Between 1920 and 1930, 1,405 farm owners lost their land and the associated $12,167,803 investment in the acreage and buildings. Thus all classes of black farmers and laborers in the Black Belt could be attentive to discussions of alternative power structures and politics.[19]

The focus on the plight of African Americans in the South was a topic discussed by the Communist Party at the highest levels in the 1920s. During the Second Congress of the Comintern (1920) Lenin provided support for the mention of the African American plight in the Black Belt. In 1928 the Sixth World Congress of the Communist International recognized the Black Belt region as an independent nation within the American South. Thus blacks in the Black Belt region became a major objective of the party. This focus by the Communist Party would gain momentum in Alabama and provide a structure for Black Power strategies.[20]

Remarkably, the black communists facilitated Black Power expansion in Alabama through its appeal to black sharecroppers and tenants during the 1930s. Robin D. G. Kelley claims that "the Communists' position on the 'Negro Question' (implicitly, at least) and its own interpretation of 'proletarian realism' unintentionally created an opening for African Americans

Table 10.3. Black Agricultural Workers in the Alabama Black Belt, 1930

County	Black Farm Laborers	Black Agricultural Wage Workers	Black Unpaid Family Workers
Barbour	1,814	1,201	1,613
Butler	2,351	947	1,364
Choctaw	1,496	481	1,015
Clarke	1,881	667	1,214
Conecuh	2,569	1,006	1,563
Crenshaw	1,380	579	801
Dallas	8,301	2,202	11,099
Escambia	1,282	1,044	238
Greene	4,965	1,693	3,272
Lowndes	4,770	1,497	3,273
Macon	4,493	1,526	2,967
Marengo	5,955	1,416	9,539
Monroe	2,820	1,007	1,813
Perry	6,328	935	5,393
Pike	2,885	1,303	1,492
Russell	3,994	1,471	2,523
Sumter	2,671	838	1,833
Washington	550	400	230
Wilcox	4,787	886	3,901
Black Belt Counties Total	**65,292**	**21,099**	**55,143**
Alabama Total	**127,931**	**45,900**	**82,031**

Source: Fifteenth Census of the United States: 1930, Census of Agriculture, 1933, 99–124, tables 13 and 20.

to articulate nationalist ideologies in spite of the Party's formal opposition to 'Negro nationalism.'" Ironically, blacks turned to communism as a way to defy the capitalist Black Belt agricultural system based in consolidated landholdings under white ownership and farmed by exploited laborers. They did not challenge one system of capitalism only to rebuild another based on black land ownership. Instead, in the quest for greater economic security the landless, predominantly, challenged the economic system that placed land and power in the hands of a few. The political potential that communism offered for expanding civil rights within the capitalist system remains underexplored.[21]

Targeting Birmingham, Alabama, as the central location within the southern region, the U.S. Communist Party opened a central committee headquarters close to the eighteen counties forming the Black Belt of Alabama and its large population of economically disadvantaged sharecroppers and agricultural laborers. The proximity of party headquarters to the proletariat helped forge a relationship between farmers, agricultural workers, and the party.[22]

Many within the U.S. Communist Party did not believe the black agricultural workers in the Black Belt had the capability to begin a movement for change. These doubts were erased, however, when the history of blacks organizing around labor issues and doing so biracially before the arrival of the communists became obvious. The process illustrates the co-racial Black Power strategy Carmichael described as sometimes necessary for blacks to reach their goals. Some blacks wrote letters requesting assistance in communist-supported publications, according to Schafer. Others used communist literature to mobilize tenants, as described in a report in the *Crisis*, in 1938. Ralph Gray and his brother Tommy rallied black tenant farmers and sharecroppers in Alabama, eventually requesting assistance from the communists. The *Morning Star* found that "the tenant farmer, having many years accepted their lot philosophically [is] now organizing but is opposed violently by the owners." Within the first couple of months of organizing, a network of reputedly over eight hundred members would soon become the Share Croppers' Union of Alabama, the largest communist black-led mass organization in the deep South during the 1930s. The Share Croppers' Union quickly drew fire from the local establishment as it tried to organize sharecroppers and tenants in the Alabama Black Belt.[23]

The union advocated for self-determination, which members defined as a continuation of food allowances until year-end settlement, cash settlement at the end of the season, the right to sell their cotton wherever they pleased, and nine months of school for their children. For these demands, they were attacked and were drawn into a campaign of armed defense in Camp Hill, Alabama, where over a hundred sharecroppers met to organize a union. Camp Hill was located in Tallapoosa County, which reported 1,044 black farm laborers in 1930. Organizer Ralph Gray was murdered and, several African Americans were arrested. A White posse made up of law enforcement personnel and citizens attacked the black community (union and non-union), attempting to stop a rumored race war and communism. The *Florence Times Daily* reported that posses of two hundred persons searched the county for union organizers and members of the *communist society*. The posse claimed that the group had threatened the life of Governor Miller and shot Sheriff Young. The *New York Times* reported that the posse burned black houses and a church during the mêlée, and several black meetings had been interrupted by the police. Police officer Wilson called the group "communist organizers" and said the police found inflammatory literature urging "members to demand social equality and intermarriage with the white race, not ask but demand what you want and if you don't get it take it." J. Louis Engdahl, secretary of the International Labor Defense, charged, however, that "Ralph Gray was murdered by Sheriff Carl Young of Tallapoosa County." He argued that Gray was on his way to attend a meeting of the Share Croppers' Union, which had been organizing during the past months. He disclosed, "The negroes of this county have been organizing against miserable starvation wages. The plantation owners planned to cut the sharecroppers off from all food advances giving a small number of sharecroppers the alternative of working in the field or saw mills at wages of sixty to ninety cents a day." Engdahl also linked the plantation owners with the police in the terrorism against blacks. These violent efforts were used to impede future organizing in the county.[24]

Terrorist activities spread as blacks continued to organize. The *Afro-American* reported that a lynch mob had murdered a tenant farmer, Jim Merriweather, because he belonged to the SCU and joined a strike to get $1 a day in wages for ten hours of work. In addition, the mob whipped his wife with a rope; the assailant, Vaughn Ryles, explained that "I want naked meat this morning." The report also highlighted that many more blacks were terrorized by the mob and about two hundred of them hid in swamps until they could escape to Birmingham.[25]

According to Michael Honey, "race hate and anticommunism together poisoned many southern whites. . . . In Alabama, authorities launched a 'little red scare' against all leftists and civil rights workers." The Communist Party recruited agricultural laborers, specifically, and workers' willingness to become members indicates the dire economic circumstances and level of rights abuses in Alabama. The interest likewise indicates that not all agricultural laborers or impoverished cash and share-rent tenants believed in private property ownership in the American capitalist tradition. Finally, rural black Alabamans' willingness to become members of the Communist Party indicates the extremes that black laborers would go to in their quest for change. The Black Power that black farmers developed required self-defense in pursuit of self-determination. This created tension in the countryside that needs further consideration.[26]

The link between the SCU and the communists was critical because at the time the sharecroppers and tenants had few supporters who were willing to assist them against the Black Belt aristocracy. This group had long ruled in the Black Belt, owning large amounts of land and exploiting black laborers, and they had no intention of allowing outside agitators to change the arrangements. The aristocracy retaliated with extreme violence against the union, and most SCU members armed themselves. Lemon Johnson, a

Lowndes County sharecropper and former secretary of the SCU, theorized: "The only thing to stop them from killing you, you got to go shooting." Internationally known communist Harry Haywood attended an SCU meeting in Alabama and stated that the group had "a small arsenal," with guns of all kinds—shotguns, rifles and pistols.[27]

Even though local black leaders and some black tenants eagerly participated, many criticized the effort. Some charged that the sharecroppers were being taken advantage of by the communists. For example, Du Bois, a critic of communist tactics in the deep South, wrote in 1933, "Without plan or apparent forethought, the Communists sent agitators down into a rural county of Northern Alabama, and induced the wretched Negro sharecroppers to form a Union." Others, however, saw the movement as a continuation of black resistance against oppression in the region. Harold Preece reported in the *Crisis* that the sharecroppers were a *potent weapon,* and he called leaders Ralph Gray and others heirs of Denmark Vesey and Nat Turner. He linked southern slave rebellions with the current union activity: "Thus Camp Hill and Reel Town stand in logical relation to almost forgotten battles of the past century.... The Sharecroppers Union is an expression of the tradition in modern terms, with only a slight change in economic symbols."[28]

This unique Black Power strategy was co-racial by design as blacks worked with a majority-white organization, the U.S. Communist Party, using the partnership as defined by Carmichael for the benefit of black agricultural workers. Assessing the SCU based on Walton and Smith's definition of power, the black communists' power base rested in the large African American population of share-rent tenants and agricultural laborers who exercised their power through their numbers and used their work in agriculture to protest current conditions and to seek innovative techniques for group improvement. These strategies fit the classic definition of Black Nationalism and the Black Power strategy that is a part of it, as they were local, black-led, and promoted black advancement for the rural landless. They did not, however, further capitalist or private ownership of the means of production, a goal that many blacks in Alabama had pursued and some had realized by 1930. Many forces sought to destroy the union and eventually were successful. As documented, violence played an important role in dismantling the union. A concerted effort by the leaders of the state also undermined the movement, as shown in correspondence between Governor B. M. Miller and top administrators at Alabama Polytechnic Institute (now Auburn University). In a letter dated July 20, 1931, L. N.

Duncan, director of the Alabama Extension Service, reported the efforts under way to undermine the SCU. The letter stated, "Two or three of our best Negro County Agents . . . have been working diligently with the Negro farmers, looking after their regular work, but at the same time making a special effort to quiet the people down, urging them to put away their guns and calling their attention to the fact that they are badly mislead [sic] by these communistic representatives." Duncan assured the governor that the Extension Service had done this type of work in the past, had "prevented conflict between the races," and was available for continued service if needed. Bradford Knapp, president of Polytechnic Institute, seconded Duncan's assurance that the Negro division of the Alabama Extension Service would "quiet down the communistic activities." The Extension Service had emerged out of Washington's self-help philosophy and had allied with land-owning farmers entrenched in black communities across the South, including Alabama. These allies appeared as conservative laissez-faire capitalists in comparison to the radical communists, and indicate the ways that the union heightened awareness of class divisions among African Americans in rural Alabama.[29]

By late 1938, schism occurred. Tenant farmers abandoned the SCU and shifted their alliances to the Farmers Union, while SCU wage laborers transferred to the Agricultural Workers Union, chartered by the American Federation of Labor as the Farm Laborers and Cotton Field Workers Union. Although the efforts of the black communists in Alabama were weakened by racism, violence, and demonstrated efforts by leaders of the state to destroy the endeavor, the communist movement nonetheless sustained Black Power ideologies.[30]

The decades between the 1930s and the 1960s showed little progress in Black Nationalist efforts in the Alabama Black Belt, yet the seeds that had been sewn earlier served as a catalyst for the Black Power activities that began in the 1960s. The civil rights protests of the 1960s reignited Black Power within the Alabama Black Belt, specifically in Lowndes County, through the work of the Student Nonviolent Coordinating Committee and black agricultural workers. Lowndes County had a history of violence against African Americans. The *New York Times* reported that many blacks deemed the county as hostile territory and claimed that "all the Negroes are either school teachers or sharecroppers, which means the Whites have strings on them all, one way or another." Under these conditions, and due to civil rights work in neighboring Dallas County, SNCC came to Lowndes County and worked with local activists. This work continued a long history of self-determination by locals under extremely adverse circumstances. Jeffries found "SNCC's brand of Black Power emerged as a direct result of organizing successes in Lowndes County." Organizers of SNCC stated that Black Power was in the bloodstream of the group and was cultivated in the racial march from Memphis to Jackson, yet the philosophy was developed when addressing the political climate of Alabama. One organizer defined the basis of the group's ideology: "It began to emerge during the voter registration drives . . . we saw the vote itself meant nothing if all we could vote for was a George Wallace. We saw the need to put black men in power."[31]

The Black Power articulated by SNCC did not have the same goals as earlier Black Power, which had focused on land acquisition and ownership and labor negotiations. SNCC, however, overtly linked Black Power to electoral participation, something prohibited to propertyless blacks under the Alabama Constitution since 1901.[32]

The connection between SNCC workers and former SCU members proved important in the fusion and continuation of Black Power in the Alabama Black Belt. Bob Mants of SNCC admitted to "leaning hard on the wisdom of the locals," such as Lemon Johnson and Charles Smith, both participants of union activities in the 1930s and also linked to the 1960s movement in Lowndes County decades later. Not everyone, however, thought this connection would benefit the group. Chamberlain theorized in the *Milwaukee Sentinel* that SNCC and Black Power had taken a backward plunge that was linked to "the period of the 1920s when [the] American Communist Party was going all out for something called 'self-determination' for the Black Belt. . . . Black power is simply another way of saying self determination." He supported his aversion to Black Power by suggesting that the black establishment, notably Roy Wilkins of the National Association for the Advancement of Colored People, supported the premise that Black Power is a reverse of the Ku Klux Klan. The strategies of SNCC also drew fire; as differences between its ideology and traditional civil rights organizations were highlighted in the national media, SNCC was described as the most controversial civil rights group, consisting of "agents of anarchy." The difference between SNCC and other groups was emphasized in the *Washington Afro-American*, when Carmichael was quoted as saying, "this is a revolution, not just another movement."[33]

As civil rights activities increased in the Black Belt during the 1960s, blacks who farmed other people's land assisted the movement, but so did blacks who owned their land. For example, soon after SNCC arrived in

Lowndes County, Matthew Jackson, a farmer and black landowner, provided SNCC a residence, a freedom house, as it was called. The independence of Jackson was in sharp contrast to the situation of most African Americans in Lowndes County, who worked as sharecroppers and tenant farmers. In addition, Jackson was a member of the Lowndes County Christian Movement for Human Rights (LCCMHR), which assisted homeless residents who had been evicted due to political activity. Eventually this group formed the Lowndes County Freedom Organization (LCFO), called the Black Panther Party of Lowndes County, which was dedicated to electing blacks to political office in the county and was critical in the development and maturation of Black Power ideology. The SNCC organization strove to put black candidates up for office in Lowndes County and other Alabama counties where blacks had a voting majority. Black electoral participation in Lowndes County had been nonexistent since the 1901 Constitution was enacted: "not a single Negro in Lowndes County had even tried to register in the last 65 years," stated Andrew Young. White resistance continued even during the movement as black sharecroppers were evicted for attempting to register, including an eighty-two-year-old man, who said that both he and his mother, a former slave, had been born on the farm. Another woman said her employer dismissed her from her $12 a week job as a maid, struck her with a broom, and told her to get out. Another was threatened by a local businessperson who stated, "I'd like to take a damn two-by-four to the side of your head for registering. Get out of my store."[34]

The LCCMHR solicited and was initially granted funds from the Office of Economic Opportunity (OEO) in 1966 and was slated to receive nearly $241,000 to assist Black Belt tenants who had been displaced. But Governor George Wallace petitioned this award, stating the grant "amounts to the poverty office in Washington financing the revolutionary black power movement in this county." Governor Wallace listed all efforts for self-advancement in Lowndes County as "revolutionary" and challenged the federal government to cease support of the LCCMHR, as it was directly linked to Carmichael and the Black Panther Party and political activities. The OEO distanced itself as an official stated: "Obviously, the OEO does not intend to finance any so called black power group, just as we wouldn't support any extremist group."[35]

Black Power continued to mature in the county as the LCFO's electoral activities were linked to agricultural activities and goals. With the help of SNCC, the LCFO worked to elect black farmers to the local Agricultural

Stabilization and Conservation Service (ASCS), which assisted local farmers. Although this effort was but a modest success, it indicated the potential for Black Power in the Black Belt.[36]

Even with promise of civil rights expansion made possible through the Civil Rights Act of 1964 and the Voting Rights Act of 1965, the economic progress of many blacks in the region remained stagnant. Some groups during the 1960s focused on land acquisition as a major factor in Black Power in Alabama. Black nationalists specifically made headway in land ownership in the state. Historically, black nationalists had preached black empowerment through land ownership and socioeconomic separatism, and the Nation of Islam (NOI) adopted this message during the 1960s. Alabama became the stage for continued Black Power strategies as the NOI attempted to purchase property there. Their quest to acquire 3,600 acres generated extreme white resistance. According to Nelson, this resistance was not so much attributed to religious affiliation of the Black Muslims as much as to their racial group membership and their desire to buy up large amounts of land.[37]

The group managed large tracts of land in other states, including Georgia and Michigan, yet they received significant resistance in Alabama. The group owned land near Pell, Alabama, and the Ku Klux Klan actively sought to run them from their property by galvanizing local whites and law enforcement against them. Retaliation in Alabama included large hostile town meetings, the poisoning of farm animals, and governmental prosecutions. Tales also spread that the group planned to seize control of the county and banish whites. These fears of black economic and political dominance can be linked to similar reactions toward black land ownership during the Civil War and Reconstruction.[38]

Under the leadership of Elijah Muhammed, the NOI used their land purchases in Alabama to further Black Power rhetoric. Muhammed stated, "The most important step people who want to be independent must take is to learn to feed, shelter and clothe themselves." He was able to pool the resources of his organization and purchase thousands of acres of farm land and build manufacturing facilities for the purpose of Black Muslim self-sufficiency. Because of these efforts, members of the Nation of Islam were called the leaders of "black capitalism" during the 1960s by the media. The theory of Walton and Smith helps explain NOI strategy. It used its large African American membership to overcome two major challenges, landlessness and economic underdevelopment, to meet its members' needs.[39]

Historically, Black Power within the state of Alabama took on many forms as agricultural workers and land owners sought self-sufficiency and advancement. These efforts were shaped by situational contexts that revealed the difficulty of black empowerment in a hostile state. Although the SCU and SNCC were short-lived, their work in the Black Belt assisted in the development of Black Power ideologies through the experiences of workers and, to some extent, owners of the land. The NOI combined Black Nationalism and land acquisition as part of a Black Power policy for racial advancement. In fact, the NOI has been one of several all-black groups that achieved significant land ownership as a strategy. The ideology of Black Power transformed black activism in the state and addressed challenges facing African Americans. Black Power in Alabama was often based in hopelessness and desperation. Yet those who owned and worked the land developed and cultivated unique and situational strategies of racial advancement that were supported by and often grounded in the land.

Notes

1. W. E. Burghardt Du Bois, "The Negro Farmer." *Special Reports: Supplementary Analysis and Derivative Tales*. Twelfth Census of the United States, 1900 (Washington, D.C.: Government Printing Office, 1906): 523.

2. Hasan Jeffries, *Bloody Lowndes: Civil Rights and Black Power in Alabama's Black Belt* (New York: New York University Press, 2009). Mary G. Rolinson, *Grassroots Garveyism: The Universal Negro Improvement Association in the Rural South, 1920–1927* (Chapel Hill: University of North Carolina Press, 2007).

3. I use the terms black and African American interchangeably throughout this chapter. "Alabama's 'Black Belt': A Region Where Colored Men Are Contented and Prosperous," *New York Times*, July 17, 1879, 3. Booker T. Washington, *Up From Slavery: An Autobiography* (New York: Doubleday, 1901). Louis E. Swanson, Rosalind P. Harris, Jerry R. Skees, and Lionel Williamson, "African Americans in the Southern Rural Regions: The Importance of Legacy," *Review of Black Political Economy* 22 (1994): 110. Joyce E. Allen-Smith, Ronald C. Wimberley, and Libby V. Morris, "America's Forgotten People and Places: Ending the Legacy of Poverty in the Rural South," *Journal of Agricultural and Applied Economics* 32 (2000): 319–29. Michael W. Fitzgerald, "To Give Our Votes to the Party": Black Political Agitation and Agricultural Change in Alabama 1865–1870," *Journal of American History* 76 (1989): 489–505, and Michael W. Fitzgerald, *The Union League Movement in the Deep South: Politics and Agricultural Change during Reconstruction* (Baton Rouge: Louisiana State University Press, 1989). Richard Bailey, *Neither Carpetbaggers Nor Scalawags: Black Officeholders during Reconstruction of Alabama, 1867–1878* (Montgomery: New South Books, 2010).

4. Hanes Walton and Robert C. Smith, *American Politics and the African American Quest for Universal Freedom,* 5th edition (New York: Longman Pearson, 2010): 105. Stokely

Carmichael and Charles Hamilton, *Black Power* (New York: Random House, 1967). Robert Smith, "Black Power and the Transformation from Protest to Policies," *Political Science Quarterly* 96 (1981): 432.

5. Raymond Franklin, "The Political Economy of Black Power," *Social Problems* 16 (1969): 286–301. Stokely Carmichael, "What We Want," *New York Review of Books*, September 22, 1966, 5.

6. Mississippi Black Code influencing Black land ownership, http://www.pbs.org/wnet/slavery/experience/legal/docs6.html. Unlike Mississippi, Alabama's Black Codes did not specify limiting black land ownership.

7. "Alabama's 'Black Belt.'"

8. James S. Fisher, "Negro Farm Ownership in the South," *Annals of the Association of American Geographers* 63 (1973): 482–83. Thomas W. Mitchell, "From Reconstruction to Deconstruction: Undermining Black Landownership, Political Independence, and Community through Partition Sales of Tenancies in Common," LTC Research Paper 132, Land Tenure Center, University of Wisconsin–Madison (March 2000), available at http://ageconsearch.umn.edu/bitstream/12753/1/ltcrp132.pdf (accessed September 20, 2011). W.E.B. Du Bois recognized there were two classes of black farmers: those who operated their own farms and those who operated farms owned by other people. In addition he defined the farming Black Belt as counties with over one-half of the farmers being black; Du Bois, "The Negro Farmer," 523–27. The states of Virginia, Mississippi, Texas, South Carolina, and North Carolina had more black owner-operated farms than Alabama; see 524, 554, 558.

9. Du Bois, "The Negro Farmer," 554, 557.

10. Charles E. Hall, *Negro Farmer in the United States*, Census of Agriculture, Fifteenth Census of the United States: 1930 (Washington, D.C.: U.S. Government Printing Office, 1933): 39, 46, 50, 52. Blacks accounted for 97 percent of the colored farmers in the United States and 99 percent of all colored farmers in the South.

11. William Nelson Jr., "Black Rural Land Decline and Political Power," in *The Black Rural Landowner—Endangered Species: Social, Political, and Economic Implications*, ed. Leo McGee and Robert Boone (Westport, Conn.: Greenwood Press, 1979): 86. Farm Population of the United States: 1981 Current Population reports, Farm Population Series P-27, No. 56, 1982.

12. Dr. Wayne Flynt, Distinguished Professor of History at Auburn University, "A Legacy of Shame," From a Rally for Constitutional Reform, Tuscaloosa, Alabama, April 7, 2000, Alabama Citizens for Constitutional Reform, www. Constitutionalreform.org/archive/speeches/speech_wf.html (accessed September 21, 2011). A photograph of delegates to the 1872 Alabama Legislature on the steps of the state capitol in Montgomery indicates the involvement of black representatives and senators during Reconstruction; see Item Q4285, Alabama Department of Archives and History Digital Archives (hereafter cited as ADAH Digital Archives). Eric Foner, ed., *Freedom's Lawmakers: A Directory of Black Officeholders during Reconstruction*, rev. ed. (Baton Rouge: Louisiana State University Press, 1996). Stephen Plass, "Dualism and Overlooked Class Consciousness in American Labor Laws," *Houston Law Review* 37 (2000), 823–58, available at http://www.houstonlawreview.org/archive/downloads/37-3_pdf/HLR37P823.pdf (accessed September 21, 2011). 1901 Alabama Constitution, Article I, Section 181.

13. Wayne Flynt, "Alabama's Shame: The Historical Origins of the 1901 Constitution," *Alabama Law Review* 53 (2001): 75. Manning Marable, "The Politics of Black Land Tenure: 1877–1915," *Agricultural History* 53 (1979): 150. Some white Alabamans favored a white-farmer state, as evident in the goals of the German Immigration Society of Birmingham, which existed to recruit white farmers. See "As to an Immigration Bureau," newspaper clipping, November 7, 1902, Items Q17438–Q17439, ADAH Digital Archives.

"Two Negroes Jailed as 'Reds' after Series of Gun Battles" (editorial), *Berkeley Daily Gazette*, December 21, 1932, 3. "Along the Color Line," *Crisis* (February 1933): 39.

14. Allen W. Jones, "Voices for Improving Rural Life: Alabama's Black Agricultural Press, 1890–1965," *Agricultural History* 58 (1984): 215. Norman Crockett, *The Black Towns* (Lawrence: University of Kansas Press, 1979); Hannibal B. Johnson, *Acres of Aspiration: The All-Black Towns in Oklahoma* (Austin, Texas: Eakin Press, 2002); Thad Sitton and James H. Conrad, *Freedom Colonies: Independent Black Texans in the Time of Jim Crow* (Austin: University of Texas Press, 2005); Associated Press, "East Alabama Landmark in Peril," *NewsOne for Black America*, May 25, 2009, http://newsone.com/nation/news-one-staff/historic-black-town-in-alabama-is-in-peril/ (accessed September 22, 2011).

15. Rochelle Hines, "Once Prolific and Prosperous, Black Towns Now Struggle to Survive," *Journal Record* (Oklahoma City), July 12, 1999. Sundiata Keita Cha-Jua, *America's First Black Town Brooklyn, Illinois, 1830–1915* (Urbana: University of Illinois Press, 2000): 153. "Historic Black Town in Alabama Is in Peril," *News One*, May 26, 2009.

16. R. H. Ellis, "The Calhoun School: Miss Charlotte Thorn's 'Lighthouse on the Hill,' in Lowndes, Alabama," *Alabama Review* 37 (1984): 183–201.

17. Reverend Pitt Dillingham, "In Aid of Colored Men: Work That Is Carried on in the Calhoun School in Alabama," *New York Times*, January 21, 1896, 9. Ms. Ida Tourtellot, letter to the editor, *New York Times*, March 5, 1936.

18. Robert E. Zabawa and Sarah T. Warren, "From Company to Community: Agricultural Community Development in Macon County, Alabama, 1881 to the New Deal," *Agricultural History* 72 (1998): 459–86.

19. Hall, *Negro Farmer*, 27, 43. Racial categories include Black (Negro), Native-Born Whites, and Foreign-Born Whites. Fisher, "Negro Farm Ownership in the South," 483.

20. Woodford McClellan, "Africans and Black Americans in the Comintern Schools, 1925–1934," *International Journal of African Historical Studies* 26 (1993): 371.

21. Robin D. G. Kelley, *Race Rebels: Culture, Politics, and the Black Working Class* (New York: Free Press, 1994): 105.

22. Robin D. G. Kelley, *Hammer and Hoe: Communists in Alabama during the Great Depression* (Chapel Hill: University of North Carolina Press, 1990). The list of Black Belt Counties includes Barbour, Greene, Perry, Butler, Lowndes, Pike, Choctaw, Macon, Russell, Crenshaw, Marengo, Sumter, Dallas, Wilcox, Clarke, Conecuh, Escambia, Monroe, and Washington.

23. John Beecher, "The Share Croppers' Union in Alabama," *Social Forces* 13 (1934–35): 124. Elizabeth Schafer, "Alabama Share Croppers Union," in *Organizing Black America: An Encyclopedia of African American Associations*, ed. Nina Mjagkij (New York: Garland Publishing, 2001): 25–27. Elaine Ellis, "Women of the Cotton Fields," *Crisis* 45 (October 1938): 342. "Sharecroppers Plight Is Vividly Described," *Sunday Morning Star*, January 17, 1937, 32.

24. "The League Charges Brutal Methods," *Evening Independent*, August 3, 1931. Census of Agriculture, 1930, 121. Lowell K. Dyson, *Red Harvest: The Communist Party and American Farmers* (Lincoln: University of Nebraska Press, 1982). Kelley, *Hammer and Hoe*, 41–42. Robin D. G. Kelley, "Share Croppers Union," *Encyclopedia of the American Left*, edited by Mari Jo Buhle, Paul Buhle, and Dan Georgakas (New York: Garland Publishers, 1990),695–97. Beecher "Share Croppers' Union," 126. "Posses Still Seek Negroes in Tallapoosa," *Florence Times Daily*, July 18, 1931, 1. "34 Await Hearings as Result of Riots," *Reading Eagle*, July 19, 1931, 13. "Volley Disperse Alabama Negroes," *New York Times*, July 17, 1931, Business and Opportunity, 30.

25. "Murder, Woman's Beating Unveiled in Three Affidavits," *Afro-American*, October 26, 1935, 10.

26. Michael Honey, *Southern Labor and Black Civil Rights Organizing Memphis Workers* (Urbana: University of Illinois Press): 250, 146.

27. Theodore Rosengarten, *All God's Dangers: The Life of Nate Shaw* (New York: Vintage Books, 1984). Frye Gaillard, *Cradle of Freedom, Alabama and the Movement that Changed America* (Tuscaloosa: University of Alabama Press, 2004): 285. Jeffries, *Bloody Lowndes*, 27. Gaillard, *Cradle of Freedom*, 285. Kelley, *Hammer and Hoe*, 45.

28. W.E.B. Du Bois, "Postscript," *Crisis* (June 1933): 140–42. Harold Preece, "Epic of the Black Belt," *Crisis* (1936): 75, 92.

29. "Correspondence to Governor Benjamin Miller, discussing violence in Camp Hill, Alabama between members of the Alabama Sharecroppers Union and county officials": quotes from L. N. Duncan, Director, Extension Service, Alabama Polytechnic Institute, to Honorable B. M. Miller, Governor of Alabama, July 20, 1931; and Bradford Knapp, President, Alabama Polytechnic Institute, to Miller, July 21, 1931, Items Q12339–Q12341, ADAH Digital Archives. Schafer, "Alabama Share Croppers Union," 27.

30. Schafer, "Alabama Share Croppers Union," 27.

31. Roy Reed, "Rights Marchers Push into Region Called Hostile," *New York Times*, March 23, 1965. Jeffries, *Bloody Lowndes*, 32. Hasan Jeffries, "SNCC, Black Power, and Independent Political Party Organizing in Alabama, 1964–1966," *Journal of African American History* 91 (2006): 188. Al Kuetthner, "SNCC and 'Black Power' Seen as Most Controversial," *Washington Afro-American*, September 13, 1966, 16.

32. Jeffries, "SNCC and 'Black Power,'" 176.

33. Timothy Tyson, "Robert F. Williams, 'Black Power,' and the Roots of the African American Freedom Struggle," *Journal of American History* 85 (1998): 546. Gaillard, *Cradle of Freedom*, 289, 285–86. Kuetthner, "SNCC and 'Black Power,'" 16 (Carmichael quote). John Chamberlain, "'Black Power' Movement Helpless without Allies," *Milwaukee Sentinel*, July 15, 1966, 16. "Agents of Anarchy," *Milwaukee Journal*, September 15, 1966, 24.

34. Gene Roberts, "Alabama Negroes Say Farmers Evict Them for Enrolling to Vote," *New York Times*, December 22, 1965, 16.

35. Gaillard, *Cradle of Freedom*, 289. Susan Youngblood Ashmore, *Carry It On: The War on Poverty and the Civil Rights Movement in Alabama, 1964–1972* (Athens: University of Georgia Press, 2008). "'New Leaders' and New Course for 'Snick,'" *New York Times*, May 21, 1966, 208. Reed, "Rights Marchers," 1. "'Black Panther': A Demo Threat in Alabama," *St. Petersburg Times*, December 16, 1965, 12-A. Gene Roberts, "For Lowndes County Anti Poverty Program Sargent Shriver Denies 'Black Power,'" *Florence Times Daily*, July 21, 1966,

3. OEO quote from "Lowndes Aid Gets Black Power Tag," *Gadsden Times*, July 20, 1966, 6. "Rights Commission Highly Critical of Black Belt Living Conditions," *Florence Times–Tri Cities Daily*, April 28, 1968, 6.

36. Gaillard, *Cradle of Freedom*, 303.

37. Anthony Gribbs, "How Blacks Lost 9,000,000 Acres of Land," *Ebony* magazine (October 1974): 98. Michael Martin and Marilyn Yaquinto, *Historical Injustices in the United States on Reparations for Slavery, Jim Crow, and Their Legacies* (Durham, N.C. Duke University Press, 2007): 594. Nelson, "Black Rural Land Decline," 88–89.

38. Hans J. Massaquoi, "Elijah Muhammed: Prophet and Architect of the Separate Nation of Islam," in "Which Way Black America: Separation? Integration? Liberation?" special issue, *Ebony* August 1970, 80. Cordell Thompson, "Black Muslims Fight to Keep Alabama Farm," *Jet* 1970, 16. Races: "Muslims in Alabama," *Time*, February 2, 1970, www.time.com/time/magazine/article; "Muslim Land Purchases Are under Investigations," *Tuscaloosa News*, November 28, 1969. Mattias Gardell, *In the Name of Elijah Muhammed: Louis Farrakhan and the Nation of Islam*, (Durham: Duke University Press, 1996), 274.

39. Dora Muhammad, "Now We Can Build," *Final Call*, April 19, 2004. "Races: The Original Black Capitalists," *Time*, May 7, 1969.

11

"You're just like mules, you don't know your own strength"

Rural South Carolina Blacks and the Emergence of the Civil Rights Struggle

CARMEN V. HARRIS

Rural African Americans provided critical support during the civil rights movement. Fannie Lou Hamer and other Mississippians who participated in Freedom Summer and members of the Lowndes County Alabama Freedom Organization, which evolved into the Black Panther Party, provide notable examples of rural black activism.[1] Less attention has been paid to the ways rural African Americans in South Carolina expected equal protection under the law. In 2003 members of the lead families in the *Harry Briggs et al. v. Elliot et al.* lawsuit that was central to the decision striking down segregation in *Brown v. Board of Education of Topeka Kansas* received the Congressional Gold Medal posthumously.[2] Little has been written about them or about other plaintiffs in the *Briggs* case who risked their personal security in the quest for civil rights legislation and enforcement.

This chapter surveys the strategies and resilience of rural Afro-South Carolinians during the 1950s and 1960s, the high water mark in the struggle for racial liberation. They used their leadership skills developed through community organizing and the support provided by civil rights activists in South Carolina and beyond to confront *de jure* racial apartheid in South Carolina. Historians have generally ignored these rural individuals—many of whom lived economically precarious lives—and have concentrated on urban activists instead. Yet much material, including contemporary media coverage, personal papers, business records, and official correspondence, corroborates the evidence that rural black South Carolinians—including farm-owning families who signed the petition that spawned the *Briggs* case—expected the government to protect their rights.[3]

Clarendon County's black citizens were among the least likely to have been expected to incite a civil rights battle. In 1930, 72 percent of all citizens in Clarendon were African American, and nearly a quarter of African American adults were illiterate, compared to 3.7 percent of whites in the county. As late as 1960, 68 percent of the county's population remained African American and impoverished.[4]

In his 1938 program of work under the heading "Problems to be met," Clarendon County white extension agent F. M. Rast declared:

> Undoubtedly the greatest single factor which will act detrimentally to our long time program is the large percent of tenants on farms in the county, and also that approximately 69% of the farming population is of the colored race. This latter fact will hinder the attainment of a higher standard of living since the colored race will *submit* [my emphasis] to a standard of living which the white race will not tolerate.[5]

Rast's words echo the defenses that whites within the region and the state crafted in response to the July 1938 *Report on Economic Conditions in the South*. While Fitzgerald Hall of the Southern States Industrial Council in Nashville, Tennessee, conceded that southern whites enforced substandard conditions on Africans Americans in their communities, his was the minority opinion.[6] The University of South Carolina extension division drafted a rebuttal report that attributed part of the state's poor showing on economic indicators to its black population.

The national report criticized the small, uneconomical size of southern farms, which encouraged the "destructive practice" of cash crop agriculture rather than a balanced program that would save the region's soil. The language of the South Carolina rejoinder was contradictory. It blamed cash crop agriculture on farm tenancy where farm size was dictated by the amount of acreage a man and his family could cultivate and asserted that usually the tenant made the decision to plant only cash crops because staple crops provided a low return. It ignored the reality that staple crops would permit a tenant family to subsist but not to pay the landlord, and landlords evicted tenants who did not repay debts. The report also included the argument that African Americans lacked the cognitive capacity for independent decision making: "Negro farm hands require constant supervision, so land owning farmers are [also] limited in the number of hands they can afford to pay and personally supervise, or by the number of supervisors they have capital to hire."[7] Views expressed in Rast's program of work and in South Carolina's rebuttal show how firmly white South Carolinians embraced notions of black inferiority and attributed to them a corollary submissive nature, with no concession to the idea that the submissiveness was coerced. Clearly, whites in Clarendon County had become accustomed to submission from the county's majority-black population.

Therefore it came as a great surprise when, a decade later, Levi Pearson and then Harry Briggs Sr. and others filed class action lawsuits on behalf of their children, seeking increased county financial support for their children's education and eventually pursued the radical solution of school desegregation. While both these lawsuits were unsuccessful on the state level, their filings were sufficiently troubling to the county's white establishment that whites embarked on a campaign of economic retaliation intended to make rural blacks cower back into submission. This time, however, African Americans were not to be deterred. With the encouragement of community leaders like Liberty Hill African Methodist Episcopal pastor E. E. Richburg, who told his listeners, "You're just like mules, you don't know your own strength," rural blacks began to use organizing skills and to cooperate with activist organizations to resist submission.[8]

As pragmatic individuals, Afro-South Carolinians found ways to adapt themselves to the racial oppression that pervaded South Carolina from the 1870s onward. As the abuses that African Americans in the South suffered became more visible nationally during the 1930s and internationally during the 1940s, individuals in the United States mobilized across the color line to fight fascism. As a consequence, members of the county's rural black families transformed their view of their place in the world. African American minister J. W. Seals asserted, as quoted in Richard Kluger's *Simple Justice*: "We ain't asking for anything that belongs to these white folks. I just mean to get for that little black boy of mine everything that any other South Carolina boy gets." Clarendon County blacks had honed their leadership skills as participants in and local leaders of community-based organizations and churches. For example, African American agriculture and home demonstration agents had worked with farm families across the state since the 1910s, involving them in clubs that the families organized and administered. Adults as well as 4-H members gained leadership opportunities through these clubs. Membership in black churches also provided opportunities for the county's rural black residents to develop leadership skills and form networks of support that proved crucial to maintaining cohesion during the years after the filing of the Pearson and Briggs cases when whites attempted to use economic reprisals to undermine black demands for equality.[9]

The degree to which agricultural extension program leadership contributed to the development of activist mentality among rural blacks cannot be definitively established.[10] Some of the names on the lists of plaintiffs and participants in extension programs overlapped. Only one person, a 4-H club member named Willie Gibson, appears in the lists of persons mentioned in the 1955 annual report of the black agricultural agent for Clarendon County, William Thompson, and of his successor, Hugene Gerald, and of the 123 signatures on the Clarendon petition for educational equality that families signed to launch the *Briggs* case. Yet a comparison of names mentioned in the same Thompson-Gerald annual report with those on a list of sixty-seven black farmers assisted by a support group called the Clarendon County Improvement Association (CCIA) yields six names on both lists, including the father of Willie Gibson. The names of three of the farmers being helped by the CCIA appear in the 1955 extension agent's report as local leaders (two of them were also members of the farm council executive committee). Three other men's names matched those of men who were identified clients in these reports.[11]

The county's white political leadership recognized the importance of organizations—such as state-funded extension work—to rural blacks and used their appropriations control to make their displeasure with the activities of rural blacks known. For example, after the filing of the Pearson case in 1948, State Supervisor for Negro Home Demonstration Work Marian Baxter Paul reported in 1949 that a Clarendon County state senator had vetoed the appropriation for and forbidden the continuation of black home demonstration work (but not black agricultural extension work) because he "was annoyed by political trends."[12]

Despite the economic dangers of assertiveness, rural blacks in Clarendon County committed themselves to the civil rights cause in earnest. The account in Richard Kluger's *Simple Justice* reveals that farmers in the county signed on to the *Briggs* case despite the reprisals they faced. Levi Pearson, who became president of Clarendon County's branch of the National Association for the Advancement of Colored People (NAACP) in 1957, was denied credit after he filed his case, and R. W. Elliott, the defendant in the *Briggs* case and a lumber mill owner, refused to accept the lumber Pearson hoped to sell to purchase fertilizer. Pearson could not borrow a harvester for his cotton either, and his other crops rotted in the fields.[13]

To counter economic backlash by white political and commercial leadership, local blacks established the Clarendon County Improvement Association, a cooperative created to serve black farmers who had been targeted for white reprisal for their involvement in the desegregation struggle. Hammett Pearson, the brother of Levi (of the *Pearson* case), was on its executive committee. The CCIA bought fertilizer for cotton and tobacco to sell to rural civil rights activists to whom retaliatory white vendors refused to sell. Seventy-three farmers used the CCIA, which was able to sell fertilizer to them at lower than market prices because the association had no overhead.[14]

The *Pearson* and *Briggs* lawsuits had been filed because local white officials refused to make any concessions to African Americans that would have improved the educational environment for their children. Whites in Clarendon became somewhat solicitous of black citizens' demands during the interregnum between the *Briggs* decision in South Carolina and the *Brown* decision in the U.S. Supreme Court. Yet when the outcome of *Brown* struck down segregation, the façade of conciliation ended, and Clarendon whites retaliated by attempting to annihilate the black community economically. According to a statement by local funeral director Billie S. Fleming, who was the organizer of the CCIA and Reverend J. A. Delaine's nephew, after the *Briggs* decision the Clarendon County superintendent of education, Reverend L. B. McCord, and S. Emory Rogers, a prominent local attorney who assisted in the defense of the school district, organized a White Citizens' Council. (Rogers went on to become executive secretary of all of South Carolina's White Citizens' Councils). The council immediately began to apply economic pressure on blacks who had been part of the case.

The persistence of these black farmers in the face of adversity demonstrates their awareness of American ideals of citizen equality despite the white minority's efforts to impose its own values of institutionalized white supremacy and black submission. In 1955 the U.S. Supreme Court seemingly handed supporters of racial segregation in schools a second defeat in *Brown II*, when the justices mandated that desegregation move forward "with all deliberate speed." Rural African Americans recognized that national acquiescence to "separate but equal" was weakening, and they intensified their local opposition to inequality to force South Carolina whites to fall in line with the national sentiment. Resistance spread to Orangeburg County, which was adjacent to Clarendon and disproportionately African American (63 percent) as well. There, in the Elloree Community, rural blacks joined the NAACP and signed a petition to desegregate their district's schools. Small landholders joined the suit although they were desperate for cash. According to their spokesman, "they have there [sic] own little land and that's all they has."[15]

White reprisal spread from Clarendon County into Orangeburg in response to black civil rights activism. Whites in Elloree responded as whites had in Clarendon County by establishing a White Citizens' Council. Howard Quint, in *Profiles in Black and White: A Frank Portrait of South Carolina*, reported that the "leaders of the Elloree Council declared their immediate purpose was to exert 'economic pressure on all persons connected with the NAACP,'" but in particular on parents who had signed the petition.[16] L. A. Blakemon, the NAACP president in the Elloree community, described the plight of farmers who had signed the petition in a letter to Roy Wilkins. Blakemon reported that black owners of their own farms were "catching the devil and need help now." The crop allotments these independent farmers received from federal programs such as those provided by the Agricultural Stabilization and Conservation Service were minimal, two to three acres at most. Both nature, in the form of almost continual rain, and white hostility conspired against the farmers, and many were threatened with the loss of their farms.[17]

The economic pressure that Levi Pearson experienced in 1957 was intense and not unique. Loans were called in; farmers who had signed on to legal actions or who were members of the NAACP were unable to buy seed or fertilizer; crops rotted away because the farmers could not rent harvesters; cotton went unsold. White landowners even refused to advance money for burial expenses for sharecroppers who used Fleming's funeral services to bury their dead. The Citizens' Council went so far as to send a letter to major lending institutions outside Clarendon County to request that credit be denied to sixty-eight persons on a list they enclosed. According to Fleming, the list included the names of Clarendon plaintiffs, many of whom were farmers. The Citizens' Council leadership promised that those blacks who withdrew from the case would no longer feel economic pressure, but that turned out not to be true.

The CCIA received financial support from outside the county, including from the NAACP, to provide "fertilizer, seed, insecticides, cash loans and other services that [farmers] could not get elsewhere." CCIA support enabled farmers like Ladson Stukes to continue their principled objection to segregation. Stukes owed the Clarendon Memorial Hospital $700 for the care of one of his children. Despite his small payments on the note, a sheriff's deputy threatened to arrest Stukes but said he would not do so if Stukes removed his name from a petition from parents seeking to integrate the schools. Stukes refused to remove his name. According to a quotation in *Jet* magazine, Stukes asserted, "I ain't taking my name off the list until Thurgood Marshall comes down here and tells me." He had to mortgage a mule to get the funds to pay for his child's release.[18] Stukes was not alone in his willingness to suffer in the civil rights struggle. At least sixteen reprisals on a list of nearly one hundred compiled by the NAACP were directed at southern farmers for signing petitions and engaging in other types of citizenship assertions.[19] Yet they persevered.

In Clarendon County where it all began, African Americans countered the economic boycott by drawing on their organizing traditions to craft methods of survival, including publicizing the condition in the public sphere. The plight of South Carolina's black farmers received national attention when Billie Fleming testified before a Senate subcommittee in 1959. Fleming reported that whites refused to gin the cotton of blacks who were associated with the *Briggs* case or with the NAACP. The gin owners posted the names of persons whose cotton they would not accept. White bankers also refused to make operating loans to black farmers "to force them into submission." Fleming further testified that white farmers refused to loan or rent black farmers harvesting equipment, and in 1957 black farmers' crops rotted because they could not get harvesters. He recalled a talk on the situation he made to a conference of the United Auto Workers in New York. The delegates collected enough money to purchase a combine. Whites in Clarendon County refused to sell Fleming a combine, but he succeeded in buying one in another county by not mentioning his affiliation with the CCIA. The combine permitted black farmers to harvest their crops and to continue to support desegregation. According to Fleming, "a number of our farmers . . . did not feel that such economic reprisals were in keeping with the American Way of life."[20]

Popular reporting regarding the conditions in Clarendon and Elloree and the endurance of rural Afro-South Carolinians resulted in financial support from outside the state that enabled residents to persist in their protest. The article in *Jet* magazine included an address for contributions for the support of the communities, but it also noted that "the hard-pressed farmers are trying to help themselves." A retired contractor came out of retirement to build houses to provide the unemployed with jobs. A snackshop owner sent chickens to suffering families. "We been fighting for our rights for six years and we're not quitting now. But we do need help."[21]

Four black ministers, three from Orangeburg and one from Summerton in Clarendon County, issued an open letter appealing for assistance for the farmers. The ministers reported that three black farmers nearly lost their farms for owing mortgages of less the $100 each. The ministers documented whites' attempted use of economic strain to coerce submission. Many farmers in Clarendon and Orangeburg counties, and in Sumter County—adjacent to Clarendon on the northwest—had been unable to borrow money for operations unless they attested that they were not members of the NAACP, that they opposed integration, and that they expressed satisfaction with their current condition. Without these assurances, "a petition signer with 350 acres, unencumbered, mechanized, and improved cannot borrow $100." The ministers encouraged the readers of their letter to collect money for loans to the farmers made on the usual terms. Loans would "hold [the farmer] to the line in the fight" and help farmers establish credit. The ministers also encouraged the sponsorship of a farm family. Such extraordinary efforts on the part of the ministers to find support suggest that rural Afro-South Carolinians' participation was vital in the fight for desegregation.[22]

To bolster community spirits the Elloree NAACP held a program in 1958 to celebrate the fourth anniversary of the *Brown* decision. By 1959 conditions in Elloree were further exacerbated by crop destruction caused by hurricane Gracie. More than one sharecropper family had their entire crop seized by their landlords. Others were unable to get credit or to secure day work as farm laborers. Some were without food or clothing.[23]

Ministerial leadership was crucial in these days of protest because other members of what constituted the black leadership in the state were constrained by conditions of their employment. South Carolina's extension program—and those in other southern states—employed African American extension agents to provide services to rural black residents. These agents carried on a nearly fifty-year tradition of interacting with rural residents as leaders, sponsors of community-based clubs, educators, and resource persons who provided information not only on government programs but on current issues of the day. Indeed, these agents' programs centered on the importance of cooperation for community uplift. As the civil rights movement progressed, however, the manner in which the agents interacted within the communities they served became increasingly complicated. Agents who practiced overt activism jeopardized their jobs. Thus, during the early stages of the civil rights movement, extension agents remained largely on the sidelines. The agents' programs followed the model associated with Booker T. Washington and his advocacy for economic advancement that deemphasized political and social equality. The agents became increasingly marginal to black community activism as rural blacks and civil rights organizations became the central forces in advancing black equality during the early 1950s. The absence of extension workers from these early battles sometimes strained relationships between some extension workers and their clients. As Marian Paul noted in her 1951 report, agents "must be aware of the exploitation of our people and must not become discouraged when these people doubt our sincerity and leadership."[24]

There likely was sympathy for the agents' situation also as all Afro-South Carolinians understood the expanse of white power. The reports of State Supervisor of Negro Home Demonstration Work Marian Paul in South Carolina captured the approaches to civil rights that existed somewhere between the Washingtonian and Du Boisian philosophies. Paul, whose reports prior to the 1950s had served as an instrument of resistance to the oppression that Afro-South Carolinian's faced, seemingly turned conservative during the 1950s. In her 1938 program, for example, Paul challenged the idea that blacks were the cause of South Carolina's problems by asserting that "the Negro is not the problem, but rather the problem is the white man's attitude toward him."[25] During the 1950s, however, Paul suggested an introspective approach; black home demonstration agents should encourage black families to seek greater economic freedom and to motivate them to become "law-abiding worthwhile citizens" and assets to the state and nation rather than liabilities.[26] "Our people are all excellent followers—they only need the right leaders." Paul suggested that extension agents were held in high esteem by their communities; she asserted that they "assum[ed] the status of a public servant and the position of a public benefactor and advisor." They shaped "sentiment for or against . . . public policy." They were trained to "mobilize all available forces" to eliminate "ignorance, poverty and misunderstanding" and to serve as leaders by example. They were expected to "act in any capacity for the uplift of the county and its citizenry . . . [and] to ease racial tensions." She said her agents' ultimate goal was to change rural blacks' behavior and encourage them "to assume responsibilities which will enlarge their capacities and *fit* [my emphasis] them for worthwhile citizenship." She wrote of the importance of teaching blacks to learn to "respect the rights, privileges, and properties of others." The home agent's task was to help blacks understand "county, state, national and international affairs," so that they, and the United States, could take their place in the new order. Paul also stated that it was the agents' "duty to direct all of her clear thinking into channels for harmony, progress and for the well being of the nation."[27]

The meaning of Paul's assertions, however, was a matter of perspective. Like the language games that enslaved African Americans played on their masters, such phrases as "respect[ing] the rights, privileges, and properties of others" could be read in multiple ways. In her report written the year that *Brown II* was decided, Paul's description of the passage of the postplantation era in South Carolina and the acknowledgement that it was rural folk who had done the heavy lifting in their own salvation was poignant:

> The old "plantation system" [was] fading away. Gone now are the corduroy or wash board roads, the lean-to cabins, the one-teacher schools that ran three months, the horse and buggy, the one-crop system with cotton planted to the cabin door, the illiterate and superstitious families and eight Negro Home Demonstration agents to work the entire state . . . we had to corral these poor, poverty stricken, illiterate people, gain their confidence and respect, then motivate them with the desire for self improvement, hence our agents had to become half-missionary, half magician. Our program was simple but sound built upon the theory that "an enlightened people can be trusted to save themselves."[28]

Rural African American resistance in the *Briggs* era was crucial to solidifying the base of the liberation struggle in South Carolina as it moved into the 1960s. Successes such as the black counter boycott that broke white reprisals in Elloree were just one manifestation of the resolve of the Afro-South Carolinian community.

As Congress passed civil rights laws and the U.S. Supreme Court overturned prior precedents such as *Plessy v. Ferguson*, rural African Americans recognized that more avenues to demand equal treatment existed. Activist groups such as the NAACP made certain that rural blacks, many of whom were members of its rank and file, became increasingly aware of their rights. Rural blacks responded by filing protests to federal government agencies regarding discrimination.

Through these activities, they made clear to local whites that they, too, were at the mercy of forces beyond their control. Rural blacks served notice that they would no longer be abused with impunity. African American farmers also began to agitate to end discrimination in federal agricultural programs. In 1960 the U.S. Department of Agriculture shut down operations for fifteen days at the Clarendon County Agricultural Stabilization and Conservation Service office to investigate Billie Fleming's allegations of discrimination in tobacco- and cotton-acreage allotments. Fleming's claims were confirmed, and the board was replaced, but little changed in the operation of the office.[29]

Attitudes regarding the potential of the Afro-South Carolinian community were also changing. Paul Webber Jr., a field representative from the Office of Economic Opportunity and a professor at South Carolina State College, addressed a meeting of the Cherokee County Council of Farm Women in 1966. Webber told them, "This is a good age or time to live in." He encouraged them to take on tough jobs. "You don't have to be the plumber's helper any more [sic]; you can be the plumber." He encouraged them "to learn all you can about all you can, read, develop local community heros [sic]," and encourage youth to pursue technical education.[30]

Despite Webber's declaration of a new age, problems persisted. Fifteen African American farmers signed a petition of protest in 1966 when the African American agent in Union County was fired, allegedly for substandard performance. The petitioners claimed that the agent was fired because he had attempted to enroll his child in a "white" school.[31] Farmers in the Elloree community of Orangeburg County continued to remain activists as well. Title VI of the Civil Rights Act of 1964 and subsequent federal memoranda made clear that all people had a right to expect equal treatment in federal services. Just as they had used the *Brown* decision to make demands on behalf of their children, they used the Civil Rights Act to make demands on behalf of themselves and African American agents in Orangeburg County. In 1968 Raymond Anderson and a committee of six other farmers from Elloree—representing a group of farmers that correspondence on this matter identifies as "low income"—wrote to Clemson President R. C. Edwards to complain that there had been no extension agent to serve them since July 1967. The one black agricultural agent in the county, according to Anderson, spent most of his time working with 4-H youth. (According to reports, the agent was also serving white clients.) The farmers complained that they had been left "without farm visits, on the farm advice and little or no information when office calls are made." Anderson admitted that black farmers received information when they requested it, but the group sought the sort of impromptu personal attention that they had received when there was a black agent who worked with black farmers (black agents served black clients exclusively during segregation). While his group recognized that it might be difficult to find "qualified" personnel, they also questioned the level of effort that had been put into the search. They demanded an immediate replacement of the black agent who had been transferred to

Laurens County in 1967. The distribution of the letter demonstrates the development of political astuteness by rural blacks. They sent copies of their correspondence to George Nutt and their state representative and senator.[32]

Demonstrating the strength of collective action, Anderson's letter initiated two months of investigation of the matter. Director Nutt told Edwards he had intended to replace the transferred agent with a "qualified Negro agricultural graduate." Nutt said Bennie Cunningham, an African American administrator, was in the process of checking the qualifications of several applicants, but they had "not found a qualified person for the position." Edwards wrote to Anderson to express his commitment to see that the farmers' needs were served.[33]

A struggle that began for improved segregated schools transformed the lives of some rural Afro-South Carolinians in ways they could not have imagined. In 1967, for example, Jonas T. Kennedy, a black farmer from Marlboro County, was one of ninety-five farmers invited to have lunch with President Johnson to discuss issues affecting farmers. Kennedy, a producer of turkeys, corn, cotton, and soybeans, gave a report to the local paper on the issues the farmers raised in the meeting. According to the article, the high point of Kennedy's day was meeting the president. "I just can't wash that hand off quite yet."[34] No rural black could have imagined this opportunity a decade earlier.

By the 1960s it became clear that rural blacks in South Carolina had not willingly submitted to the conditions under which they lived, as had been asserted in the 1930s. Rural blacks had aspirations for themselves and especially for their children that extended beyond the sharecroppers' shacks to which dependency on white landowners confined them.

Organization of rural groups in Clarendon and Elloree and later in other communities in other counties provides examples of civil rights organizing called the "indigenous perspective." Aldon Morris posited this model in 1984 as a modification of the "resource mobilization" theory. The resource mobilization theory emphasizes factors beyond charismatic leadership that can ignite social movements, including "formal and informal organizations, leaders, money, people, and communication networks." The theory takes account of the "larger political environment" as a critical factor in activating protest movements. Such protests are "rational ... grow[ing] out of preexisting social structures and political processes." Theorists argue, however, that social movements are often driven by professional leaders and funding external to the community. The model also minimizes the importance of "grievances, psychic strain, and other psychological states of the participants." Organizational skills, according to the model, are more important to the development of such movements than are long-held grievances.[35]

As Morris rightly points out, the traditional resource mobilization approach centers attention on the role of outside elites in initiating social change. Alternatively, indigenous perspective focuses on "dominated groups" who are "excluded from one or more of the decision-making processes that determine the quantity and quality of social, economic, and political rewards that group receives from a society." As a result the dominated group attempts to "change their situation of powerlessness by engaging in nontraditional and usually nonlegitimized struggles with power holders." The success of these groups depends on "(1) certain basic resources, (2) social activists with strong ties to mass-based indigenous institutions, and (3) tactics and strategies that can be effectively employed against a system of domination." In these movements it is the activists who play the central role in merging internal resources and strategies to form a movement. "Outside resources . . . are triggered by the strength and force of indigenous movements." The strategies and tactics used by these groups are intended "to generate widespread disruption of a social order [which] . . . generates the collective power of masses used by dominated groups in their struggle to redistribute power."[36]

Morris confines his narrative to the interaction between the black church and visible civil rights organizations. Although he discusses the citizenship schools that were established on the South Carolina Sea Islands and spread throughout the South, and shows that their successful form was the result of local initiative, his treatment focuses on organization—the subject of his study—rather than the human dimension.[37]

The indigenous perspective must include a fourth dimension that is equally crucial: the importance of individuals whose "grievances, psychic strain, and other psychological states" reached the critical point. At that moment these people find resonance in the calls for protest within their indigenous institutions. This moment occurred across South Carolina for rural Afro-South Carolinians during the civil rights era. As a result, they took the initiative in creating multiple "local movement centers" which permitted their communities to "produce, organize, coordinate, finance, and sustain protest." Clearly, the black church played a role in spurring organization. Yet secular institutions such as extension programs also contributed to the organizing tradition. Extension programs enabled rural African Americans to realize the benefits of collective cooperation. Additionally, extension work enabled farmers to increase their self-sufficiency and inspired them to demand equality and autonomy and to achieve it through effective coordination. Eventually, as in the case of the Clarendon and Elloree movements in particular, these various threads of institutional organization came together to form local resistance movements.

Notes

1. Monographs that focus on rural black activism during the civil rights era tend to focus on Mississippi and Alabama. See, for example, John Dittmer, *Local People: The Struggle for Civil Rights in Mississippi* (Champaign: University of Illinois Press, 1995); Charles Payne, *I've Got the Light of Freedom: The Organizing Tradition and the Mississippi Freedom Struggle*, 2nd edition (Berkeley: University of California Press, 2007); and Hasan Jeffries, *Bloody Lowndes: Civil Rights and Black Power in Alabama's Black Belt* (New York: New York University Press, 2009).

2. Petition of Harry Briggs et al. to the Board of Trustees for School District No. 22, November 11, 1949, digitized and available at Teaching American History in South Carolina, http://www.teachingushistory.org/ttrove/briggsvelliott.htm (accessed September 16, 2011).

3. "House Passes Congressman Clyburn's Bill to Honor Clarendon County Desegregation Heroes," press release, Congressman James E. Clyburn, November 19, 2003, http://clyburn.house.gov/press/031119goldmedals.html (accessed 29 July 2010). *Harry Briggs, Jr., et al. v. The Board of Trustees for School District Number 22, Clarendon County, South Carolina, R. W. Elliott, Chairman, et al.*, 1950 Case No. 2505; and *Harry Briggs, Jr., et al. v. R. W. Elliott, et al.*, 1950 Case No. 2657. These cases originated in the U.S. District Court for the Eastern District of South Carolina. The decision in *Briggs v. Elliott* (1950 Case No. 2657) was appealed to the U.S. Supreme Court (*Harry Briggs et al. v. Elliott et al.*, 342 U.S. 350 [SCOTUS, 1952]) and was consolidated into *Brown v. Board of Education*.

4. Historical Census Browser, University of Virginia, Geospatial and Statistical Data Center, http://mapserver.lib.virginia.edu/index.html (accessed July 28, 2010).

5. F. M. Rast, "The 1938 County Agricultural Program for Clarendon County," p. 6, Cooperative Extension Service Records, series 33, box 27, folder 740, Special Collections, University Libraries, Clemson, South Carolina (hereafter cited as CUL).

6. "Fitzgerald Hall and Lowell Mellett, *Attack and Response: Hall's Comments and Mellett's Response*," in *Confronting Southern Poverty in the Great Depression: "The Report on Economic Conditions of the South" with Related Documents*, ed. David L. Carlton and Peter A. Coclanis (Boston: Bedford Books of St. Martin's Press, 1996), 139–40.

7. University of South Carolina, Extension Division, *Discussion of Economic Conditions of South Carolina: Annotations and Comments Relating to the Report Prepared for the President of the United States by the National Emergency Council*, Bulletin of the University of South Carolina Extension Division (Columbia: University of South Carolina, c. 1938), 17–18. This document is a reproduction of the national report with inserts regarding South Carolina in red. The page citations include the commentary from the national report and the South Carolina response.

8. See *James Pearson, an infant, by Levi Pearson, his next friend and Levi Pearson v. County Board of Education for Clarendon County, et al.* 1948 Case No. 1909; *Briggs, v.*

Trustees for School District Number 22, 1950 Case No.: 2505; and *Briggs v. Elliott* 1950 Case No. 2657. For a discussion on the historical context in Clarendon County at the time of the filing of the suits see Richard Kluger, *Simple Justice* (New York: Vintage Books, 1975), 3–17, 21–23. Richburg is quoted on page 24.

9. Kluger, *Simple Justice*, 24.

10. While program reports for the years the cases were filed are not extant, the participation of plaintiffs—beyond the named one in the lawsuit—has been stated by Dr. Barbara Williams Jenkins, the daughter of Mr. E. N. Williams who was State Agent for Negro Agricultural Extension work at the time of the case, and the late Mrs. Altamese B. Pough, a Negro Home Demonstration agent and State Negro Girls' 4-H agent. Transcript of recorded oral interview with Mrs. Rosa Odum, Mrs. Altamese B. Pough, and Mrs. Sara A. Waymer (black Home Demonstration agents in the state of South Carolina); Dr. Barbara Williams Jenkins (Librarian, Miller F. Whitakker Library, South Carolina State University and daughter of a former State Agent for Negro Agricultural Extension Work); and Dr. William Hine, Professor of History, South Carolina State College. Interview conducted by Carmen Harris at Miller F. Whittaker Library, South Carolina State University, Orangeburg, South Carolina, and transcribed by Carmen Harris, Master of Arts in History Candidate, Clemson University, July 1988. Transcript in author's possession.

11. Statement of Conditions, Clarendon County Improvement Association, April 4, 1961, NAACP papers, part 20, reel 11, frames 99–100; William Thompson and Hugene Gerald, "Annual Report: Negro Agricultural Agent's, Clarendon County South Carolina," 2–3, 11, 15, 23; Petition of Harry Briggs et al., November 11, 1949. This analysis does not include persons who may have signed the petition and did not seek assistance of the CCIA or who left the area.

12. Marian Baxter Paul, "South Carolina Annual Narrative Report, 1948," 6. Interestingly, the agricultural agent, William Thompson, a twenty-six-year veteran of extension work, continued to work as agricultural agent in Clarendon County until his retirement in 1955. E. N. Williams, Annual Report, 1951, p. 3, series 33, box 215, folder 3903, CUL.

13. For a discussion of the white response to the initial filings of the *Pearson* and *Briggs* cases, see Kluger, *Simple Justice*, 17–26. All the sources say that the crops rotted in the fields without providing any other detail.

14. Statement of Conditions, Clarendon County Improvement Association, April 4, 1961, NAACP papers, part 20, reel 11, frames 99–100; William Thompson and Hugene Gerald, "Annual Report: Negro Agricultural Agent's, Clarendon County South Carolina," 2–3, 11, 15, 23.

15. L. A. Blakemon (former extension agent) to Roy Wilkins, May 23, 1956, NAACP papers, part 20, reel 11, frames 14–16, quote in frame 15.

16. Re: Bills, Suits, injunctions, etc., NAACP papers, part 20, reel 7, frame 783, supports Howard Quint's statement on Elloree and Clarendon in Howard Quint, *Profiles in Black and White: A Frank Portrait of South Carolina* (Washington, D.C.: Public Affairs Press, 1958), 51–53. This book is not Quint's work but is actually the work of his student, Idus A. Newby. A comparison of its contents with those of Newby's master's history thesis, "South Carolina and the Desegregation Issue, 1954–1956" (University of South Carolina, 1957), shows that the works are almost identical. In his preface, Quint states that the book "could not have been written without the assistance of a young scholar who is a Southerner.

Legitimately his name should be on the title page but he desires for personal reasons, to remain anonymous. Both the research and a preliminary draft of a major portion of this study were done by him.

17. L. A. Blakemon to Roy Wilkins, May 23, 1956, NAACP papers, part 20, reel 11, frames 14–16 (quotation in frame 14; crop allotment information in frame 15).

18. "Statement of Billie S. Fleming, President of the Clarendon County, South Carolina, Improvement Association before the Senate Subcommittee on Constitutional Rights, April 16, 1959," NAACP papers, part 20, reel 11, frames 44–51; Billie S. Fleming to Dr. John Morsell, September 1, 1959, NAACP papers, part 20, reel 11, frame 60; Kluger, *Simple Justice, 24*; the Stukes quotation is from "South Carolina's Plot to Starve Negroes," *Jet*, October 20, 1955, 11–12.

19. Re: Bills, Suits, injunctions, etc., NAACP papers, part 20, reel 7, frames 776–85.

20. Billie S. Fleming to Mr. John Morsell, December 1, 1958, Memorandum from John A. Morsell, December 3, 1958, NAACP papers, part 20, reel 11, frames 28–29. Once it became known that the CCIA was selling its fertilizers to black petitioners, it also found its credit cut off and made a frantic appeal to the national offices of the NAACP for a cash infusion so that they could supply their farmers. See also NAACP papers, part 20, reel 11, frames 31, 34; "Statement of Billie S. Fleming, President of the Clarendon County, South Carolina, Improvement Association, before the Senate Subcommittee on Constitutional Rights, April 16, 1959," NAACP papers, part 20, reel 11, frames 44–51.

21. "South Carolina's Plot to Starve Negroes," 13.

22. Reverend M. D. McCollom, Reverend E. E. Richburg, Reverent Henry L. Parker, and Reverend Alfred Isaac, "An Open Letter," n.d. [c. 1956], NAACP papers, part 20, reel 11, frames 184–85.

23. L. A. Blakeman to Roy Wilkins, May 23, 1956, NAACP papers, part 20, reel 11, frames 14–16; "The Achievement of Full Citizenship, Human Dignity, Equalization of Opportunity Demands SACRIFICE, COOPERATION AND RESPONSIBILITY: Do Your Part," NAACP papers, part 20, reel 11, frames 21–23; Reverend I. DeQuincey Newman to John A. Morsell, December 4, 1959, NAACP papers, part 20, reel 11, frames 80–81.

24. Paul, "Annual Report, County Home Demonstration Work, 1951," 20; Paul, "Annual Report, Cooperative Extension Work, 1957," 7.

25. Paul, "South Carolina Narrative Annual Report, 1938–1939," series 33, box 33, folder 914, CUL, p. 1.

26. Paul, "Annual Report, County Home Demonstration Work, 1951," 20; Paul, "Annual Report, Cooperative Extension Work, 1957," 7.

27. Paul, "Annual Narrative Report, Home Demonstration Work among Negroes, 1955," 40; Paul, "Annual Report Cooperative Extension Work, South Carolina, 1958," 7.

28. Paul, "Annual Narrative Report, Home Demonstration Work among Negroes, 1955," 40; Paul, "Annual Report Cooperative Extension Work, South Carolina, 1958," 7.

29. Billie S. Fleming to Dr. John W. Morsell, July 8, 1960 (with news article "Clarendon ASC Undergoes Probe" attached), NAACP papers, part 20, reel 11, frames 88–89; Billie S. Fleming to Dr. John Morsell, April 5, 1961, NAACP papers, part 20, reel 11, frame 97.

30. Minute Book, Cherokee County Council of Farm Women, April 22, 1966, in possession of the author.

31. C. B. Bankhead and six others to the Honorable William N. Seabron, Assistant to

the Secretary, c. May 1966; Cal Jeter and seven others to the Honorable William N. Seabron, May 3, 1966, series 32, box 31, folder 4, CUL.

32. Raymond Anderson and six others to Dr. R. C. Edwards, May 3, 1968, series 32, box 30, folder 13, CUL.

33. R. C. Edwards to Mr. Raymond Anderson, May 13, 1968, series 32, box 30, folder 13, CUL.

34. "Kennedy Has Lunch with LBJ," February 24, 1967, series 32, box 29, folder 10, CUL. The article has written across it: "clipped from front page, county paper."

35. Aldon Morris, *The Origins of the Civil Rights Movement: Black Communities Organizing for Change* (New York: Free Press, 1986), quotes on 279.

36. Ibid., 279–83.

37. Ibid., 149–57.

12

Between Forty Acres and a Class Action Lawsuit

Black Farmers, Civil Rights, and Protest against the U.S. Department of Agriculture, 1997–2010

VALERIE GRIM

Black farmers historically have had a difficult relationship with the U.S. Department of Agriculture (USDA) since 1862. Many believed that the U.S. government was going to play a major role in helping black families become independent landowners and farmers after slavery ended in 1865. This, however, did not happen. The majority of newly freed families did not receive either a mule or forty acres; nor did they gain admittance to state-based land grant colleges established by the Morrill Act of 1862. Not until 1890 did the USDA respond to African American petitioners who sought access to public education and experiment stations and the right to participate in other USDA programs with passage of the Morrill Act of 1890. The assistance that the federal government provided to white elite and yeomen farmers did not readily extend to black farmers.

By the mid-twentieth century, in the immediate aftermath of post–World War II agricultural changes, only haphazard help was given to selected black farm families who protested that they should have access to USDA services, particularly access to resources available through its Federal Extension Service (FES) and agricultural experiment stations. Help was and has been little and sparse. But African American farmers have not been silent about the lack of service. They have claimed neglect and protested against what they believed constituted unfair treatment due in part to the color of their skin.

This chapter profiles some of the black farmers' encounters with national and local USDA offices and the failures the farmers experienced as they pursued equal access to and participation in USDA programs. Farm owners believed that government advice could help them negotiate changing markets, crop and stock science, and technological changes. They believed that they should be involved with and be allowed to benefit from all federal agricultural programs, specifically those created in the 1930s as part of the New Deal and modified in the decades since. The Civil Rights Act of 1964 guaranteed black farmers' access, but many African American farmers recognized that federal policy implementation could ignore their civil rights. This led black farmers to label the USDA as the "Last Plantation." The struggles black farmers have engaged in since the 1980s indicate the failure of civil rights legislation and prove that the quest for civil rights in the United States is largely unfinished.

Landowners made up the backbone of civic and political life in rural black communities. In fact, black landowners were among the first to join and support the civil rights movement in the rural South. Black landownership peaked during the 1910s with 218,972 individuals owning nearly 15.7 million acres (more than 8.8 million acres owned free and clear; 4.0 million acres mortgaged, and 2.8 million acres owned in part). Between 1910 and 1920 the number of African Americans owning farms declined even though the number operating farms increased from a total of 893,370 in 1910 to 925,710 in 1920. By 1992 the number of all minority farms had fallen from the 1910s high to around 60,000. For African Americans, the number fell from 925,000, or 14 percent of all farms, in 1920 to only 18,000, or 1 percent of all farms, in 1992.[1]

Most African American farmers have been small operators who specialized in the production of cash crops, livestock, and fruit and vegetable produce.[2] Between 1920 and the 1990s a number of factors affected African American farmers' ability to remain economically viable, and agents of the USDA and the federal government offered little support because, according to James Cobb, government policy designed support for large operators who happen to be majority white. This applies especially in the case of New Deal programs, such as the Agricultural Adjustment Act (AAA) and its successor, the Agricultural Stabilization and Conservation Service (ASCS). Both failed to serve blacks equitably. Cobb has shown that large planters in the Yazoo-Mississippi Delta were sustained by depression era federal agricultural relief programs, while the poor farmers starved.[3]

Legalized segregation facilitated creation of unequal public programs. Furthermore, elite white farmers proved more successful than blacks at lobbying for regulatory legislation that protected their individual and institutional interests.[4] Nonetheless, black landowning families gained access during the 1930s through their involvement with each state's Agricultural Extension Service. A few New Deal settlement communities, such as Tillery, North Carolina, served black constituents, and the Farmers Home Administration (FmHA) assisted some families with land purchases, houses, and buildings and with technical and scientific information to make farms more profitable. Most black farm families, however, remained unserved.[5] According to Pete Daniel, powerful white farmers and bureaucrats controlled all the resources and programs made available by the federal government through the USDA.[6] Black farm families, on the other hand, received little or no help and were forced to beg for access through segregated offices.

The racial segregation created a climate that marginalized African Americans as a whole from USDA decision making. Consequently, prior to 1964 no African American served on a county committee. Whites seemed comfortable with the politics as they were. But the absence of blacks and other minority farmers simply showed that little had changed for black farm laborers, owner-operators, and farm managers. Amid growing criticism and rising black activism of the mid-1960s, the USDA attempted a serious assessment of offerings to blacks.[7]

The U.S. Commission on Civil Rights, an independent agency created by the Civil Rights Act of 1957 to investigate and report on a broad spectrum of discriminatory practices, focused on USDA programs. In 1965 the commission released a highly critical study, *Equal Opportunity in Farm Programs*. The study revealed how the ASCS, the FmHA, and the FES stubbornly refused demands to share power with African Americans. The commission also cooperated with the Sharecroppers Fund and the National Association for the Advancement of Colored People (NAACP), sharing complaints and suggesting approaches to end discrimination.[8] In light of the report, on April 22, 1965, Secretary of Agriculture Orville L. Freeman issued a memorandum demanding that the USDA staff "put into effect with dispatch" comprehensive policies that would ensure an end to discrimination. "The right of all our citizens to participate with equal opportunity in both the administration and benefits of all programs of this Department is not only legally required but morally right," he explained.[9] But despite the secretary's insistence, black farmers lost more ground in the 1960s because the USDA did not control the implementation of its policies at the state and local levels, and neither did it address any of the complaints made by those claiming discrimination. Thus the civil rights laws that should have ensured equal rights and parity were undermined by powerful whites who had all the money, machines, chemicals, and government subsidies and who dominated local and state USDA offices.[10]

USDA officials procrastinated in implementing detailed recommendations issued by the U.S. Commission on Civil Rights in 1968 to bring the USDA into compliance with the Civil Rights Act. Subsequent reports provided more details about continued injustices, particularly on the part of the FmHA, the major public lending institution for family farmers.[11] The department failed to ensure equal opportunity and instead acquiesced to local patterns of racial segregation and discrimination.[12]

Complaints against the USDA increased during the 1970s. Not only were African American farmers complaining about experiencing abuse and intimidation from agents at the state and local offices of the ASCS and FmHA, but they also claimed that their civil rights were violated. Black farmers claimed that racism was as prevalent as it had been prior to the Civil Rights Act of 1964. They believed that unfair treatment by some agents of the USDA local offices undermined their efforts to farm successfully and compromised their ability to keep their land. The USDA needed to address several problems, including the office's commitment to civil rights, the program delivery of local offices, and the need to include minority and black representation on the local agricultural committees.[13]

The failed civil rights policies and practices of the 1970s, however, made it difficult for the USDA to establish a strong civil rights record in agriculture and farming in the 1980s. Based on past practices, the department's Civil Rights Policy Analysis and Coordination Center found that less than 1 percent of the department's full-time equivalent resources and budgetary resources were allocated to civil rights. Civil rights budgets were seriously reduced in the 1980s and have not fully recovered. The Civil Rights Leadership Council indicated that related agencies did not provide adequate resources to carry out the compliance and oversight activities needed to enforce civil rights laws and regulations.[14]

Black farmers also charged that the USDA had consistently tolerated discrimination in the distribution of program benefits predominantly to white farmers. They blamed farm program regulations that excluded minority and limited-resource farmers and ranchers from benefits. And they blamed the USDA's insensitivity to the differing needs of minority and limited-resource farmers and customers and neglect of its responsibility to reach out and serve all who needed USDA assistance.[15] Many black farmers and those working for the USDA viewed the 1980s as the critical period, a time when alleged racist practices and retaliation against those complaining became the most entrenched. The resurgence of conservatism during this time was accompanied by a rapid decline in the participation rate of black farmers in certain public agricultural programs.[16]

During the 1990s the USDA attempted to respond to some of the criticism but seemed unable to establish the right kind of policies that black and small farmers needed. By the 1990s black farmers and their advocates complained that the way in which the USDA allowed the local county committee to function disrupted their ability to farm successfully and profitably. At least 94 percent of all county committees had no female or minority representation even though many southern farmers were female and minorities. Minority producers were 4.7 percent of eligible voters, but held only 2.9 percent of county committee seats. Women constituted 28.8 percent of eligible voters, but held only 1.5 percent of county committee seats. The General Accounting Office found that in 1995, only thirty-six of the 101 counties with the largest concentration of minority farmers had at least one minority county committee member.[17]

During the-mid 1990s, some important legislation appeared. In 1994, for example, Congress implemented a measure that attempted to address the problem of inadequate representation of black and minority farmers on county committees. The legislation required that the county committees reflect the demographics of the agricultural producers in the county or multicounty area. In counties with relatively high concentrations of minority farmers without elected minority county committee members, the Farm Service Agency (FSA, which replaced ASCS and FmHA) was to require an appointment of minority advisors to increase the minority awareness of programs, including elections. Minority advisors were to convey problems and viewpoints for consideration in all FSA actions. USDA believed that this addressed the problem that minority and black farmers claimed was one of the reasons they were losing their farms.[18] But black farmers suggested that the unchecked power of local committee members caused them to lose their land. They believed that committee members deliberately delayed and denied loans to force foreclosure of their farms so the white members and/or their friends could buy the land at public auction with the USDA handling the sale.

Continuing to address issues of discrimination in the implementation of federal farm programs, the USDA created a debt relief program for minority and limited resource farmers. During the 1990s this resourceful program served as a conservation contract debt reduction program, called "Debt for Nature." It encouraged reduction in a landowner's debts in return for his/her placing a portion of the land under contract as a conservation easement for a specified length of time, usually fifty years. Use of the program allowed minority or limited-resource farmers to retain ownership of their land and continue farming on a large enough portion to remain profitable, while contributing to the conservation of highly erodible land, wetlands, endangered species habitats, and other fragile lands. Much to the chagrin of black farmers, however, these contracts were considered debt write-downs; therefore, their use disqualified the landowners from further FSA loans. A change in legislation to end that prohibition made "Debt for Nature" contracts more helpful to minority and limited-resource customers and increased benefits to fragile ecosystems.[19]

A third development that allowed the USDA to address criticism about its compliance process was the establishment of a new, independent appeals unit in 1994, the National Appeals Division (NAD). The director of NAD reported directly to the secretary of agriculture and bore responsibility for improving the appeals process. It was designed to provide farmers with information and render decisions quickly. Any farmer could appeal to NAD after going through at least one stage of appeal within the USDA. Black farmers still complained, however, that if NAD overturned an agency's decision in favor of the farmer, the agency, usually FSA, could appeal to NAD's director to have the decision reversed.[20]

Despite the suite of farm legislation created to help minorities remain in agriculture, the number of African American farmers decreased by 98 percent by 1997, while the number of white Americans who farmed declined by 66 percent. Documentation of black land loss dates to 1971 when the Black Economic Research Center sponsored a two-day conference at Clark College in Atlanta. The Emergency Land Fund grew out of these efforts.[21] R. S. Browne produced a report of the 1971 conference in 1973 that described the outcome of approximately a dozen projects dealing with land loss. Browne's comprehensive report argued that between 1950 and 1969, the number of acres of farmland fully or partly owned by blacks dropped from 12 million to 5.5 million.[22] The reduction in ownership of acres continued because black farmers could not acquire capital and also, as some black farmers believed, because the USDA allowed large white landowners to manipulate local USDA offices to maintain their domination of agricultural life and production.[23]

During the 1990s black farmers became increasingly vocal in blaming the USDA's relatively autonomous local delivery structure for racial discrimination. They charged that USDA has long tolerated unequal distribution of program benefits and misuse of power to influence land ownership and farm profitability. They blamed farm program regulations that intentionally or not prevented minority and limited-resource farmers and ranchers from the benefits of the same programs that had helped larger nonminority producers survive the changes in agriculture since the 1930s. And they blamed USDA's insensitivity to the differing needs of minority and limited-resource farmers and customers and neglect of its responsibility to reach out and serve all who needed USDA's assistance.[24]

The 1990s were ripe for protest. And some black farmers took advantage, began to press for greater inclusion and participation, and demanded action with expected results. On December 12, 1996, for example, black farmers representing each region of the country demonstrated outside the White House and called upon President Bill Clinton to ask for fair treatment in the implementation of federal agricultural lending programs. Thereafter Secretary of Agriculture Daniel R. Glickman established the Civil Rights Action Team (CRAT) within the USDA to investigate the charges black farmers were making. Glickman authorized listening sessions to take place throughout the country to field complaints of black and minority farmers and ordered that a findings report be submitted to the USDA in a timely manner.

The USDA sponsored twelve listening sessions in eleven locations in January 1997. The purpose was to learn about the experiences of black and minority farming from the farmers, especially the socially disadvantaged ones. Nine listening sessions were held with farmers and producers, typically called the customers, and three with USDA staff employees. Each session was designed to address concerns regarding gender and race, as they related to interactions between USDA local offices and African Americans, American Indians, Hispanics, and Asians. Farmers and staff employees who did not speak at the listening sessions were allowed to submit recorded or written statements to CRAT. In addition, the USDA established an e-mail address, a fax number, and a hotline for civil rights comments.[25]

Throughout the country thousands of self-proclaimed farmer-victims attended the sessions. At the sessions, those who spoke voiced concerns about program delivery and civil rights issues. Details varied from family to family, but the general themes of the stories farmers told to CRAT personnel focused on loan processing, delays in delivery of approval of loans, and the lack of information and help needed to participate in USDA programs. Farmers, too, orally documented their concern about declining minority farmers and farms. Many black farmers indicated they believed that the USDA was involved in a conspiracy to take land from minority farmers so that wealthy landowners could gain access to more land.[26]

At these sessions, farmers also described a pattern of discriminatory behavior. The most serious accusation concerned how the black farmer was treated as a person and how minority farm business was not treated as an agricultural enterprise. Within this context, some claimed that their paperwork had not been taken seriously and that they were disrespected because of their skin color. Other complaints emphasized loans that arrived long after planting season, arbitrary reductions in loan amounts, and a much higher rejection rate than white applicants received. An overwhelming majority of black farmers also accused the USDA of ignoring research that would help small-scale and limited-resource farmers, and of failing to include minority populations in outreach efforts to raise awareness of federal programs. Finally, minority farmers indicated that official complaints of discrimination were processed slowly, if at all, and that the USDA often continued with foreclosure proceedings even when a relevant discrimination complaint had been filed. Members of CRAT heard more than thirty different complaints at the USDA-authorized listening sessions where USDA representatives supervised meetings, gathered data, and began processing the scope and nature of the problems black and other farmers were alleging.[27] These were the same issues they had raised before Glickman established his "action" team.

Although the listening sessions created a forum for dialogue, none of them produced any real solutions to problems or answers to questions that positively and significantly affected black farmers' ability to survive. But the USDA ordered CRAT to gather data, and plenty of it was found. Only a fraction of the findings from the oral testimonies from the twelve listening sessions was included in the February 1997 CRAT Report. Yet the report made possible a black farmers' lawsuit, because CRAT personnel indicated discrimination had taken place and that the USDA was liable.[28] Overall, the CRAT Report found little accountability within the USDA, especially in its local offices, and county officials who had allegedly discriminated against minority farmers went unpunished.[29]

Meanwhile, some black farmers and their advocates developed grassroots strategies to be heard. Their activism included protest marches in Washington, D.C., Detroit, Chicago, Atlanta, and other major cities. They organized letter writing campaigns, sent messages to churches, emailed messages to local and national politicians, conducted major fundraisers to help farmers, and founded national and regional farm organizations to address media questions concerning the struggle. Among the many issues raised by the protests, none seemed more pressing than the fight against foreclosure of farms owned by black farmers and the snail's pace at which the USDA handled complaints. Black farmers clearly linked these two issues to the ready loss of land and of farms.[30]

More than 90 percent of the farmers were concerned about the slow pace and ineffective process of handling complaints. In 1997 the Office of General Counsel notified CRAT that USDA did not have any published regulations with clear guidance on the process or timelines involved in program discrimination complaints. When a farmer alleged discrimination, preliminary investigations were typically conducted by the agency involved. This, according to USDA's compliance office, took more time, time that black farmers had indicated they did not have because of growing debts and threats to their land. Because expediency seemed to be lacking in processing claims, black farmers also charged that while complaints worked their way through the agency, USDA proceeded with farm foreclosures. Seemingly, the USDA did not respond to all complaints. On the few occasions when a complaint had been acted upon and discrimination was documented, black farmers claimed the USDA refused to pay damages. They charged the USDA with forcing them into court to seek justice, rather than working with them to address grievances.[31]

Farmers described a complaints processing system which they believed made the matters worse. When USDA denied a loan, payment, or any other benefit, the customer almost always had appeal rights. Agency appeals processes varied, but typically, an appeal went to a higher level agency official in the county, state, or region and then to the agency's national office or to the department. Until 1995 the FSA's appeals process was handled entirely within the agency. If the farmer did not agree with the national decision, he or she could appeal to the courts. Yet many farmers, especially small farmers who managed to appeal their cases to FSA, charged that even when decisions were overturned, local offices often did not honor the decision. They claimed that decisions favoring farmers were simply not enforced. Farmers also mentioned the backlog and length of time needed to appeal and the lack of timely communication to inform them of the status of their cases.[32]

National black farm organizations, specifically the Black Farmers and Agriculturalists Association (BFAA) led by Gary Grant, the National Black Farmers Association (NBFA) led by John Boyd, and the Federation of Southern Cooperatives (FSC) led by Ralph Paige took the leadership on the racial discrimination charges against the USDA. The FSC especially had provided a consistent and uninhibited voice against discrimination in farm policy since the 1960s. The FSC had lobbied for land loss prevention, paying particular attention to reclamation processes and ways that black farmers could diversify their operations and maintain land ownership. In terms of the 1997 black farmer class action lawsuit, however, the BFAA and NBFA took the forefront, leading the charge for compensation for the discrimination that black farmers had suffered. They represent, through membership, thousands of black farmers from each region of the country. These organizations have had the support of a leading watchdog, the Environmental Working Group (EWG), which keeps abreast of issues relating to alleged injustices. EWG has issued numerous reports concerning the status of black farmers and their quest for justice.[33]

In August 1997 three African American farmers representing a putative class of 641 black farmers filed a proposed class action lawsuit against the USDA, *Timothy C. Pigford et al. v. Dan Glickman, Secretary, U.S. Department of Agriculture*. Attorneys Pires and Fraas handled the case. At an initial status conference on October 30, 1997, plaintiffs' attorneys requested that the case be referred to Magistrate Judge Alan Kay of the U.S. District Court of the District of Columbia (DDC) for the purpose of discussing settlement. The government opposed that request, and the DDC did not require the government to engage in settlement negotiations. Regardless, the DDC made it clear that the process would move swiftly. Although much legal maneuvering took place on many issues, both sides believed there were problems that had to be resolved for the case to proceed. A second proposed class action lawsuit was filed on July 7, 1998, *Cecile Brewington et al. v. Dan Glickman, Secretary, U.S. Department of Agriculture*, and included black farmers who alleged discrimination but who had missed the deadline for joining the Pigford class action. On October 9, 1998, the DDC granted a motion for a class certification in *Pigford*. On January 5, 1999, the two cases petitioned to consolidate and join the classes. In December of 1999 Judge Friedman certified *Pigford* as a class action lawsuit. This allowed the debate over racial discrimination within the USDA to begin.[34]

Initially, nearly 15,000 African Americans joined the class action lawsuit. The USDA offered each certified claimant a settlement of $50,000 and forgiveness of debt owed the USDA (but not to private lenders). Claimants could also choose arbitration, in which the settlement equaled actual cash damages. These two options became known as Track A for $50,000 and Track B for an unspecified amount. In the end, a consent decree was established, thereby making way for cases to be filed, reviewed, and compensated if discrimination was found.[35]

Black farmers and their advocates criticized the terms of the class action and consent decree because they believed the terms were insufficient to address the long-term effect of discrimination and their need for compensation options. Their criticism suggested they believed that the proposed consent decree was unfair; that compensatory damages were too limited in Track A and too difficult to obtain in both Tracks A and B; that the timing of the settlement and the extent of discovery was also not considerate of the farmers' experiences; that the definition of "class" needed to be clearer and in keeping with the experiences the class action addressed; that the issue of collusion needed to be settled before any claims were settled; that a notice of opportunity needed to be heard in reaction to the class action; and that the issue of recovery had to be addressed as if the case would proceed to trial.[36] In this endeavor several other organizations supported the farmers, including Concerned Black Farmers of Tennessee, Arkansas, Mississippi, Georgia, and North Carolina, the Coordinating Council of Black Farm Groups, Land Loss Prevention Project, NAACP, National Council of Community Based Organizations in Agriculture, and National Family Farm Coalition.[37] Together, these organizations, with BFAA, NBFA, and FSC, demanded greater clarity, fairness, and resources to address adequately the debts black farmers had incurred due to USDA discrimination and lack of funding support that would have helped them secure their land.

Some resolution did come in the wake of the criticism articulated. To resolve conflict, the court ruled that adequate notice had to be provided to all members of the class and that a fairness hearing had to be conducted. Notices were provided through black media outlets, announcements in churches and other institutions in the black community, and through advertisements in local newspapers. But after a fairness hearing was conducted, the court found that the "settlement is fair, adequate and reasonable, and was not the product of collusion between the parties."[38]

A review of the history of the case revealed that sufficient discovery was provided and reviewed and that the term "class" in this class action lawsuit was correctly defined. It was expected that the government would provide the plaintiffs with the files of "class members." Consequently, the class action included all African American farmers who: (1) farmed or attempted to farm between January 1, 1981 and December 31, 1996; (2) applied to the U.S. Department of Agriculture during that period for participation in a federal farm credit or benefit program and who believed that they had been discriminated against on the basis of race in USDA's response to that application; and (3) filed a discrimination complaint on or before July 1, 1997, regarding USDA's treatment of such farm credit or benefit application. Some wanted the class to be broadened to include all African American farmers who claimed to have faced discrimination in credit transactions or benefit programs with the USDA, even if they had not filed a complaint of discrimination by July 1, 1997, or by July 7, 1998, in a second case, *Cecil Brewington et al. v. Dan Glickman, Secretary, U.S. Department of Agriculture.* Others, especially those in the USDA and the U.S. Justice Department, were concerned that the broadening of the class would inject legal and factual issues into the case that were not present at the time and would, therefore, hinder a fair and reasonable settlement for the African American farmers who were legitimately a part of the class action, as per the definition of the case.

Any negative court determination had the potential of undermining black farmers' ability to maintain ownership of their land. Issues of foreclosures, statute of limitation, and proof of discrimination had to be resolved. Judge Friedman and President Bill Clinton, with the support of officials and politicians, responded to associated issues.[39] In 1998 Congress provided relief to plaintiffs with respect to the statute of limitations for all those who filed discrimination complaints with the USDA before January 1, 1997, and who alleged discrimination at any time during the period beginning January 1, 1981 and ending on or before December 31, 1996. A moratorium on foreclosures was also issued.[40] On January 5, 1999, Judge Friedman consolidated the *Pigford* and *Brewington* lawsuits under *Pigford* and issued preliminary approval of a consent decree that had been negotiated between Department of Justice attorneys and class counsel.[41] With these developments, it was clear that the court would not hear tens of thousands of individual cases at taxpayers' expense but expected the federal government to give black farmers legal support against foreclosures and moratoriums while their cases were in deliberations.

With these resolutions other kinds of criticism evolved. Some conservatives, some anti-black organizations, and persons opposed to black farmers being paid weighed in. By their estimate, the class action lawsuit was a sham. They called the suit a reparation payment for black enslavement. Others referred to it as a shakedown for segregation and the discrimination blacks have experienced in the work force. Some others dismissed the suit by claiming that it was simply a big lie against the government to make this country look bad and that the discrimination charge was a figment of black farmers' (and by extension the black community's) imagination. Still others proclaimed that the class action invited blacks to continue complaining and hustling money from white taxpayers. The class action was believed to have encouraged scoundrels and thieves, lawyers who joined the case simply for the money, and one woman even posed as a lawyer so she could get money. Eventually, black farmers criticized the lead attorneys, Pires and Fraas, for being incompetent, greedy, and for not genuinely caring about the discrimination black farmers had faced and the subsequent land loss they experienced.[42] The lawsuit proceeded in spite of these and other criticisms.

The consent decree established a dual track system to handle the claims filed. Once a claim package was submitted and accepted, the claimant was required to choose one of the two tracks. As the judge described them, the consent decree provided those class members with little or no documentary evidence an automatic cash payment of $50,000 and forgiveness of debt owed to the USDA (Track A), while those entitled to a larger payment had to prove their cases with documentary or other evidence (Track B). Under the original consent decree, claimants had to file their claims with the facilitator (Poorman-Douglas Corporation) within the 180 days of the consent decree, or no later than October 12, 1999. For those determined to be eligible class members, the facilitator was to forward the claim to the adjudicator (JAMS-Endispute, Inc.), if it was a Track A claim, or to the arbitrator (Michael Lewis, ADR Associates), if designated as a Track B claim. If the facilitator determined that the claimant did not qualify as a class member, the claimant could seek review by the court-appointed monitor Randi Roth. If the facilitator ruled that the claim was filed after the initial deadline, the adversely affected party could request permission to file a late claim under a process ordered by the court.[43]

An overwhelming majority of the claimants qualified for Track A. Through midsummer 2010, at least twenty thousand payments had been made to persons in Track A, while Track B, the more difficult claim, had only fifty successful claimants. Most of these claims were settled between 2000 and 2004. The small number of successful claimants resulted from a small pool of clients who, with other potential claimants, argued that insufficient notice and time had been given to file. According to data reported by Louis T. March, in the year 2000, there were 50,551 decisions on cases with a 60 percent success rate; in 2002, there were 42,831 with a 60 percent success rate; in 2003, 43,260 decisions with a 61 percent success rate; and in 2004, 22,138 decisions with a 61 percent success rate. Consistently, 39 percent of claimants failed to secure settlement.[44] While these data and these numbers seem high and somewhat inconsistent with the staggering number of reports addressing the failure and success rate of cases and the number of persons who filed, March claimed that these percentages represented the most accurate data between 2000 and 2004, because they are reported by the Department of Justice. Yet this 60 percent success rate seems suspicious, as if some people decided that a 60 percent win rate would be publicly acceptable and would be satisfying because this acknowledged the discrimination, while at the same time suggesting it was not as serious as the black farmers and their lawyers and advocates claimed.[45]

It is worth noting, however, that in the adjudication process, the adjudicator's decisions are final. The decisions are subject to review only by the court's appointed monitor, whose job it is to review appeals from either side. Decision-making power concentrated in the hands of one person in this way did not satisfy black farmers. Reports show that the appeal process has been used primarily by black farmers constituting the 40 percent failed rate due to a negative decision or to additional debt requiring more documentation.[46] Moreover, documentary evidence shows that the process has been brutal, with debate and bickering back and forth among the parties and with some farmers being required to refile their cases with more supporting evidence. Some black farmers have had success getting compensation for discrimination; others claimed they have neither had their case heard nor had it reviewed and therefore have not received any compensation. For those who claimed they never had the opportunity to be included, Pires, the attorney for the class action, sought to have the case reopened and the deadline extended to include a new filing date. A new era in this struggle was dawning and the fight for a positive outcome for black farmers intensified.[47]

The year 2000 held many battles. No period of time during this year seemed more contested and significant than July 2000, when growing concern about the class action escalated. Written and loud verbal demands for a new class action were drawing considerable negative attention to the USDA, President Clinton and his administration, and the Department of

Justice. To arrest fears and to quiet the political mayhem circling this issue, Judge Friedman intervened again and on September 15, 2000, established a new filing date for late claimants and lowered the requirements for the new filers, who could now forego the actual claim package and provide an explanation as to why they had to file late. As a result, a record 61,400 additional farmers joined the class action. Most of the claimants lived in the South. According to news reports and e-mail communications from the leaders of the black farm organizations, these claimants have not secured justice and have not been compensated.[48]

The extension drew criticism. Some believed the USDA was the victim of another shakedown. They claimed that this decision was about politics because 2000 was a presidential election year, and groups of anti-Democrats believed the new file date for late claimers was a gift to the black farmers to keep the black community loyal to the Democratic Party.[49] Criticism also came from black farm leaders, and it did not show concerns for the Democratic Party or its nominee but for the black farmers. Black farm advocates believed that the court and the government were not doing enough to get justice and compensation for either the group who filed in time to be considered as part of the original class action in *Pigford I* or this new group of black farmers comprising *Pigford II*. This belief remains today, and there is continuous concern, even after BFAA filed a $20.5 billion class action lawsuit in September 2004 on behalf of approximately 25,000 farmers who alleged racial discriminatory practices between January 1997 and August 2004.[50] The failure of the 2004 attempt to establish a new lawsuit and class action certification meant that the question of justice and compensation for black farmers continued with little success for an overwhelming majority in *Pigford I* and for nearly all of those in the subsequent *Pigford II* case. Even President Barack Obama suggested that not enough was being done to "close this chapter" on the country's racial history.[51]

In actuality, black farmers' struggles with the USDA over civil rights violation do not seem to be nearing an end. More sad episodes keep emerging. The Shirley Sherrod debacle is an example. It connects to this struggle not only in terms of her family being one of the black farm and landowning families who joined the class action lawsuit against the USDA in 1997 but also in her work as an employee of the USDA. Sherrod was head of the rural development office in Georgia. She was released from this position following a claim that she had behaved in a racist manner toward a white farm family. News of this claim and the edited video that accompanied it created a fuss with Sherrod being forced to resign. But she made her forced resignation a public issue and she fought back, thereby forging an investigation of her situation, which ultimately showed that she had been wrongly terminated. In this situation the USDA appeared inefficient and ineffective, as additional reporting made clear that Sherrod had been a victim of partisan politics and had been treated shamefully. Those connected to her, especially some of the 1960s civil rights workers, many black farmers and leaders of national black farm organizations, and members of the national rural coalition were stunned at this treatment. Sherrod's experience with the USDA provides an example of the kind of business blacks have claimed is the norm when working with USDA offices and agents, locally and nationally. The Sherrod incident proved an embarrassment, and it signaled that the USDA is still very confused around the notions of civil rights and how best to enforce its policies. Because of this incident, a leader of one of the black farm organizations called for the resignation of Secretary of Agriculture Tom Vilsack.[52]

Toward the end of the first decade of the twenty-first century, other developments created mixed results for black farmers. A provision in the 2008 Farm Bill permitted any claimant in the *Pigford* decision who had not previously obtained a determination on debt payments or foreclosure on the merits of a *Pigford* claim to petition in civil courts to obtain such a determination, but the provision has not helped many farmers. Further, President Obama announced during May 2009 that the Farm Bill would contain language to address the larger issue of justice and compensation, but in June 2010, after the House passed a bill appropriating funds for *Pigford II* settlements, the U.S. Senate voted against funding *Pigford II* in the "Extenders Bill." Then during July 2010, the Republicans, according to Democrat Senator Harry Reid, stalled justice once again. This time, they blocked a measure that would have settled compensatory disputes between the USDA and black farmers (*Pigford II*) and between the USDA and Native American farmers (*Cobell*). For the fourth time in three months, Reid explained, the Republicans prevented fairness and justice to minority farmers, and as Reid continued, "Their obstruction has not only hurt our economic recovery and our growth as a nation, [but] it is now preventing individuals and families who suffered discrimination for decades from receiving a long-overdue resolution to their grievances."[53]

Taken together, these developments made it very difficult for the Obama Administration to follow through on promises made to black farmers in February 2010. At that time the Obama Administration expressed support for an additional $1.15 billion to settle *Pigford II*, which Congress had to appropriate by March 31, 2010. Administration officials praised the agreement, especially Secretary of Agriculture Tom Vilsack, who indicated his approval by thanking President Obama "for bringing the [struggles] of African American farmers to a rightful solution."[54] Vilsack explained that he looked "forward to a swift solution to this issue, so that the families affected can move on with their lives . . . and the department [USDA] has made it a top priority to ensure that all farmers are treated fairly and equally. . . . We have worked hard to address [this issue] and its checkered past so that we can get to the business of helping farmers succeed."[55]

But not one of these promises was realized as of late summer and early fall of 2010. In fact, all developments seemed to be pointing in the opposite direction, with the U.S. Senate continuously denying all claims related to *Pigford II*. For example, a Senate vote on July 25, 2010, prevented payments from going forward. Then again on August 6, 2010, despite broad support, legislation to finalize $4.6 billion in settlements with black farmers and American Indians stalled in the Senate because of partisan politics. Lawmakers on both side of the aisle claimed they supported resolving the problem between two minority farm groups and the USDA, but senators appeared unclear and often confused as to how to pay for the settlement. For black farmers, *Pigford II* represents the unfulfilled 1999 class action decision. Reports indicate that the federal government has paid out more than $1 billion to about 16,000 farmers, with most getting payments of $50,000. The money, not yet appropriated, was earmarked for farmers numbering between 70,000 and 80,000 who were denied earlier payments because they missed filing deadlines.[56]

In 2008 a report from the Office of the Monitor, written by a representative who had been certified by Judge Friedman to be involved in this case, suggested quite a different story. Data showed that cases were being resolved and that the filing was not at the level reported by Louis T. March in his 2004 study, even though March indicated that the numbers he reported were from the Justice Department. Further, according to a 2008 monitor's report, 22,547 decisions in Track A had been made, with adjudications approving 15,640 cases (69 percent); adjudication denied 6,895 cases (31 percent). In terms of Track A payouts for $50,000, compensation totaled $756,900,000. Payouts in non-credit awards total $1,299,900, while another $36,655,757 had been awarded for debt relief. IRS tax payments for Track A claimants have amounted to $189,225,000, and the IRS received

$6,307,903 in payments for debt-relief compensation. By the end of 2008 the government had paid a total of $990,387,660 to compensate some of those involved in *Pigford I*.[57]

Two years later, by December 2010, some gain had been made in the number of black farmers receiving settlements. A 2010 Congressional Research Service Report indicated a slight increase in funds dispensed and cases evaluated: 22,550 decisions in Track A, with adjudications approving 15,640 cases (69 percent); adjudication denied 6,910 cases (31 percent). In terms of Track A payouts for $50,000, compensation was provided in the amount of $768,200,000. Payouts in non-credit awards amounted to $1,512,000, while another $39,180,011 was awarded for debt relief. IRS tax payments for Track A claimants have amounted to $192,050,000 and the IRS had received $6,690,517 in payments for debt-relief compensation. By the end of 2010, the government had paid a total of $1,007,632,528 to compensate some of those involved in *Pigford I*.[58]

More important, by the end of 2010, the federal government, Congress, and the USDA achieved their greatest results relating to *Pigford II*. The U.S. Senate finally decided that *Pigford II* was legitimate and worthy of compensatory damages, thereby clearing the way for late claimers in the black farmers' class action lawsuit to be awarded. Late in the evening of November 19, 2010, the U.S. Senate passed a bill to fund *Pigford II*, largely with the support and work of Senators Harry Reid of Nevada and Chuck Grassley of Iowa. Yet efforts to appropriate the $1.25 billion necessary to fund *Pigford II* stalled in the U.S. Senate, even though the money was twice appropriated by the U.S. House in 2010. The November 2010 decision was tied to the *Cobell* settlement, a Native American suit that the federal government also settled due to Native Americans' claims that for centuries, the U.S. Department of the Interior engaged in land abuse and mismanagement of royalty funds that belonged to their communities of peoples.[59]

In the wake of the U.S. Senate vote in November 2010, there has been strong opposition from many who believe the settlement is a farce. Objections have been raised by Reps. Steve King (R-Iowa) and Bob Goodlatte (R-Virginia), for example. In one instance Rep. Michele Bachmann (R-Minnesota) told Fox News she would fight the settlement because she has been informed by insiders that many blacks were getting money they did not deserve. Bachmann suggested that if discrimination was as widespread at the USDA as claimed, the office should have been shut down. These politicians are not alone in their belief that *Pigford II* is fraudulent. On dozens of Web sites, comments from American citizens indicate outrage with President Obama, Congress, and the USDA.[60]

In spite of the hardships that black farmers endured trying to obtain compensatory damages, their long and slow journey to secure justice has not deterred other groups from coming forward. Women and other minority farm groups indicated that they have also been neglected and negatively affected by the USDA. These cases include *Keepseagle* (Native Americans), *Garcia* (Hispanics), *Love* (women), and *Green* (farmers not part of a "protected" racial, ethnic, or gender class). *Green* has been dismissed by a U.S. District Court and the others remain in various stages of litigation.[61]

The quest of black farm owners to survive represents a larger civil rights struggle. Some believe that the eighteen thousand African Americans still farming could survive by diversifying their income through crop choices, using less hired labor, and bringing idle farmland back into production. This compares to a larger movement to revitalize diversified production in the face of global monoculture. Others believe that black farmers should focus on high-value vegetable crops to compensate for the small sizes of their farms. This compares to the slow-food movement's goal to create more markets for local produce. Still others suggest that survival could be enhanced through the development of alternative marketing strategies designed specifically for small-scale farmers. Some black farmers believe that their chances of remaining farm owners would be improved if new approaches could be developed, specifically direct or cooperative marketing strategies, engaged and profit-earning youth outreach programs, and legal services aimed specifically at encouraging black farmers to write wills that protect their land and estates.

Other black farmers believe that agribusiness could provide the answer. To that end, a number of projects by black organizations try to link black farmers to mainstream supermarkets and consumers. The USDA's National Commission on Small Farms has responded by targeting credit to minority farmers, developing direct marketing and value-added activities, increasing funding to programs that work with limited-resource farmers, and implementing the CRAT recommendations. Increased access to credit may lead to permanent indebtedness unless black farmers also use technologies that increase productivity.[62]

Thinking of ways to use the land other than in the production of crops may increase the survival rate of black owner-operators as well. In 1994, Jones's study of federal agricultural programs found that the forestry and conservation incentive programs could provide major opportunities for blacks who do not have the credit or capital to continue to produce commercial crops. This is an area of federal farm program participation where blacks lagged far behind whites in participation rates. Research shows that some African American farmers have earned an income from their lands by leasing acreages to hunting and fishing lodges as well as to paper companies to grow trees. However, although these appear to be ideas that can help black farmers, many continue to claim that information concerning these alternative enterprises has not been well disseminated to them and their community, especially to owners of small acreages and plots who possibly could benefit greatly from this relevant information and the additional income that can be earned from these kinds of alternative uses of their land.[63]

Ultimately, the will and strategy to survive depends on the choices that black farmers make. Several studies suggest that personal characteristics of farmers affect success or failure rates. Successful black farmers have been early adopters of new technologies and managerial techniques, have participated in government programs, and have high educational aspirations for their children as well as a strong work ethic.[64] Education and off-farm income relate more closely to increased incomes than do value-added farm activities. This means that many black farmers have not made much money in farming and do not see their income generating opportunities. Increasing farm income often means that farmers have to take risks, and this proves difficult for many black farmers because they are averse to risk, lack access to capital, and do not have information on new management practices.[65] Many depend on off-farm jobs rather than their farms to survive, and those off-farm jobs may not always be lucrative because farmers' age, education levels, and lack of job skills limit their ability to find off-farm work. Of special concern is the reality that low earning potential will remain consistent, since most black farmers are concentrated in counties and states with few nonfarm employment opportunities. To help with this need for cash and credit, the Housing Assistance Council has encouraged legislation that would allow USDA agencies to provide loans to black farmers who are co-owners of heir property, even when they do not have clear title to the entire property, so that they can continue farming. Such a policy would make it possible for those interested in farming not to be hindered by conflicts with heirs over land.[66]

The United States remains a nation vested in liberty and justice for all. Thus the future of African American farmers could be guaranteed more by the enforcement of the nation's civil rights laws than by market competition. To achieve this objective, the USDA must implement and monitor relevant recommendations suggested by the Civil Rights Action Team. These include: (1) taking action to remedy past discrimination; (2) strengthening USDA's outreach efforts to underrepresented farmers and producers; (3) strengthening USDA's research and educational assistance to the socially disadvantaged; (4) removing barriers to serving underrepresented customers at USDA service centers; (5) increasing involvement of small and disadvantaged businesses in USDA's programs; (6) consolidating USDA's civil rights functions into one office; (7) making the Office of the General Counsel accountable for civil rights; (8) establishing civil rights offices in each agency associated with the USDA; (9) removing USDA employees who do not perform adequately on civil rights or who abuse their authority; and (10) ensuring that the department has measurable outcomes for treating farmers fairly and equitably.[67]

Taking actions and establishing plans that create activities and positive outcomes in the aforementioned areas would help the USDA realize its goal of ensuring that each farmer and producer is treated equitably and fairly. More important, achieving this outcome would mean that this longstanding department would no longer be viewed as the "Last Plantation" and that it would finally have solved the persistent problem of racial discrimination. But the African American community should also play a role. To date, an overwhelming majority of members of the black community have largely ignored the land loss crisis. Other than the Black Caucus in Washington, D.C., no independent self-proclaimed black leader has made the issue visible, and few black publications other than *Jet* and *Ebony* have reported on it. Few black churches, black-owned businesses, black athletes and entertainers with high profiles, black fraternities and sororities, or academicians have taken an interest in what is arguably the largest class action law suit in U.S. history launched on the basis of alleged race discrimination. Community groups and activists of all ages who believe in social justice could ally to encourage the Justice Department to settle all claims swiftly. Only then will some black farmers regain security in the right to own their land. The longer settlement issues continue, the more visible black farmers and black land loss will become as an international human rights issue of global consequence. Harry Young, a black farmer in Kentucky who lost his farm because of the valuable minerals and resources his land contained, said it best: "Until the rights of black people are recognized, nothing they own is secure."[68]

Notes

1. Debra Reid, "African American Land Loss in Texas: Government Duplicity and Discrimination Based on Race," *Agricultural History* 77, no. 2 (2003): 258. Acreages at the 1910s peak were 15,691,536 acres (8,835,857 acres owned free and clear; 4,011,491 acres mortgaged, and 2,844,188 acres owned in part).

2. Bruce J. Reynolds, *Black Farmers in America, 1865–2000: The Pursuit of Independent Farming and the Role of Cooperatives* (Washington, D.C.: U.S. Department of Agriculture, 2002): 2–8.

3. James C. Cobb, *The Most Southern Place on Earth: The Mississippi Delta and the Roots of Regional Identity* (New York: Oxford University Press, 1992), 208.

4. Reid, "African American Land Loss," 262.

5. Lester M. Salamon, "The Time Dimensions in Policy Evaluation: The Case of the New Deal Land Reform Experiments," *Public Policy* 27, no. 2 (Spring 1979): 130–83. The family of Gary Grant, president of the Black Farmers and Agriculturalists Association, benefited from the Tillery, North Carolina, resettlement community.

6. Pete Daniel, "African American Farmers and Civil Rights," *Journal of Southern History* 1, 23 (February 2007): 5.

7. United States Commission on Civil Rights, *The Decline of Black Farming in America: A Report of the United States Commission on Civil Rights* (Washington, D.C.: Government Printing Office, 1982). "Racial Bias in Workings of U.S. Farm Aid Is Criticized by Federal Civil Rights Unit," *Wall Street Journal*, March 1, 1965; "Calls U.S. Unfair to Negroes," *Chicago Tribune*, March 1, 1965, 5; U.S. Commission on Civil Rights, *Equal Opportunity in Farm Programs: An Appraisal of Services Rendered by Agencies of the United States Department of Agriculture* (Washington, D.C., Government Printing Office, 1965).

8. U.S. Commission on Civil Rights, *Equal Opportunity*. See also Valerie Grim, "Black Participation in the Farmers Home Administration and Agricultural Stabilization and Conservation Service, 1964–1990," *Agricultural History* 70, no. 2 (Spring 1996): 321–36. See also U.S. House of Representatives, Committee on Government Operations, *Minority Farmer: A Disappearing American Resource—Has the Farmers Home Administration Been the Primary Catalyst?* House Report no. 101-984 (Washington, D.C. Government Printing Office, 1990).

9. "Title VI, Civil Rights Act—Compliance," box 4255, Civil Rights, General Correspondence, 1906–1975, Records of the Secretary of Agriculture, Record Group 16, National Archives and Records Administration, College Park Maryland.

10. Pete Daniel, "African American Farmers," 8–11.

11. Reid, "African American Land Loss," 262–63.

12. For a discussion of the U.S. Commission on Civil Rights' involvement with this issue, see U.S. Commission on Civil Rights, *The Mechanism for Implementing and Enforcing Title VI of the Civil Rights Act of 1964: U.S. Department of Agriculture, 1968* (Washington, D.C.: U.S. Commission on Civil Rights, 1968); and Paul Good, *Cycle to No Where*, prepared for the U.S. Commission on Civil Rights (Washington, D.C.: Government Printing Office, 1968).

13. J. Schor, "Fantasy and Reality: The Black Farmer's Place in American Agriculture," *Agriculture and Human Values* 9, no. 1 (1992): 72–78. See also his "Black Farmers/Farms:

The Search for Equity," *Agriculture and Human Values* 13, no. 3 (1996): 48–63. For a discussion and an example of the way the federal government's efforts at addressing some aspects of civil rights concerns and violation, see U.S. Commission on Civil Rights, *The Federal Civil Rights Enforcement Effort: One Year Later* (Washington, D.C.: Government Printing Office, 1971; U.S. Commission on Civil Rights, *The Federal Civil Rights Enforcement Effort—A Reassessment* (Washington, D.C.: Government Printing Office, 1973); and U.S. Commission on Civil Rights, *The Federal Civil Rights Enforcement Effort—1974* (Washington, D.C.: Government Printing Office, 1974). See also U.S. House of Representatives, Committee on Agriculture, Subcommittee on Department Operations, Oversight, Nutrition, and Forestry, *USDA's Civil Rights Programs and Responsibilities,* House Report no. 106-37 (Washington, D.C.: Government Printing Office, 1999).

14. U.S. Department of Agriculture, Citizens' Advisory Committee on Equal Opportunity, *Report to the Secretary,* December 1980, 1–6. U.S. Department of Agriculture, Civil Rights Action Team, *Civil Rights at the U.S. Department of Agriculture* (Washington, D.C.: Government Printing Office, 1997), 12 (hereafter cited as CRAT Report). See also N. Baharanyi, R. Zabawa, and W. Hill, eds., *Access and Equity Issues in Agriculture and Rural Development* (Tuskegee, Ala.: Tuskegee University, 1998).

15. CRAT Report, 14. For supporting documentation, see V. J. Banks, *Black Farmers and Their Farms,* ERS-59, U.S. Department of Agriculture (Washington, D.C.: Government Printing Office, 1986); D. Glickman, "Access and Equity Issues in Agriculture and Rural Development: Lessons from the Past," in *Access and Equity Issues in Agriculture and Rural Development,* ed. N. Baharanyi, R. Zabawa, and W. A. Hill (Tuskegee, Ala.: Tuskegee University, 1998), 7–13.

16. Grim, "Black Participation in the Farmers Home Administration," 257–71. See also V. Grim, "The Politics of Inclusion: Black Farmers and the Quest for Agribusiness Participation, 1945–1990s," *Agricultural History* 69, no. 2 (Spring 1995): 257–71; J. S. Hickey and A. A. Hickey, "Black Farmers in Virginia, 1930–1978: An Analysis of the Social Organization of Agriculture," *Rural Sociology* 52, no. 1 (Spring 1987): 75–88.

17. CRAT Report, 20. C. Beale, "Black Farmers: Why Such a Severe and Continuing Decline?" *Rural Development Perspectives* 7, no. 2 (February–May 1991): 12–14; and E. Y. Beauford and M. C. Nelson, "Business Approach to the Survival of the Family Farm: Status and Prospects of Improving the Economic Conditions of Minority Owned Farms in the South," in *Keys to Rural Community Development . . . the 1890 Land Grant Universities Approach,* ed. T. T. Williams (Tuskegee, Ala.: Tuskegee University, 1988).

18. CRAT Report, 20. The General Accounting Office found that between October 1, 1994, and March 31, 1996, 33 percent of minority applications and 27 percent of nonminority applications in the Agricultural Conservation Program were disapproved. Approval rates for FSA direct and guaranteed loan programs in 1995 and 1996 varied by region and by state and showed no consistent picture of disparity between minority and nonminority rates. But recent studies requested by Congress and FSA have found lower participation and lower loan-approval rates for minorities in most FSA programs.

19. CRAT Report, 22. See also U.S. Department of Agriculture, National Commission on Small Farms, *A Time to Act: A Report of the USDA National Commission on Small Farms* (Washington, D.C.: Government Printing Office, 1998).

20. CRAT Report, 23. For a discussion concerning how the USDA has attempted to

address this issue using various methodologies, see also U.S. Department of Agriculture, National Agricultural Statistics Service, *Agricultural Economics and Land Ownership Survey*, vol. 3, part IV (Washington, D.C.: Government Printing Office, 1999).

21. J. Gilbert, G. Sharp, and S. Felin, "The Loss and Persistence of Black-Owned Farms and Farmland: A Review of the Research Literature and Its Implications," *Southern Rural Sociology*, 18, no. 2 (2002): 1–30, see 7. See also J. Brooks, "The Emergency Land Fund: A Rural Land Retention and Development Model," in *Black Rural Landowner—Endangered Species: Social, Political, and Economic Implications*, ed. L. McGee and R. Boone (Westport, Conn.: Greenwood Press, 1979), 117–34.

22. R. S. Browne, *Only Six Million Acres: The Decline of Black Owned Land in the Rural South* (New York: Black Economic Research Center, 1973). For other points of view regarding this issue, see C. Gilbert and Q. Eli, *Homecoming: The Story of African American Farmers* (Boston: Beacon Press, 2000); R. D. Christy, "The African American, Farming, and Rural Society," in *Social Science Agricultural Agendas and Strategies*, ed. G. L. Johnson and J. T. Bonnen (East Lansing: Michigan State University Press, 1991); J. S. Hickey and A. A. Hickey, "Black Farmers in Virginia, 1930–1978: An Analysis of the Social Organization of Agriculture," *Rural Sociology* 52, no. 1 (1987): 75–88; R. Marshall and A. R. Thompson, *Status and Prospects for Small and Nonwhite Farmers in the South* (Atlanta: Southern Regional Council, 1976); and J. A. Lewis, *White and Minority Small Farm Operators in the South*, ERS-353, U.S. Department of Agriculture (Washington, D.C.: Government Printing Office, 1976).

23. Reid, "African American Land Loss," 260–63. Virgil L. Christian Jr. and Pepelasis Adamantios, *Farm Size and the Rural South* (Austin: University of Texas, Center for the Study of Human Resources, 1971).

24. CRAT Report, 14.

25. CRAT Report, 94. See also transcripts for nine customer listening sessions in Albany, Georgia; Memphis, Tennessee; Halifax, North Carolina; Tulsa, Oklahoma; Brownsville, Texas; Window Rock, Arizona; Salinas, California; Washington, D.C.; and Belzoni, Mississippi; and one employee listening session in Woodland, California, located in the black farmers' files at the USDA. Two additional employee listening sessions occurred at New Orleans, Louisiana; and Washington, D.C.

26. CRAT Report, 2–10, 93–95.

27. CRAT Report, 58–92.

28. See CRAT Report in its entirety.

29. Gilbert et al., "Loss and Persistence of Black-Owned Farms," 11.

30. See updates and reports of the black farmers' class action lawsuit located on the Web sites of the Black Farmers Agriculturalist Association (Gary Grant); the National Black Farmers Alliance (John Boyd); and the Federation of Southern Cooperatives (Ralph Paige). These organizations maintain daily and weekly updates on this lawsuit.

31. See CRAT Report.

32. CRAT Report, 23.

33. Environmental Working Group, "Obstruction of Justice," www.ewg.org/reports/blackfarmers.

34. *Timothy C. Pigford et al. v. Dan Glickman, Secretary, U.S. Department of Agriculture*, Civil Action No. 97-1978 (PLF) (DDC, April 14, 1999). Consolidated with *Cecil Brewington*

et al. v. Dan Glickman, Secretary, U.S. Department of Agriculture, Civil Action No. 98–1693 (PLF) (DDC April 14, 1999). Pigford consent decree approved, 185 F.R.D. 82 (DDC 1999); consent decree affirmed, 206 F.3d 1212 (D.C. Cir. 2000); subsequently referenced as *Pigford v. Veneman, Pigford v. Johanns, Pigford v. Schafer, Pigford v. Vilsack.*

35. Ibid.
36. Ibid.
37. Ibid.
38. Ibid.
39. CRAT Report, 3. Individuals involved included Secretary of Agriculture Glickman; Attorney General Janet Reno; members of the Black Caucus represented by Maxine Waters, Democrat of California, Senator Charles Robb, Democrat of Virginia, Charles Grassley, Republican senator of Iowa, and Republican House Speaker Newt Gingrich of Georgia.
40. CRAT Report, 16–31.
41. Ibid.
42. Ibid.
43. Tad Lock Cowan and Jody Feder, CRS Report for Congress, "The Pigford Case: USDA Settlement of a Discrimination Suit by Black Farmers," Congressional Research Service, Library of Congress, Washington, D.C., September 11, 2008, 5.
44. Louis T. March, *Harvest of Lies: The Black Farmer Lawsuit against the U.S. Department of Agriculture* (North Carolina: Representative Government Press, 2004), 124.
45. Ibid., 125–34.
46. See *Pigford v. Glickman*, Monitor's Reports.
47. Ibid.
48. See press releases of the Federation of Southern Cooperatives.
49. March, *Harvest of Lies*, 11–20.
50. Cowan and Feder, CRS Report for Congress, "The Pigford Case."
51. See December 2001 Associated Press series on black farmers.
52. See regular updates and reports about *Pigford* on the Web sites of the BFAA, NBFA, and FSC.
53. Senator Harry Reid, press release, Washington, D.C., August 6, 2010.
54. Ibid.
55. Updates on the BFAA, NBAA, and FSC Web sites.
56. Ibid.
57. See *Pigford v. Glickman*, Monitor Reports, June 2008.
58. Cowan and Feder, CRS Report for Congress, "The Pigford Case," 6.
59. "U.S. Senate Passes Funding for Pigford II: Black Farmer Racial Discrimination Lawsuit," http://www.wichitanaacpblog.com/2010/11/us-senate-passes-funding-for-pigford-ii.html (accessed November 23, 2010).
60. Publius, "Lawmakers Warn $1.2 Billion Pigford Payout to Black Farmers Rife with Fraud," http://bigovernment.com/publius/2010/11/24/lawmakers-warn-1-2-billion-pigford-payout (accessed November 24, 2010). See also Judson Berger, "Lawmakers Warn $1.2 Billion Payout to Black Farmers Rife with Fraud," http://www.foxnews.com/politics/2010/11/23/lawmakers (accessed November 24, 2010); Jason Hancock, "King: Pigford Settlement Boils Down to 'Paying People for their Skin Color,'" *Iowa Independent*,

November 23, 2010, 1; Fred Lucas, "USDA Denies Discrimination against Black Farmers but Pays Out $1.25 Billions," *CNSNews.com,* December 8, 2010; "Pigford I and Pigford II—An Obama Regime Scheme Rife with Fraud and Malfeasance in Ridiculous Favor of One Ethnic Minority—No Wayyy," *NwoDaily.com* (accessed November 23, 2010); Abraxas, "Pigford's Fraud on the American Taxpayer," (Right Wing News), *Uncoverage.net* (accessed December 11, 2010); Abraxas, "The Pigford Class Action Lawsuit: The Machinery of Greed," *Uncoverage.net* (accessed December 28, 2010); and Gary Hewson, Peter Schweizer, and Andrew Breitbart, "The Pigford Report—The Pigford Shakedown: How the Black Farmers' Cause Was Hijacked by Politicians, Trial Lawyers, and Community Organizers—Leaving Us With a Billion Dollar Tab," http://biggovernment.com/pigford-investigation-resources/ (accessed December 28, 2010).

61. For the four related cases, see (1) *George B. Keepseagle et al. v. Dan Glickman, Secretary, U.S. Department of Agriculture*, Civil Action No. 1:99CV03119 (DDC, initiated November 1999; fourth amended class action complaint filed October 11, 2000); subsequently *Keepseagle v. Veneman, Keepseagle v. Johanns, Keepseagle v. Schafer, Keepseagle v. Vilsack*. (2) *Guadalupe L. Garcia, Jr. et al. v. Dan Glickman, Secretary, U.S. Department of Agriculture*, No. 1:00CV02445 (DDC, filed October 13, 2000; second amended filed February 8, 2001); consolidated with *Love*; subsequently *Garcia v. Veneman, Garcia v. Johanns, Garcia v. Schafer, Garcia v. Vilsack*. (3) *James D. Green et al. v. Ann E. Veneman, Secretary, U.S. Department of Agriculture*, Civil Action No. 3:00CV366LN (S.D. Miss., filed April, 2, 2001); dismissed. (4) *Rosemary Love et al. v. Dan Glickman, U.S. Secretary of Agriculture*, No. 00-2502 (DDC, filed October 19, 2000); consolidated with *Garcia*; subsequently *Love v. Veneman, Love v. Johanns, Love v. Schafer, Love v. Vilsack*.

62. CRAT Report, recommendations.

63. H. S. Jones, "Federal Agriculture Policies: Do Black Farm Operators Benefit?" *Review of Black Political Economy* 22, no. 4 (1994): 25–50.

64. Gilbert et al., "Loss and Persistence of Black-Owned Farms," 13–14.

65. Ibid., 14.

66. USDA, *A Time to Act*.

67. CRAT Report, 58–92.

68. Monica Davis, "82 Year Old Black Farmer Arrested on Terroristic Threatening Charges," April 24, 2009, www.indybay.org/newsitems/2009/04/18591062.php.

Researching African American Land and Farm Owners

A Bibliographic Essay

DEBRA A. REID

Color-conscious record keeping generated historical data that can make it easy to identify an individual by race, but other data systematically deemphasized African American achievements, particularly land ownership, thus veritably obliterating black landowning farmers from the historical record. For example, the manuscript returns generated by the federal population and agricultural censuses, specifically those of 1870 and 1880, provide significant data. Researchers can cross reference names of individuals and their race with names of farmers, their property and production, and then can corroborate the findings with other local public records such as mortgages, deeds, plat maps, and tax assessments. Researchers can use data that they generate through this time-consuming process to compare farmers across race, ethnicity, age, family size, and economic status. Census compendia, however, did not consistently report farm tenure based on race. Prior to 1900 the national compendium did not include black farmers by tenure at all, and between 1930 and 1970, the period coincident with significant land loss by black farmers, neither state nor national compendia provided detailed information about black landowners as the compilations did for white owners. This made less obvious the rapid loss of land that black farmers experienced, it makes statistical comparison impossible, and it leaves researchers little choice but to conduct original research in local records and census manuscripts.

Despite the inadequacies of mid-twentieth century data compiled on black landowners, the U.S. government issued reports on African American farmers during the height of black land ownership in the early twentieth century, some with substantive analysis. An early example is W. E. Burghardt Du Bois, "The Negro Farmer," in *Negroes in the United States*, Bureau of the Census, Bulletin

8 (Washington, D.C.: Government Printing Office, 1904), 69–98; reissued in *Special Reports: Supplementary Analysis and Derivative Tales. Twelfth Census of the United States, 1900* (Washington, D.C.: Government Printing Office, 1906), 511–79; reprinted in Herbert Aptheker, compiler and editor, *Contributions by W.E.B. Du Bois in Government Publications and Proceedings* (Millwood, N.Y.: Kraus-Thomson, 1980): 229–346. *Negro Population in the United States, 1790–1915* (Washington, D.C.: Government Printing Office, 1918; repr., New York: Arno Press and *New York Times*, 1968).

Further reports include Charles E. Hall, *Negro Farmer in the United States*, Census of Agriculture, Fifteenth Census of the United States: 1930 (Washington, D.C.: U.S. Government Printing Office, 1933); U.S. Bureau of the Census, *U.S. Census of Agriculture: 1959*, Vol. 2: *General Report, Statistics by Subjects* (Washington, D.C.: U.S. Government Printing Office, 1962), Chapter 10: Color, Race, and Tenure of Farm Operator, 1004–5; and U.S. Bureau of the Census, *U.S. Census of Agriculture: 1969*, Vol. 2: *General Report* (Washington, D.C.: U.S. Government Printing Office, 1973), Chap. 1: General Information, Procedures for Collection, Processing, Classification, Table 34: Farms Operated by Negro and Races Other than White: 1900 to 1969, 96–97. Calvin L. Beale compiled data during the mid-1960s that appeared in reference works: "The Negro in American Agriculture," in *The American Negro Reference Book*, edited by John P. Davis (Englewood Cliffs, N.J.: Prentice-Hall, 1966), 161–204; revised as "The Black American in Agriculture," in *The Black American Reference Book*, edited by Mabel M. Smythe (Englewood Cliffs, N.J.: Prentice-Hall, 1976), 284–315.

Social scientists active during the heyday of black land ownership in the early twentieth century conducted field work to generate data. One of the most prolific, W. E. Burghardt Du Bois, published three major reports in addition to the first analysis of black farmers as reported in the U.S. census returns: *The Negroes of Farmville, Virginia: A Social Study*, U.S. Department of Labor Bulletin 3, no. 14 (Washington, D.C.: Government Printing Office, January 1898), 1–38; *The Negro Landowner in Georgia*, U.S. Department of Labor, Bulletin 6, no. 25 (Washington, D.C.: Government Printing Office, July 1901), 647–777; and *Souls of Black Folk* (Chicago: A. C. McClurg and Company, 1903; unabridged edition, New York: Dover Publications, 1994). Robert Preston Brooks analyzed the ways that geography, demographics, labor availability, and crop and stock values affected the rate of black farm ownership in *The Agrarian Revolution in Georgia, 1865–1912* (Madison: University of Wisconsin, 1914, repr., Westport, Conn.: Negro Universities Press, 1970). Samuel T. Bitting documented African American land ownership at its peak in *Rural Landownership among the Negroes of Virginia, With Special Reference to Albermarle County* (Charlottesville: University of Virginia Press, 1915). Private foundations also commissioned contemporary studies, such as that produced by Donald Dewey Scarborough, *An Economic Study of Negro*

Farmers as Owners, Tenants and Croppers, Phelps-Stokes Foundation Studies, no. 7 (*Bulletin of the University of Georgia*, vol. 25, September 1924), and Carter Godwin Woodson, *The Rural Negro* (Washington, D.C.: Association for the Study of Negro Life and History, 1930).

The New Deal prompted more research into conditions in the rural South. Arthur Raper and other sociologists conducted extension field work with social reform as a goal. For an example of products of such research, see *Preface to Peasantry: A Tale of Two Black Belt Counties* (Chapel Hill: University of North Carolina Press, 1936). During the 1960s social scientists analyzed contemporary statistical data documenting black farmers, including owners. Demographers James D. Cowhig and Calvin L. Beale compared white and black farmers in "Socioeconomic Differences between White and Nonwhite Farm Populations in the South," *Social Forces* 42, no. 13 (March 1964): 354–62, and "Relative Socioeconomic Status of Southern Whites and Nonwhites, 1950 and 1960," *Southwestern Social Science Quarterly* (September 1964): 113–24.

Early histories of black landowners focused on free blacks during the antebellum era. See, for example, Carter G. Woodson, editor and compiler, *Free Negro Owners of Slaves in the United States in 1830; Together with Absentee Ownership of Slaves in the United States in 1830* (Washington, D.C.: Association for the Study of Negro Life and History, 1924); Harold Schoen, "The Free Negro in the Republic of Texas," *Southwestern Historical Quarterly* 39–41 (April 1936–July 1937); Luther Porter Jackson, "The Virginia Free Negro Farmer and Property Owner, 1830–1860," *Journal of Negro History* 24 (October 1939): 390–439; and John Hope Franklin, *The Free Negro in North Carolina, 1790–1860* (Chapel Hill: University of North Carolina Press, 1943).

The new social history movement of the 1960s and 1970s facilitated scholarship on freedmen's aspirations, as evidenced in LaWanda Cox, "The Promise of Land for the Freedmen," *Mississippi Valley Historical Review* 45 (December 1958): 418–40; Edward H. Bonekemper III, "Negro Ownership of Real Property in Hampton and Elizabeth City County, Virginia, 1860–1870," *Journal of Negro History* 55, no. 3 (1970): 165–81; Peter Kolchin, *First Freedom: The Responses of Alabama's Blacks to Emancipation and Reconstruction* (Westport, Conn.: Greenwood Pres, 1972); Gary B. Mills's study of one colony founded by freed slaves and farmed by slaves, *The Forgotten People: Cane River's Creoles of Color* (Baton Rouge: Louisiana State University Press, 1977); and Claude Oubre, *Forty Acres and a Mule: Freedmen's Bureau and Black Landownership* (Baton Rouge: Louisiana State University Press, 1978).

Relatively little secondary scholarship exists to put African American land owners after Reconstruction into historic context. Studies include Robert Higgs, *Competition and Coercion: Blacks in the American Economy, 1865–1914* (Chicago: University of Chicago Press, 1977) and Stephen J. DeCanio, "Accumulation and

Discrimination in the Postbellum South," *Explorations in Economic History* 16 (April 1979): 182–206. DeCanio, in *Agriculture in the Postbellum South: The Economics of Production and Supply* (Cambridge, Mass.: The MIT Press, 1974), esp. 239–40, argued that black farmers were not less productive due to the "legacy of slavery" but other factors accounted for real differences in productivity based on a farmer's race and tenure (239–40). During the 1980s an article by Robert Higgs, "Accumulation of Property by Southern Blacks before World War I," *American Economic Review* 72, no. 4 (September, 1982): 725–37, generated a dialog: Robert A. Margo, "Accumulation of Property by Southern Blacks before World War I: Comment and Further Evidence," *American Economic Review* 74, no. 4 (September, 1984): 768–76; Higgs, "Accumulation of Property by Southern Blacks before World War I: Reply," *American Economic Review* 74, no. 4 (September 1984): 777–81.

Loren Schweninger's *Black Property Owners in the South, 1790–1915* (Urbana: University of Illinois Press, 1990) remains the most comprehensive study of property acquisition by African Americans, including farmers, and a model of source analysis. Schweninger spent nearly a decade identifying the names of 41,000 African Americans who owned at least one hundred dollars in real and/or personal property in fifteen states and the District of Columbia. He consulted an array of primary sources, including three decennial manuscript census returns. He corroborated that evidence with additional data drawn from state and county tax assessments; county court records such as deeds, mortgages and wills; probate and estate inventories; published sources such as newspapers; and biographical dictionaries and archival and manuscript collections. Schweninger explains his approach and the limitations of the data in "An Essay on Sources and Methodology," 371–91.

Few authors have produced monographs on rural African American property owners or the communities that they created, but those who have done so have delved into an array of primary sources. See sociologist Stewart E. Tolnay, "Appendix: Southern Black Farm Families in the 1910 and 1940 U.S. Census," in his comprehensive study *The Bottom Rung: African American Family Life on Southern Farms* (Urbana: University of Illinois Press, 1999), 179–90. For an example of a historian's analysis of one county, see Jeannie M. Whayne's study of Poinsett County, Arkansas. Her study did not focus on African American landowners, but her field work—which included data drawn from population returns from four townships in six decennial U.S. population census returns: 1860, 1870, 1880, 1900, 1910, and 1920, corroborated with U.S. agricultural census returns for 1880, county tax and mortgage records and numerous additional sources—allowed her to identify owners and put them into the context of the larger county experience. She explained the process in "Appendix: Quantitative Methods," *A New Plantation South: Land, Labor and Federal Favor in Twentieth-Century Arkansas*

(Charlottesville: University of Virginia, 1996), 237-44. Sociologist Elizabeth Rauh Bethel explored the collective memory expressed among those with first-hand knowledge of Promised Land, South Carolina, a black farming community founded by freedmen in 1870. She put the living memory and collective consciousness into historic perspective in *Promiseland: A Century of Life in a Negro Community* (Philadelphia: Temple University Press, 1981; rev. ed., Columbia: University of South Carolina Press, 1997).

Studies have addressed family-based solutions to securing and retaining property. Examples include Dylan C. Penningroth, *The Claims of Kinfolk: African American Property and Community in the Nineteenth-Century South* (Chapel Hill: University of North Carolina Press, 2003), and Sharon Ann Holt, *Making Freedom Pay*, first an essay in the *Journal of Southern History*, later expanded into the book *Making Freedom Pay: North Carolina Freedpeople Working for Themselves, 1865-1900* (Athens: University of Georgia Press, 2000).

Few studies assess land acquisition and loss to the 1950s, but examples include Valerie Grim, "African American Landlords, 1865-1950: A Profile," *Agricultural History* 72, no. 2 (Spring 1998): 399-416; Mark R. Schultz, "The Dream Realized? African American Landownership in Central Georgia between Reconstruction and World War Two," *Agricultural History* 72, no. 2 (Spring 1998): 298-312; and Peggy G. Hargis, "Beyond the Marginality Thesis: The Acquisition and Loss of Land by African Americans in Georgia," *Agricultural History* 72 (Spring 1998): 241-62.

The New Deal prompted significant outmigration, but sharecroppers and tenants left while owners persisted. The loss of croppers, tenants, and laborers has generated significant study, but scholars have paid less attention to the persistence of land owners or the factors that caused the number of owners to remain steady through the mid-twentieth century. Yet economist Victor Perlo documented the increase in subsistence and part-time farming partially due to reverse migration of city workers; see Perlo's *The Negro in Southern Agriculture: The Plantation, Sharecropping, Farm Labor, Land Ownership, Mechanization, and Living Standards since World War II* (New York: International Publishers, 1953). African American farm owners held onto the land until economic pressure intensified to participate in the capital-intensive post–World War II production agriculture that "get bigger, get better or get out" USDA policy supported. For context see Donald L. Winters, "Agriculture in the Post–World War II South," *The Rural South since World War II*, edited by R. Douglas Hurt (Baton Rouge: Louisiana State University Press, 1998), 8-27, and Debra A. Reid, "'The Whitest of Occupations'? African Americans in the Rural Midwest, 1940-2010," *The Rural Midwest since World War II*, edited by J. L. Anderson (DeKalb: Northern Illinois University Press, forthcoming). Valerie Grim has incorporated African American owner experiences into modern agricultural literature through essays such as "The Politics of Inclusion: Black Farmers and the Quest for Agribusiness

Participation, 1945–1990s," *Agricultural History* 69, no. 2 (Spring 1995): 257–71; "The Impact of Mechanized Farming on Black Farm Families in the Rural South: A Study of Life in the Brooks Farm Community, 1940–1970," *Agricultural History* 68, no. 2 (Spring 1994):169–84; and "The High Cost of Water: African American Farmers and the Politics of Irrigation," *Agricultural History* 76, no. 2 (Spring 2002): 338–53.

Social scientists have also compared property acquisition among rural blacks and whites from the antebellum era to the mid-twentieth century to determine how factors such as skin color and access to credit and to education affected the opportunities available to rural residents. See Howard Bodenhom, "The Complexion Gap: The Economic Consequences of Color among Free African Americans in the Rural Antebellum South," *Advances in Agricultural Economic History* 2 (2003): 41–73; Neil Canaday, "The Accumulation of Property by Southern Blacks and Whites: Individual-Level Evidence from a South Carolina Cotton County," *Explorations in Economic History* 45, no. 1 (2008): 51–75; and Neil Canaday and Charles Reback, "Race, Literacy, and Real Estate Transactions in the Postbellum South," *Journal of Economic History* 70, no. 2 (June 2010): 428–45.

Once African Americans acquired land, they faced challenges in retaining it. Farm owners often held less than $100 in property and may not have trusted their local courts to protect their property interests. Lower-class property owners who did not secure clear title to real estate or who did not probate estates had trouble protecting their legal interests. The heirs did not appear in the public record because they did not file legal paperwork. The Emergency Land Fund produced a report in 1980 that explored the relationship between clear title, heir rights, and land ownership. See "The Impact of Heir Property on Black Rural Land Tenure in the Southeastern Region of the United States" (1980), submitted to the U.S. Department of Agriculture/Farmers Home Administration in 1984. Staff of the Federation of Southern Cooperatives/Land Assistance Fund identified heir ownership as the most pressing cause of land loss and lack of estate planning as a close second; see Miessha Thomas, Jerry Pennick, and Heather Gray, "What Is African-American Land Ownership?" (2004), available at http://www.federationsoutherncoop.com/aalandown04.htm (accessed February 21, 2011). Even with estate planning, black landowners often faced challenges from family members who forced partition sales or from white heirs who contested wills that had granted their black relatives farmland. See Janice F. Dyer and Conner Bailey, "A Place to Call Home: Cultural Understandings of Heir Property among Rural African Americans," *Rural Sociology* 73, no. 3 (2008), 317–338, and Gene Stowe, *Inherit the Land: Jim Crow Meets Miss Maggie's Will* (Jackson: University Press of Mississippi, 2006).

For analytical studies of contested legal title and its effect on black landowners, see Thomas W. Mitchell, "From Reconstruction to Deconstruction: Undermining

Black Landownership, Political Independence, and Community through Partition Sales of Tenancies in Common," *Northwestern University Law Review* 95, no. 2 (Winter 2001): 505–80. Mitchell challenges scholars to devote more attention to property ownership under "tenancy in common," the form of ownership that best described most black farm family property. Only then can the full extent of land loss through partition sales of heirs' property be fully understood. See Mitchell, "Destabilizing the Normalization of Rural Black Land Loss: A Critical Role for Legal Empiricism," *Wisconsin Law Review* 2005, no. 2 (2005): 557–615.

Inadequate traditional historic sources, including lack of public records such as legal title, have deterred some scholars from pursuing research in African American rural and political history. Yet Thad Sitton and James H. Conrad indicate that other sources exist to document rural black community life; see their *Freedom Colonies: Independent Black Texans in the Time of Jim Crow* (Austin: University of Texas Press, 2005). A micro-level study focused in and around one city indicates how material evidence, public records, private papers, oral histories, city directories, and newspapers can create a more complete picture of the complexity of land and property ownership; see Michelle M. Mears, *And Grace Will Lead Me Home: African American Freedmen Communities of Austin, Texas, 1865-1928* (Lubbock: Texas Tech University Press, 2009).

State departments of agriculture offer incentive programs to farm families with a century or more in continuous occupation of and production on the same farm land. R. Douglas Hurt's *American Farms: Exploring Their History* (Malabar, Fla.: Kreiger Publishing, 1996), provides directions that most families can follow to document their farming history. African Americans have applied for and received such designations. Those records can yield valuable information about well-documented farms. Yet incomplete data that frustrates genealogists can also frustrate those researching family farms.

Sometimes research starts with one name. Some scholars have shared names of individuals they identified in their research, and these lists of names can be the foundation for more focused studies on black farm families. Schweninger included the list of those with property valued at more than $20,000 as "Appendix Six: Biographical Listing of Prosperous Blacks in the South, 1870s–1915," 295–300. Steven Hahn compiled 3,878 names that he defined as local and state leaders in former Confederate states. He provided only a brief description of the set, but he encouraged readers to contact him if they wanted to see it and his analysis of it. See "Appendix: Black Leaders Data Set," in *A Nation under Our Feet: Black Political Struggles in the Rural South from Slavery to the Great Migration* (Cambridge, Mass.: Belknap Press of Harvard University Press, 2003), 479–80. Hahn documented property ownership and occupation for each political leader he identified. Some biographers have addressed the rural and farm backgrounds of political leaders, as did John F. Marszalek, *A Black Congressmen in the Age of*

Jim Crow: South Carolina's George Washington Murray (Gainesville: University Press of Florida, 2006).

Schweninger, Hahn, Tolnay, and other scholars who have incorporated African American landowning farm families into their research have focused on the region of the country where the majority of black farmers lived, the South. Yet some studies exist of black families and the strategies they used to acquire land, establish rural communities and farm alongside their white peers in the Northeast, Midwest, Plains states, and Far West. Sociologist George K. Hesslink studied a farmer-entrepreneur community founded in Calvert Township in southwest Michigan during the 1830s to understand race relations over time; see his *Black Neighbors: Negroes in a Northern Rural Community* (Indianapolis: Bobbs-Merrill Company, 1968). Stephen A. Vincent focused on the rise of black farming communities during the antebellum era in Indiana and then traced their development and eventual decline in *Southern Seed, Northern Soil: African American Farm Communities in the Midwest, 1790–1900* (Bloomington: Indiana University Press, 1999). Juliet E. K. Walker documented the life of Francis "Free Frank" Mc-Whorter, who established New Philadelphia, a black farming community in Pike County, Illinois, about the same time the first black resident arrived in Calvert Township, Michigan. See *Free Frank: A Black Pioneer on the Antebellum Frontier* (Lexington: University Press of Kentucky, 1983).

Several factors affected development of all-black farming communities and ultimately black towns. Landowners played a major role, but the dependency between community and farm owners needs more study. See Susan Eva O'Donovan, *Becoming Free in the Cotton South* (Cambridge: Harvard University Press, 2007); Vincent, *Southern Seed, Northern Soil*; Sitton and Conrad, *Freedom Colonies*; and Kenneth Marvin Hamilton, *Black Towns and Profit: Promotion and Development in the Trans-Appalachian West, 1877–1915* (Urbana: University of Illinois Press, 1991), which focuses on communities in Mississippi, Kansas, and Oklahoma. For a more detailed analysis of relationships between landownership and power in multi-racial Oklahoma, see David A. Chang, *The Color of the Land: Race, Nation, and the Politics of Landownership in Oklahoma, 1832-1929* (Chapel Hill: University of North Carolina Press, 2010). For the Exoduster movement see, for example, Nell Irvin Painter, *Exodusters: Black Migration to Kansas after Reconstruction* (New York: Alfred A. Knopf, 1977). Exodusters became farmers; some gained worldwide renown. Anne P. W. Hawkins included Junius Groves, the Potato King of the World, who farmed near Edwardsville, Kansas, in her article, "Hoeing Their Own Row: Black Agriculture and the Agrarian Ideal in Kansas, 1880–1920," *Kansas History* 22, no. 3 (Autumn 1999): 200–13. Studies of African Americans outside the South rarely focus on their agricultural pursuits, though any mention of black farmers or ranchers helps make more complete the story of minority rural property ownership. For example, Betti Vanepps-Taylor includes black homesteaders and their involvement in cattle ranching and horse breeding in *Forgotten Lives: African Americans in South Dakota* (Pierre: South Dakota State Historical Society, 2008).

African American farm owners outside the South, particularly those operating after World War I, beg further study because a greater proportion of the black farm population outside the South owned their land than did those in the South. They, like their white peers, left farming as their family-based way of life became obsolete and farming became more a capital-intensive business. Valerie Grim's state-level study, "African Americans in Iowa's Agricultural and Rural Life," in *Outside In: African History in Iowa*, edited by Hal Chase (Des Moines: State Historical Society of Iowa, 2001), 166–90, surveyed the changes from settlement through the production revolution for black farmers in Iowa. Reid's "'The Whitest of Occupations'?" addresses black midwestern farmers' responses to the production revolution but also considers the back-to-the-country movements that began before World War II and continued thereafter. Some urban blacks, many of whom could trace their roots to the rural cotton South, became hobby farmers in northern agricultural ghettos within commuting distances of city jobs after World War II. More could be done to see if this occurred in the South or West.

More could also be done to understand the relationships between urban and rural African Americans. Several scholars have assessed migrants and their attitudes, but the significance of the influence between the two remains a ripe topic. For the potential to link rural and urban history see Debra A. Reid, "African Americans and Community Building: Lifting Despite Racism and Racial Separatism," *Journal of Urban History* 33, no. 1 (November 2006): 1–11. For examples of migration studies see Morton Rubin, "Migration Patterns of Negroes from a Rural Northeastern Mississippi Community," *Social Forces* 39, no. 1 (October 1960–May 1961): 59–66; Valerie Grim, "From the Yazoo Mississippi Delta: Conversations with Rural African American Women Concerning Their Experiences in Urban Communities of the Midwest, 1950–2000," in *Frontier: Journal of Women's History* 2, no. 1 (Summer 2001), 126–44; and Bernadette Pruitt, "For the Advancement of the Race: African-American Migration to Houston, 1914-1941," *Journal of Urban History* 31, no. 4 (May 2005): 435-78.

Seasonal cycles and crop cultures affected farming culture, but few studies convey clear relationships between crops and stock and farm labor needs and practices. Scholars who study African American landowners need to be conversant about such things in their geographic area of study. To this end, compendiums produced from agricultural census returns as well as special reports prove useful. See, for example, Eugene W. Hilgard, *Report on Cotton Production in the United States*, Part I: *Mississippi Valley and Southwestern States*; Part II: *Eastern Gulf, Atlantic, and Pacific States*, Tenth Census of the United States, 1880 (Washington, D.C.: Government Printing Office, 1884); Bureau of Agricultural

Economics, U.S. Department of Agriculture, *Cotton Farming in the Southern Piedmont, 1930–1951,* Agricultural Information Bulletin no. 90 (Washington, D.C.: Government Printing Office, June 1952); and J. B. Killebrew, *Report on the Culture and Curing of Tobacco in the United States* (Washington, D.C.: Government Printing Office, 1884).

Secondary surveys of agriculture in a region or comparisons of crop cultures within and across regions can provide important context as well. For broad overviews of agriculture, farming, and rural life in the United States see John Schlebecker, *Whereby We Thrive: A History of American Farming, 1607–1972* (Ames: Iowa State University Press, 1975); R. Douglas Hurt, *American Agriculture: A Brief History* (Ames: Iowa State University Press, 1994; rev. ed., Bloomington: Indiana University Press, 2002); and David Danbom, *Born in the Country: A History of Rural America* (Baltimore: Johns Hopkins University Press, 1995; 2nd ed., 2006). For surveys on southern agriculture see Lewis Cecil Gray, *History of Agriculture in the Southern United States to 1860,* 2 vols. (Washington, D.C.: Carnegie Institution of Washington, 1933; repr., Gloucester, Mass.: Peter Smith, 1958), and Gilbert C. Fite, *Cotton Fields No More: Southern Agriculture, 1865–1980* (Lexington: University of Kentucky Press, 1984). For northern agriculture see Percy Wells Bidwell and John I. Falconer, *History of Agriculture in the Northern United States, 1620–1860* (Washington, D.C.: Carnegie Institution of Washington, 1925; 1941); Howard S. Russell, *A Long Deep Furrow: Three Centuries of Farming in New England* (Lebanon, N.H.: University Press of New England, 1976; abridged edition, 1981); Hal S. Barron, *Mixed Harvest: The Second Great Transformation in the Rural North* (Chapel Hill: University of North Carolina Press, 1997). For a series of economic histories see Fred Albert Shannon, *Farmer's Last Frontier: Agriculture, 1860–1897* (New York: Farrar and Reinhart, 1945; repr., M. E. Sharp, 1989); Paul Wallace Gates, *The Farmer's Age: Agriculture, 1815–1860* (New York: Holt, Rinehart and Winston, 1960); and Gilbert C. Fite, *The Farmers' Frontier: 1865–1900* (New York: Holt, Rinehart and Winston, 1966). For a survey of farmer revolts including African American involvement, see Theodore Saloutos, *Farmer Movements in the South: 1865–1933* (Lincoln: University of Nebraska Press, 1960). For a comparative study of crop cultures that includes substantive information on black landowners, see Pete Daniel, *Breaking the Land: The Transformation of Cotton, Tobacco and Rice Cultures since 1880* (Urbana: University of Illinois Press, 1985). Land policy studies should begin with Paul Wallace Gates, *The History of Public Land Law Development* (Washington, D.C.: U.S. Government Printing Office, 1968; repr., New York: Arno Press, 1979).

Sociologists E. M. Beck and Stewart E. Tolnay show the potential for quantitative studies to understand relationships between agricultural production, markets, and violence that often targeted the most successful farm owners. See "The Killing Fields of the Deep South: The Market for Cotton and the Lynching of

Blacks, 1882–1930," *American Sociological Review* 55 (August 1990): 526–39. For a study of race relations in the context of cotton culture, see Neil Foley, *The White Scourge: Mexicans, Blacks and Poor Whites in Texas Cotton Culture* (Berkeley: University of California Press, 1997); for the South in general see Jack Temple Kirby, *In Rural Worlds Lost: The American South, 1920–1960* (Baton Rouge: Louisiana State University Press, 1987), and for Virginia see Jo Ann S. Hickey and Anthony Andrew Hickey, "Black Farmers in Virginia, 1930–1978: An Analysis of the Social Organization of Agriculture," *Rural Sociology* 52, no. 1 (1987): 75–88.

Scholars produced the aforementioned studies using historical sources available in original or microfilm form in archives and libraries. Much can be gained from careful searching of newspapers, and major African American newspapers have become more accessible with the spread of electronic search engines and live-text searchable databases. Historically, publisher Claude Barnett, who founded the Associated Negro Press (ANP) in 1919, did more than most journalists to focus national attention toward the plight of black farmers. His influence on the ways readers understood African American farmers warrants further study in the same vein that scholars analyzed the influence of television on the Civil Rights Movement. ANP stories appeared in all major daily and weekly African American newspapers, and the extensive collection of Barnett's papers, photographic files, and ANP records in the Chicago History Museum can provide much needed context for the content of the ANP stories on black farmers.

Journalists helped fix attention on black farmers' lives. See Edwin Ware Hullinger, *Plowing Through: The Story of the Negro in Agriculture* (New York: Morrow, 1940). Most journalist accounts after World War II featured the plight of black farmers, but some celebrated accomplishments, implying that success could be realized regardless of race if farm families worked hard, prayed hard, and relied on family labor. See William Brinkley, "Degrees by the Dozen on $40 a Week," *Life* (September 19, 1955), 188–90, 192, 194, 196, 198, 200, 202, 204. Reporting after the farm crisis of the late 1970s and early 1980s focused on the negative as did Thad Martin, "The Disappearing Black Farmer," *Ebony* (June 1985): 145–46, 148, 150–51; and the 2001 three-part story that resulted from an eighteen-month investigation by Associated Press writers—Todd Lewan and Dolores Barclay, "Torn from the Land, Part I: Black Americans' Farmland Taken through Cheating, Intimidation, Even Murder" (December 2, 2001); Todd Lewan, Dolores Barclay, and Allen G. Breed, "Torn from the Land, Part II: Landownership Made Blacks Targets of Violence and Murder, an AP Investigation Shows" (December 3, 2001); Dolores Barclay, "Torn from the Land, Part II: A Man Is Jailed for Defending His Land" (December 3, 2001); Todd Lewan, "Torn from the Land, Part II: Taking Away the Vote—and a Black Man's Land" (December 3, 2001); Todd Lewan and Dolores Barclay, "Torn from the Land, Part III: Today, Developers and Lawyers Use a Legal Maneuver to Strip Black Families of Land" (December 9, 2001); Todd

Lewan, "Torn from the Land, Part III: With Help from Their White Lawyer, a Black Mississippi Family Loses a Farm" (December 9, 2001), available through *The Authentic Voice*, http://www.theauthenticvoice.org/Torn_From_The_Land_ Intro.html (accessed August 9, 2010). Other reports featured perseverance as did Wil Haygood, "The Promised Land: Bigotry and Bankruptcy Haven't Driven Ricky Haynie from the Fields His Ancestors Worked as Slaves," *Washington Post* (October 3, 2004), W12.

Digitization has made primary sources including census data sets, library special collections, and archival and three-dimensional museum collections available. These can add new dimensions, literally, to research on black farm owners. Researchers must be cautious and remember that not all extant materials have been digitized, but the variety of material can be overwhelming. Libraries feature genealogical resources tailored to the needs of those researching African American history. Massive microfilming projects undertaken by the Church of Jesus Christ of Latter Day Saints (LDS) and available through local LDS reading rooms or via electronic, live-text searchable sources such as FamilySearch.org or Ancestry.com have revolutionized genealogy research. Most state libraries and archives or state history museums have special portals devoted to African American history, funneling researchers to collections of local historical societies and museums. At present these mostly contain digitized photographic collections, but other types of data will be added. The Illinois State Museum, for example, maintains AudioBarn as a portal to transcribed oral history interviews that document rural and agricultural experiences in the state. These interviews include several African Americans sharing their life stories as rodeo operators, members of cooperatives, production farmers, or retired hobbyists. More relevant to the majority black farmer experience, starting in 2007 significant photographic collections held in the archives of historically black colleges and universities, including several 1890 land grant institutions, were digitized with support from the Andrew W. Mellon Foundation. This is critical to the preservation of records that document not just the reformers' agendas but the involvement of landowning farm families over the more than one-hundred-year history of the institutions.

Examples of special collections available digitally include the Jackson Davis Collection at the University of Virginia. Davis traveled throughout the southeast taking photographs of African American training schools from 1908 into the 1930s. Many feature private schools that African American rural reformers such as Joseph Elward Clayton and Robert Lloyd Smith founded as well as public schools maintained by black rural communities; see http://www2.lib.virginia.edu/small/collections/jdavis/search.html (accessed February 24, 2011). Enter the term *black farmer* into the search engine of "Documenting the American South," a clearing house of digitized primary sources maintained by the University Library of the University of North Carolina at Chapel Hill, and it returns 2,240 hits, a mere fraction of the relevant material; http://docsouth.unc.edu/ (accessed February 24, 2011). Data sets made available through Historical Census Browser from the University of Virginia, Geospatial and Statistical Data Center (2004), can simplify quantifying selective data; see http://fisher.lib.virginia.edu/collections/stats/histcensus/index.html (accessed August 18, 2010). The task of locating scattered sources remains time-consuming and daunting, but the returns justify the commitment.

Historians can benefit from interdisciplinary approaches, particularly when studying under-documented minority farmers. Material culture can prove most enlightening to this endeavor. For theoretical and methodological insight, see Leora Auslander who discusses the merits of integrating material evidence as historic evidence in "Beyond Words," *American Historical Review* 110, no. 4 (October 2005): 1015–45. Giorgio Riello provides three approaches to writing about history using objects in "Things that Shape History: Material Culture and Historical Narrative," in Karen Harvey, editor, *History and Material Culture: A Student's Guide to Approaching Alternative Sources* (London: Routledge, 2009), 24–46. For an article that indicates the potential for systematically analyzing farm owners' furniture, houses, and cooking utensils, among other things, see Debra A. Reid, "Furniture Exempt from Seizure: African American Farm Families and Their Property in Texas, 1880s–1930s," *Agricultural History* 80, no. 3 (Summer 2006): 336–57.

Scholars unsure about doing their own field work can draw on gray literature that contract historic archaeologists prepare for properties they excavate. These provide rich evidence of material culture excavated at sites threatened by construction projects of varying sorts, from cellular phone towers to interstates. Each state historic preservation officer has an inventory of the sites excavated and the material found. Multiple volume site reports can be secured through interlibrary loan. See, for example, Randall W. Moir and David H. Jurney with Susan A. Lebo, "Farmstead Site Descriptions," in *Pioneer Settlers, Tenant Farmers, and Communities*, Richland Creek Technical Series, vol. 4, edited by Randall W. Moir and David H. Jurney (Dallas, Tex.: Archaeology Research Program, Institute for the Study of Earth and Man, Southern Methodist University, 1987), 70–75, 100–106; or Steven D. Smith, *A Comparison of the Documentary Evidence of Material Culture and the Archaeological Record: Store Ledgers and Two Black Tenant Sites, Waverly Plantation, Mississippi*, Volumes in Historical Archaeology 12 (Columbia: University of South Carolina, 1991), 87.

Some site reports have gained wider distribution as articles. See, for example, Linda France Stine, "Social Inequality and Turn-of-the-Century Farmsteads: Issues of Class, Status, Ethnicity, and Race," *Historical Archaeology* 24, no. 4 (1990): 37–49. Rural communities could become volatile, as Kenneth Brown discusses in "Material Culture and Community Structure: The Slave and Tenant Community at Levi Jordan's Plantation, 1848–1892," in *Working Toward Freedom: Slave Society and Domestic Economy in the American South*, edited by Larry E. Hudson Jr. (Rochester, N.Y.: University of Rochester Press, 1994), 95–118.

Monographs likewise provide models of how to integrate material evidence into historic narrative. See Charles E. Orser, *The Material Basis of the Post-Bellum Tenant Plantation* (University of Georgia Press, 1988); Theresa Singleton, *I, Too, Am America: Archaeological Studies of African American Life* (Charlottesville: University of Virginia Press, 1999); Paul R. Mullins, *Race and Affluence: An Archaeology of African America and Consumer Culture* (New York: Kluwer Academic Press, 1999); and Laurie A. Wilkie, *Creating Freedom: Material Culture and African American Identity at Oakley Plantation, Louisiana, 1840–1950* (Baton Rouge: Louisiana State University Press, 2000).

Cultural geography can provide important context for understanding black farm families' relationships to the landscape and environment in which they functioned. Charles S. Aiken established a model with *The Cotton Plantation South since the Civil War* (Baltimore: Johns Hopkins University Press, 1998). Historians who have adopted cultural geographic approaches include J. William Harris, *Deep Souths: Delta, Piedmont and Sea Island Society in the Age of Segregation* (Baltimore: Johns Hopkins University Press, 2001). Studies such as this can prove indispensible in understanding how farmers in the Black Belt cotton region faced different pressures and different crises than a potato farmer in Kansas or a wheat or tobacco farmer in Virginia. Cultural geographers have even focused on black farm ownership. See, for example, James S. Fisher, "Negro Farm Ownership in the South," *Annals of the Association of American Geographers* 63 (1973): 478–89.

Scholars can focus on land use to understand black farm families' attitudes toward their rural environment. Some studies have emphasized cultural distinctiveness, arguing that Africans carried their agroecological practices to the places where they toiled as slaves, and retained the traditions as they established freedmen communities and became landowning farmers. Others have linked African American agrarianism to the legacy of white political philosophy, particularly agrarianism as articulated by Thomas Jefferson. For the range of approaches, see Kimberly Smith, *African American Environmental Thought: Foundations* (Lawrence: University of Kansas Press, 2007) and essays in two collections, *"To Love the Wind and the Rain": African Americans and Environmental History*, edited by Dianne D. Glave and Mark Stoll (Pittsburgh: University of Pittsburgh Press, 2006), and *Land and Power: Sustainable Agriculture and African Americans— A Collection of Essays from the 2007 Black Environmental Thought Conference*, edited by Jeffrey L. Jordan, Edward Pennick, Walter A. Hill, and Robert Zabawa (Waldorf, Md.: Sustainable Agriculture Research and Education, 2009). Much remains to be done to understand farm owners' environmentalism.

Place mattered to black landowners. Sociologist Arthur Raper, in *Preface to Peasantry*, noted that black owners maintained a permanent residence, in contrast to mobile African American tenants and sharecroppers, who moved every two to three years. This generated an "abiding interest . . . in the community" where they lived (22). Thus community studies can provide tangible evidence of real and personal property accumulation and black farmer influence. Sitton and Conrad focused on such extended kinship communities in *Freedom Colonies: Independent Black Texans in the Time of Jim Crow*. They include a list of communities, not comprehensive but indicative of the scope of community formation in one southern state. For a survey of the culture that rural communities could sustain, see Valerie Grim, "African American Rural Culture in the Twentieth Century," in *Rural African Americans in the Twentieth Century*, edited by R. Douglas Hurt (Columbia: University of Missouri Press, 2003), 108–28. For studies that indicate the ways progressive reformers engaged black agricultural communities see Debra A. Reid, "African Americans, Community Building, and the Role of the State in Rural Reform in Texas, 1890s–1930s," in *The Countryside in the Age of the Modern State: Political Histories of Rural America*, edited by Catherine McNicol Stock and Robert D. Johnston (Ithaca, N.Y.: Cornell University Press, 2001), 38–65. For a social history of people and place, see Valerie Grim, "Black Farm Families in the Yazoo-Mississippi Delta: A Study of the Brooks Farm Community, 1920-1970," Ph.D. Dissertation, Iowa State University, 1990.

Historians have used another traditional anthropological approach, oral interviews, to deepen their understanding of black farm owners and their communities. Bethel's *Promiseland* indicates the benefits of taking the memories of those with firsthand experience seriously for the ways they can make the historic evidence more complete. Oral sources can document nuanced interactions between rural residents, including black farm owners. Most of this research focuses on southern farmers. See Orville Vernon Burton, "Race Relations in the Rural South since 1945," in *The Rural South since World War II*, edited by R. Douglas Hurt (Baton Rouge: Louisiana State University Press, 1998), 28–58, and Mark R. Schultz's study based on interviews with more than two hundred residents in one Georgia county, *Rural Face of White Supremacy: Beyond Jim Crow* (Urbana: University of Illinois Press, 2007).

Oral history can also yield information on gender relations among farm owning families, a history underrepresented in the written record. See Valerie Grim, "'Tryin' to Make Ends Meet': African American Women's Work in Brooks Farm, 1920–1970," in *Unrelated Kin: Race and Gender in Women's Personal Narratives*, edited by Gwendolyn Etter-Lewis and Michéle Foster (New York: Routledge, 1996), 124–40. Rebecca Sharpless explored the significance of multiethnic relations in cotton country in *Fertile Ground, Narrow Choices: Women on Texas Cotton Farms* (Chapel Hill: University of North Carolina Press, 1999). For upland southern studies see Melissa Walker, *All We Knew Was to Work: Rural Women in the Upcountry South, 1919–1941* (Baltimore: Johns Hopkins University Press, 2000), and LuAnn Jones, *Mama Learned Us to Work: Farm Women in the New South* (Chapel Hill: University of North Carolina Press, 2002). For women as farmers, see Valerie Grim, with Anne Effland and Denise Roger, "Women as Agricultural Landowners: What Do We Know about Them?" *Agricultural History* 67, no. 2 (Spring 1993): 235–61.

Studies of programs aimed at improving life for rural families usually focus on farm owners because reformers directed programs toward that constituency historically. Jim Crow legislation segregated agricultural reform programs for black families from those for whites, and the separation based on race created self-conscious documentation within government agencies such as the Federal Extension Service (FES). Agents working in all eleven former confederate states and in Kentucky, Maryland, Missouri, Oklahoma, and West Virginia targeted landowning families because the agents knew that these families could decide what to do with their own labor and land. The agents celebrated their successes in detailed county and state reports that described their work with agricultural extension, home demonstration, and youth programs such as 4-H.

Government publications consolidated the positive news drawn from annual reports into serial publications. These can provide important context for understanding black farm owners even though they present the FES perspective. Three appeared within a decade of formation of the "Negro" divisions at the state level: W. B. Mercier, *Extension Work among Negroes, 1920*, USDA Circular 190 (Washington, D.C.: Government Printing Office, 1921); James A. Evans, *Extension Work among Negroes: Conducted by Negro Agents, 1923*, USDA Circular 355 (Washington, D.C.: Government Printing Office, 1925); and O. B. Martin, *A Decade of Negro Extension Work, 1914–1924*, Miscellaneous Circular no. 72 (Washington, D.C.: USDA, 1926). Other surveys documented work during the 1930s and 1940s: Erwin H. Shinn prepared *A Survey of the Manner of Procedure Followed in Developing County Programs of Negro Extension Work in Agriculture and Home Economics*, Miscellaneous extension publication 11 (mimeographed; Washington, D.C., March 1933); and see Doxey A. Wilkerson, *Agricultural Extension Services among Negroes in the South* (Washington, D.C.: Conference of Presidents of Negro Land-Grant Colleges, 1942).

Much attention has been paid to the influence of the Tuskegee Institute—see Allen W. Jones's, "Improving Rural Life for Blacks: The Tuskegee Negro Farmers' Conference, 1892–1915," *Agricultural History* 65, no. 2 (Spring 1991): 105–14, and his "The Role of Tuskegee Institute in the Education of Black Farmers," *Journal of Negro History* 60, no. 2 (April 1975): 252–67—but less to farmer attitudes about the programs offered. Karen J. Ferguson provides a corrective to this in "Caught in 'No Man's Land': The Negro Cooperative Demonstration Service and the Ideology of Booker T. Washington, 1900–1916," *Agricultural History* 72, no. 1 (Winter 1998): 33–54, as does Gary Zellar, "H.C. Ray and Racial Politics in the African American Extension Service Program in Arkansas, 1915–1929," *Agricultural History* 72, no. 2 (Spring 1998): 429–45. George Washington Carver, the most influential agriculturalist at Tuskegee Institute, has drawn similar attention: Linda O. McMurry, *George Washington Carver: Scientist and Symbol* (New York: Oxford University Press, 1981); Gary R. Kremer, *George Washington Carver: A Biography* (New York: Greenwood, 2011); and Mark D. Hersey, *My Work Is That of Conservation: An Environmental Biography of George Washington Carver* (Athens: University of Georgia Press, 2011).

Studies of the "Negro" divisions of the state-level agricultural extension services that existed in all southern states concentrate on the programs that agricultural and home demonstration agents delivered. Studies address the racist policy that defined the lines of authority and communication within the service and the politics among agents and constituents. See the bibliographic essay in Debra A. Reid, *Reaping a Greater Harvest: African Americans, the Extension Service, and Rural Reform in Jim Crow Texas* (College Station: Texas A&M University Press, 2007). Critiques of an early extension promotional film, *Making Negroes Better Farmers* (1920), address racism. See J. Emmett Winn, "Documenting Racism in an Agricultural Extension Film," *Film and History* 38, no. 1 (Spring 2008): 33–43. Rarely, however, do scholars assess the extension service from the perspective of the farm families served. Much remains to be done to discern the attitudes farm families and rural communities had toward the service, and ultimately researchers need to assess the reasons why the comprehensive public program that existed to preserve farming failed to do so.

The farm owners who persisted did so because of their preexisting involvement in public programs. Reid, in *Reaping a Greater Harvest*, argued that owners survived because they had access to information and personal contacts that entitled them to participate in New Deal programs, but she concentrated on evidence provided by the extension service records rather than farm-level data. Other studies have concentrated on specific government agencies or services, such as Joel Schor, "The Black Presence in the U.S. Cooperative Extension Service since 1945: An American Quest for Service and Equity," *Agricultural History* 60, no. 2 (Spring 1986): 137–53; Douglas Helms, "Eroding the Color Line: The Soil Conservation Service and the Civil Rights Act of 1964," *Agricultural History* 65, no. 2 (Spring 1991): 35–53; and Valerie Grim, "Black Participation in the Farmers Home Administration and Agricultural Stabilization and Conservation Service, 1964–1990," *Agricultural History* 70, 2 (Spring 1996): 321–37, reprinted as a supplementary report in the U.S. Department of Agriculture, *Civil Rights at the United States Department of Agriculture: A Report by the Civil Rights Action Team* (Washington, D.C.: USDA, February 1997), 110–25.

Congress established the U.S. Commission on Civil Rights in 1957 to investigate complaints of civil rights infractions and submit reports addressing the problems. The commission released *Equal Opportunity in Farm Programs: An Appraisal of Service Rendered by Agencies of the U.S. Department of Agriculture* (Washington, D.C.: U.S. Government Printing Office, February 1965), and *The Decline in Black Farming in America: A Report of the United States Commission on Civil Rights* (Washington, D.C.: n.p., February 1982). Between these reports, an important private study appeared, directed by Robert S. Browne of the Black Economic Research Center, entitled *Only Six Million Acres: The Decline of Black Owned Land in the Rural South*, a report sponsored by Clark College of Atlanta, Georgia, and funded by the Rockefeller Brothers Fund (June 1973; repr., March 1975). Also, Leo McGee and Robert Boone edited *The Black Rural Landowner—Endangered Species: Social, Political and Economic Implications* (Westport, Conn.: Greenwood Press, 1979), which included an article by McGee and Boone, "Black Rural Land Ownership: A Matter of Survival," that had appeared in the *Review of Black Political Economy* 8, no. 1 (1977); 62–69, an article by Manning Marable on landownership in historic context, and a discussion of the Emergency Land Fund by Joseph Brooks.

Since the 1970s, numerous studies have emphasized the civil rights injustices that farmers, including owners, have faced: Jeannie Whayne, "Black Farmers and the Agricultural Cooperative Extension Service: The Alabama Experience, 1945–1965," *Agricultural History* 72, no. 3 (Summer 1998): 523–51; Carmen V. Harris, "'The Extension Service Is Not an Integration Agency': The Idea of Race in the Cooperative Extension Service," *Agricultural History* 82, no. 2 (Spring 2008): 193–219; Pete Daniel, "African American Farmers and Civil Rights," *Journal of Southern History* 73, no. 1 (February 2007): 3–38. Greta de Jong focuses on civil rights activism in her study *A Different Day: African American Struggles for Justice in Rural Louisiana, 1900–1970* (Chapel Hill: University of North Carolina Press, 2002), but considers farm owners in the context of larger activism. More general in nature, Charlene Gilbert and Quinn Eli focus on contemporary issues that assail black farmers in *Homecoming: The Story of African American Farmers* (Boston: Beacon Press, 2000), and Waymon R. Hinson and Edward Robinson provide a broad overview in "'We Didn't Get Nothing': The Plight of Black Farmers," *Journal of African American Studies* 12, no. 3 (2008): 283–302.

Scholars from several disciplines study black land ownership today, as do rural sociologists Jess Gilbert, Spencer D. Wood, and Gwen Sharp, in "Who Owns the Land? Agricultural Land Ownership by Race/Ethnicity," *Rural America* 17, no. 4 (Winter 2002): 56–62. Historians Valerie Grim and Anne Effland have co-written several articles on contemporary farmers, including "Experiences of Small Scale African American Farmers in the Delta Region," in *Making a Difference for America's Small Farmers and Ranchers in the Twentieth-First Century* (Washington,

D.C.: U.S. Department of Agriculture, January 2006), 95–105, and "Helping Farmers Succeed: Conversations with Small-Scale Operators in the Mississippi Delta," research findings included in *Meeting the Challenge of A Time to Act: USDA Progress and Achievements on Small Farms, 1998–1999* (Washington, D.C.: USDA, 2000). Carol Stack, an anthropologist, followed reverse migrants who left the urban North for the rural South in *Call to Home: African Americans Reclaim the Rural South* (New York: Putnam, 1996).

Several opportunities exist for scholars interested in using land ownership as the framework to gain greater understanding of African American experiences. The studies can expand temporally to the recent past and can expand topically to address discrete and hitherto understudied topics, such as non-elite property owners, crops other than cotton, and regions of the country other than the South. Scholars should engage in more comparative studies based on class or gender in addition to race. More micro-level studies of individual and family experiences in and outside of heavily black-populated cotton-producing counties must be undertaken to understand fully the breadth of black landowning farm family experiences.

Contributors

Omar H. Ali is associate professor of African American and Diaspora Studies at the University of North Carolina at Greensboro. He has written two books on the history of independent black politics: *In the Lion's Mouth: Black Populism in the New South, 1886–1900* (2010) and *In the Balance of Power* (2008), the latter named "a landmark work" by the *National Political Science Review*.

Evan P. Bennett is assistant professor of history at Florida Atlantic University and is completing a manuscript on the history of tobacco agriculture in the Old Bright Belt of the Virginia–North Carolina Piedmont.

Scott E. Casper is Dean of the College of Arts, Humanities, and Social Sciences, and Professor of History at the University of Maryland, Baltimore County. He previously taught at the Univeristy of Nevada at Reno. His books include *Sarah Johnson's Mount Vernon* (2008) and *Constructing American Lives* (1999), for which he won the book prize of the Society for the History of Authorship, Reading, and Publishing.

Valerie Grim is chairperson and professor of African American and African Diaspora Studies at Indiana University. Her articles have appeared in *Agricultural History*; *Oral History Review*; *Frontiers: A Journal of Women Studies*; *Black Women, Gender & Families*, and *Rural Development Perspectives*. Grim's "Life at Brooks Farm: Stories of African American Rural Experiences in the Yazoo-Mississippi Delta, 1910–1970," is under contract and her book-length study, "Between Forty Acres and a Class Action: Black Farmers' Protest against the United States Department of Agriculture, 1995–2010," is in progress.

Carmen V. Harris is associate professor of history at the University of South Carolina Upstate. She received the Vernon Carstensen Memorial Award from the Agricultural History Society for her article "'The Extension Service Is Not an Integration Agency': The Idea of Race in the Cooperative Extension Service," *Agricultural History* (Spring 2008).

Kelly A. Minor is adjunct assistant professor of history at Santa Fe College. She has published articles on rural women's reform programs in *Migration and the Transformation of the Southern Workplace since 1945*, edited by Robert Cassanello and Colin J. Davis (2009), and *Entering the Fray: Gender, Politics, and Culture in the New South,* edited by Jonathan Daniel Wells and Sheila R. Phipps (2010).

Adrienne Petty is assistant professor at the City College of New York (CUNY). She and Mark Schultz received a grant from the National Endowment for the Humanities for Breaking New Ground: A History of African American Farm Owners after the Civil War. The project generated hundreds of interviews with farm owners, archived in the Southern Oral History Collection at the University of North Carolina at Chapel Hill. Her book, *Standing Their Ground: Small Farmers in North Carolina since the Civil War* (2013), addresses the transformation of rural society.

Debra A. Reid is professor of history at Eastern Illinois University and adjunct professor in the College of Agricultural, Consumer, and Environmental Sciences at the University of Illinois at Champaign-Urbana. Her first book, *Reaping a Greater Harvest: African Americans, the Extension Service, and Rural Reform in Jim Crow Texas* (2007), received the T. R. Fehrenbach Award from the Texas Historical Commission.

Jarod Roll is associate professor of history at the University of Mississippi. He previously taught at the University of Sussex in England and directed the Marcus Cunliffe Centre for the Study of the American South. He is the author of *Spirit of Rebellion: Labor and Religion in the New Cotton South* (2010) which won the C. L. R. James Award and the Missouri History Book Award. Most recently he is the co-author (with Erik S. Gellman) of *The Gospel of the Working Class: Labor's New Deal Prophets* (2011).

Mark Schultz is professor of history at Lewis University and author of *The Rural Face of White Supremacy: Beyond Jim Crow* (2005). He and Adrienne Petty collaborated on Breaking New Ground: A History of African American Farm Owners after the Civil War, an ambitious oral history project documenting the rise, experience, and legacy of black farm owners in the South.

Loren Schweninger is the Elizabeth Rosenthal Excellence Professor at the University of North Carolina at Greensboro. He has written a number of scholarly articles and seven books, including *Black Property Owners in the South, 1780–1915* (1990) and with John Hope Franklin, *In Search of the Promised Land: A Slave Family in the South* (2006). Between 1991 and 2009 he served as director of the Race and Slavery Petitions Project, now online as the Digital Library on American Slavery.

Keith J. Volanto is professor of history at Collin College in Plano, Texas. He specializes in early twentieth-century U.S. and Texas history. His first book, *Texas, Cotton, and the New Deal* (2005), was a finalist for the Texas State Historical Association's Coral Horton Tullis Memorial Prize for Best Book on Texas History.

Veronica L. Womack is associate professor of political science and public administration at Georgia College and State University. Her research focuses on rural economic development and politics in the southern Black Belt. She has published an article in the *Harvard Journal of African American Public Policy* and has completed a manuscript on underdevelopment in the Black Belt which she describes as America's Third World.

Index

Page locators with t indicate tables, f indicate figure captions, m indicate map captions

Abolition debates, 158–59
Accotink village, Virginia, 42
Activism, 1, 91, 249; political, 9, 11, 14, 207, 231, 232, 245–48, 273
ADR Associates, 283
Africa, 134
African American associations, 52, 55, 113, 127n10, 281; building, 47; support Black Populism, 109, 110. *See also* Association for the Advancement of Negro Country Life (AANCL)
African American businesses and business owners, 7, 28, 39, 55; clubs, 39; financial institutions, 84, 112, 139, 184, 188; middle or professional class, 29, 45, 99; trades and tradesmen, 39, 55
African American death rate in Florida (1939), 221
African American fraternal and civic organizations, support of, 93, 139, 214. *See also* "Afro-Americans"
African American name lists as research tool, 303–4
African Americans: living conditions of, 146–47; physical health of, 146, 221–22, 232
African American settlements. *See* Communities settled by African Americans
African American women club leaders: goals differ from national/state objectives, 207, 209, 211, 214–15, 219, 226n6; status and influence, 206–7, 209, 214, 219–24; tenure of, 220–21, 223
African Methodist Episcopal church, 56, 110, 116, 139, 195, 256
Afro-American (newspaper), 243
Afro-American Farmers Alliance, 125. *See also* Colored Alliance
"Afro-Americans" (fraternal organization), 139
Agrarianism, Jeffersonian, 6–7, 84, 92, 163–64, 166–68, 310. *See also* Idealism, rural
Agribusiness, 86, 289
Agricultural Adjustment Act (AAA), 143, 145, 146, 148, 196, 272; Cotton Section, 148; failed tenant farmers, 196
Agricultural Adjustment Administration (AAA), 75, 92
Agricultural Conservation Program, 293n18
Agricultural extension agents, 92, 100, 185, 187–90, 196, 206; African American, 15, 74, 86, 95–96, 97, 102n7, 139, 189, 193, 195, 196, 206, 208, 214, 245, 256–57, 261–62, 264, 268n12; fired, 264; Florida structure of, 14, 206, 213, 219; government publications of, 312; lack of civil rights activism by, 261–62; petition for replacement, 264; provide little help, 272, 274, 286, 312; reports, 185, 187, 188, 189–90, 193, 195–96, 210, 214; target land-owning families, 312; transferred, 264; white, 86, 92, 188, 193, 208, 209, 255. *See also* Home demonstration agents
Agricultural extension services, 273; segregated, 312, 313; studies of, 312, 313. *See also specific state services*
Agricultural History Society, 4
Agricultural programs: debt forgiveness, 276, 281, 283, 287–88; decline of use by African Americans, 275; federal assistance and subsidy, 92, 96, 99–100, 105n42, 141–43, 145–46, 196, 247, 273–74, 279, 282, 293n18, 313; federal crop reduction, 75, 143, 146, 148, 183, 196–99, 259, 264; federal tobacco, 183, 197–99; racism found in, 30, 92, 141–42, 146–47, 166, 198–99, 206, 207, 211, 225, 257, 259, 263–64, 271–75, 277–78; use of by African Americans lagging, 289–90
Agricultural Stabilization and Conservation Service (ASCS), 247–48, 259, 263, 272, 273–74, 275
Agricultural Workers Union, 245
Agriculture: cash crop, 231, 232, 255, 272 (*see also* Cotton: as cash crop; Tobacco: as a cash crop; Wheat: as a cash crop); centralization, 149; depression, 29, 84; diversified, 12, 71, 74, 77, 138, 156–57, 159, 168–72, 193, 255, 280, 289; Golden Age of, 167; one crop production, 30, 168, 198, 263; scientific, 84–85, 86, 87, 91, 94, 96, 99–100, 111, 113, 147, 272, 273, 278, 290. *See also* Plantation agriculture

Agriculture—*continued*
—African American: economic viability of, 28, 39, 47, 84, 85, 159, 169, 276, 290; future survival strategies of, 289–91; household production/consumption through, 48, 57, 71, 74, 90, 94, 137, 143, 168, 207, 210t, 220; multi-generational family farms, 3, 63; viability threatened, 259, 281, 272, 274–75
Alabama, 79n6; Constitutional Convention of 1901, 237–38, 246, 247; farms in (1930), 235–36; state legislature, 250n12; studies of, 23. *See also* Black Belt: Alabama
Alabama Agricultural Extension Service, 84, 245; Negro Division, 87, 245
Alabama Colored Agricultural Wheel. *See* Colored Agricultural Wheels: Alabama state
Alabama Polytechnic Institute, 244–45
Alachua County, Florida, 216, 222
Alamance County, North Carolina: extension agent report, 193; rates of African American land ownership (1900–1950), 186t
Albany, Georgia, 294n25
Alexander, Sandy, 45, 47; farm location of, 46m
Alexandria, Virginia, 39–40, 42–43, 45, 51, 54–55, 56–57; Cameron Street, 55; as a commercial center, 54, 57; court, 51, 55; hub of slave trade, 40; markets, 55
Alfred Street Baptist Church (Alexandria, Virginia), 39, 54–55
Ali, Omar H., 11
All-black communities. *See* Communities settled by African Americans
Allen, Blanche Washington, 66
Allen, J. W., 115
Alliance Advocate, 112, 118, 127n18, 129n45
American Country Life Association, 86, 93
American Federation of Labor, 245
American Indians. *See* Native Americans
American Tobacco Company, 188
Anderson, Ethel, 220–21, 223, 225
Anderson, Raymond, 264–65
Anti-African American organizations, 282–83. *See also* Ku Klux Klan
Anti-slavery, 158–59
Arkansas, 123, 163, 175n7; drought of 1930–31 affects, 141; state assembly, 124,
Arkansas Colored Agricultural Wheel. *See* Colored Agricultural Wheels: Arkansas state
Artwork, 47
Ashville, Alabama, 8f, 9
Asians, 277
Associated Negro Press (ANP), 307
Associated Press, 2
Association for the Advancement of Negro Country Life (AANCL), 85, 87, 93, 100, 101n4; 1929 pamphlet, 93
Atlanta, Georgia, 95; protests in, 279
Atlanta Baptist College, 86. *See also* Morehouse College
Atlanta Journal, 97
Auburn University. *See* Alabama Polytechnic Institute
Auction: public, 275; tobacco, 188, 189, 191, 192f, 193
Augusta, Georgia, 5, 95
Austin, Texas, 63, 73
Austin Hotel, 73, 81n21
Automobiles, 76; accident, 76, 82nn28,29; sale of, 94

Bachmann, Michele, 288
Bailey, John, 47, 48, 55–56; family of, 54
Bailey, Louisa, 47, 48, 50–52, 55, 56, 60n19, 62n28; family of, 50, 52
Bakersville, Virginia, 1
Ballard, Rosa, 222–23
Ballenger, Charles, 43
Baltimore, Maryland, 39
Bankhead Act, 146
Baptism, 54, 116
Baptist, 110, 116
Baptist Pilot, 129n45
Barbour County, Alabama: African American agricultural workers (1930), 241t; African American farm owners, tenants, and sharecroppers (1930), 237t; farms in (1930), 236t; farms under African American operation (1930), 236t
Barns, 168; dairy, 96; livestock, 194f. *See also* Tobacco: barn
Beaufort, South Carolina, 134
Beautification, house and yard, 98, 218, 219f
Belzoni, Mississippi, 294n25
Bember, Bennie, 136–37
Bennett, Evan P., 2, 7, 26–27, 57n1
Berries, picking, 28
Bethlehem Baptist Church (Gum Springs, Virginia), 42, 47, 54–55, 56–57, 62n29; cemetery, 55–56
Bethune, Mary McLeod, 93
Biblical rhetoric, 136–38, 142, 144
Birmingham, Alabama, 241, 243
Black, Bill, 171, 178n27
Black Belt, 181, 235; African American farm owners, tenants, and sharecroppers (1930), 237t; Alabama, 14–15, 64, 231–32, 234; Alabama African American agriculture workers (1930), 241t; Alabama African American

farm owners, tenants, and sharecroppers (1930); definition, 250n6; farms by Alabama county (1930), 236t; farms by Alabama county under African American operation (1930), 236t; political-geographic area of, 231, 232, 251n22
"Black capitalism," 248
Black Caucus, 291, 295n39
Black Codes: of Alabama, 250n6; in Black Belt, 233, 238; of Illinois, 155, 156; of Indiana, 156; of Mississippi, 250n6; of Ohio, 156
"Black Eagle, the," 125
Black Economic Research Center, 2, 276
Black Farmers and Agriculturalists Association (BFAA), 1, 280, 281, 285, 292n5, 294n30
Black Muslims, 15, 231, 248. See also Nation of Islam (NOI)
Black Nationalism: ideology of, 231–32, 244; precursor to Black Power, 231–32. See also Communities settled by African Americans; Garveyism; Separatism
Black Panther Party, 247; of Lowndes County, 247, 254
Black Populism, 22, 137; as an activity, 115; distinct from white populism, 11, 109, 115, 121–22; longevity of, 109
Black Power, 4; adaptable ideology of, 232–33, 246–47, 249; origins of, 231–32; power theories related to, 232–33, 244, 248; strategies, 231, 233, 238, 240, 242, 244, 246, 248
Black Power (Carmichael and Hamilton), 233
Black Property Owners in the South, 1790–1915 (Schweninger), 5
"Black Republicans," 115
Blacksmith/blacksmithing, 58n9, 91, 103n24
Blakemon, L. A., 259
Bloomington, Wisconsin, 155
Blue Ridge Mountains, 184, 187
Blytheville, Arkansas, 136, 138
Bolivar County, Mississippi, 135, 142
Boll weevil, 88, 93, 100, 240
Bonhomme Township, Missouri, 170–72
Booker T. Washington Park (Limestone County, Texas), 75
Boutwell, George S., 130n55
"Boutwell Report," 130n55
Boycotts, 112, 118–19
Boyd, John, Jr., 1, 198, 280, 294n30
Boydton, Virginia, 127n18
Boyed, Harry, 169, 178n24; family of, 169
Bradfordville, Florida, 215
Brick works, 43
Briggs, Eliza, 15
Briggs, Harry, Sr., and family, 15, 254, 256. See *also* Courts and lawsuits: *Harry Briggs et al. v. Elliot et al.*
Brown, Clarence, 50–51, 53, 55
Brown, Florence (née Ford), 39–40, 48, 50–55; family of, 50–52, 54; marriage license of, 49f
Brown, Linwood, 198
Brown, Lovelace, 45, 52
Brown, Ulysses, 45, 52
Brown, Wilbert P., 39–40, 42, 47–48, 50–55, 56, 62n28; family of, 50–52, 54; marriage licenses of, 49f
Browne, Robert, 2, 276; *Only Six Million Acres*, 2
Brownsville, Texas, 294n25
Brown v. Board of Education. See Courts and lawsuits: *Brown v. Board of Education of Topeka Kansas*
Bruce, Philip A., 6–7
Brunswick County, Virginia: percentage change of improved farm acreage (1860–1920), 201n12t; percentage change of owner or tenant operated farms (1880–1920), 201n12t; percentage change of total farms (1860–1920), 201n12t; rates of African American land ownership (1900–1950), 186t
Buffalo soldiers, 165
Butler County, Alabama: African American agricultural workers (1930), 241t; African American farm owners, tenants, and sharecroppers (1930), 237t; farms in (1930), 236t; farms under African American operation (1930), 236t
Butler Springs, Alabama, 12, 13f
Butterfield, Kenyon L., 86, 91–92, 93; promotes country life, 86, 98. See also American Country Life Association; Country Life Movement
Byers, Mrs. J. Clinton, 75
Bynum, Mollie, 136
Byram, Rev. B. W., 142

Cain, Rev. E. D., 141
Calhoun Colored School, 239
Camilla-Zach Log Cabin Center, 97f
Campbell, Thomas, 84
Campbell County, Virginia, rates of African American land ownership (1900–1950), 186t
Camp Hill, Alabama, 242, 244
Canaday, Neil, 6, 26
Canning, 71, 74, 91, 205, 207, 208f, 210f
Canning plant (cooperative), 96
Capital, lack of, 10, 112, 114
Capitalism, 7, 15, 92, 241, 243, 244–45. See also "Black capitalism"
"Caravan to Washington," 2

Caregiving, 208
Carmichael, Stokely, 233, 242, 244, 246, 247; *Black Power*, 233
Carondelet Township, Missouri, 169
Carothers, Andrew J., 114
Carr, North Carolina, 181f, 194f
Carriages, 70, 71t
Carter, L. C., 12, 13f
Carter, J. W., 121
Carver, George Washington, 239, 313
Cash tenants. *See* Farmers/farm operators (tenants): Cash tenants
Caskets, 75
Casper, Scott E., 10
Caswell County, North Carolina: farmers develop curing bright tobacco, 188; percentage change of improved farm acreage (1860–1920), 201n12t; percentage change of owner or tenant operated farms (1880–1920), 201n12t; percentage change of total farms (1860–1920), 201n12t; rates of African American land ownership (1900–1950), 186t
Cattle, 45, 70–71, 71t, 74, 168; dairy, 45, 95, 172; ranching, 77, 165, 305; slaughter, 75
Caucasian, 122
Cedar Grove Township, Orange County, North Carolina, 179–81, 191, 194; African American farm ownership in, 179–82
Cemeteries: church, 47, 55–56; family, 47
Census, 63, 184; enumerators, 39, 40, 57, 169, 172, 182; of 1850, 129n38; of 1860 (Slave Schedule), 78n3; of 1870, 42, 63, 79n4, 80n12, 128n37, 173n1, 297; of 1870 lists freedpeople, 65; of 1880, 43, 67–68, 128n36, 297; of 1900, 43; of 1910, 39, 47, 176n13; of 1920, 56, 176n13; of 1930, 57, 182, 240. *See also* Census of Agriculture
Census of Agriculture, 175n11, 305; of 1870; of 1880, 65, 297; problems with, 31; of 2002, 183; of 2007, 183
Chamberlain, John, 246
Chapel Hill, North Carolina, 179
Charleston, Missouri, 145, 148
Charleston, South Carolina, 114, 123
Charlotte County, Virginia: extension agent report, 195; marketing cooperative in, 195; percentage change of improved farm acreage (1860–1920), 201n12t; percentage change of owner or tenant operated farms (1880–1920), 201n12t; percentage change of total farms (1860–1920), 201n12t; rates of African American land ownership (1900–1950), 186t

Chatham County, North Carolina: percentage change of improved farm acreage (1860–1920), 201n14, 202n14t; percentage change of owner or tenant operated farms (1880–1920), 201n14, 202n14t; percentage change of total farms (1860–1920), 201n14, 202n14t; rates of African American land ownership (1900–1950), 186t
Chemicals, 274
Cherokee County Council of Farm Women, 264
Chesapeake region: colonial planting of wheat in, 158–59; tobacco fields of, 190
Chicago, Illinois, 140, 167; markets, 171; protests in, 279
Chicago Defender, 138
Chicago Tribune, 163–64
Chicken houses (cooperative), 95, 96
Chickens, 51, 74, 94–95, 168, 260
Child care and rearing, 50–51, 53, 55, 205, 208, 218; by grandmother, 40; child abuse, 73; child support, 51–52
Chinn, J. L., 139
Choctaw County, Alabama: African American agricultural workers (1930), 241t; African American farm owners, tenants, and sharecroppers (1930), 237t; farms in (1930), 236t; farms under African American operation (1930), 236t
Christian piety, 86
Churches: African American, 44, 52, 55, 222, 279; as cultural center, 86, 194; dues, 50; elder of, 194–95; leadership learned in, 116, 256; at Log Cabin Community, 85; notified of *Pigford v. Glickman*, 281; repaired by home extension clubs, 215; support civil rights and desegregation, 260–61, 266; support through, 93, 109, 110–11, 112, 214. *See also specific churches, denominations*
Cigarettes, 182; manufacturers, 188
Citizenship, denial of, 22
"City View" farm (near Gum Springs, Virginia), 43
Civil rights, 141, 145, 147, 232, 240–41, 246, 248, 291; legislation, 254, 263, 275 (*see also* Civil Rights Act of 1957; Civil Rights Act of 1964); petitions, 255, 257–61; protests, 245, 277, 279; studies of, 314; supported from African American landless and land owners, 246–47, 272; violated, 15–16, 114, 120–21, 274, 277, 278, 280, 285, 314; workers, 243, 245, 254, 258, 286
Civil Rights Action Team (CRAT), 277–78,

279; recommendations, 289–91; report, 278, 279, 291
Civil Rights Act of 1957, 273–74
Civil Rights Act of 1964, 2, 15, 248, 272, 274; Title VI, 264
Civil Rights Leadership Council, 274
Civil Rights Policy Analysis and Coordination Center, 274
Civil War: African American migration before, 64, 157; change of land tenure after, 184; veterans, 155
Clarendon County, South Carolina: African American majority in, 255–56; African Americans take lead in civil rights effort, 255, 256–58, 261, 267; extension agent report, 255, 257; rural civil rights activism, 15
Clarendon County Improvement Association (CCIA), 257, 260; financial support provided to, 259, 260, 269n20; formed as purchasing cooperative, 258
Clarendon Memorial Hospital, 259
Clark, Irie Mae, 217–18
Clark College, 276
Clarke County, Alabama: African American agricultural workers (1930), 241t; African American farm owners, tenants, and sharecroppers (1930), 237t; farms in (1930), 236t; farms under African American operation (1930), 236t
Class, African American middle or professional, 29, 99, 162–63
Clayton, Joseph Elward, 167, 308
Clayton, Missouri, 171
Clemson University, 264
Cleveland Gazette, 123, 125
Clinton, Bill, 277, 282, 284
Clinton, Mississippi, 119, 129n54
Clothes, 50, 71, 217, 220, 261; overalls, 50; shoes, 50
Cobb, Cully, 148
Cobb, James, 272
Cobb, Phoebe, 112
College: African American produce sold to, 96; degrees, 98; farms, 90. *See also specific colleges*
Colored Agricultural Wheels: Alabama state, 115; Arkansas state, 124; work with the Colored Alliance, 110
Colored Alliance, 127n18
Colored Alliance: activities of, 110–11, 113, 120–21, 125, 126; Alabama chapter, 114, 115; Arkansas chapter, 114; attacks against, 119; attempts to create cooperative exchanges, 114; class differences within, 113, 115, 121–22; collapse of, 124, 125; conventions of, 114, 118, 120, 125, 128n23; cooperation with white alliances, 118, 125; Cotton Pickers League off-shoot of, 120; covert actions of, 111; Florida chapter, 125; founding of, 109–10, 114; Garveyism unaligned with, 135, 137; general superintendent of, 111, 113; Georgia chapter, 114, 121, 124, 125; initial purpose of, 109–10, 112, 113–14, 121; Kentucky chapter, 114; lecturers of, 114, 118, 121, 125; legacy of, 124–26; Louisiana chapter, 114; membership numbers of, 1, 109–10, 112, 114, 118; merger with National Colored Alliance, 114; Mississippi chapter, 114, 130n57; newspapers, 112, 124, 127n18, 128n23; North Carolina chapter, 114, 115, 116, 118, 127n18; offices of, 110, 111, 115; organizational structure of, 110, 111–12, 114–15, 120; parade of force, 119; presidents of, 110, 114, 118, 121; promotes agrarian reform, 109–10, 111, 118, 124, 126, 145; rallies of, 112; rituals of, 111; secretaries of, 110, 114; South Carolina chapter, 114, 125; strategic differences within, 113, 121, 124; superintendents of, 115, 125, 127n18; Tennessee chapter, 114; Texas chapter, 112, 114, 125; trustees of, 110; Virginia chapter, 114, 115, 127n18; white organizers in, 109, 110, 113, 115, 118; white resistance to, 111, 112–13, 119; women leaders in, 112
Colored Civic League, 139
Colored Farmers Alliance. *See* Colored Alliance
Colored Farmers Association, 110–11
Colored Farmers Home Improvement Lodge, 110–11
Colored Farmers National Alliance and Co-Operative Union, 109, 114. *See also* Colored Alliance
Colored Homestead Companies, 112
Colored Orphanage Asylum, 117
Colored State Fair Association, 87
Columbia, Tennessee, 172f
Comanche Crossing (Limestone County, Texas), 75
Commodity prices, 143; low, 91, 117, 121, 138, 140
Commonwealth, 142
Communist Party, 146, 232, 245, 246; anticommunist reaction to, 242–45; helps organize the SCU, 241–42, 244; literature and publications, 242; opposes Black Nationalism, 241; recognizes Black Belt as

Communist Party—*continued*
  independent nation, 240; recruitment, 15, 242–43; Second Congress of the Comintern, 240; Sixth World Congress of the Communist International, 240; taking advantage of sharecroppers, 244, 245
Communities settled by African Americans, 6–7, 165, 166, 231, 233, 308; Arkansas, 167; called for, 136, 145, 165; Calvert Township, Michigan, 304; Gum Springs, Virginia, 39, 42–45, 46m, 48, 50, 53–57, 59–60n14, 62n29; Hobson City, Alabama, 238–39; Illinois, 158; Indiana, 158, 304; James City, North Carolina, 118; Langston City, Oklahoma, 165; laws forbidding, 233, 238, 250n6; leaders of, 39, 45, 92; Louisiana, 299; Mason Neck, Virginia, 44; Michigan, 158; Mississippi, 167; Missouri, 138; Mound Bayou, Mississippi, 135, 137, 140, 142–43; Nicodemus, Kansas, 164; Ohio, 158; Oklahoma, 134, 238; planned, 143; Promised Land, South Carolina, 301; Spring Bank, Virginia, 43–45, 48, 54–57; studies of, 27, 303–4; supported through philanthropic efforts, 86, 87, 93, 96, 97, 99–100, 105n42, 222, 239; Texas, 27–28, 134, 238; Tillery, North Carolina, 1, 273, 292n5. *See also* Log Cabin Community
Composting, 212
Concerned Black Farmers of Tennessee, Arkansas, Mississippi, Georgia, and North Carolina, 281
Conecuh County, Alabama: African American agricultural workers (1930), 241t; African American farm owners, tenants, and sharecroppers (1930), 237t; farms in (1930), 236t; farms under African American operation (1930), 236t
Confederate States of America, 175n7; veterans, 113, 114
Conquest, The (Micheaux), 167, 177n21
Conrad, James H., *Freedom Colonies*, 27; study of communities settled by African Americans, 27–28
Contracts: land conservation, 276; landowner/tenant, 233–34
Convict-lease system, 111
Coolidge, Texas, 63, 75–77, 82n29
Coolidge Herald, 75
Cooperatives, 21, 86, 94, 99–100, 308; canning plant, 96; chicken houses, 95, 96; corn mill, 96; creamery, 96; exchanges, 112, 114, 118, 127n10; gas station, 96; health clinics, 96 (*see also* Mary Otis Willcox Health Clinic); land, 84, 85–86, 91, 94–99, 127n10; marketing, 74, 84, 113, 132, 138–40, 142, 147, 166, 167, 195, 289; poultry plant, 95; purchasing, 84, 86, 132, 138–40, 142, 167, 258; recreation centers, 96, 97, 97f, 98; saw mill, 96; storehouses, 127n10; stores, 90, 96, 113, 119–20, 124; sweet potato curing plant, 96; wheat mill, 96
Cooperative Workers of America: South Carolina state, 115; work with the Colored Alliance, 110
Coordinating Council of Black Farm Groups, 281
Corbett, Bedford, 195
Corbett, Benjamin, 180, 197
Corbett, Charlie, 180
Corbett, Doc, 179–80, 182, 190, 191, 197, 199; family of, 182, 183, 197; farm of, 194f; as model African American farmer, 180, 193–94
Corbett, Richard, 180, 184, 194
Corbett, Teash, 180, 184, 194
Corn laws, 159
Corn mill (cooperative), 96
Cotton, 3, 64, 259; allotment, 75, 146, 264; bales of, 12, 13f, 68; as cash crop, 12, 71, 74, 263; farmer, 12, 27, 70, 113, 181, 242, 265; farms, 76, 109, 122f, 122–23, 158, 257–58; gin owner, 124, 260; not grown in St. Louis area, 169; pickers/picking, 68, 74, 111, 113, 121–23, 122f, 145, 240; plantations, 24, 25, 123; prices, 88, 94, 121; production, 26, 68, 93–94, 119, 137, 146, 168; reduced through federal program, 75; supplanted by tobacco, 185. *See also* Cotton Belt; Cotton South
Cotton Belt, 119, 121, 123, 235; southwest, 134. *See also* Cotton South
Cotton Farmer, 137
Cotton Pickers' League, 121–24
Cotton South, 181, 231, 305. *See also* Cotton Belt
Country Life Commission, 86, 167
Country Life Movement, 85, 92, 98
Courses, to disseminate scientific agriculture, 93
Courts and lawsuits: against USDA, 2, 198–99, 280; *Brown II*, 15, 258, 263; *Brown v. Board of Education of Topeka Kansas*, 15, 175n11, 254, 258, 261, 264; *Brown vs. Brown*, 52–54, 60nn17,19; *Cecile Brewington et al. v. Dan Glickman, Secretary, U.S. Department of Agriculture*, 280, 282; circuit court office, 55; class action, 32, 256, 280–89, 291; *Cobell*, 286, 288; county court, 164; court clerk, 39; distrust of, 302; divorce and proceedings, 50–56, 60nn17,18,19; federal district, 105n44; *Garcia*,

289, 296n61; *Gillespie v. Palmer*, 156; *Green*, 289, 296n61; *Harry Briggs et al. v. Elliot et al.*, 15, 254–55, 256–58, 260, 263; *James Pearson, an infant, by Levi Pearson, his next friend and Levi Pearson v. County Board of Education for Clarendon County, et al.*, 256–58; judges, 55, 155, 164, 176n17, 198; jurors, 50–52, 120, 279, 286; *Keepseagle*, 289, 296n61; lawyers, 21, 50–53, 55, 60n19, 258, 280, 282, 283, 284; legal defense, 52; *Love*, 289, 296n61; *Plessy v. Ferguson*, 263; U.S. Court of the District of Columbia (DDC), 280; U.S. District Court, 289; U.S. Supreme Court, 15, 258, 263. See also *Pigford II*; *Pigford v. Glickman*
Crates, citrus packing, 217
Craven County, North Carolina, 118, 129n47
Crawford, Lecturer, 124
Creamery (cooperative), 96
Credit, 181; access to, 95, 114; available, 184, 188; denied, 94, 257, 259, 269n20; eschewed, 137; programs, 112, 261, 289–90; seasonal, 188. See also Farm loans
Credit unions, 188. See also African American businesses and business owners: financial institutions
Crenshaw County, Alabama: African American agricultural workers (1930), 241t; African American farm owners, tenants, and sharecroppers (1930), 237t; farms in (1930), 236t; farms under African American operation (1930), 236t
Crisis, 242, 244
Crisp, Eddie, 180
Crisp, Lacy, 197, 204n50
Crisp, Wesley, 179–80, 197, 204n50; family of, 182, 183, 204n50; farm of, 181f
Cromwell, Oliver (African American farmer), 118–19, 129nn52,54
Crop culture, 12–14, 156, 186, 190, 305–6
Crop liens, 3, 181, 182, 188, 231, 234
Crops: apples, 169; beets, 172; berries, 96; cabbage, 172; corn, 71, 74, 94, 159, 168, 170, 172, 173, 265; cow peas, 94; fruit, 95, 96, 272 (*see also* Trees: fruit); grain, 42; grapes, 172; hay, 74, 77, 159, 163, 169, 194f; Indian corn, 169; Irish potatoes, 172; lettuce, 172; melons, 140; oats, 172; okra, 172, 212f; peas, 74, 172; potatoes, 94, 169, 304; produce, 45, 52, 207; rice, 25; rotted, 257, 259, 260, 268n13; soybeans, 265; straw, 168; sugar cane, 26, 75; sweet potatoes, 96; vegetables, 3, 75, 95, 96, 168, 172, 211, 272, 289 (*see also* Gardens); velvet beans, 94. See also Cotton; Tobacco; Wheat

Cultural hearth theory, 158
Cunningham, Bennie, 265

Dairying, 45, 54; barn, 96; butter, 45, 71, 172; cheese, 45; cream, 94–95, 96, 172; milk, 45, 52, 54, 172; milk crocks and cans, 45
Dallas, Texas, 81n18, 127n18
Dallas County, Alabama, 234; African American agricultural workers (1930), 241t; African American farm owners, tenants, and sharecroppers (1930), 237t; civil rights work in, 245; farms in (1930), 236t; farms under African American operation (1930), 236t
Dances, 191
Daniel, Pete, 30, 198, 273
Danville, Virginia, 184
Darmstadt, 169
Davidson County, North Carolina: percentage change of improved farm acreage (1860–1920), 201n14, 202n14t; percentage change of owner or tenant operated farms (1880–1920), 201n14, 202n14t; percentage change of total farms (1860–1920), 201n14, 202n14t; rates of African American land ownership (1900–1950), 186t
Davis, J. P., president of NFCF, 141, 143
Dean, J. R., 8–9, 8f
Debt, farm, 29, 92, 117, 139–40, 235, 239, 255, 279; forgiveness, 276, 281, 283, 287–88
"Debt for Nature," 276. See also U.S. Department of Agriculture (USDA): debt relief program of
Deep Souths (Harris), 6
de Jong, Greta, 57n1
Delaine, Rev. Joseph, 15, 258
Delaware, studies of, 23
Democratic Party, 22, 115, 120, 124; anti-, 285; disaffected members of, 125; modify Jeffersonian agrarian ideal, 6; monopoly on Southern politics, 109, 120, 126
Demonstrations to disseminate scientific agriculture, 84
Desegregation. See Schools: desegregation
Detroit, Michigan, protests in, 279
Dial, J. M., 119
Dial, Jack, 119
Dillingham, Mabel W., 239
Dillingham, Rev. Pitt, 239
Diseases and illnesses: appendicitis, 73; diphtheria, 221; hookworm, 221–22; malaria, 221; pneumonia, 72; smallpox, 221; typhoid, 221

328 · Index

Disfranchisement, 9, 22, 238. *See also* Suffrage, African American
DNA analysis, 64, 67, 79n7
Domestic work, 48, 51; basket weaving, 28; cooking, 48, 71; laundry, 48, 71; sewing, 28
Dougherty County, Georgia, 181
Douglass, Frederick, 166
Draft animals, 94, 171
Driskill Hotel, 81n21
Drought of 1930–31, 141
Dual tenure, 28, 74, 121, 187, 190, 193
Du Bois, W. E. B., 2, 5, 101n2, 181, 250n8, 262; critical of communist union efforts, 244; incremental approach to land ownership, 8, 162; land ownership obstacles indentify by, 234–36; notes class differences in Farmville, Virginia, 7, 162; *Souls of Black Folk, The*, 181
Duncan, L. N., 245
Dunlap, Kansas, 164, 165f, 176n18
Durant, Mississippi, 119
Durham, North Carolina, 188; tobacco auction house, 191, 192f
Durham County, North Carolina: extension agent report, 196; rates of African American land ownership (1900–1950), 186t
Duval County, Florida, 210f, 220, 223, 224

Earle, Carville, 157
East Dubuque, Iowa, 155
Ebony, 291
Economic: dependence, 232, 313; exploitation, 27, 231, 241; exploitation by white landlords, 233–34; mobility, 134, 189; opportunities, 27, 40, 114, 193–94, 302; opportunities through ease of transportation, 54, 64, 164; retaliation, 15, 256–61, 263; rights, 32, 147, 240
"Economic Status of the Negro, The," 99
Education, 290; financial support of, 256; industrial, 90, 103n4, 239; political, 136; poor, 232; promoted, 84, 86, 96, 98, 239, 242; regressive, 91, 103n24; technical, 84, 264; trade, 90–91. *See also* Schools; *specific schools; specific colleges*
Education of Booker T. Washington, The (West), 22
Edwards, R. C., 264–65
Edwardsville, Kansas, 304
Eggs, 95, 169
Electric light company, 57; linesman, 57
Electrification, 75, 189
Elites, 26
—African American: within NFCF, 139; within rural Garveyism, 134
—White: allied with Democratic Party, 120; benefit from federal programs, 92, 146, 157, 183, 234, 271, 273–75; control federal programs, 92, 166, 196–99, 233–34, 237–38, 247, 273, 276–77; power to assist or thwart African American aspirations, 27, 84, 133, 143, 163, 181, 248, 255; reaction to NFCF, 141–43; suppress violence; 85–86
Elliott, R. W., 257. *See also* Courts and lawsuits: *Harry Briggs et al. v. Elliot et al.*
Ellis County, Texas, 68–69
Ellison, Currie, 195
Elloree Community, Orangeburg County, South Carolina, civil rights efforts by, 15, 258–61, 263, 264, 267
Ellzey, Jef, 140–41
Ellzey, Jessie, 141
Ely, Melvin, 7; *Israel on the Appomattox*, 7
Emancipation Proclamation, 39. *See also* Juneteenth
Emergency Land Fund (ELF), 2, 276, 302, 314
Eminent domain, 2
Endangered species, 276
Engdahl, J. Louis, 243
Enterprising Southerners (Kenzer), 28
Environmental Working Group (EWG), 16n2, 280
Equal Opportunity in Farm Programs, 273
Erby, Adaline, 66
Erby, Cynthia, 66
Erby, Eli, 66, 80n12. *See also* Lillie, Eli
Escambia County, Alabama: African American agricultural workers (1930), 241t; African American farm owners, tenants, and sharecroppers (1930), 237t
Exodusters, 83, 164–65, 304

Factories, 141, 248; tobacco, 188
Fairfax County, Virginia, 39, 43, 45, 54; chancery commissioner, 51; chancery court, 51, 57n1; circuit court, 55; court clerk, 39; district of, 43
Fairs, 86; to disseminate scientific agriculture, 84. *See also* Colored State Fair Association
Farm: capital intensive, 159, 301, 305; foreclosures, 145, 275, 278, 282; mechanization, 92, 95, 103n24, 149, 159, 171–72, 182, 196, 261; percent managed by African Americans by Midwest state or region (1900), 160–61t; percent tenant operated by Midwest state or region (1900), 160–61t; value by Midwest state or region (1900), 160–61t
Farm agent. *See* Agricultural extension agents; Home demonstration agents
Farm Bill of 2008, 286

Farm Credit Administration (FCA), 145, 146
Farm equipment and tools, 239; binders, 172f; combine, 260; comparison of value per farm by state (1930), 95; cotton gin, 94; harvester, 257, 260; kerosene tractor, 172f; lack of, 48, 95; plows and harrows, 45; reaper, 156, 159, 164, 171, 174n3; thresher, 96; tractors, 96, 103n24; wagons, 47, 55, 94, 116, 194f. *See also* McCormick reaper
Farmers/farm operators: census obfuscation, 31 (*see also* Census of Agriculture, problems with); common values, 133 (*see also* Producerism); effect of class, 21, 26, 92; effect of race, 5–6, 10, 23–24, 28, 29–30, 31–32, 163, 166; land use/crop culture, 25–26, 159, 168–69, 182, 189–91, 193; similarity despite race, 5–6, 12, 156, 171, 188, 305; size of acreage/operation, 21, 92, 121, 133, 185, 197, 275, 279
—African Americans as: agricultural diversification used by, 74, 77, 159, 280; in Alabama (1930), 236–37; in Alabama Black Belt counties (1930), 236t; alternative use of land run by, 289; dependency on whites, 237; federal programs not attuned to, 272–73; growth within the Orange County, North Carolina, 180; as hobby, 305; Hubert lays out goals for, 96; market woman, 40, 52, 55; multi-generational, 63; as percentage of colored farmers in U.S. and the South, 239, 250n11; revolts, 306; in San Jacinto County, Texas, 64, 74, 77; small holdings of, 272; syrup producing, 75; tobacco grown by, 180, 183; women, 39–40, 43–44, 47, 134, 194
—Whites as, 156; decline in number, 276; farmed much of Mount Vernon area, 57; in Limestone County, Texas, 71
—Women as, 183, 264, 312; discrimination against, 275, 277; lawsuits by, 289; property inheritance, 45; white tenants, 179
Farmers/farm operators (owners): racism affecting ownership, 23–24, 29–30, 156–57, 164; role of elites, 27; size of farms, 23–25, 31. *See also* Farmers/farm operators; Elites; Landowners
—African Americans as: 184–85, 187, 235, 250n8, 273, 289; agricultural extension agents targeting, 312; children attending college, 86, 98, 99, 102n7, 180, 195; discrimination against, 2, 22, 26, 85, 182–83, 198–99, 259, 263–64 (*See also* U.S. Department of Agriculture [USDA]: discrimination of African American by); historical invisibility of, 3–4, 7, 29, 84–85, 183, 291, 297; home demonstration agents targeting, 207, 209, 312; in contrast to landless, 4; independence, 29–30, 92, 155–56, 168 (*See also* Separatism); status/leaders, 4, 5–6, 163–64; stereotypes of, 29, 83, 133, 182, 183, 189; in U.S. (1900), 235; in U.S. (1910), 272; in U.S. (1920), 272; in U.S. (1992), 272; submissive behavior, 27
—Whites as: rate of farm ownership by region (1900), 159, 162
Farmers/farm operators (sharecroppers), African American: abandon SCU, 245; with African American landlords, 74, 76, 180; in Alabama (1900), 235; in Alabama Black Belt (1930), 237t; crop reduction program effect on, 146, 147; crops seized, 261; disenfranchised, 238; evicted, 247; factor in civil rights movement, 231, 239; flight to urban life, 301; growth with tobacco crop, 184–85, 187, 189; houses provided by FHA, 105n43; limits opportunities for children, 84, 239; membership in Colored Alliance, 110, 121; mentioned, 245; mobility of, 311; numbers stable (1910–20), 176n13; political power of, 9, 14–15, 238; relationship within NFCF, 139–40, 145, 147, 148; relationship within UNIA, 134; restrictive contracts with, 233–34; retaliation after civil rights efforts, 15, 247, 259, 261; stereotypes of, 29; system prevents land ownership, 83, 234; uncommon at Mt. Vernon, 61n22; unionization of, 14–15, 146–47, 148, 240–44. *See also* Share Croppers' Union of Alabama (SCU)
Farmers/farm operators (tenants): percentage change (1880–1920) in Piedmont area, 201t
—African Americans as: 24; abandon SCU, 245; with African American landlords, 94; in Alabama (1900), 235; in Alabama (1930), 237t; census ambiguity, 31, 297; crop reduction program effect on, 143, 146, 147, 196–97; disenfranchised, 238; evicted, 247, 255; experience with scientific agriculture, 94, 100; factor in civil rights movement, 239; factor in separatist movements, 231; flight to urban life, 301; high rates in Alabama, 232; limited assistance through federal programs, 92; mechanization by, 171; membership in Colored Alliance, 110, 111, 113; mobility of, 311; murder of, 243; numbers increase, 29; numbers stable (1910–20), 176n13; operated farm value per acre (1930), 240; operated percentage of farms by Midwest state or region (1900), 160–61t; and owner, 160–61t; path to land ownership, 43, 91, 100, 105n42, 139, 143, 189; political power of, 9; relationship within NFCF, 139, 142, 143–44, 147, 148;

Farmers/farm operators—*continued*
  relationship within UNIA, 134; restrictive contracts with, 234; system prevents land ownership, 93, 144, 235, 255; tobacco farming, 182, 184–85, 187, 189–90, 193; unionization of, 146–47, 240–44; use of land bank, 97, 105n42
—Cash tenants, African American, 14, 43, 160–61t; with African American landlords, 190, 236; in Alabama (1900), 235; in Black Belt Alabama (1930), 237t; census ambiguity, 31; condition preferred to land ownership, 169–70, 171, 243; disenfranchised, 237–38; paid for seasonal labor, 169–72; relationship within NFCF, 139, 143
—Share tenants, African American, 160–61t; in Alabama Black Belt (1930), 237t; condition preferred to land ownership, 243; disenfranchised, 237–38; relationship within NFCF, 143; unionization of, 244
—Whites as, 147; mechanization by, 171; women, 179
Farmer's Alliance History and Agricultural Digest, The (Humphrey), 128n23
Farmers Home Administration (FmHA), 273, 275; lending inequalities by, 274
Farmers Home Association (FHA), 92, 99, 105n43
Farmers' Improvement Society of Texas, 84, 110–11, 128
Farmers' Legal Action Group (FLAG), 1–2
"Farmers' Sunday," 142
Farmers Union, 245; work with the Colored Alliance, 110
Farming, power, 96. *See also* Farm: mechanization
Farming, scientific. *See* Agriculture: scientific
Farming, truck, 172, 184
Farm laborers, 91, 128n37, 170f; Colored Alliance efforts with, 110–11, 113, 118, 121–23, 126; Democratic Party hushes up massacre of, 120; employed by African Americans farmers, 72, 169–70, 172; employed by white farmers, 14, 43, 121–23; factor in civil rights movement, 240; machinery displacing, 171; political impotence of, 14, 237; skilled, 187–88; strikes by, 11, 121–23; unionization of, 14–15, 240–44; white Farmers Alliance disregard for African American and white, 121, 130n65
Farm Laborers and Cotton Field Workers Union, 245
Farm loans: called in, 259; delayed or denied, 32, 183, 260, 275, 276, 278, 293n18; personal, 69–70; provided by the government, 143, 196, 275, 276, 278, 290, 293n18; provided through African American institutions, 69, 84, 97, 114, 188, 259, 261
Farm Security Administration (FSA), 1, 26–27, 147; Photographic Division, 179–80
Farm Service Agency (FSA), 275–76, 279, 293n18
Farm size. *See* Landowners (large acreage), Landowners (small acreage)
Farmville, Virginia, 7, 162
Fascism, 256
Federal Emergency Relief Administration, 146
Federal Farm Board, 143
Federation of Southern Cooperatives (FSC), 1–2, 280, 281, 294n30; Land Assistance Fund, 21
Feggins, Ebert, 189
Feggins, Joseph, 189
Fence, 219f
Ferry, 175n10
Fertilizer, 171, 190, 257–58, 259, 269n20; commercial, 94; natural, 94, 212. *See also* Soil preparation
Ficara, John Francis, 3
Fielder/Fedder, Fanny F., 174n3
Fields, Barbara J., 30; *Slavery and Freedom on the Middle Ground*, 30
Firewood, 13, 50, 172
Fisher, James S., 234, 240
Fite, Gilbert, 95
Fleming, Billie S., 258, 259, 260, 263–64
Florence Times Daily, 242
Florida, turpentine industry moves to, 25
Florida Agricultural and Mechanical University (FAMU), 206, 209
Florida Agricultural Extension, 206
Florida Farmers Union, 115
Florida Home Extension, 206, 210, 214, 221; Junior Home Demonstration Council, 206; "Negro" District Home Demonstration, 14, 206, 208, 226n4
Florida State Board of Health, 222
Florida State College for Women (FSCW), 206
Flour, 95, 96, 159; sacks, 95, 96, 97, 217. *See also* Mills: wheat
Flowers and bulbs, 218
Floy, Britt, 214
Fodder, 168
Ford, Emma, 39, 48, 50–53, 55
Ford, George, 39, 48, 50–56; guard at Washington's tomb, 56
Ford, West, 42–43, 45, 47, 57, 62n29; family of, 42–45, 48, 52

Forestry, 289
Forsyth County, North Carolina: percentage change of improved farm acreage (1860–1920), 201n14, 202n14t; percentage change of owner or tenant operated farms (1880–1920), 201n14, 202n14t; percentage change of total farms (1860–1920), 201n14, 202n14t; rates of African American land ownership (1900–1950), 186t
"Forty acres and a mule," 3, 271
Foster (landlord), 193
4-H clubs and members, 206, 220, 222, 224, 256–57, 264, 268n10, 312; camps segregated, 211
Fowl, barnyard, 169. See also Chickens
Fox News, 288
Franklin County, Virginia, 201n12t (note b); rates of African American land ownership (1900–1950), 186t
Fredericksburg, Virginia, 39
Free African Americans (pre-Civil War), 5, 7, 28, 129n38, 299; migration of, 83, 175n10; Mount Vernon's, 40, 42, 44
"Freedom colonies," 27, 85, 100, 164, 303. See also Communities settled by African Americans
Freedom Colonies (Sitton and Conrad), 27
"Freedom house," 247
Freedom Summer, 254
Freedpeople, 65f, 67f; African American community founded by, 301, 310; accounts documented by WPA, 175n11; as leaders in Black Populist activities, 116; becomes land seller to African Americans, 44; celebrate Juneteenth, 75; descendents of, 32, 180; eligible to vote, 65; evicted as sharecroppers, 247; found African American community, 301; integration into communities, 5, 164; migrate with former owner's kin, 155, 156, 157; migration patterns, 158; Mount Vernon's, 39–40, 42, 48, 52–53, 56; non-reliance on former owners, 175n10; obsession to acquire land, 184; path to land ownership, 8–9, 28, 77; political impotence of, 92, 237; promises unfulfilled to, 271; restrictive contracts created for, 233; studies of, 299; success in Arkansas reported, 163; take owner's surname, 67; use farming techniques they learned as slaves, 156–57, 159. See also Migrations
Free labor, 157
Freeman, Orville L., 273–74
French settlers, 169
Friction of space theory, 158
Friedman, Paul, 280, 282, 283, 285, 287

Frontier thesis, 158, 175n7
Fundraising, 89, 239, 260–61, 279; Brunswick stew, 191
Funeral parlors, 55–56
Funerals, 116, 259
Furniture and household items, 47, 50, 309; bedding, 51, 59–60n14; books, 47, 59–60n14; china, 47; cooking utensils, 309; curtains, 47, 217; dinner-plates, 47; dresser, 50; fancywork, 47; feather beds, 42; furniture, 94, 217; pillow shams, 47; pincushions, 47; rocking chair, 76; sideboard, 47; stoves, 47, 51, 71, 217; table and chairs, 47, 51, 76, 219; tablecloths, 217; tub, 71; washboards, 71
Futrell, Junius M., 148

Gardens (gardening): as college offering, 90–91; cottage, 211; dooryard, 212; home, 211, 212f; for home consumption, 12, 28, 71, 94, 207, 211; market, 10; slave-cabin, 212; symmetrical, 212; traditional, 211–13; vegetable, 211
Garvey, Marcus, 133, 136, 138; founder of UNIA, 132, 134; incarceration and deportation of, 138
Garveyism: adherents to, 132–38; strongholds, 134–35, 140; supported by whites, 138, 142, 148, 233; tenets of, 132–33, 134, 136–38, 139–40, 144
Gas station (cooperative), 96
Gender, 40, 55; bias, 14, 206; relations studies, 311–12; roles, 40, 53, 55; stereotypes, 51
Genealogy, 48, 63, 79n7; resources, 303, 308
General Accounting Office, 275, 293n18
General Association of the Colored Baptists of North Carolina, 116
General Education Board, 89
Georgetown, South Carolina, 134
Georgia, 248; African American land ownership in (1900), 100; agriculture assistance in, 21, 23; cooperative in, 140; jury commissioners, 120; most hostile toward African American land ownership, 11, 100, 235; state assembly, 124; studies of, 7, 23–25, 29–30; tobacco auctions starting in, 191; turpentine industry moves to, 25; value of farm equipment in (1930), 95
Georgia State College, 98
Georgia State Industrial College for Colored Youth, 98, 103n14; academic focus changed at, 89–90; Department of Agriculture, 90; educational offerings of, 88, 91, 92, 93, 94, 97; expansion of, 89; farm, 90; funding of, 89; insolvency of, 87; led by Hubert, 85, 87–94, 97–99, 167

Gerald, Hugene, 257
German immigrants, 169–71
German Immigration Society of Birmingham, 251n13
Ghess, Rev. M. T., 139
Gibson, Willie, and family, 257
Gilbert, Charlene, 2–3
Gilbert, Jess, 198
Gilmore, Glenda, 209
Gingrich, Newt, 295n39
Ginn, R. L., 141
Glave, Dianne, 211–12, 215, 218
Gleason, Flavia, 214
Glickman, Daniel R., 276–78, 295n39. See also *Pigford v. Glickman*
God, 32, 76, 136–37, 224
Goode, John, 189
Good-food advocacy, 3
Goodlatte, Bob, 288
Goodwyn, Lawrence, 111
Gossips, 50–51, 55, 60n19, 156, 207
Grain cradles, 170f
Grain elevator: operators, 169; storage charges, 169
Granary, 168
Grant, Gary, 1, 280, 292n5, 294n30
Grant, W. A., 124
Grant County, Wisconsin, 155
Granville County, North Carolina, 116, 129n38; editorial extolling tobacco farming in, 189; land prices in, 187; percentage change of improved farm acreage (1860–1920), 201n12t; percentage change of owner or tenant operated farms (1880–1920), 201n12t; percentage change of total farms (1860–1920), 201n12t; rates of African American land ownership (1900–1950), 186t
Grassley, Chuck, 288, 295n39
Graveyards. *See* Cemeteries
Gray, Joseph, 148
Gray, Ralph, 242–43, 244
Gray, Tommy, 242
Great Depression, 74–75, 83, 89, 91, 98, 99–100, 139–41, 145–47
Great Migration, 3, 83–84, 88, 137
Green, Hardy, 173
Green, John, 155, 168, 173, 173n1, 175n11; family of, 155–56, 164, 168, 173, 173n1; spelling of family name, 173n1
Green, Lillie, 155, 168, 173n1, 175n11
Green, Thomas, 9, 156, 157f, 173, 175n11
Greene, Thomas, and family, 173n1
Greene County, Alabama: African American agricultural workers (1930), 241t; African American farm owners, tenants, and sharecroppers (1930), 237t; farms in (1930), 236t; farms under African American operation (1930), 236t
Greenwood, Mississippi, 142
Griffith, Daniel A., 155, 164, 174n3, 176n17; family of, 155–56, 164, 174n2
Griffith, Eliza, 155
Griffith, Fannie F., 156
Griffith, John Hunter, 155–56, 174n3
Griffith's Mill, 164, 176n17
Grim, Valerie, 15–16
Groceries, 12, 50, 55; and notions, 47
Grocery store (cooperative), 96
Groves, Junius, 304
Guilford County, North Carolina: extension agent report, 195; marketing cooperative failure in, 195; rates of African American land ownership (1900–1950), 186t
Guineas, 74
Gunston Hall plantation, 44

Hackney's Landing, Arkansas, 124
Hagood, Margaret Jarman, 179–81
Hahn, Steven, 6, 9
Halifax, North Carolina, 294n25
Halifax, Virginia, 168
Halifax County, Virginia: percentage change of improved farm acreage (1860–1920), 201n12t; percentage change of owner or tenant operated farms (1880–1920), 201n12t; percentage change of total farms (1860–1920), 201n12t; rates of African American land ownership (1900–1950), 186t
Hall, Fitzgerald, 255
Hamer, Fannie Lou, 254
Hamilton, Charles, 233; *Black Power*, 233
Hammond, Lily H., 5, 7, 162–63
Hampton Institute, 90, 239; educational model, 91, 103n24
Hancock County, Georgia, 24–25, 29, 85; African American land ownership growth, 97–98; boll weevil infestation in, 88, 93–94; race relations in, 86, 100; taxable income drops in, 94
Hargis, Peggy, 25
Harness making, 103n24
Harris, Carmen, 15, 211, 225n1, 227n16
Harris, J. William, 4, 6, 30
Harris, Leon R., 143–45
Hart, Mary Ida, 129n41
Harvest, 94, 111, 121, 170, 260; corn, 74; cotton, 68, 74, 121–23, 122f, 240; grain, 170f,

171; hay, 74; peas, 74; tobacco, 191; wheat, 159, 169, 172–73, 172f
Harvester World, 12, 13f
Haywood, Harry, 244
Haywood, Ruth, 224
Health clinics, 86, 221; cooperative, 96. *See also* Mary Otis Willcox Health Clinic
Heidleberg, J. H., 69–70
Heidleberg, Octavia, 69–70
Heir property, 2, 34n24, 290, 302
Henry County, Virginia, rates of African American land ownership (1900–1950), 186t
Herald Journal (Greensboro, Georgia), 95
Hessen, 169
Hesslink, George. *See* Friction of space theory
Higgs, Robert, 5, 24
Hinds, Thomas, 80n8
Hispanics, 21, 277, 289
Hoey, Clyde, 180
Hogs, 71t; as diversification strategy, 13, 71, 74, 95, 168, 169, 172
Holmes, Vicki, 63, 76, 78n1
Holmes, William, 119
Holmes County, Mississippi, 142
Holms, George, 239
Holt, Sharon Ann, 28; *Making Freedom Pay*, 28
Homecoming, 3
Home demonstration agents, 95; African American men, 206; African American women, 205–25, 210f, 256, 262–63, 268n10; adaptability and flexibility of, 14, 205–7, 209, 211, 213, 214–15, 218–20, 223, 225; backgrounds of, 205; constraints of, 209; Florida, 14, 205–25; funding sources of, 14, 208, 211, 213–14; funding vetoed, 257; gain trust of African American families, 205, 207–9, 214–15, 221–25, 262–63; government publications of, 312; health programs of, 220–23; mistrust of, 205, 207–8, 213, 224–25, 225n1; promotional strategy, 218–19; removal, 213–14, 225; reports, 205, 210, 220, 221, 222, 224–25, 227n16, 257, 262; respectability of, 208–9, 262; in South Carolina, 225n1, 227n16, 256, 257, 262; stereotypes, 207; target African American farm owners, 207, 209, 312; in Tennessee, 215; use of new scientific methods, 205, 207, 209; white women, 206, 208, 209, 214, 215
Home demonstration clubs: empowerment through, 220–21, 223–24; to improve rural African American lives, 205–7, 209, 211, 213, 215, 217–25, 261–63. *See also* 4-H clubs and members
Homemaking, 208–9, 218
Home Seekers Land Company, 239

Homestead Act of 1862, 234
Homesteader, The (Micheaux, book), 167, 177n21
Homesteader, The (Micheaux, film), 167, 177n21
Homesteading, 83, 112, 135, 164, 167, 177n21, 304. *See also* Migrations
Honey, Michael, 243
Hoover, Herbert, 99, 105n42, 143
Hope, John, 93
Horner, William, 157, 159, 174n5; family of, 159
Horses, 96, 263; breeding, 168, 305; buggy, 47, 263; buggy whip, 73; as personal property, 45, 47, 69, 70, 71t, 169, 172; used in parade, 39
Horton, Adolph, 119
Hotels, African American produce sold to, 96. *See specific hotels*
Houses, 48, 50, 71, 165, 168, 189, 273, 309; closets in, 50; dilapidated, 94; improved, 8, 196, 213, 215–18, 216f, 217f 219f; lawn, 212; out-; 189; poor drainage around, 221; porches of, 8, 72f, 213f, 219f, 72f; unpainted, 27; wallpaper, 50; windows, 8
Housing Assistance Council, 290
Houston, Texas, 114, 127n18, 167
Houston County, Texas, 109, 114
Hover, Hiram, 115
Howard University, 84, 98; College of Arts and Sciences, 84
Hubbard, Nelson, 170
Hubert, Benjamin Franklin, 84, 89f; autocratic style and characteristics of, 90, 99; birth date confusion of, 101n5; creates African American agrarian model, 11, 85, 94, 168 (*see also* Log Cabin Community); delivers speech before Georgia's legislature, 89; drafts position paper for Hoover, 99; formal education of, 85–86; founder of AANCL, 93; helps direct Europe's agricultural reconstruction, 87; personal papers of, 101n4; president of Georgia State Industrial College for Colored Youth, 85, 87–94, 97–99, 103n14, 167; promotes AANCL, 85, 87, 167–68; purchases parents' land, 94; refuses Tuskegee Institute presidency, 87, 88, 102–3n14; South Carolina state positions of, 87; supervises Alabama Agricultural Extension Service, Negro Division, 87; work at South Carolina State Agricultural and Mechanical College, 86–87; work at Tuskegee Institute, 87
Hubert, Camilla, 85–86, 94, 101n5
Hubert, James, work at the Urban League, 87–88, 91, 101n5, 102n7
Hubert, John Wesley, 88
Hubert, Zach, 85–86, 88, 94, 99, 101n5; family of, 85–86, 88, 101n5, 102n7

334 · Index

Hubert, Zachary Taylor, 102n7
Humphrey, Rev. Richard M., death of, 127n22; general superintendent of the Colored Alliance, 111–12, 113–14, 115; writings of, 113, 128n23
Hunt, Henry A., 145–46
Hunting, 28
Hunting and fishing lodges, 290
Hyde, Arthur, 138, 141

Idealism: Lockean, 163; rural, 91, 133, 139, 163–64, 168. *See also* Agrarianism, Jeffersonian
Igleheart, Thomas, 72
Illegitimate children, 45, 64, 66
Illinois: average size of African American farm (1900), 160–61t; percentage of African American farm ownership (1900), 160–61t, 162
Illiterate/illiteracy, African American: 6, 24, 255, 263; compared to whites, 26, 79n5, 255
Immunizations, 215, 221
Incarceration, 52, 123, 124, 138, 242
Indiana: average size of African American farm (1900), 160–61t; percentage of African American farm ownership (1900), 160–61t
Indian Territory, 175n7. *See also* Oklahoma
"Indigenous perspective" theory, 265–66
Industrialization, 196
Insecticides, 259
Interest rates, excessive, 112, 114, 118
International Harvester, 171
International Labor Defense, 243
Internet, resources, 308–9; technology, 64, 277, 279, 285, 289, 294n30
Iowa: average size of African American farm (1900), 160–61t; percentage of African American farm ownership (1900), 160–61t; value of farm equipment in (1930), 95
Ireland, 169
Irrigation, 31
IRS tax payments, 287–88
Isolationism, 27–28, 166
Israel on the Appomattox (Ely), 7

Jackson, Henry, 170
Jackson, Jesse, 23
Jackson, Luther Porter, 5
Jackson, Matthew, 247
Jackson, Mississippi, 246
Jackson College, 102n7
Jacksonville, Florida, 220, 223
Jamaica, 134
James, Epistle of, 136
James Lee, 124

JAMS-Endispute, Inc., 283
Jeanes Teachers, 100, 102n7
Jefferson, Thomas (farmer), 168–69; family of, 169
Jefferson City, Missouri, 152n51
Jefferson Davis County, Mississippi, 142
Jeffries, Hasan, 4, 231, 246
Jenkins, Barbara Williams, 268n10
Jenkins, Estelle, 218, 219f
Jenkins, Martha, 55
Jet, 260, 291
Jewelry, 47; earrings, 47
Jim Crow era: laws and inequities of, 85, 93, 136, 147, 312; stereotypes of African American during, 27; violence common during, 27, 29, 92, 137, 232, 238
John, Alex, 112
Johnson, Andrew, 92
Johnson, Griffin, 43, 45
Johnson, Lemon, 243–44, 246
Johnson, Lyndon Baines, 81n21, 265
Johnson, Nathan, 44, 51, 52
Johnson, Rev., 136
Johnson, Sarah, 44, *See also* Robinson, Sarah
Joint Stock Club of Gum Springs, 44, 48, 52, 59n11
Jones, Anthony, 189
Jones, H. S., 289
Jones, Junius, 189
Jones, R., 139
Jones, Robert, 136
Jordan, Barbara, 79n6
Juke joints, 220
Julius Rosenwald Foundation, 89, 96, 100
Juneteenth, 75

Kansas: average size of African American farm (1900), 160–61t; percentage of African American farm ownership (1900), 160–61t; value of farm equipment in (1930), 95
Kansas City, Missouri, 77
Kay, Alan, 280
Kelley, Robin D. G., 240
Kennedy, Jonas T., 265
Kentucky, 175n10, 291; wheat to, 159; wheat production, 158
Kenzer, Robert C., 28; *Enterprising Southerners*, 28
Kerosene, 172f
King, Patrick, 64, 66, 68, 78nn1,3, 79n5, 82n31
King, Steve, 288
Kingfisher County, Oklahoma, 132
Kluger, Richard, 256, 257

Knapp, Bradford, 245
Knights of Labor: Georgia state, 115; North Carolina state, 115; southern branch of, 110; work with the Colored Alliance, 110, 112, 125
Ku Klux Klan, 119, 138, 246, 248

Labor/laborers, 169, 204; agricultural/farm, 10, 14, 110, 113, 121, 122, 130n65, 170, 237, 241t, 243, 244; African American child, 64, 68, 71–74, 77, 144–45, 170f, 188, 194; African American women, 144–45, 170f, 188, 194; blue collar, 90; free black labor, 69; to make ends meet, 47; manual, 48; piece, 110; stereotypes of, 29; wage, 29, 51, 53–55, 111, 112, 121, 146–47, 245; wage, at Mt. Vernon, 44, 48, 53, 56; wage, with railroad, 39, 47–48, 52–53, 56, 61n22; work for whites, 29. *See also* Landless African Americans
LaCour, Arthur B., 143
Land: alternate use for, 289–90; average values in 1930, 240; cheap, 24; confiscation and redistribution of, 92, 234; conservation, 276, 290; consolidation through FHA, 92; cooperatives, 84, 85–86, 91, 94–99, 127n10; cost per acre for African American, 26, 184, 187; cost per acre for mulattoes, 26; cost per acre for whites, 26; inequality in sale price, 26, 157; Native American, 165, 167; prices, 184–85, 187, 189; public, 157; redistribution of, 198
Land acquisition, African American and: through changes in land use, 25–26; through confiscation and redistribution, 92, 234; within context of space and time, 26, 28; through credit from African American financial institutions, 112, 139, 184, 188; as an expression of Black Power, 14, 232, 238; local factors influencing, 25–26, 28; through family ties, 10–11, 26, 43–45, 47, 85, 99, 116; through gifts, 26, 97; through inheritance, 26, 27–28, 42, 45, 47, 48, 50, 56, 234, 302; through land transfer, 80n12; path to, 26–27, 43, 45, 91, 100, 105n42, 157–58, 187, 189; through philanthropy, 239; Piedmont region of North Carolina and Virginia (1900–1950), 185, 186t, 187; political weakness hinders, 237; through purchase, 8–9, 26, 43–45, 47–48, 52–53, 64, 69–71, 85, 94, 157, 184, 188, 234–35; by purchase of land at higher prices / acre, 26, 184, 188; studies of, 5–6, 301; substantial holdings, 42, 45, 52, 57, 180, 193; through tenancy, 43, 143, 189, 234–35; through white land abandonment, 25, 85, 91, 97, 184, 187; through white patronage, 6, 11, 26–27, 42, 69, 85–86, 99–100, 138, 142, 143, 147, 187; through whites willing to sell, 23–24, 97, 184, 187. *See also* Land banks
Land Act of 1820, 174n5
Land Act of 1866, 234
Land banks, 44, 97, 105n42, 239–40. *See also* Joint Stock Club of Gum Springs
Land grant colleges, 271; African American, 85, 88, 91, 93, 209, 214, 308; Georgia's neglect of, 88, 90; white, 93; withdrawal of federal support to, 88
"Landholdership," 44
Landless African Americans: civil rights as hope for, 240–41, 246–47; Colored Alliance efforts with, 113, 118, 121; compared to Argonauts by Du Bois, 181; condition preferred to land ownership, 243; contracts with white landowners, 234; displaced by agricultural machinery, 169, 171; government programs to help, 146–47; hired by African Americans landowners, 170; lacked government support, 92, 145, 147–48, 273; lacked support from white farmer alliances, 118, 121–22, 130n65; leave SCU for Farm Laborers and Cotton Field Workers Union, 245; NFCF efforts with, 145–48; NOI strategy for, 248; path to land ownership, 43; reprisals against, 15, 261; resettlement of, 143, 145–46; stereotypes of, 7, 29; strikes of, 11, 121–24; support of Garveyism, 133; supported by Hubert's efforts, 92; synonymous with farm wage laborer, 110; tobacco growing opportunities for, 187, 189; unionization of, 146–48, 241–45; unique experience from most whites, 31, 118, 121; work for white landlords, 43, 234, 237
Landlords: African American farmer set out to impress, 193; evicts tenants, 255; home extension agents avoid, 207; negotiate rates with cash tenant farmers, 169; puts tenants in cycle of dependency, 255.
—African Americans as: of African American cash tenant farmers, 190, 235–36; of African American sharecroppers, 22, 74, 76, 180; of African American tenant farmers, 94; over plantations, 22.
—Whites as: of African American landless, 14, 43, 234, 237; resistance to aims of Colored Alliance, 111, 118, 119; resistance to aims of the NFCF, 142; restrictive contracts created by, 233–34; seize crops, 261.
Landlord-Tenant Act, 130n65
Land Loss Prevention Project, 281

336 · Index

Landowners, African Americans as: 43, 55, 163; as achievement, 27, 30, 137; afford equal protection, 110, 113, 133, 143, 156–57, 164, 254, 258, 267; archeological resources available about, 309; average size of farm by Midwest state or region (1900), 160–61t; cash crop dependency, 255, 272; civil rights studies involving, 314; clear title to land, 76, 290, 302; community leadership of, 4, 30, 75, 77, 116, 134, 137, 141, 180, 193–94; contemporary, 314; creates class differences, 4, 7, 9, 115, 146, 162–63, 245, 250n8; cultural geography studies of, 310; decline, 2, 9, 56–57, 98, 240, 272, 305; decline due to low tobacco prices, 195–96; decline due to suburbanization, 57, 196–97; decline due to underfunding agricultural extension, 211; decline due to USDA policies, 16, 197–98, 276–77, 278, 279; decline ignored, 291; in 1890, 235; farms in Alabama (1900), 235; farms in Alabama (1910), 235–36; farms in Alabama (1920), 235–36; farms in Alabama (1930), 235–36, 240; farms in Alabama Black Belt (1930), 237t; as financial security and/or independence, 3, 28, 29–30, 44, 69, 74, 84, 85, 87, 90–92, 93, 96, 99–100, 132–34, 136–37, 141, 142, 143, 147, 158, 164, 166, 168, 173, 207, 234, 235, 247; geographic disparities of, 23–24, 26; government studies of, 297–98; historical perspective studies of, 299–300; impacts on race relations, 22–26, 28, 100, 157, 163; in Log Cabin community, 97–98; journalistic resources for, 307–8; kept off the public record, 27, 302–3; land retention studies, 302–3; legal barriers to, 157–58 (see also Black Codes); legitimizes citizenship, 5, 6–7, 11, 132–33, 137, 144–45, 149, 162–63, 239, 258; location creates class differences in Mt. Vernon area, 40, 52–55; material culture studies of, 309; before 1910, 7, 24; in 1910, 83; in 1910, 23, 25, 29, 31, 272, 292n1; in 1920, 83; non-farming, 28, 43, 47–48, 56–57, 139; within the Old Bright Belt, 182–91, 193–99; as a part of American farming experience, 22–23, 24, 30, 163, 164, 166, 168, 191; percentage by Midwest state or region (1900), 160–61t, 176n13; against powerful landowners, 24–25, 235, 238, 243; records incomplete, 297; small holdings, 26, 28, 31, 43, 44–45, 47–48, 50, 64, 75, 93, 95, 114, 121, 134, 162, 193, 198, 258–59, 272, 290; sociological studies of, 298–301; source analysis, 297, 300; in spite of racism, 28; studies, 22–32; studies on sense of place, 311; studies outside The South, 304–5; "tenancy in common," 44, 236, 290, 303; underlying racism against, 23–28, 30–32, 84, 182, 187, 193–94, 198–99, 248, 273, 278; wealth building, 23, 24, 28, 52, 74, 91, 132, 139, 167, 168; white resentment of, 7, 27, 86, 138, 139, 187, 306–7; women as, 43–45, 47, 48, 52, 57. *See also* Farmers/farm operators (owners)

Landowners (large acreage): African American, 22, 165, 193; white, 24–25, 30–31, 32, 45, 83

Landowners (small acreage): African Americans, 25, 45, 47, 92, 155–57, 159, 160–61t; commonality with small-scale white farmers, 5–6, 10, 24–26, 31–32, 166, 168–69; 189–91; limited by class relations, 24–25, 26, 32; prime land not available to, 21, 24, 25; tenant decisions to not buy land, 171

Land quality: endangered species habitat, 276; forest, 65, 92, 185; "hard," 48; highly erodible, 276; improved, 185, 261; marginal, 24, 25, 182, 189; poor, 48, 239; premium, 24, 25, 164, 240; rocky, 24; sandy, 75; tillable, 65, 68, 168–70, 172, 178n24; undeveloped, 24, 65, 185, 189; wetland, 276; wooded, 172

Land-rush settlers, 158, 166–67

Landscaping. *See* Beautification: house and yard

Langhorne, Orra, 162

Langston College, 102n7

Laurens County, South Carolina, 265

Laurent, L. D., 131n76

Lead mining, 157

Lee County, Arkansas, 123

Lee's Chapel Baptist Church, 195

Leflore County, Mississippi, 119–20, 130n57, 141–42

Leftists, 243

Lenin, Vladimir, 240

Leon County, Florida, 205, 211, 215, 217, 221, 224

Lewis, Michael, 283

Liberty Hill African Methodist Episcopal church (Summerton, South Carolina), 256

Lillie, Eli, 80n12. *See also* Erby, Eli

Limestone County, Texas, 63–64, 69, 75

Lincoln High School (Charleston, Missouri), 145

Lincoln University, 152n51

Littig, Texas, 167

Little Rock, Arkansas, 148

Livestock: barn, 194f; care for, 172; college, 90; comparison of value per farm by state (1930), 95; farming, 42, 159, 169, 178n24, 272 (*see also* Cattle: ranching; Horses: breeding); lack of, 48; provided by landlord, 234; raising crops for, 12, 143, 159, 168; sale of, 94, 191, 196

Lobbying: for agrarian reform by Colored

Alliance, 112, 113, 118, 124; for agrarian reform by Cotton Pickers' League, 124; for agrarian reform by STFU, 146; for extension agent, 225; success by white elites, 273
Lodge, Henry Cabot, 120
Log Cabin Community: administrative papers of, 101n4; church at, 85; cooperative ventures of, 95–97; created by Hubert, 11, 85, 94, 168; decline of, 98–99; private African American school at, 85, 86, 88, 95, 98; size of, 85, 97–98; success of, 85, 94–99. *See also* Springfield, Georgia
Lornell, Kip, 191
Los Angeles, California, 77
Louisiana, 175n7; drought of 1930–31 affects, 141; studies of, 23
Louisiana Farmers' Union (LFU), 146–47
Love, Louisa, 136
Love, Rev. E. F., 127n10
Lovelady, Texas, 114
Lowe, Rev. George W., 124
Lowndes County, Alabama, 64, 78n3, 239, 245–46; African American agricultural workers (1930), 241t; African American farm owners, tenants, and sharecroppers (1930), 237t; civil rights work in, 245–47; farms in (1930), 236t; farms under African American operation (1930), 236t
Lowndes County Alabama Freedom Organization, 254
Lowndes County Christian Movement for Human Rights (LCCMHR), 247
Lowndes County Freedom Organization (LCFO), 247
Lowry, Robert, 119
Lumber, 257
Lunenburg County, Virginia: percentage change of improved farm acreage (1860–1920), 201n12t; percentage change of owner or tenant operated farms (1880–1920), 201n12t; percentage change of total farms (1860–1920), 201n12t; rates of African American land ownership (1900–1950), 186t
Lytle, Lutie, 112

Machinery, 50, 159, 169, 171, 178n24, 182, 274; leads to fewer laborers, 171
Mackenzie, Mary Todd, 222
Macon, Georgia, 95, 127n10
Macon County, Alabama: African American agricultural workers (1930), 241t; African American farm owners, tenants, and sharecroppers (1930), 237t; farms in (1930), 236t; farms under African American operation (1930), 236t
Madden, Rev., 47
Madison, Rev. H. M., 139
Making Freedom Pay (Holt), 28
Mants, Bob, 246
March, Louis T., 284, 287
Marengo County, Alabama: African American agricultural workers (1930), 241t; African American farm owners, tenants, and sharecroppers (1930), 237t; farms in (1930), 236t; farms under African American operation (1930), 236t
Margo, Robert A., 5, 24
Marks, Stella Youngblood, 78n1
Marriage, 39, 48, 52; desertion, 50–51; divorce and proceedings, 50–54, 56; licenses, 39, 40, 49f, 68, 116; weddings, 48, 54
Marshall, Thurgood, 260
Martin, John, and family, 171–72
Maryland, studies of, 23, 29
Maryland, wheat production, 159
Mary Otis Willcox Health Clinic, 98
Mason, George, 40, 43. *See also* Gunston Hall plantation
Mason, Sallie E., and family, 43
Massachusetts Agricultural College, 86
McCall, Harry G., 115
McCondichie, W. G., 234
McCord, Rev. L. B., 258
McCormick family, 159, 164
McCormick Harvesting Machine Company, 159
McCormick reaper, 159, 164
McGilbra, Israel, 110
McWhorter, Frank, 175n10, 304; family of, 175n10
Meat processing, 173
Mebane, North Carolina, 204n50
Mechanical science, 87
Mecklenburg County, Virginia: extension agent report, 189; land sales in, 184–85; percentage change of improved farm acreage (1860–1920), 201n12t; percentage change of owner or tenant operated farms (1880–1920), 201n12t; percentage change of total farms (1860–1920), 201n12t; rates of African American land ownership (1900–1950), 186t
Medicine, patent, 192f
Memphis, Tennessee, 123, 143, 246, 294n25
Meridian, Mississippi, 118
Merriweather, Jim, and wife, 243
Methodist church, 79
Methodist Episcopal Church cemetery (Alexandria, Virginia), 56

Mexia, Texas, 76
Micanopy, Florida, 216f
Micheaux, Oscar, 167, 177n21
Michigan, 248; average size of African American farm (1900), 160–61t; percentage of African American farm ownership (1900), 160–61t; wheat to, 159
Midland Express, 112, 127n18
Migrations, 9, 25, 134; Back-to-Africa, 141, 167; back-to-the-land, 11, 167–68, 305; east-to-west, 158, 175n7; to Illinois, 83, 175n7; to Indiana, 83; influenced by white ancestry, 158; to Iowa, 175n7; to Kansas, 83, 158, 164–65, 175n7 (*see also* Exodusters); to Michigan, 83; to Minnesota, 175n7; use of Mississippi River, 156; to Nebraska, 175n7; to North Dakota, 164–65, 175n7; north-to-south, 315; to Ohio, 83; to Oklahoma, 83, 132, 158, 165; to South Dakota, 164–65, 167, 175n7; south-to-north, 83, 175n7; studies of, 304–5; to Texas, 64, 79n6; to Wisconsin, 83, 155–56, 158, 168, 175n7; to Wyoming, 165
Military, 39, 73
Militia, 112, 124
Miller, B. M., 242, 244–45
Miller, Julia, 226n4
Miller, Kelly, 84, 98
Miller (occupation), 155
Mills: commercial, 96; cooperative, 96; corn, 96; lumber, 257; saw, 96, 116, 243; syrup, 75; wheat, 96, 158–59, 164
Mills, Ruby, 224
Milwaukee Sentinel, 246
Minnesota: average size of African American farm (1900), 160–61t; percentage of African American farm ownership (1900), 160–61t
Minor, Kelly A., 14
Minority farmers: discriminated against, 274, 278; land loss by, 272; lawsuits by, 286–87, 289
Miscegenation, 163, 232
Mississippi: drought of 1930–31 affects, 141; studies of, 23
Mississippi River, 175n7; Delta, 26; flood of 1927, 138; travel along, 156, 175n10; Valley, 169
Missouri: average size of African American farm (1900), 160–61t; drought of 1930–31 affects, 141; percentage of African American farm ownership (1900), 160–61t; state guard, 138; wheat production, 158
Missouri, Kansas, and Texas Railroad, 164
Mitchell, Thomas, 234
Mobile, Alabama, 114

Modern Farmer, 138
Monopolies: banking, 118; Democratic Party rule in the South, 109, 120, 126; railroad, 118; storage, 112; transportation, 112
Monroe County, Alabama: African American agricultural workers (1930), 241t; African American farm owners, tenants, and sharecroppers (1930), 237t; farms in (1930), 236t; farms under African American operation (1930), 236t
Montezuma, Georgia, 3
Moore, Rev. John L., 125–26
Moore, Shade, 233–34; family of, 234
Mooree Quarter, Oxford, Alabama, 238
Morehouse College, 86, 102n7
Morning Star, 242
Morrill Act of 1862, 271
Morrill Act of 1890, 271
Morris, Aldon. *See* "Indigenous perspective" theory; "Resource mobilization" theory
Morris, John, and family, 170
Morris, Scott, 119
Mosquitoes, 213f, 221
Mothers of the South (Hagood), 179
Moton, Robert R., 84, 105n42; board member of AANCL, 93; drafts position paper for Hoover, 99; president of Tuskegee Institute, 87, 88, 102n14
Mount Vernon, 39–40, 42, 44–45, 52–54, 56; district, 40, 42–45, 47–48, 54, 56, 61n22; district map, 41m, 45, 46m; free workers or employees, 39, 42, 44, 48, 52–54, 56; grounds keeping, 48, 53; guard at Washington's tomb, 56; guide books, 52; lunchroom, 52; map showing, 46m; tourists and visitors, 44, 52–53, 56
Mount Vernon Ladies' Association, 44, 48, 52, 54, 56
"Moveable school," 84
Movements: Black Populist, 109–26; civil rights, 4, 272; civil rights, in South Carolina, 254–67; communist, 240–46; Country Life, 85, 92, 98; large-scale farming, 86; populist, 22, 92; slow-food, 289. *See also* Garveyism
Mt. Vernon, historic preservation, 44, 56
Mt. Zion African Methodist Episcopal church, 195
Muhammed, Elijah, 248
Mulatto, 28; afforded better opportunity as, 27; census designation, 63, 68, 78n3, 79nn4,5, 80n12, 128n36, 129n38
Mulatto cash tenant farmers, 170
Mulatto landowners, 168

Mules, 69, 70, 71t, 172, 260
Murphysboro, Illinois, 167
Murray, George Washington, 124
Music, 191

National Alliance, 112, 124, 127n18, 128n23
National Association for the Advancement of Colored People (NAACP), 21–22, 137, 147, 260, 263, 281; civil rights work in South Carolina, 257–61, 263; Clarendon County, South Carolina, branch, 257; Elloree community, 15, 258, 261; members discriminated against, 257–61; Southern Regional Conference, 147; supplants NFCF, 147; supplies money to CCIA, 269n20; work with U.S. Commission on Civil Rights, 273
National Black Farmers Association (NBFA), 1, 14, 16n2, 198, 280, 281, 294n30
National Colored Alliance, 114
National Council of Community Based Organizations in Agriculture, 281
National Economist, 124
National Family Farm Coalition, 281
National Federation of Colored Farmers (NFCF): Alabama units of, 139; Arkansas units of, 139; attacks against, 142; broadside, 144f; conventions of, 139, 140, 142–43, 145–56, 148, 152n51; cooperation with UNIA, 140–41, 143; courts rich whites, 143, 147–48; disillusionment of white elites with, 141–42; dissolution of, 12, 146; founded, 138; Georgia units of, 139; goals of, 12, 132, 138–40, 146, 147, 167; leaders of, 139; Louisiana units of, 139; membership of, 12, 138–40, 141, 142, 147, 148, 180; Mississippi units of, 138–39, 140–41, 142; Missouri units of, 139, 145; *Modern Farmer* newspaper of, 138; organizational units of, 138–40, 142, 145; political activities of, 12, 139, 141–43, 145–46, 147; Tennessee units of, 139; Tennessee units of, 140; UNIA similarities to, 138–39, 145, 148; white resistance to, 139, 141–42
National Guard, 119
National Home Demonstration Week, 220
National Negro Health Week (NNHW), 222, 228n23
National Self-Help Association, 167
Nationhood. *See* Garveyism: tenets of
Nation of Islam (NOI), 15, 248–49
Native Americans, 277, 286–87, 288; land, 165, 167
Nat Turner's rebellion, 159. *See also* Turner, Nat
Nebraska: average size of African American farm (1900), 160–61t; percentage of African American farm ownership (1900), 160–61t
Negro Landholder of Georgia, The (Du Bois), 101n2
"Negro Question," 240
Negro Star, 142
Negro World, 132, 134, 136, 137, 140, 141
Nelson, Estella, 225
Nelson, William, Jr., 237, 248
Neosho River (Kansas), 164
New Bright Belt, 188
Newby, Idus A., 268–69n16
New Deal agriculture programs, 143, 145, 273, 313; factor in flight from farms, 301; fail small farmers, 32, 92, 145–47, 272. *See also* Agricultural Adjustment Act (AAA); Agricultural Adjustment Administration (AAA); Resettlement Act (RA)
New Encyclopedia of Southern Culture, The (Walker and Cobb), 22
New Mississippian, 119
New Orleans, Louisiana, 114, 294n25
New Philadelphia, Illinois, 175n10, 304
Newspapers, 2, 76, 113, 265, 281; African American, 85, 97, 191; company, 171; cover home extension activities, 210, 223; feature Hubert, 85, 88, 93, 97; interview son of escaped slaves, 175n11; promote separatism, 164; Republican, 163, 171; white, 85, 97, 115, 120, 122, 124. *See also specific newspapers*
New York, 169; migrants from, 43
New York City, New York, 140; Harlem, 134, 137
New York Times, 23, 101n5; African American farm ownership covered by, 2, 234, 239; reports on Alabama's "Black Belt," 232, 234, 239, 242, 245; reports on violence against African Americans, 242, 245
Nichols, Willis, 110
Noblesse oblige, 26
Norfolk, Virginia, 114
North Carolina, Cape Fear region, 25–26; marketing cooperative in, 195; Piedmont area, 26, 184–85; Piedmont region rates of African American land ownership (1900–1950), 185, 186t, 187; rate of African American farm owners, 185, 187; studies of, 23; tobacco regions, 116, 182, 184, 188, 200–201n12
North Carolina A&T University, 195
North Dakota: average size of African American farm (1900), 160–61t; percentage of African American farm ownership (1900), 160–61t
Northern Farmers Alliance, 118, 125

340 · Index

Nottoway County, Virginia: percentage change of improved farm acreage (1860-1920), 201n12t; percentage change of owner or tenant operated farms (1880-1920), 201n12t; percentage change of total farms (1860-1920), 201n12t; rates of African American land ownership (1900-1950), 186t
Nutrition, 74, 207, 208, 222
Nutt, George, 265

Obama, Barack, 285, 286-87, 289
Ocala, Florida, 120, 128n23
Occupations, multiple. *See* Dual tenure; Laborer: to make ends meet; Off-farm income
Occupations (non-farm): artisan, 162; author, 167; banker, 260; carpenter, 42, 48, 50; chief engineer, 165; clock and watch maker, 43; college professor, 102n7; concrete work, 48, 53, 56; construction, 90; contractor, 260; cooper, 159; deputy, 124; doctor, 28, 98; film director, 177n21; film maker, 167; funeral parlor director, 258; funeral parlor embalmer, 56; grocer, 96, 162; grounds keeping, 48, 53; guard, 56; hotel worker, 8f, 9, 73, 81n21; house servant, 47; housekeeper, 44; janitor, 73, 81n18, 90; laundress, 47; maid, 247; merchant, 111, 112, 118-19, 140; minister, 102n7, 134, 142, 191, 194, 260-61 (*see also specific ministers*); nurse, 43, 98; peddler, 191, 192f; physician, 45; police officer, 242-43, 248; principal, 102n7; railroad worker, 39, 47, 48, 55; register of deeds, 116; sailor, 58n9; school superintendent, 116-17, 258; school teacher, 45, 73, 76, 79n6, 98, 116, 128n36, 134, 162, 222, 239, 245; sheriff, 242-43; sheriff's deputy, 259; shoemaker, 91, 103n24; snack-shop owner, 260; storekeeper, 47, 137; wagon maker, 159; whitewasher, 58n9; wholesaler, 140
O'Daniel, W. Lee "Pappy," 76
Odd Fellows lodge, 55
Odum, Howard, 180-81
Off-farm income, 194, 198, 290
Office of Economic Opportunity, 247, 264
Office of General Council, 279
Ogburn, Charlie, 189
Ohio, 169; average size of African American farm (1900), 160-61t; percentage of African American farm ownership (1900), 160-61t; wheat to, 159
Oil, cylinder, 172f
Okfuskee County, Oklahoma, 134
Oklahoma, 165

Old Bright Belt, 182, 188, 189-90, 196, 198-99; included highest ratio of African American land ownership, 182
Oliver, E. E., 148
Omaha, Nebraska, 131n76
Only Six Million Acres (Browne), 2
Oral history, 2, 63, 68, 73, 175n11; resources, 303, 308, 311
Orangeburg, South Carolina, 87, 260
Orangeburg County, South Carolina: extension agent needed in, 264; resistance to civil rights in, 258-59, 261
Orange County, North Carolina, 179; rates of African American land ownership (1900-1950), 186t
Orchard, 168
Orphanages, 117. *See also* Colored Orphanage Asylum
Outbuildings, 168, 189
Overby (land seller), 184
Overman, R. E., 148
Oxford, North Carolina, 116, 127n18

Pacific Northwest, 171
Paige, Ralph, 280, 294n30
Paper companies, 290
Parades: Colored Alliance, 119; Emancipation Day parade, 39-40, 45, 55, 61n22; and other civic celebrations, 55
Parma, Missouri, 139, 140
Parrish, Amanda, 205, 215, 224-25
Pasturage, 45, 71
Paternalism, 6-7, 26, 100, 118, 138
Patrick County, Virginia: percentage change of improved farm acreage (1860-1920), 201n14, 202n14t; percentage change of owner or tenant operated farms (1880-1920), 201n14, 202n14t; percentage change of total farms (1860-1920), 201n14, 202n14t; rates of African American land ownership (1900-1950), 186t
Patten, Edward A., 79n6
Patten, Norman, 79n6
Patten, Silas, 79n6
Patterson, Ben, 123-24
Pattillo, Rev. Walter A., 116-18, 117f, 125, 128nn36,37, 129nn41,45; family of, 129n41
Patton, Mathias, 169
Paul, Marian Baxter, 257, 262-63
Peabody, George Foster, 93
Pearson, Hammett, 258
Pearson, Levi, 15, 256-59; family of, 256. *See also* Courts and lawsuits: *James Pearson, an*

infant, by Levi Pearson, his next friend and Levi Pearson v. County Board of Education for Clarendon County, et al.
Pell, Alabama, 248
Pemberton, Ida, 220, 224–25
Pennsylvania, wheat production, 159
People's Party, 110, 112, 113; Colored Alliance precursor to, 112–13, 125–26; conventions of, 125, 128n23, 131n76; formation of, 125–26, 128n23; segregation within, 125; Texas state, 115
Perry, H. H., 118
Perry County, Alabama: African American agricultural workers (1930), 241t; African American farm owners, tenants, and sharecroppers (1930), 237t; farms in (1930), 236t; farms under African American operation (1930), 236t
Personalism, 29
Person County, North Carolina: percentage change of improved farm acreage (1860–1920), 201n12t; percentage change of owner or tenant operated farms (1880–1920), 201n12t; percentage change of total farms (1860–1920), 201n12t; rates of African American land ownership (1900–1950), 186t
Pests, 171
Petersburg, Virginia, 45
Petitions, 260, 261; for access to USDA programs, 271; civil courts, 286; for education equality, 255, 257, 258, 259, 271; for replacement of extension agent, 264
Petty, Adrienne, 10
Photographs, 2, 47, 59–60n14, 76, 171, 250n12; collections for research resources, 308–9; of extension work, 210, 217; by Farm Security Administration, 179–80, 191
Pigford, Timothy, 32. See also *Pigford II*; *Pigford v. Glickman*
Pigford I. See *Pigford v. Glickman*
Pigford II: created from extension given to *Pigford v. Glickman*, 284–85; criticism of, 288–89; funding of, 286–87, 288; members of the class, 285; settlements of, 287
Pigford v. Glickman, 16n2, 198–99; appeals process, 283–84; *Brewington* consolidated under, 282; claimants' success rate, 283–84, 287–88; as class action lawsuit, 2, 15, 280–84, 291; competency of lawyers questioned, 283; consent decrees of, 2, 16n2, 281, 282, 283; criticism of, 281, 282–83, 285; members of the class, 280, 281, 282, 283, 285; Office of the Monitor report, 287; *Pigford II* created from extension given, 284–85; settlements of, 2, 22, 281, 283, 287–88; supported by farming and civil rights organizations, 281; U.S. District Court for the District of Columbia (DDC), 280. See also *Pigford II*

Pike County, Alabama: African American agricultural workers (1930), 241t; African American farm owners, tenants, and sharecroppers (1930), 237t; farms in (1930), 236t; farms under African American operation (1930), 236t
Pike County, Illinois, 175n10
Pike County, Mississippi, 134, 140
Pine City, Arkansas, 136
Pinkard, E. W., 136
Pinnix, Lawson, 194
Pires, Alexander, 284
Pires and Fraas, 280, 282, 283
Pittsylvania County, Virginia, 190; percentage change of improved farm acreage (1860–1920), 201n12t; percentage change of owner or tenant operated farms (1880–1920), 201n12t; percentage change of total farms (1860–1920), 201n12t; rates of African American land ownership (1900–1950), 186t
Plantation agriculture, 25; African American landlords, 22; cotton, 24, 25, 168; domination by, 42–43, 168, 235; rice, 25; sugar, 26; tobacco, 26, 168; uncommon at Mt. Vernon, 61n22
Plantation belt, 25; average size of farms, 95; of Virginia-North Carolina Piedmont, 185, 187, 200–201n12
Plantation division, 182, 184–85
Plantation manager, 124
Plantation slavery, 185
Plantersville, Alabama, 135
Plants: native, 211; potted, 218, 219f
Plattville, Wisconsin, 175n11
Pleasant Ridge, Wisconsin, 157f, 159, 168, 173; former slave family success in, 9, 155–57, 164, 173; race relations in, 155–57, 163, 166
Poinsett County, Arkansas, 26, 300
Pointer, Nathan, and family, 168
Politics/political, 25, 28, 30–31; African American officials and candidates, 79n6, 110, 113, 116, 124–25, 247–48, 250n12, 303–4; activist race, 233; agrarian protest, 145; color-line, 163–64, 166, 232; conservatism, 275, 282; co-racial, 233, 242, 244; education, 136; Garveyism and, 132–33; impotency, 183, 237–38, 246–47; representation denied, 183, 233, 237–38, 246; smear campaign, 116;

Politics/political—*continued*
strategies differ between farm owners and tenants/sharecroppers, 9. *See also* Colored Alliance: political activities of; Third-party politics; Republican Party: fusion
Polk, Leonidas, 122
Polk County, Texas, 63–65, 78n3
Poole, Alice, 221
Poole, M. L., 136
Poorman-Douglas Corporation, 283
Populists/Populism, 11, 22, 92, 109, 115, 121–22, 125. *See also* Black Populism
Ports of call, 159; British, 159
Post, Marion, 179–81, 191
Pough, Altamese B., 268n10
Poultry, 71, 74; not allowed to sell, 234. *See also* Chickens; Guineas
Poultry plant (cooperative), 95
Powell, Ethel M., 210f, 220
Power house, 48
Prairie Farmer, 171
Prairie View State Normal and Industrial College, 90
Prayer, 3, 109, 136
Preece, Harold, 244
Prejudice, against whites, 21, 23, 165, 285
Price fixing, 112, 113, 119
Produce, not allowed to sell, 234
Producerism, 132–33, 135–36, 144
Profiles in Black and White (Howard), 259, 268–69n16
Progressive Farmer, 122, 127n18
Proletarian realism, 240
Proletariat, 241
Property, African Americans compared to whites: 24–25, 26, 29, 31, 35n37, 42–43, 57, 299, 302
Protests: agrarian, 22, 147, 148, 244, 277, 279 (*see also* Strikes); civil rights, 245, 266, 277, 279; counter boycott, 263
Prussia, 169

Quander, Lewis, 42, 59–60n14; family of, 42, 45, 62n28
Quander, Susan, 42; farm location of, 46m
Quint, Howard, 259, 268–69n16

Race relations: African American land acquisition due to better, 23–24; African American separatism supporting, 7, 11, 99–100, 138, 141, 142, 148; between agrarian alliances, 118; in Calvert Township, Michigan, 304; current day, 23; followed by extension agents, 208–9, 261–62; in Hancock County, Georgia, 86, 99–100; in higher education, 87; not factor in African American land ownership, 25–26, 28; philosophy challenged, 242; in Pleasant Ridge, Wisconsin, 157, 163, 175n11; practiced by "Squire" Youngblood, 74, 75, 77; Washington's philosophy of, 22
Race war, rumored, 242, 248
Racial inferiority: education strategy supporting, 91; African American unable to farm due to, 6, 183, 193, 199, 211, 255–56; as reason to not sell land to African Americans, 24. *See also* White supremacy
Radio, 75, 194
Railroads, 76; cars, 96, 140; electric/electric trolley, 39, 47–48, 54–57; freight charges, 169; segregated cars, 55, 121. *See also* Monopolies: railroads
Ranchers/ranches, 63, 274, 277; cattle, 77, 165, 305
Randall, George, 57
Randall, Henry, 43–44, 47, 52, 59n11; family of, 47–48, 50, 52, 54, 57
Randall, Mary, 47, 57
Randall, William, 57
Randolph County, North Carolina: extension agent report, 185, 187; percentage change of improved farm acreage (1860–1920), 201n14, 202n14t; percentage change of owner or tenant operated farms (1880–1920), 201n14, 202n14t; percentage change of total farms (1860–1920), 201n14, 202n14t; rates of African American land ownership (1900–1950), 186t
Raper, Arthur, 4
Rast, F. M., 255–56
Raymond, C. Elizabeth, 57n1
Reaper crews, 164, 171
Reback, Charles, 6, 26
Reconstruction Act, 66
Recreation centers, 86; cooperative, 96, 97, 97f, 98
Red Cross, 141–42, 222
Redlining, 24
Reed, Adolph, 9
Reeltown, Alabama, 244
Reid, Debra, 13, 30, 57n1
Reid, Harry, 286, 288
Reno, Janet, 295n39
Report on Economic Conditions in the South, 255
Republican-Greenback fusion, 125
Republican Party, 157, 166, 286; African American involvement in, 113, 116, 124–25, 141, 232; fusion, 125–26; radicalism, 157, 164

Resettlement, 1, 105n43, 143, 168, 234, 273, 292n5
Resettlement Administration (RA), 146–47
"Resource mobilization" theory, 265–66
Restaurants, African American produce sold to, 96
Reunions, family, 77, 82n31, 98
Richardson, E., 121
Richburg, Rev. E. E., 256
Richmond, Virginia, 188
Ridley, W. P., farm of, 172f
Riots, 129n54
Robb, Charles, 295n39
Robert, Joseph C., 184
Roberts, Roy, 29
Robinson, Ashton, 57n1
Robinson, Sarah, 40, 42, 44–45, 47–48, 51–56; employed at Mount Vernon, 39, 52–53; family of, 44, 47. See also Johnson, Sarah
Robinson, William, 40, 43–45, 47, 48, 52–56, 59–60n14; family of, 43–44, 47, 54
Rockbridge County, Virginia, 159
Rockefeller Foundation, 222
Rock Hill Community, Florida, 212f
Rockingham County, North Carolina, 188; percentage change of improved farm acreage (1860–1920), 201n12t; percentage change of owner or tenant operated farms (1880–1920), 201n12t; percentage change of total farms (1860–1920), 201n12t; rates of African American land ownership (1900–1950), 186t, 187
Rodeo operators, 308
Rodgers, H. P., 123
Rogers, Joseph J., 115, 127n18
Rogers, S. Emory, 258
Rolinson, Mary, 134
Roll, Jarod, 11
Roosevelt, Franklin Delano, 143, 196; "black cabinet" of, 145, "kitchen cabinet" of, 99. See also New Deal agriculture program
Roosevelt, Theodore, Country Life Commission of, 86
Rosenwald, Julius, 93. See also Julius Rosenwald Foundation
Rosenwald Foundation. See Julius Rosenwald Foundation
Rosenwald school. See Schools: Rosenwald
Roth, Randi, 283
Rural Face of White Supremacy, The (Schultz), 24
Russell, Lester F., 101n5
Russell, Sandy, 189

Russell County, Alabama: African American agricultural workers (1930), 241t; African American farm owners, tenants, and sharecroppers (1930), 237t; farms in (1930), 236t; farms under African American operation (1930), 236t
Ryles, Vaughn, 243

Saddler, R. M., 110
Salinas, California, 294n25
Sam Huston College, 73
Sandfield Cemetery (San Jacinto County, Texas), 66
Sanitation, 207, 215, 221–22
San Jacinto County, Texas, 63, 68, 82n31; Deed Record, 80n12
San Jacinto River (Texas), 64
Sapiro, Aaron, 195
Savannah Morning News, 97
Savannah State College, 87. See also Georgia State Industrial College for Colored Youth
Savings banks, 94, 188
Saw mill (cooperative), 96
Schafer, Elizabeth, 242
Schools, 73, 86, 99, 155, 163, 166; desegregation, 15, 256, 258, 260, 261; public, 42, 112; white, 264
—African American, 239; citizenship, 266; lunch program, 222; at Log Cabin Community, 85, 88, 95, 98, 99; in Mount Vernon district, 42, 44, 48; one-teacher, 263; Rosenwald school, 98; support of, 93; unsanitary, 221–22; See specific schools
Schultz, Mark, 11, 24, 26, 29; *Rural Face of White Supremacy, The*, 24
Schweninger, Loren, 5, 23, 45, 184
Scott, Garrett, 115
Seals, R. Grant, 211
Seals, Rev. J. W., and family, 256
Secretary of Agriculture, 198. See specific secretaries
Seed, 259; catalogues, 3; sacks, 217
Segregation: of agrarian alliances, 114–15, 118, 119, 125, 128n23; of agricultural extension services; of bunk rooms, 191; of extension organizations, 206–7, 208, 209, 214, 222, 264, 273; of 4-H camps, 211; legalized, 5, 22, 77, 205, 223–24, 254–55, 258, 259–60, 273; of railroad cars, 55, 121; of restaurants, 191; overcoming, 23; petitions against school, 257, 258–60, 265; of stores, 191. See also Schools: desegregation
"Separate but equal," 258
Separate-coach law, 121

Separatism, 6, 27, 164–67, 238, 248; against assimilation, 166; emphasized by newspapers, 164; followed by home extension agents, 211, 223; Garveyite, 15, 91, 132–33, 134–35, 137–38, 140–41, 144, 147, 231–33 (*see also* Garveyism: tenets of); as ideal, 166; Washington's philosophy of, 235. *See also* Communities settled by African Americans
Sermons, 116, 141, 142
Sharecroppers. *See* Farmers/farm operators (sharecroppers); Farmers/farm operators (tenants): Share-tenants
Sharecroppers Fund, 273
Share Croppers' Union of Alabama (SCU), 146–47, 243, 249; creation of, 242, 244; decline and undermining of, 244–45; demands of, 242–43; members arming, 243–44; supported by the Communist Party, 146, 232, 242–44; violence against, 242–43
Share tenants. *See* Farmers/farm operators (tenants): Share tenants
Shaw University, 116
Sheds, 8, 13f
Shepard family, 156–57, 173
Sherrod, Shirley, 21–23, 32, 285–86; family of, 285
Shrubs, 212, 213f
Shuffer, Jacob J., 110, 114
Simple Justice (Kluger), 256, 257
Singleton, Benjamin "Pap," 176n18
Sitton, Thad: *Freedom Colonies*, 27; study of communities settled by African Americans, 27–28
Slavery and Freedom on the Middle Ground (Fields), 30
Slavery or slaves, 64–66, 68, 263; Alexandria, Virginia, as trade hub of, 40; census designation, 129n38; escaped, 155, 168; inherited, 78; not required for wheat farming, 159; owners, 40, 44, 53, 56, 64–65, 78n3, 79n6, 80n8, 155, 157; plantation, 185; sexual relations with, 64, 78n3; sold, 64; traditions carried on as freedpeople, 212, 310; as wealth, 64–65, 155; as wedding present, 66; work for African Americans, 299. *See also* Free African Americans (pre–Civil War); Freedpeople
Smith, Annie M., 45, 47, 52, 59–60n14; family of, 45, 47
Smith, Charles, 246
Smith, Dandridge, 39–40, 42, 44–45, 47–48, 52, 56, 59–60n14; family of, 42, 45
Smith, Gertrude, 224
Smith, Lenora Youngblood, 63–65, 78nn1,2

Smith, Mrs., 212–13, 213f
Smith, Robert C. *See* Black Power: power theories related to
Smith, Robert Lloyd, 84, 128n24, 308
Snow Hill, Alabama, 234
Social and economic status improvement: attached to successful farm ownership, 4, 30, 92, 180, 189, 193, 232; determined by estate, 42; differentiated within African American community, 52, 56; due to position at Mount Vernon, 10, 44; through involvement in home demonstration clubs, 220–21, 223–24. *See also* Communities settled by African Americans: leaders of
Socialists, white, 146
Soil preparation, 8, 68, 74, 84, 168, 172, 175n10. *See also* Fertilizers
Souls of Black Folk, The (Du Bois), 181
South, The: deep South less conducive to African American land ownership, 23–24; Solid South, 29; upper South more conducive to African American land ownership, 23–24
South Carolina, 123; African American land ownership in (1900), 100; civil rights work in, 254–67; extension agent report, 255–56, 257, 262; Food Administration Board, 87; marketing cooperative in, 195; Negro Agricultural Extension, 261–62, 266–67, 268n10; Negro Home Demonstration Work, 257, 263; Sea Islands, 266; studies of, 6, 29
South Carolina State Agricultural and Mechanical College, 87; Agricultural Extension Service, 86–87
South Carolina State College, 264
South Dakota, 167; average size of African American farm (1900), 160–61t; percentage of African American farm ownership (1900), 159, 160–61t
Southern Farmers Alliance, 114, 115, 118, 119–20, 125; cooperation with Colored Alliance, 118, 125, 128n23; opposes Colored Alliance strategy, 121–22, 130n65; opposes Lodge Bill, 120
Southern hospitality and gentility, respectability, 44, 47, 52–53
Southern Mercury, 112
Southern States Industrial Council, 255
Southern Tenant Farmers' Union (STFU), 146–48
Sparta, Georgia, 94–95
Speeches: of Benjamin F. Hubert, 89; of Shirley Sherrod, 21–23
Spelman College, 102n7
Spencer, H. J., 110, 114

Spooner, Eloise, 23
Spooner, Roger, 21, 23, 32; family of, 23, 285
Springfield, Georgia, 86, 95, 96, 98, 99, 168; economic depression of, 93–94, 104n31; founded, 85. *See also* Log Cabin Community
Springs, 42
St. Charles, Missouri, 155–56, 168, 174n2
St. Charles County, Missouri, court, 164
St. Cloud, Vincent, 115
St. Ferdinand Township, Missouri, 168
St. Louis, Missouri, 128n23, 131n76, 169, 172; markets, 171, 172, 175n10
St. Louis County, Missouri, 169
St. Louis County Watchman, 171
St. Paul's College, 195
Stack, Nicholas, 115
Staples, Todd, 63
Stewart family, 216, 216f
Stock market crash of 1929, 138
Stokes County, North Carolina, rates of African American land ownership (1900–1950), 186t
Store equipment: cake cases, 47; coffee mill, 47; counter scales, 47; show cases, 47; tea canisters, 47; tobacco cutter, 47
Storehouses (cooperative), 127n10
Stores, 45, 53, 72, 141, 247; accounts, 47; books, 55; cooperative, 90, 96, 113, 119–20, 124; country, 90; furniture, 75; general, 47, 85
Strikes, 112, 122, 146, 148, 243; cotton pickers, 11, 113, 121–24; workers fired during, 123
Stryker, Roy, 180
Student Nonviolent Coordinating Committee (SNCC), 231, 245, 249; criticism of, 246; historical linkage to SCU and Communist Party, 246; ideology of, 246; promotes civil rights, 246–47
Stukes, Ladson, and family, 259–60
Suburban experience, African American: 54–57; in rural area, 86, 212, 216
Suffrage, African American: in Arkansas, 163; Democratic Party limiting, 166; federal election oversight, 110, 113, 120; "Force Bill," 120; in Hancock County, Georgia, 105n44; Lodge Bill, 120; at Log Cabin Community, 85, 99, 105n44; poll tax, 110, 113; Reconstruction Act, 65; restricted for landless in Alabama, 237–38, 246, 247; related violence, 232, 247; voter registration drives, 246, 247; voter registration rolls, 65; voting, 85, 105n44, 120; voting requirements, 237–38; Voting Rights Act of 1965, 237, 248; in Wisconsin, 156. *See also* Disfranchisement
Sugar, production, 26

Summer, John, and family, 165f
Summerton, South Carolina, 260
Sumter County, Alabama: African American agricultural workers (1930), 241t; African American farm owners, tenants, and sharecroppers (1930), 237t; farms in (1930), 236t; farms under African American operation (1930), 236t
Sumter County, South Carolina, 261
Sun-Maid Raisin Cooperative, 195
Supermarkets, 289
Surry County, North Carolina: percentage change of improved farm acreage (1860–1920), 201n14, 202n14t; percentage change of owner or tenant operated farms (1880–1920), 201n14, 202n14t; percentage change of total farms (1860–1920), 201n14, 202n14t; rates of African American land ownership (1900–1950), 186t, 187
Swamps, hiding in, 119, 243
Swann-Wright, Dianne, 44
Sweet potato curing plant (cooperative), 96
Swimming pool, 98

Taliaferro County, Georgia, 25
Tallapoosa County, Alabama, 242
Talmadge, Eugene, 148
Tax assessments, 65, 69
Tax records, personal property, 48
Taylor, Rev. Samuel K., 54
Technology, 182, 218, 226n6, 272, 289–90; harvesting, 159, 164, 171, 257, 260
Tenants. *See* Farmers/farm operators (tenants)
Tennessee: studies of, 26; wheat to, 159; wheat production, 158
Texas, 113, 123, 175n7; Big Thicket area, 63; Capitol Building, 73; Highway 171, 82n29; as home to African American agrarian organizations, 110–11; House of Representatives, 79n6
Texas Agricultural Extension Service, Negro Division, 74, 75, 84
Texas Department of Agriculture, 167; Family Land Heritage Program, 63, 78n1
Third-party politics, 11, 116, 124–26, 166, 240–47
Thompson, William, 257, 268n12
Thorn, Charlotte, 239
Threshing crews, 171
Time merchant, 182, 239
Timothy C. Pigford et al. v. Dan Glickman, Secretary, U.S. Department of Agriculture. See *Pigford v. Glickman*

Tobacco: allotment, 183, 196, 197–98, 264; as cash crop, 168, 182–97; auctioneer, 193; auctions and auction houses, 188, 189, 191, 192f, 193; bright leaf, 13, 182, 188–89, 190; buyer, 193; church supported through profits from, 195; cooperative, 195; curing, 188, 193; curing barns, 181, 191, 197; education supported through profits from, 195; factories, 188; farm decline, 182–83, 196–98; farmers, 181–99, 192f, 258; farming culture, 13–14, 182, 190–91, 193; farms abandoned, 197–98; foreign production, 197; growing regions, 13, 182; land prices, 184–85, 187, 189; manufacturers of chewing, 188; markets, 191; opportunities for African American and whites, 182, 184; plantations, 26; prices, 184, 187, 188–89, 195–97; production, 26, 182–97; profitability, 182, 188–89, 193, 196–97; as reminder of slavery, 182, 191; replaces cotton, 185; shipping, 188; soil needed for, 190; stemmers, 188; strip houses, 182; tax, 197; Virginia "shipping," 188; warehouse owner, 193; warehousemen, 188, 191, 192f

"Tobacco Kingdom," 184

Tobacco Road, 183

Trade, global, 182

Trans-Mississippi West, 175n7

Transportation, 122; and commuting, 54–57, 61n22; ease of, 54, 64; by ferry, 175n10; infrastructure, 158–59, 171; price gouging, 113; by railroad, 118, 164; by river, 164; by steamboats, 64; by wagon, 55. *See also* Monopolies: transportation

Trees, 290; fruit, 168; gum, 42; pine, 25, 92, 98–99

Trinity River (Texas), 64

Tri-State Tobacco Grower, 195

Tri-State Tobacco Growers' Cooperative, 195

Truatt, Rev. Alexander, 39, 54

Truck, 194f

Truck produce, 96, 172

Tulsa, Oklahoma, 294n25

Turkey farmer, 265

Turkeys, 74

Turner, A. A., 206

Turner, Frederick Jackson. *See* Frontier thesis

Turner, Mrs. A. A., 226n4

Turner, Nat, 244. *See also* Nat Turner's Rebellion

Turpentine industry, 25

Tuskegee Farm and Improvement Company, 239

Tuskegee Institute, 84, 87, 88, 90, 228n23, 232, 235; Department of Agriculture, 87; develops land bank, 239; studies of the influence of, 312–13; trustees of, 87; Vocational Teacher Training, 87

Tylertown, Mississippi, 140

U.S. Army, 65

U.S. Army camp (Camp A. A. Humphreys), 54

U.S. Commission on Civil Rights, 273–74, 314

U.S. Congress, 293n18; Congressional Gold Medal, 254; Congressional Research Service Report, 288; defeats Lodge Bill, 120; first African American from Texas elected to, 79n6; involvement with *Pigford v. Glickman* and *Pigford II*, 282, 287, 288–89; modifies farm programs, 197, 275; passes civil rights laws, 263; passes Reconstruction Act, 65; Senate Committee on Agriculture and Forestry, 128n23

U.S. Department of Agriculture (USDA), 21, 215; appoints minority advisors, 275; complaints against, 271–75, 276–80; create and fund extension services, 86, 214; debt relief program of, 276; discrimination of African Americans by, 2, 14, 15–16, 22, 32, 197–99, 271–89; discrimination of women, Native Americans, Hispanics, and others by, 289; enforcement civil rights laws, 272, 274, 291; experiment stations, 271; extension services rejected, 139–40; farm foreclosure issues of, 275, 278, 279, 282; favored rich, large, and/or white farmers, 32, 271–72, 274, 275, 276–78; Federal Extension Service (FES), 210, 271, 273, 312; forecasters, 197; interactions with the NFCF, 141, 143; investigations, 2, 16n2, 147, 263–64, 273, 277; issues memo to end discrimination, 273; lack of control at state and local levels, 15–16, 273–75, 276–77, 278, 279; lack of female and minority representation at state and local level, 15, 146, 183, 198, 273–75; lack of process for discrimination complaints, 278, 279–80; as "Last Plantation," 15, 272, 291; listening sessions, 277–78, 294n25; National Appeals Division (NAD), 276; National Commission on Small Farms, 289; opened to lawsuits, 278, 280; violates civil rights, 274, 277, 278, 280, 285

U.S. Department of Justice, 282, 284–85, 287

U.S. Department of the Interior, 288

U.S. House of Representatives, 286, 288

U.S. Public Health Service, 228n23

U.S. Senate, 286–87, 288; subcommittee, 260

U.S. Supreme Court, 15, 258, 263

Unemployment, 39, 48, 51, 260–61
Unfree labor, 69
Uniforms, caregiver-white, 209
Union County, South Carolina, extension agent fired, 264
Union Labor Party, 124
Union League, in Alabama, 232
Unions, 146–48, 232, 242–46, 249
United Auto Workers, 260
United Brethren church, and cemetery, 155
Universal Negro Improvement Association (UNIA), 167; caters to prosperous African Americans, 12, 134; collapse of, 12, 138, 146; conventions of, 136; cooperation with NFCF, 140–41, 142; divisions, 135; founded by Garvey, 132, 134; goals of, 12, 134; membership of, 12, 132–34, 136–37, 138, 140–41; *Negro World* newspaper of, 132; organizational divisions of, 133–35, 135m, 136, 138, 140; political indifference of, 137, 141, 145, 147; race relations of, 138; similarities to NFCF, 138–39, 145, 148
University of Florida (UF), 206
University of Georgia: Board of Regents, 91; Hargrett Rare Book and Manuscript Library, 101n4
University of North Carolina, 180
University of South Carolina, extension division, 255
Urban: markets, 13; wealth, 92
Urban League, 87–88, 102n7
Urban life: of African Americans, 3, 29, 61n22, 98; flight to, 86, 90–91, 93–94, 95, 98, 162, 173, 182, 301; and rural studies, 305. *See also* Great Migration
Urban middle class, 83–84, 86, 98–100
Utopianism: African American, 165; agrarian, 156, 168

Vaccinations. *See* Immunizations
Vance County, North Carolina: African Americans inclined toward tobacco farming in, 189; murder in, 187; percentage change of improved farm acreage (1860–1920), 201n12t; percentage change of owner or tenant operated farms (1880–1920), 201n12t; percentage change of total farms (1860–1920), 201n12t; rates of African American land ownership (1900–1950), 186t
Vesey, Denmark, 244
Vigilantism, 119, 123–24
Vilsack, Tom, 286, 287
Violence: church burning, 242; common during Jim Crow era, 14, 27, 29, 137, 232, 238; death threats, 119; domestic, 50–51, 53; factor in creation of "freedom colonies," 27, 238; house burning, 187, 242; intimidation, 120, 123, 142, 248, 274; lynching, 124, 243; massacre, 119–20, 130n57; mob, 119, 124, 243; murder, 21, 52, 119–20, 124, 187, 242–43; poisoning farm animals, 248; suffrage related, 232, 247; against successful African American farmers, 306; suppressed, 86, 100, 138; terrorism, 243; torture, 124; against unions, 242–45; whipping, 243; against white leaders of Colored Alliance, 115
Virginia, 44, 51, 128n23, 198; African American land ownership in (1900), 100; Accotink Turnpike, 43, 57; congress, 159; highest rate of African American farm owners, 184–85, 187; marketing cooperative in, 195; Mount Vernon Parkway, 57; Piedmont area, 184–85; Piedmont region rates of African American land ownership (1900–1950), 185, 186t; Route 1, 57; Southside area, 26, 184–85; studies of, 7, 23; Tidewater region, 184; tobacco regions, 182, 184, 188, 200–201n12; wheat belt, 159; wheat production, 158, 159
Vital Flores survey, 80n12
Volanto, Keith J., 10–11
Volusia County, Florida, 220

Wages, 111, 112; demand for higher, 121–22, 146, 243; low, 123; lowered, 117, 120; maximizing, 53, 54; necessary to purchase a house, 50; "starvation," 136, 243; urban, 171. *See also* Laborers: wage
Wagstaff, Harvey, 193
Wake County, North Carolina, rates of African American land ownership (1900–1950), 186t
Walker, Melissa, 133, 215
Walker, Rosa, 211–13, 212f, 217–18, 217f
Wallace, George, 246, 247
Wallace, Henry, 148
Walton, Hanes. *See* Black Power: power theories related to
Warehousemen, tobacco, 188, 191, 192f
Warren County, North Carolina: percentage change of improved farm acreage (1860–1920), 201n12t; percentage change of owner or tenant operated farms (1880–1920), 201n12t; percentage change of total farms (1860–1920), 201n12t; rates of African American land ownership (1900–1950), 186t, 187
Warren County, Virginia, 159; marketing cooperative in, 195

Washington, Alexandria and Mt. Vernon Railway, 55
Washington, Booker T.: creates land bank, 239; Du Bois criticizes, 101n2; followers of, 73–74, 77, 84, 87–89; initiates National Negro Health Week, 222; as Jeffersonian agrarian, 84, 232; race relations philosophy of, 22–23, 77, 91, 261–62 (*see also* Race relations); self-reliance philosophy of, 135, 245; separation philosophy of, 137, 235
Washington, Bushrod, 42
Washington, D.C., 39, 51, 53, 56, 166, 294n25; dairy products provided for, 45; protests in, 2, 277, 279; and suburbs of, 54, 57
Washington, George, 40, 44, 56, 57; family of, 42, 44, 53; tomb of, 56; will of, 42. *See also* Mount Vernon
Washington, John Augustine, 44, 53
Washington, Lloyd, 44, 59–60n14; family of, 44–45
Washington, W. G., 95
Washington Afro-American, 246
Washington County, Alabama: African American agricultural workers (1930), 241t; African American farm owners, tenants, and sharecroppers (1930), 237t
Washington County, Florida, 208t
Washington Post, 39
Washington's philosophy, 77. *See also* Racial inferiority
Watch, 42
Water rights, 31
Waters, Maxine, 295n39
Water service, 189
Watkins, Norman, and family, 169
Watkins (homesteading recruiter), 165
Watson, James, 65, 67f, 68, 80n12
Watson, Mary (née Youngblood; owner of "Squire's" mother), 65, 67f, 68
Watson family, 65, 66, 78n3
Waxahachie, Texas, 68
Weapons: brick, 50; guns, 244, 245; hammer, 50; hoes, 124; knives, 124; pistols, 244; rifles, 244; shotguns, 244; sticks, 124
Weather, 138, 140, 141, 259, 261
Weaver, P. J., 234
Webb, Nathan, 59n11
Webber, Jr., Paul, 264
Wells, Charlie, 182, 194
West, Michael Rudolph, 22–23; *Education of Booker T. Washington*, 22
West Virginia, studies of, 23
Wheat, 13, 97; bushels of, 156, 169, 172; as cash crop, 156–57, 158, 165, 169, 171; farmer, 156–59, 163–65, 168–73, 175nn7,10; markets, 158–59, 171; mill (cooperative), 96; sheaves, 170f
Wheat belt: Midwestern, 158, 164, 168; expansion of, 156, 159, 171, 175n7; northern, 158–59
Whig Party, 85
White, Sampson, 190
White Citizens' Councils, 258–59
White farm occupations not open to African Americans, 193–94
White House, 277
White Oak Grove Baptist Church, 194
Whites: hiring African American laborers, 29, 42, 136; hiring white laborers, 43; refusing to sell land, 24–25, 235, 237; support African American middle-class, 162–63
White supremacy, 6–7, 16, 157, 170f, 209, 258, 262; leads to violence, 15; Log Cabin Community buffer from, 11, 84; paternalism a facet of, 100; supported by
White washing, 217
Widow's benefit, 55
Wilcox County, Alabama: African American agricultural workers (1930), 241t; African American farm owners, tenants, and sharecroppers (1930), 237t
Wilkins, Roy, 246, 259
Willcox, Mary Otis, 93. *See also* Mary Otis Willcox Health Clinic
Williams, E. N., 268n10
Wills, 42, 47, 59–60n14, 68, 69, 88, 289; of George Washington, 42; lack of, 27, 47, 59–60n14
Wilson, B., 234
Wilson, Martha, 90
Wilson, Woodrow, 87
Wilson (police officer), 242
Wind from Nowhere, The (Micheaux), 177n21
Window Rock, Arizona, 294n25
Wisconsin: average size of African American farm (1900), 160–61t; legal tolerance for African American in, 156; percentage of African American farm ownership (1900), 160–61t; Supreme Court, 156; wheat production, 156
"Wizard of Tuskegee." *See* Washington, Booker T.
Womack, Veronica L., 14
Women: elites, 52; pregnancy, 50; racism against, 14, 194, 206, 207, 211, 225; sexism against, 14, 194, 206, 207, 209, 211, 225. *See also* Farmers/farm operators, women
Women's Christian Temperance Union, 125
Woodcutting, 13, 172
Woodland, California, 294n25

Woodland Cemetery (Mexia, Texas), 76
Woodlawn plantation, 42
Woodman, Harold, 31
Woodward, C. Vann, 31
Workshops to disseminate scientific agriculture, 93, 97
Works Progress Administration (WPA), 175n11
World War I, economic boom during, 180, 184, 187, 189
World War II, African American support of, 193–94

Yadkin County, North Carolina: percentage change of improved farm acreage (1860–1920), 201n14, 202n14t; percentage change of owner or tenant operated farms (1880–1920), 201n14, 202n14t; percentage change of total farms (1860–1920), 201n14, 202n14t; rates of African American land ownership (1900–1950), 186t, 187
Yarborough, Anderson "Bud," 194
Yarbrough, Mary Elizabeth "Bettie" (née Watson), 68, 79n5
Yarbrough, family, 64, 68–69, 73, 74, 77, 80n8
Yarbrough, John, 68–69
Yarbrough, Mattie, 68, 80n8
Yarbrough, Rev. Solomon Shaw, 68–69, 79–80n8
Yarbrough, Thomas, 69
Yarbrough, William, 68–69, 80n12
Yazoo-Mississippi Delta, 119, 135, 142, 272
Yeoman farmers, African American, 92; white, 32, 187, 271
Young, Andrew, 247
Young, Carl, 242–43
Young, Harry, 291
Youngblood, Alfred (son of "Squire" and Willie Lou), 70, 71, 72, 81n18
Youngblood, Alvin (grandson of "Squire"), 73, 76, 82n28
Youngblood, Alvin, Jr. (great-grandson of "Squire"), 78n1
Youngblood, Arlene, 78n1
Youngblood, Billie (son of "Squire" and Mattie), 72
Youngblood, Booker T. (son of "Squire" and Willie Lou), 70, 72, 73, 74
Youngblood, Clarence Edward (son of "Squire" and Mattie), 73
Youngblood, David (great-grandson of "Squire"), 78n1, 78n3
Youngblood, Delillian (child of "Squire" and Willie Lou), 70, 73

Youngblood, Eddie Lee (daughter of "Squire" and Mattie), 63, 72–77, 78n1, 80n12
Youngblood, Eliza (mother of "Squire"), 66, 67f, 68, 79n5, 80n12, 82n31
Youngblood, Ennis. See Youngblood, James Edward ("Squire"): as Ennis Youngblood
Youngblood, Eula Williams, 63–65, 78n1
Youngblood, Harriett (daughter-in-law of "Squire"), 73
Youngblood, Helen (daughter of "Squire" and Mattie), 73
Youngblood, Henry Miles (son of JMY), 79n7
Youngblood, J. E. (grandson of "Squire"), 76
Youngblood, J. J. (possible great-uncle or grandfather of "Squire"), 78n3
Youngblood, Jacob (great-grandfather of "Squire"), 78n3, 79n7
Youngblood, Jacob (son of JMY), 79n7
Youngblood, James (son of JMY), 79n7
Youngblood, James Edward ("Squire"), 10, 63, 70f, 72f, 82n31; as Ennis Youngblood, 66, 67f; farm laborer, 11, 64, 66, 68; follows of Washington's philosophy, 73–74, 77; generosity of, 75–76, 77; helps create park, 75; house destroyed, 76; involved in railroad accident, 76, 82n28; listed as Squire Watson in census, 68; lives with Yarbrough family, 68–69, 73, 74, 77; marriages of, 70, 72; nicknamed "Squire" or "Squar," 11, 63; successful farm ownership of, 11, 69–76; temper of, 69, 73
Youngblood, James Thomas (father of "Squire"), 63–67, 65f, 67f, 78n3, 79nn5,7, 80n12; descendants of, 66–67, 82n31; family bible of, 66, 78n3; identified as mulatto in census, 78–79n4; migration to and success in Texas, 10–11, 64–66
Youngblood, Jewell (daughter-in-law of "Squire"), 73
Youngblood, John Miles (JMY), 67, 79n7
Youngblood, Jr., John Miles (son of JMY), 79n7
Youngblood, Julie, 78n1
Youngblood, Mourning Elizabeth "Lizzie" (sister of "Squire"), 66, 78n3, 79n6
Youngblood, Mary. See Watson, Mary
Youngblood, Mary (daughter of "Squire" and Willie Lou), 70, 71, 72
Youngblood, Mary (daughter of JMY), 79n7
Youngblood, Mary (half-sister of "Squire"), 66
Youngblood, Matilda (née Alexander), 64–65, 68, 78n3, 79n5
Youngblood, Mattie (née Hobbs; second wife of "Squire"), 72, 74, 76, 82n29

Youngblood, Oscar (son of "Squire" and Mattie), 72, 76
Youngblood, Robert Grover (son of "Squire" and Willie Lou), 70, 71, 72–73, 76
Youngblood, Rudolph (son of "Squire" and Mattie), 81n19
Youngblood, Shallie (son of "Squire" and Willie Lou), 70, 73
Youngblood, Ted III (great-grandson of "Squire"), 77, 78n1
Youngblood, Ted Jr. (grandson of "Squire"), 73, 76, 82n28
Youngblood, Theodore Roosevelt (son of "Squire" and Willie Lou), 70, 72, 73, 74, 76, 81n21
Youngblood, Theresa (great-granddaughter of "Squire"), 78n1
Youngblood, Thomas (son of JMY), 79n7
Youngblood, Thomas B. (grandfather of "Squire"), 64–65, 67, 68, 79n7
Youngblood, Tracy (son of "Squire" and Mattie), 73, 82n29
Youngblood, Ulysses (son of "Squire" and Willie Lou), 70, 72–73
Youngblood, Willie Lou (née Stephens; first wife of "Squire"), 69–70, 72
Youngblood Family Cemetery (San Jacinto County, Texas), 78n3
Youth clubs, 289; to disseminate scientific agriculture, 84. *See also* 4-H clubs and members

www.ingramcontent.com/pod-product-compliance
Lightning Source LLC
Chambersburg PA
CBHW021848230426
43671CB00006B/306